COUNTRY AMERICANA

PRICE GUIDE

Edited by
Kyle Husfloen

Antique Trader Books
Dubuque, Iowa
Division of Landmark Communications, Inc.

STAFF

Assistant Editor . . . . Elizabeth Stephan
Editorial Assistant . . . . Ruth Willis
Editorial Assistant . . . . Marti Hansel
Designer . . . . Darryl Keck
Design Assistant . . . . Lynn Bradshaw
Art Director . . . . Jaro Sebek
Customer Service/Order Fulfillment . . . . Bonnie Rojemann

ISBN: 0-930625-26-9
Library of Congress Catalog Card Number: 95-83765

Antique Trader Publications
Publishers of:

The Antique Trader Weekly
Toy Trader
Collector Magazine & Price Guide
Baby Boomer Collectibles
DISCoveries
The Big Reel
Postcard Collector
Military Trader
Antique Trader Books

To order additional copies of this book
or a catalog please contact:

Antique Trader Publications
P.O. Box 1050
Dubuque, Iowa 52004
1-800-334-7165

TABLE OF CONTENTS

EDITOR'S NOTE

What is "country Americana?" That is a tricky question since the term implies that only artifacts made and used in rural America should be included. Of course, much of what is collected today as "country" was mass-produced in cities and has now become lumped under the general collecting title of "country" because these items reflect our yearning for the charm and nostalgia of the "good old days."

In deciding what to include in this general guide, my staff and I went over long lists of possible collecting categories which might fall under the heading of 'country-related.' It wasn't always easy to decide what should be included and what not, but in the end we felt it made sense to try and focus in on a diverse range of topics which reflected a wide range of collecting tastes. With only 400 pages to work with, we had to limit somewhat what could be included but we hope you'll find our selections of interest and value.

The collecting of "country Americana" has a long and fascinating history with its real roots stretching back to the Centennial Exhibition of 1876 when "colonial" American artifacts were displayed and caught the fancy of many of the thousands of visitors to Philadelphia that year. Not long after, Colonial Revival furniture was being produced and by the 1890s there was a dedicated core of collectors, mostly in the New England region, who were scouring the countryside for furniture, glass, china, and other artifacts which they felt reflected the historic charm of early American life. By the 1920s "Colonial Revival" was really 'hot,' and major manufacturers mass-produced all types of furniture and decorative accent pieces with an 'antique' appeal. The 1920s also saw the growth of major Americana collections

by such notables as Wallace Nutting, Henry Ford and Henry duPont Winterthur and many of their collections of the finest early American antiques now reside in museums. The average collector could settle for less expensive and simpler pieces for their homes. During the Depression, when prices for antiques fell, many Americans decorated with "country" items out of simple necessity but as times improved by the late 1930s rooms full of "pumpkin pine" furniture, accessorized with old bottles and decorative old china showed up in many popular mass-market magazines as well as the growing number of specialty publications aimed specifically at the burgeoning antiques collecting market.

The "country look" continued to be popular with a certain segment of the antique-loving public right through the 1940s to the 1970s, but what seems to have spurred the most recent craze for all things with a country "look" was the publication in the early 1980s of books specifically aimed at the home decorating market where page after page of color photos showed off charming groupings of baskets, woodenwares, primitive furniture and even newer "handcrafted" items. Although that frenzied period of gathering nearly anything and everything may have ebbed, there will most certainly always continue to be an interest in and demand for the wide range of antiques and collectibles which harken back to simpler times and add colorful appeal to any domestic setting, rural or urban.

Here's wishing you good luck and great enjoyment in your pursuit of your favorite category of "country Americana!"

Kyle Husfloen, Editor

ACKNOWLEDGMENTS

This book was made possible only through the combined efforts of the staff of Antique Trader Books and the generous efforts of a number of specialist collectors and authorities. My staff and I were most fortunate to receive the enthusiastic support and input of a large number of people whose particular knowledge of certain categories has ensured that they will provide you, the reader, with the broadest, most in-depth and accurate overview of these collecting fields. A special note of thanks goes to Tom Porter of Garth's Auctions, Delaware, Ohio, who prepared our special introductory feature. Garth's, as many of you are aware, is one of the premier auction houses today specializing in the sale of all types of country antiques and collectibles. We appreciate Mr. Porter's willingness to share some insights gathered during his career as auctioneer and collector.

Below we list, by category, the names of the many folks who unselfishly shared of their time and knowledge to provide special introductions, price listings and photographs for the following chapters covering the world of "Country Americana."

Further listings and addresses of collector clubs are included in a special appendix at the back of this book.

GENERAL CATEGORIES

Bootjacks
Harry A. Zuber
Houston, TX

Bottle Openers
Charles Reynolds
Reynold's Toys
2836 Monroe St.
Falls Church, VA 22042

Cash Registers
William Heuring
Hickory Bend Antiques
2995 Drake Hill Rd.
Jasper, NY 14855

**Children's Dishes &
Doll Furniture and Accessories**
Doris Lechler
Columbus, OH

Christmas Collectibles
Robert Brenner
Princeton, WI

Cookbooks
Barbara DePalma
Deer Park Books
27 Dear Park Rd.
Gaylordsville, CT 06811

Currier & Ives Prints
Robert L. Searjeant
Box 23942
Rochester, NY 14692

Kitchenwares

General
Carol Bohn
KOOKS (Kollectors of Old Kitchen Stuff)
Mifflinburg, PA 17844

Margaret "Bunny" Upchurch
Boyce, VA

Coffee Mills
Mike White, Editor
The Grinder Finder
Fraser, CO 80442

Egg Beaters
Don Thornton
Beat Books
1345 Poplar Ave.
Sunnyvale, CA 94087

Graniteware
Jo Allers
Cedar Rapids, IA 52410

Irons
Jimmy & Carol Walker
Iron Talk
Waelder, TX 78959-0068

Juice Reamers
Bobbie Zucker Bryson
Tuckahoe, NY

Lighting Devices

Aladdin Lamps
Thomas W. Small
Tom's Mantle Lamps
79 Pine St.
Frostburg, MD 21532

Kerosene Lamps
Catherine Thuro-Gripton
Toronto, Canada

Lightning Rod Balls and Weathervanes & Roof Ornaments
Phil Steiner
Weather or Knot Antiques
15832 So. C.R. 900 W.
Wanatah, IN 46390

Salesman's Samples
Allan Hoover
Peru, IL

Sewing Adjuncts
Estelle Zalkin
Miami Beach, FL

Wayne Muller
P.O. Box 903
Pacific Palisades, CA 90272

Stoves
Clifford Boram
Antique Stove Information Clearinghouse
417 No. Main St.
Monticello, IN 47960

Tobacciana
Tony Hyman
Treasure Hunt Publications
P.O. Box 3028
Pismo Beach, CA 93448

Tools
Ronald Barlow
Windmill Publishing Co.
2147 Windmill View Rd.
El Cajon, CA 92020

Trade Cards
Dave Cheadle
3706 S. Acoma St.
Englewood, CO 80110

Tramp Art
Michael Cornish
Cigar Box Antiques
92 Florence St.
Roslindale, MA 02131

Windmill Weights
Richard S. Tucker
Argyle Antiques
406 Country Club Road
Argyle, TX 76226

CERAMICS

Blue & White Pottery
Stephen E. Stone
18102 East Oxford Dr.
Aurora, CO 80013

Pennsbury Pottery
Susan N. Cox
237 E. Main St.
El Cajon, CA 92020

Red Wing Pottery
Charles W. Casad
Monticello, IL

Stoneware
Vicki & Bruce Waasdorp
P.O. Box 434
Clarence, NY 14031

Watt Pottery
Dennis M. Thompson
P.O. Box 26067
Fairview Park, OH 44126

PHOTOGRAPHY CREDITS

Bootjacks
Harry A. Zuber

Bottle Openers
Charles Reynolds

Cash Registers
Hickory Bend Antiques

Ceramics

Blue & White Pottery
Stephen E. Stone, Aurora, Colorado

Pennsbury Pottery
Susan N. Cox
Lucile Henzke, Texas
Laura DeMerchant, San Diego, California
  Photos from the collection of George
  Fedele, Newport Avenue Antiques Mall,
  4836 Newport Ave., San Diego, California

Red Wing
Charles W. Casad
Stanley Baker, Minneapolis, Minnesota
Gail DePasquale
Woody Auction Service, Douglass, Kansas
Dorothy Beckwith, Platteville, Wisconsin

Children's Dishes
Anna Green
Lynn Welker of the Strong Museum
Doris Lechler

Christmas Collectibles
Robert Brenner

Coffee Mills
Micheal White

Graniteware
Jo Allers

Irons
Carol & Jimmy Walker

Kerosene Lamps
Ken Bell, Ontario, Canada

Kitchen Collectibles
Carol Bohn
Don Simmons

Saleman Samples
Allan Hoover

Sewing Adjuncts
Estelle Zalkin
Stuart Muller

Tobacciana
Tony Hyman

Trade Cards
Dave Cheadle
Englewood, Colorado

Watt Pottery
Dennis M. Thompson
Fairview Park, Ohio

Windmill Weights
Richard S. Tucker

For permission to use photographs and listings for various categories, we also wish to extend thanks to the following auction houses:

Christie's
New York, NY

Collector's Sales and Service
Middletown, RI

DeFina Auctions
Austinburg, OH

Dunning's
Elgin, IL

Garth's Auctions
Delaware, OH

Gary Guyette ~ Frank Schmidt, Inc.
West Farmington, ME

Gene Harris Antique Auction Center
Marshalltown, IA

Morton M. Goldberg Auction Galleries
New Orleans, LA

Neal Auction Company
New Orleans, LA

Skinner, Inc.
Bolton, MA

Sotheby's
New York, NY

ON THE COVER: Top Center: a beetle bootjack with overall green & black paint, ca. 1920, Courtesy of Harry A. Zuber; Center: a 19th century stoneware crock decorated with a slip-quilled stag and house, Courtesy of Vicki and Bruce Waasdorp, Clarence, New York; Bottom: a group of painted Shaker-made buckets, Photograph courtesy of Skinner, Auctioneers and Appraisers of Antiques and Fine Art, Boston and Bolton, Massachusetts.
Cover design: Jaro Sebek

Shown above is a grouping of country antiques sold at Garth's Auctions in 1995. Included are an early theorem, an early American Empire wall mirror, a paint-decorated ladder-back side chair and a three-legged painted pine Windsor candlestand. On the candlestand is a fine turned ash burl bowl which sold for $7,250.00 in 1995. A similar bowl sold in the $4,000.00 to $4,300.00 range back in 1991.

INVESTING IN ANTIQUES— THE GOOD, THE BAD AND BLACK SATIN GLASS

By Tom Porter of Garth's Auctions, Delaware, Ohio

Carolyn and I bought our first antique in 1957. We were newlyweds living in Maryland. I was a private in the Army and making $22.00 a week. Carolyn, a registered nurse working for a federally funded children's hospital, made $121.00 a week. We thought we were making a lot of money and could afford the best, until we went to look at new furniture. We needed a dining room table. The price of the new one that we liked was $900.00. After we recovered from sticker shock, we started wandering through antiques shops. We found an inlaid cherry Hepplewhite drop-leaf table for $125.00. We sold it 15 years, four kids and five moves later for $350.00. Little did we know that with the purchase of that table we were investing in our future.

Bottom line, we became interested in antiques because we couldn't afford anything else. We stayed interested in antiques because we recognized quality and appreciated craftsmanship, as well as individualistic expression of styles. Not to mention the practicality and functionality of certain items. Of course we came to admire and collect the weird, the colorful, the curious—items that don't have a thing to do with practicality and functionality but, perhaps most important to us, are fun.

In 1962, we met Garth Oberlander. By that time, Garth had been holding auctions for about 10 years,

but had been a dealer for 25. Carolyn and I subsidized our growing family by "picking" and we went to Garth's auctions to learn more about antiques and what they were worth. Garth was always willing to educate. And boy, did we learn. We were lucky enough to join Garth in business in 1967. He remained our partner, mentor, and friend until his death in 1973. Whenever we are asked to evaluate past trends, current values and future growth of the antiques market, Carolyn and I continue to follow Garth's Golden Rules.

RULE NUMBER ONE: BUY WHAT YOU LIKE

Invest in antiques like you invest in a relationship. Take time to learn about what you like. Ask questions. Get comfortable. Grow. Don't assume anything.

In the mid-1960s I was just sure that black satin glass was going to be the hottest thing since sliced bread. I didn't particularly like the stuff, but hey, if it was going to make me the next John Paul Getty, why not try to corner the market? Let me tell you, I bought and bought and bought. To this day, there has never been a strong market for black satin glass.

Sold at Garth's in 1995, this grouping includes a decorated Pennsylvania blanket chest by Jacob Knagy, a large burl bowl and two treenware covered jars. The larger one on the left sold for $500.00 in 1990 while at the 1995 sale it had jumped to $1,900.00.

So, I was stuck with a lot of something that I didn't even like. And I lost money. Since then, Carolyn and I have bought what appealed to us. We haven't always made money on our choices, but who can put a monetary value on enjoyment?

RULE NUMBER TWO: THE BEST GETS BETTER

Buy the best that you can afford.

When an especially great piece of furniture or an exemplary item in any category would go across the auction block, Garth would say, "Buy the best and here it is...don't be sorry tomorrow that you didn't bid today." Truly great pieces get better with time and with any luck increase in value.

RULE NUMBER THREE: BUYING STOCK ISN'T AS FUN AS BUYING ANTIQUES

I'd rather sit on a Windsor chair than sit on a stock.

I buy antiques that make me smile. For me, that is a quality of life investment because I have yet to see a Brink's truck following a hearse. This philosophy isn't for everyone, but it works for us. Carolyn and I decided many years ago that we were going to invest in antiques instead of stocks. We couldn't afford to do both. Investing in antiques satiated our buying habit, furnished our home and brought us countless hours of enjoyment. Selling the antiques that we collected put our four daughters through college and kept Uncle Sam satisfied.

Compare the sale prices of some of the antiques in this photo, sold at Garth's in early 1995, with what new furniture and accessories would sell for. The large oil on canvas in gilt frame brought $500.00; the country Hepplewhite tavern table in cherry, $400.00; the ladder-back armchair with an old dark finish, $85.00; the two larger bentwood boxes on the left sold together for $260.00 while the smaller two on the right made $125.00. The small dome-top dovetailed box with a green stain reached $55.00 and the cast-iron boot scraper with two full-bodied horses and an old repaint made it to $250.00.

Buying antiques as investments isn't unlike playing the stock market, however. There is risk involved. Sometimes you win, sometimes you lose. But how often does a losing stock certificate make you grin?

RULE NUMBER FOUR: IF YOU AREN'T MAKING MISTAKES, YOU AREN'T DOING ENOUGH

Read. Listen. Watch. Buy. Learn.

Nobody's perfect. Mistakes are inevitable. But Carolyn and I have found that even mistakes can be invaluable. Once you invest your hard earned money into an antique, conjecture becomes reality—your reality. Once you have lost money in an antique you bought, for whatever reason, you tend not to make the same mistake again. Consider your mistakes as a tuition payment in your "continuing antiques education." Every successful antiques dealer and collector I know has invested a lot of money into their continuing education—learning from their bad investments has made them successful.

RULE NUMBER FIVE: HINDSIGHT IS 20/20

The antiques industry is self-perpetuating; just like people, things get older by the day. Unfortunately, that does not mean they automatically become more valuable.

Trends in the antiques market are created when a group of people decide that something is desirable. American Indian artifacts were extremely popular in the 1970s; prices dropped in the 1980s and just recently have begun to rise. Prices for Shaker furniture were stronger in the late '80s than they are currently.

Some trends remain the same and many antiques are economically accessible. It is still consistently possible to buy antique furniture and accessories more reasonably than it is to purchase new furniture and accessories. Have you visited Ethan Allen lately?

As for future trends? I wish I knew. Who would have thought that a PEZ candy container would be worth 400 times its original value? And why hasn't black satin glass ever taken off?

Which brings me back to **Rule Number One.**

In August, 1995, these pieces sold at Garth's. The Hepplewhite-style grandfather's clock made of inlaid cherry was an old hand-made reproduction and brought $1,300.00. The country chest of drawers in refinished cherry reached $275.00 and the set of six (four shown) porcelain plates marked "Imperial Crown China, Austria," each with a different floral design, sold for $100.00. The attractive leaded glass window, 27 × 50$^{1}/_{2}$", brought $375.00.

Garth's sold this interesting group of "smalls" back in 1992. The miniature Ohio-made blanket chest with original grain painting sold for $2,650.00 while the large seated sewerpipe pottery dog to its right made it to $1,000.00. In 1985 a similar dog brought $700.00. The covered burl bowl sold for $3,200.00, up from a 1984 price of $1,250.00. The small Ohio white clay dog with painted trim sold for $275.00. Finally, the four-tube miniature tin candle mold brought $350.00; in 1981, a similar one brought $200.00.

Furniture and Canton china were highlighted in this grouping sold at Garth's in the fall of 1995. The country-style plantation desk in cherry brought $550.00 while the country cherry chest of drawers made $400.00. The small oil painting on board reached $110.00 and the larger oil on canvas made $300.00. The various Canton pieces and groups sold in the $100.00 to $300.00 range with the highest single piece being the 9" h. covered pitcher which sold for $550.00.

This wide range of small items was part of a Garth's spring 1995 sale. Most notable was the carved wood seated cat in the second row which sold for $1,500.00. Back in 1982, it went for only $20.00. The facing carved wood dog by the same maker sold for $1,300.00, compared with $95.00 in 1982.

This simple grouping of pieces sold at Garth's in early 1995. The pair of country Chippendale walnut side chairs sold for $195.00 each while the cherry Chippendale candlestand between them brought $425.00. On the stand a Canton porcelain tray and Nanking porcelain covered vegetable dish rest below a small four-arm brass late 19th century chandelier which sold for $375.00.

This grouping was included in a May, 1995 Garth's sale. The stoneware pitcher with applied and tooled leaves & flowers sits beside an unusual house-shaped spice box of painted poplar. At the upper right is a pen & ink and water-color page from a 19th century exercise book. The unique decorated letter at the upper left was done in pen & ink and water-color, an ornate piece of hand-painted folk art. It sold for $2,050.00 compared to its sale price of just $900.00 back in 1992.

CHAPTER
1

BASKETS

Fig. 1-2   *Courtesy of Christie's*

Since prehistoric times Native American artisans have woven baskets for utilitarian and ceremonial purposes. Many types of natural materials were used by these first American basket makers including woven wicker, reeds, splint, tree bark, and even porcupine quills. When European settlers began arriving in the New World they brought with them their own basket making skills and also learned from the Native Americans how to use locally available materials. Baskets have been produced for a myriad of purposes in many shapes and sizes. One very collectible style is today referred to as a "buttocks" basket because of its double-lobed form, but square, round, oval, and rectangular baskets, especially any with special decorative treatments, are also choice finds. On Nantucket Island a special plain and sturdy style of basket was developed and all Nantucket baskets are prized by collectors today. Whatever their form of construction, size or original purpose, old baskets in good condition add a special accent to any country-style setting.

"Buttocks" basket, 22-rib construction, woven splint, rounded sides w/bentwood handle, natural patina w/some soiling, 5¹/₂ × 5¹/₂", 3¹/₄" h. **$248.00**

"Buttocks" basket, 16-rib construction, woven oak splint, pronounced bulges & God's-eye crossing splint handle, Pennsylvania, 19th c., 4¹/₂" h. plus bentwood handle (Fig. 1-2, upper left) **633.00**

"Buttocks" basket, 30-rib construction, woven splint, light color w/slight patina, some age, bentwood handle, 9" d., 4³/₄" h. plus bentwood handle **94.00**

"Buttocks" basket, 32-rib construction, woven splint, deep rounded sides w/wrapped rim & bentwood handle, dark red paint, 8¹/₂ × 9¹/₂", 4³/₄" h. **413.00**

"Buttocks" basket, 22-rib construction, woven splint, painted reddish brown, probably from Virginia, first half 19th c., 5" h. plus bentwood handle (Fig. 1-1) **1,380.00**

"Buttocks" basket, 18-rib construction, woven splint, wrapped rim & bentwood handle, some damage, 10¹/₂ × 11¹/₂", 6" h. plus bentwood handle **50.00**

"Buttocks" basket, 24-rib construction, woven oak splint, large defined collar, God's-eye crossing splint handle, Pennsylvania, 19th c., 6³/₄" h. plus bentwood handle (Fig. 1-2, lower left) **1,093.00**

"Buttocks" basket, 28-rib construction, woven oak splint, integrated collar, pronounced bulges & God's-eye crossing splint handle, Pennsylvania, 19th c., 6³/₄" h. plus bentwood handle (Fig. 1-2, lower right) **633.00**

"Buttocks" basket, 26-rib construction, woven splint, bentwood handle, good color, some damage, 12 × 14¹/₂", 7" h. plus bentwood handle **99.00**

"Buttocks" basket, 28-rib construction, woven splint, oblong w/slightly lobed base, wrapped rim & bentwood handle, good color, some damage, 12 × 16¹/₂", 7¹/₄" h. . . . **72.00**

"Buttocks" basket, 40-rib construction, woven splint, deep oblong form w/wrapped oval rim & bentwood handle, heavy varnish finish, 12 × 13", 7¹/₂" h. plus bentwood handle **127.00**

Fig. 1-1

"Buttocks" basket, 66-rib construction, woven splint, deep oblong form w/a wrapped rim & bentwood center handle, old patina, w/some stains & minor damage, 12 × 15", 7¹/₂" h. plus bentwood handle **94.00**

"Buttocks" basket, 34-rib construction, woven oak splint, large defined collar, pronounced bulges, Pennsylvania, 19th c., 15" h. plus bentwood handle (Fig. 1-2, upper right) **4,370.00**

Cheese basket, woven splint, round, low bentwood sides supporting a tightly woven square lattice design, branded "C.F.P.," wear, 24¹/₂" d. **83.00**

Eel basket, woven ash splint, a long slender cylindrical form w/a wooden plug & cork float w/rope handle, several small breaks, approximately 21" l. **220.00**

Gathering basket, woven splint, squared upright sides w/wrapped rim & bentwood handle, old black paint, 6¹/₄ × 6¹/₂", 4" h. plus bentwood handle **220.00**

Gathering basket, woven splint, a wide, rounded crescent-shaped form w/deep sides & a wrapped rim, two small bentwood handles on one side & a single round upright straight handle on the other rim, worn red stain, some wear & damage, 16 × 21", 9" h. plus handles **550.00**

Fig. 1-3

Fig. 1-4

Fig. 1-5

Fig. 1-6

Half basket, hanging-type, coiled rye straw, oblong shape w/upright sides & small bentwood hanging handle, Pennsylvania, 19th c., 4³/₄" h. (Fig. 1-11, top left) **288.00**

Half basket, hanging-type, woven oak splint, pronounced cheek construction, bentwood hanging handle, Pennsylvania, 19th c., 6¹/₂" h. plus handle (Fig. 1-3) **575.00**

Key basket, decorated leather, the tapering oval form w/sides incised w/stars, diamonds, hearts & running vines along w/the initials "J.R. McK.," the initials "G" & "F" flanking a six-pointed star on the bottom inside diamond, the stationary center handle w/applied leather hearts, the exterior in dark green, the interior in red leather, probably Richmond, Virginia, ca. 1830, 5¹/₂ × 8", 7¹/₈" h. (Fig. 1-4) . . . **41,400.00**

Key basket, tooled leather, oblong shaped sides decorated w/wide bands of scalloped tooling, fitted w/a center strap handle, probably Shenandoah Valley, Virginia, mid-19th c., some damages & cracks, 11¹/₄" l., 8¹/₂" h. (Fig. 1-5) **1,955.00**

Key basket, stamped leather, rigid black leather oval form w/upright sides centered by a stationary handle, embossed w/large stylized flowerheads flanked by diamonds between bands of interlacing chain bands, mounted w/a silver metal plaque inscribed "L.C. Brooks, 1883," probably Richmond, Virginia, 4¹/₄ × 8", 9" h. (Fig. 1-6) **6,900.00**

Knife box basket, woven splint, rectangular w/wrapped rim & center divider, traces of

Fig. 1-8   *Courtesy of Christie's*

old paint, minor damage, 10½ × 13½",
4½" h. plus bentwood handle (Fig. 1-7,
center row) **880.00**

Market basket, woven splint & cane, round
w/wrapped rim & bentwood swing handle,
light natural patina, Taghkanic, Columbia
County, New York, 7" d., 4½" h. plus
bentwood handle (Fig. 1-7, top row) **270.00**

Market basket, woven splint, rectangular
base w/oval wrapped rim, worn old varnish
on exterior, handle dated "1934," minor
damage, 9½ × 12½", 4½" h. plus bentwood
fixed handle (Fig. 1-7, bottom left) **83.00**

Market basket, woven splint, round
w/wrapped rim & swing bentwood handle,
old natural patina, some rim damage,
Taghkanic, Columbia County, New York,
9½ × 10¼", 5½" h. plus bentwood handle
(Fig. 1-7, bottom right) **171.00**

Market basket, woven splint, rectangular w/a
wrapped rim & bentwood center handle,
grey patina, slightly twisted, 10½ × 17",
6" h. plus bentwood handle **61.00**

Fig. 1-7   *Courtesy of Garth's Auctions*

Fig. 1-9

Courtesy of Sotheby's

Market basket, woven splint, rectangular w/wrapped rim & small bentwood end rim handles, dark varnish finish, some damage, 14 × 17", 6½" h. plus handles **50.00**

Market basket, coiled rye straw, large deep oval-sided form w/an attached center bentwood handle, Pennsylvania, 19th c., 7" h. (Fig. 1-11, top center) **1,295.00**

Market basket, woven oak splint, a deep rectangular collar over flat sides & rounded ends, lashed bentwood center handle, Pennsylvania, 19th c., 5¼" h. (Fig. 1-8, center bottom) **575.00**

Market basket, woven oak splint, a deep rectangular collar above flat sides & flaring, rounded ends, lashed squared bentwood handle, Pennsylvania, 19th c., 6¾" h. (Fig. 1-8, far right) **633.00**

Market basket, 16-rib construction, woven oak splint, deep rounded form w/a wrapped rim & lashed bentwood center handle, Pennsylvania, 19th c., 7¾" h. plus bentwood handle (Fig. 1-8, top center) **322.00**

Market basket, woven splint, deep rounded sides wrapped rim & bentwood swing handle, old grey patina, some damage, 16" d., 8¾" h. plus bentwood handle **110.00**

Market baskets, woven splint, one in ash splint of rectangular form w/wrapped rim & wrapped center handle, the second of oak splint in a shallow oblong form w/wrapped rim & wrapped bentwood handle, Pennsylvania, 19th c., 3½" h. & 7¾" h., 2 pcs. (Fig. 1-8, far left) **345.00**

"Melon" basket, 16-rib construction, woven splint, half-round oval form w/end-to-end bentwood handle, worn yellow & brown paint, 5 × 7¾", 4½" h. plus bentwood handle **193.00**

Nantucket basket, finely woven cane w/splint staves, deep round sides w/wrapped rim & wooden bottom, in bands of natural & brown, bentwood rim secured w/copper tacks & w/a bentwood swing handle, old paper label reads "Made by Ferdinand Sylvaro, 97 Orange St. Nantucket, Mass.," very minor damage, 10" d., 6" h. **880.00**

Nantucket baskets, finely woven ash splint, nesting "lightship"-type, each w/an arched ash bentwood swing handle & ash trim w/cross-over weaving continuing to turned

Fig. 1-11   *Courtesy of Christie's*

maple bases, seven stamped on the bottom "R. Folger - Maker - Nantucket - Mass.," six incised on the handles "Fellowes" & incised w/Roman numerals, lacking numbers I & VII, Nantucket, Massachusetts, late 19th c., sizes ranging from 6½" h. to 16½" h., set of 8 (Fig. 1-9) **6,900.00**

Potato basket, woven oak splint, half-round slat-sided form w/end-to-end bentwood handle, Kutztown area, Pennsylvania, 19th c., 14¼" d., 6½" h. plus bentwood handle (Fig. 1-10, center) **1,265.00**

Storage basket, woven splint, deep round slightly swelled sides w/a wrapped rim & squared bentwood handle, some damage, 12" d., 9½" h. plus bentwood handle **50.00**

Storage basket, woven splint, deep round sides w/wrapped rim & base band, bentwood handle, good age & patina, 15" d., 9½" h. plus bentwood handle **226.00**

Storage basket, woven splint, round w/deep sides, wrapped rim w/small bentwood rim handles, bentwood foot, worn old patina & some well-executed repairs, 21" d., 10" h. **303.00**

Fig. 1-10   *Courtesy of Christie's*

Storage basket, woven oak splint, deep cylindrical form w/a wrapped rim, Pennsylvania, 19th c., 26" d., 18¾" h. (Fig. 1-10, left) **288.00**

Storage basket, woven oak splint, deep slightly swelled cylindrical form w/a wrapped rim, circular bentwood foot, Pennsylvania, 19th c., 28" d., 29¼" h. (Fig. 1-10, right) **748.00**

Fig. 1-12   *Courtesy of Christie's*

Utility basket, woven splint, wide round
shallow sides w/wrapped rim & early paint,
a few holes in the sides, Maine, 9$^{1}/_{2}$" d.,
3$^{1}/_{2}$" h. **66.00**

Utility basket, coiled rye straw, circular
bowl-form w/flaring sides & openwork
rim, on a round foot, possibly Lancaster
County, Pennsylvania, 19th c., 4$^{3}/_{4}$" h.
(Fig. 1-11, top, far right) **518.00**

Utility basket, coiled rye straw, deep slightly
flaring oval sides w/woven end handles,
Pennsylvania, 19th c., 5$^{3}/_{4}$" h. (Fig. 1-11,
bottom left) **460.00**

Utility basket, coiled rye straw, deep slightly
tapering round sides w/two shaped
applied bentwood rim handles, on a
bentwood round foot, Pennsylvania,
19th c., 7$^{3}/_{4}$" h. plus handles (Fig. 1-11,
bottom right) **1,093.00**

Utility basket, woven splint, oval upright sides
& wrapped rim w/small bentwood end rim
handles, original yellow paint, 7" l. **413.00**

Wool gathering baskets, woven splint, large
half-round form w/integrated rim & side
holding handles, Pennsylvania, 19th c.,
32$^{1}/_{2}$" d., 14$^{1}/_{2}$" h. & 35" d., 15$^{1}/_{2}$" h., 2 pcs.
(Fig. 1-12) **2,990.00**

A cast-iron lobster bootjack.

CHAPTER
2

BOOTJACKS

The Bootjack is a utilitarian device used to remove a boot, and often an American art form at the same time. As with so many everyday items created in the 19th and early 20th centuries, the way something looked was as important to its creator as its use. United States patent records from 1790 to 1873 indicate the first patent for a bootjack was issued April 6, 1852 to Sardis Thomson of Hartsville, Massachusetts (Patent #8865). Normally, the bootjack has been produced from cast iron or wood and ranges from extremely fine casting and carvings to crude ones-of-a-kind. While they were quite often produced for advertising purposes and as novelties, they were also necessary for both men and women in removing ill-fitting boots.

Occasionally, a casting from brass was produced as in the case of a comic strip character by the name of "Foxy Grandpa" created by C. E. Schultze and appearing on the front pages of the *New York Herald* Sunday comic section on January 7, 1900. Foxy Grandpa disappeared by 1930.

In the late 19th century in Northeastern Oklahoma, Colonel George W. Miller amassed a 110,000 acre ranch he named "101 Ranch" which came from his "101" brand. This was not only a working ranch but the home of 101 Ranch Wild West Show which provided the average American with the color and romance of the soon to disappear frontier. Many items were sold at the 101 Ranch as souvenirs, including bootjacks. Today any item from 101 Ranch is extremely sought after. The ranch ceased operations in the early 1930s.

The most common form is the cricket or beetle in cast iron. In the 1860s and 1870s two foundries were producing cricket bootjacks. In Reading, Pennsylvania, Harbsters Bros. & Co. was listed in *The Business Director* of 1869-70 as a producer of sad irons and miscellaneous hardware. In Rumney, New Hampshire, Daniel Kidder had a foundry (ca. 1860) in which he produced not only the bootjack bearing his name on the underside, but more importantly he was instrumental in building the first engine used on the Mount Washington (N.H.) Cog Railway. Another common form is the "Naughty Nellie" which has been produced in many sizes and varying details of the anatomy. One collector in New York has 50 different varieties.

As with so many collectible items bootjacks are heavily reproduced, especially crickets and "Naughty Nellies"—castings are lightweight and of a poor quality. Prices on early fine castings and carvings have risen steadily in the last five years but prices for the more common varieties are still reasonable.

—Harry A. Zuber

Fig. 2-1

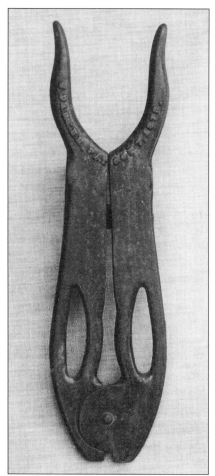

Fig. 2-2

Fig. 2-3

Brass, figural "Foxy Grandpa," ca. 1900-1910, 12" (Fig. 2-1) **$900.00**

Cast iron, adjustable cut-out arms w/wing nut on underside, marked "C. Parker, Pat Oct 7, 1873," 11" (Fig. 2-2) **400.00**

Cast iron, advertising, original gold paint, geometric & scroll design w/embossed words "Use - Musselmans - Bootjack - Plug - Tobacco," early 20th c., 9½" (Fig. 2-3) . . . **165.00**

Cast iron, closed loop at the top to hold both boot & heel, cut-out wagon wheel in center, ca. 1880, 20½" (Fig. 2-4) **275.00**

Cast iron, cut-out lettering "BOSS," ca. 1880s, 15" (Fig. 2-5) **300.00**

Cast iron, cut-out scroll design w/cut-out wording "DOWNS & CO" in center ('N,' '&' & 'S' in reverse), date unknown, 13½" (Fig. 2-6) **125.00**

Cast iron, embossed lettering "Wittier's" above & "American Centennial Boot Jack - 1876" around a cut-out star, above another star

circled by "Hyde Park" all above "Mass - 1776," 13" (Fig. 2-7) **350.00**

Cast iron, figural Devil w/painted white horns & arms, cut-out circular eyes & triangular nose above a painted red mouth & cut-out stomach, w/some original paint, ca. 1880-90, 10½" (Fig. 2-8) **275.00**

Cast iron, figural female weightlifter holding barbell w/rope & rings in her outstretched arms, late 19th c., 10" (Fig. 2-9) **800.00**

Cast iron, figural mermaid w/outstretched arms lying atop green seaweed, w/original paint, ca. 1900, 11" (Fig. 2-10) **450.00**

Cast iron, figural "Naughty Nellie" w/original wine-red-painted dress & light brown skin, ca. 1875-85, 9½" (Fig. 2-11) **300.00**

Cast iron, figural "Naughty Nellie" w/hands away from her head, painted gold, date unknown, crude casting, 10" (Fig. 2-12) . . **500.00**

Cast iron, figural "Naughty Nellie" w/original paint, late 19th c., 10½" (Fig. 2-13) **550.00**

Fig. 2-4

Fig. 2-5

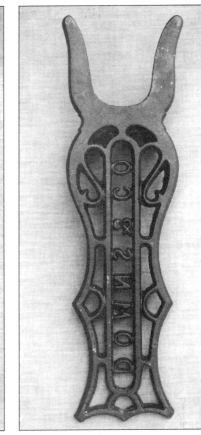

Fig. 2-6

Fig. 2-7

Fig. 2-8

Fig. 2-9

Fig. 2-10

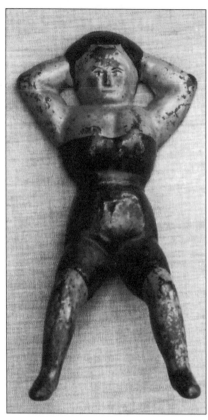

Fig. 2-11

Fig. 2-12

Fig. 2-13

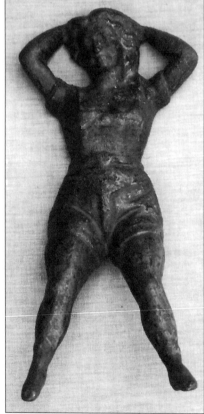

Fig. 2-14

Fig. 2-15

Fig. 2-16

Cast iron, figural "Naughty Nellie" w/head slightly turned to left, w/original red paint, fine detail, paint worn, 11½" (Fig. 2-14) . . **275.00**

Cast iron, model of a cricket w/original paint, decorated in brown, red, blue & yellow on a black ground, ca. 1900 (Fig. 2-15) **125.00**

Cast iron, model of a cricket w/bulging black eyes, painted all-over w/green & black speckled paint, ca. 1920, 10½" (Fig. 2-16) . . **95.00**

Cast iron, model of a folding pistol, marked "Phelps Dodge - Palmer - Chicago," ca. 1890, 8½" (Fig. 2-17) **275.00**

Cast iron, model of a lobster, marked "Keen Kutter" on underside, w/some original paint, 10¼" (Fig. 2-18) **125.00**

Cast iron, model of a lyre, ca. 1890, 12" (Fig. 2-19) **275.00**

Cast iron, model of a pair of upside-down dress boots above two scrolls, ca. 1870s, 13" (Fig. 2-20) **375.00**

Cast iron, model of a snail, date unknown, 13" (Fig. 2-21) **125.00**

Cast iron, model of a stag head above scroll design, ca. 1880, 11" (Fig. 2-22) **500.00**

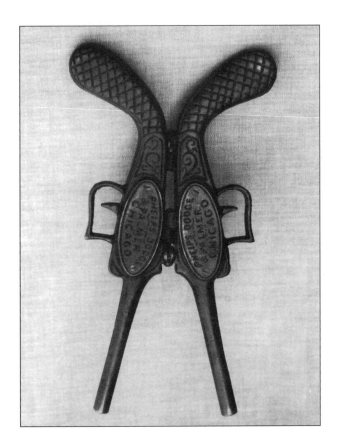

Fig. 2-17

Fig. 2-18

Fig. 2-19

Fig. 2-23

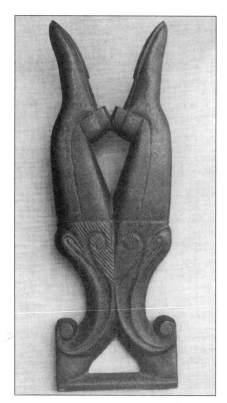

Fig. 2-20

Fig. 2-21

Fig. 2-22

Fig. 2-24

Fig. 2-25

Cast iron, model of a stear head, marked "101 Ranch" below w/Pat. Pend on underside, ca. 1910, 11½" (Fig. 2-23) **600.00**

Cast iron, model of the Tree of Life w/unusual vulture heads, cut-out heart at base, ca. 1890, 11¾" (Fig. 2-24) **125.00**

Cast iron, original red paint, elaborate floral & scroll designs w/inverted heart in center & hole at bottom, ca. 1880-90, 12¼" (Fig. 2-25) **250.00**

Cast iron, traveling-type, pivoting arms fit size of heel, cut-out vine design, style pat'd. Oct. 29, 1867 by A. P. Seymour, Hecla Works, N.Y., 8¾" open, 5⅛" closed (Fig. 2-26) **95.00**

Cast iron, Victorian scroll design, ca. 1900, 11" (Fig. 2-27) **400.00**

Wooden, folding-type, hand-carved pistol, brass hinges & pins, ca. 1860-70, 10" (Fig. 2-28) **300.00**

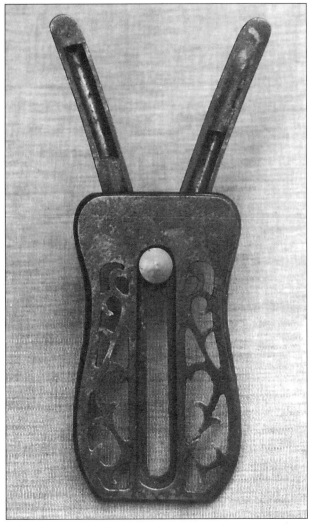

Fig. 2-26

Fig. 2-27

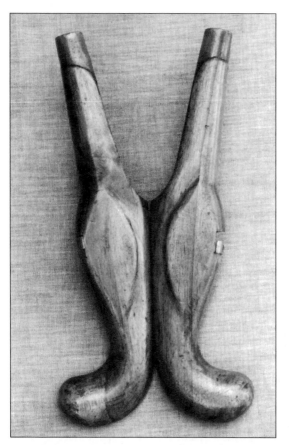

Fig. 2-28

Fig. 2-29

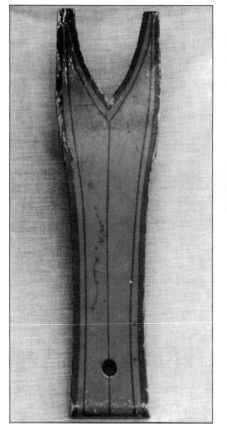

Fig. 2-30

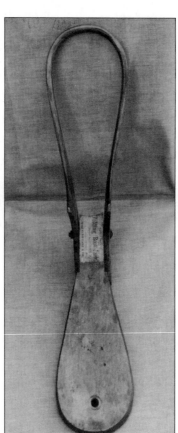

Fig. 2-31

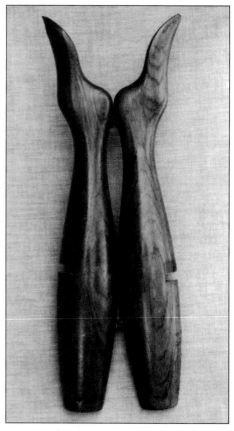

Fig. 2-32

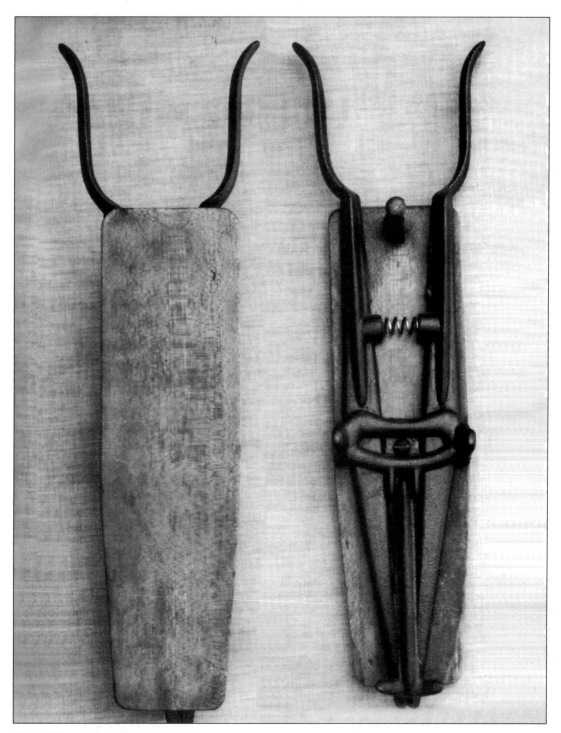

Fig. 2-33

Wooden, folding-type, long narrow boards w/brass hinges & pins, possibly Shaker, ca. 1870-80, 10½" (Fig. 2-29) **250.00**

Wooden, original red paint w/black pin striping, slender design w/small hole at bottom, ca. 1850, 16" (Fig. 2-30) **200.00**

Wooden, folding-type, w/closed loop, w/original label "Folding Boot-Jack - Wheeler Case & Co.," pat'd. Dec. 7, 1869,

Utica, New York, 23" open, 14¾" closed (Fig. 2-31) **175.00**

Wooden, walnut, folding ladies' legs w/pointed toes, brass hinges & pins, ca. 1860-70, 10" (Fig. 2-32) **350.00**

Wood & Cast iron, mechanical, spring-operated mechanism, oblong wood platform on iron base, ca. 1900, 13½" (Fig. 2-33 of front & reverse) **125.00**

A cast-iron beer drinker wall-mount bottle opener.

BOTTLE OPENERS

Fig. 3-1

Before the turn-of-the-century, the crown cap for bottled drinks was invented and immediately there was a need for a bottle cap remover or bottle opener.

There are many variations of openers, some in combination with other tools, others are utilitarian with fancy handles. Perhaps the most important type of bottle opener today is the figural bottle opener. There are 22 classifications or types of figural bottle openers, with Type 1 being the most important and sought after by collectors. Figures for openers include people, animals, birds, pretzels, keys, etc. Wall-mount openers are mostly faces of people or animals with the opener located in or near the mouth.

The important early producers (ca. 1940-50) of iron & pot-metal (zinc) figural openers were Wilton Products, John Wright Inc., Gadzik Sales, and L & L Favors. Figural openers were made primarily as souvenirs from vacation spots around the country.

Today, new original figural openers are produced in limited numbered editions and sold to collectors. Manufacturers such as Reynolds Toys have produced over 40 different figural bottle opener editions since 1988.

There are two clubs for bottle opener collectors: Figural Bottle Opener Collectors (F.B.O.C.) and Just For Openers (J.F.O.). J.F.O. a club primarily for beer opener collectors, but includes collectors of figural openers, corkscrews, and can openers.

The numbers used at the end of the entries refer to *Figural Bottle Openers Identification Guide*, a new book printed by F.B.O.C.

—Charles Reynolds

BOTTLE OPENERS BY TYPE

Type 1 - Figural bottle openers, free-standing or in its natural position or wall-mounted, the opener an integral part of the figure.

Type 2 - Figural openers with corkscrew, lighter or nutcracker, etc.

Type 3 - Figural openers, three-dimensional on both sides but do not stand.

Type 4 - Figural openers with loop openers an integral part of design.

Type 5 - Figural openers with a loop inserted in the casting process. The loop or opener is not part of the casting process.

Type 6 - Same as Type 5 with an added can punch.

Type 7 - Same as Type 5 with an added corkscrew or lighter.

Type 8 - Flat, back not three-dimensional, loop part of casting.

Type 9 - Same as Type 8, loop inserted in the casting process.

Type 10 - Same as Type 8 with a corkscrew.

Type 11 - Openers are coin or medallion shape, one or two sided, with an insert or cast integral loop opener. (These are very common.)

Type 12 - Figural stamped openers, formed by the stamping process (steel, aluminum, or brass).

Type 13 - Extruded metal openers.

Type 14 - Johnny guitars or figural holders: Johnny Guitars are figures made of wood, shells, string, etc.; they have a magnet that holds a stamped steel (Type 12) opener; figural holders or display holders are cast holders that have a clip that holds one or two cast figural openers.

Type 15 - Church keys with a figure riveted or cast on the opener. Some do not have a punch key.

Type 16 - Figural church key openers with corkscrew.

Type 17 - Decorated church key openers. (Church key loop or wire loop openers with names and jewels attached).

Type 18 - Base opener (opener molded in bottom as integral part).

Type 19 - Base opener added (opener added to bottom by brazing or soldering).

Type 20 - Base plate opener (opener screwed in base of figure).

Type 21 - Wooden openers/Syroco openers (metal insert, cast stamped or wire type).

Type 22 - Knives, hatches, scissors, etc., with openers.

RARITY

A - Most Common
B - Difficult
C - Very difficult
D - Very hard to find
E - Rare
Rare to Very Rare (few known)

FIGURAL (FULL-DIMENSIONAL)

◆ Type 1

All-American, cast iron, figure of a man in an orange football jersey w/the letters "Z B T" across his chest, standing on base marked "Joe Alexander," rarity E, 4¼" h., F-38 (Fig. 3-1) . . . . **$350.00 to 550.00**

Alligator w/boy, cast iron, figural group of black boy being bitten in the behind by an alligator, rarity B, 3" h., F-133 (Fig. 3-2, left) . . . . **75.00 to 150.00**

Alligator & boy w/hands Up, cast iron, figural group of black boy w/his hands raised above his head, being bitten in the behind by an alligator, rarity B, 2¾" h., F-134 (Fig. 3-2, right) . . . . **75.00 to 150.00**

Aviator, aluminum, figure of pilot dressed in brown flight suit & goggles w/his right hand raised, rarity B, 3¾", N-591 (Fig. 3-3, left) . . . . **75.00 to 150.00**

Barking at the moon, aluminum, figural group, a barking brown & white dog sitting at the base of a crescent moon, 2" h., N-529 (Fig. 3-4, left) . . . . **75.00 to 150.00**

Fig. 3-2

Fig. 3-3

Bar wolf, cast iron, rarity C, 9½" l.
(F-149) . . . . **150.00 to 250.00**

Bear, baby, aluminum, model of Baby Bear
wearing a red top, blue pants & holding a
cap in his hand, rarity C, 3" h., N-562
(Fig. 3-5, right) . . . . **150.00 to 250.00**

Bear, mama, aluminum, model of Mama Bear
wearing a yellow & green dress, rarity C,
4" h., N-561 (Fig. 3-5, center) . . **150.00 to 250.00**

Bear, papa, aluminum, model of Papa Bear
wearing a blue jacket, red vest & grey pants,
rarity C, 4⅝" h., N-560 (Fig. 3-5,
left) . . . . **150.00 to 250.00**

Bear at fence, aluminum, model of a bear
standing at a fence marked "FIGURAL -
BOTTLE - OPENERS," rarity B, 4⅝" h.,
N-582 (Fig. 3-6) . . . . **75.00 to 150.00**

Fig. 3-4

Fig. 3-6

Fig. 3-5

Fig. 3-7

Fig. 3-8

Fig. 3-9

Fig. 3-10

Beer drinker, cast iron, figure of a portly man wearing a hat, blue shirt & brown pants holding a bear mug, rare, 5½" h., F-192 (Fig. 3-7) . . . . **550.00 and up**

Bicycle FBOC 1990, aluminum, model of a gold bike on a base marked "FBOC," 2⅝" h., N-572 (Fig. 3-8, center) . . . . **75.00 to 150.00**

Billy goat, cast iron, figure of a goat w/head tilted back, rarity C, 2¾" h., F-74 (Fig. 3-9, right) . . . . **150.00 to 250.00**

Bird's Birch Beer, aluminum, model of a grey bird perched atop a branch, the bird marked "Birds," the branch marked "Birch Beer," 3" h., N-574 (Fig. 3-8, left) . . . . . . **50.00 to 75.00**

Black horse, aluminum, model of a rearing horse, rarity A, 3¾" h., N-584 (Fig. 3-10, left) . . . . **50.00 to 75.00**

Buffalo, aluminum, 2" h., N-595 (Fig. 3-4, right) . . . . **50.00 to 75.00**

Caddy, cast iron, figure of a black boy wearing a red shirt, black pants & red shoes, holding a golf bag w/clubs & resting his hand on a white sign that reads "19," rarity D, 5⅞" h., F-44 (Fig. 3-11) . . . . **250.00 to 350.00**

Canvasback duck, cast iron, colorfully painted duck w/red head & neck & a yellowish white body, 1¹³/₁₆" h., F-107 (Fig. 3-12, left) . . . . **75.00 to 150.00**

Fig. 3-12

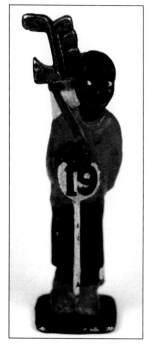

Fig. 3-11

Fig. 3-13

Cathy Coed, cast iron, figure of a young woman wearing a yellow hat, blue V-neck blouse, short flared yellow skirt & black Mary Jane-type shoes, standing on a base marked "Women's Weekend," rarity E, 4⁵⁄₁₆" h., F-39 (Fig. 3-13, right) . . **350.00 to 550.00**

Chili pepper '93, cast Iron, model of a red chili pepper, rarity B, 5⁷⁄₈" h., N-658 (Fig. 3-14, top) . . . .**75.00 to 150.00**

Cockatoo, cast iron, colorfully painted, 3" h., F-121 (Fig. 3-15, center) . . . . **75.00 to 150.00**

Cocker Spaniel, cast iron, model of dog w/white body & brown ears, neck & hind end, standing w/one foot raised, rarity A, 2³⁄₄" h., F-80 (Fig. 3-16, right) . . . . **50.00 to 75.00**

Cool penguin, zinc, model of walking penguin wearing a top hat, rarity C, 4" h. (Fig. 3-17, right) . . . . **150.00 to 250.00**

Fig. 3-14

Fig. 3-15

Fig. 3-16

Fig. 3-17

Fig. 3-18

Cowboy w/cactus, pot metal, figural group of cowboy wearing cowboy hat & plaid shirt clutching a cactus, rarity D, 4⅝" h., F-23 (Fig. 3-18, right) . . . . **250.00 to 350.00**

Crystal beetle, pot metal & crystal, model of a beetle w/cut crystal circular body w/metal legs & head, rare, 4⅜" (Fig. 3-19, right) . . . . **550.00 and up**

Devil, aluminum, figure of Devil dressed in red robes holding pitch fork, rarity B, 4" h., N-563 (Fig. 3-20, left) . . . . **75.00 to 150.00**

Fig. 3-19

Fig. 3-20

Fig. 3-21

Fig. 3-22

Dodo bird, cast iron, model of a bird w/black body, colorful markings on wings, head & an orange beak, rarity E, 2¹³/₁₆", F-122 (Fig. 3-21, left) . . . . **350.00 to 550.00**

Dolphin, aluminum, model of stylized goldish green dolphin w/tail curled over its head, 4" h., N-616 (Fig. 3-36, right) . . . **75.00 to 150.00**

Donkey, aluminum, w/3" ears, rarity D, 3³/₈" h., F-59 (Fig. 3-22, center) . . . . **250.00 to 350.00**

Donkey, brass, body of donkey marked "Phila. - 1948," rarity D, 3³/₄" h. (Fig. 3-22, right) . . . . **250.00 to 350.00**

Donkey, brass, base marked "Norwood," rare, 4¹/₈" h. (Fig. 3-22, left) . . . . **550.00 and up**

Fig. 3-23

Donkey, cast iron, figure of standing donkey
w/white teeth, rarity D, 3¹/₂" l., N-613
(Fig. 3-23, right) . . . . **250.00 to 350.00**

Dragon, cast iron, model of dragon w/open
mouth, arched back & curled tail, rarity E,
5" h. (Fig. 3-24) . . . . **350.00 to 550.00**

Dumbbell, cast iron, rare, 4⁵/₈"
(F-220) . . . . **550.00 and up**

Elephant, cast iron, rarity E, 3¹/₄"
(F-47) . . . . **350.00 to 550.00**

Elephant, cast iron, model of walking
elephant w/mouth open & trunk raised,
rarity D, 4¹/₄" l., N-616 (Fig. 3-23,
left) . . . . **250.00 to 550.00**

Eskimo ice, aluminum, figural group of
Eskimo dressed in a parka holding the
leash of the dog sitting in front of him,
3" h., N-575 (Fig. 3-4, center) . . . **75.00 to 150.00**

Father Christmas, aluminum, rarity C, 4¹/₂" h.,
N-558 (Fig. 3-25, center) . . . . . **150.00 to 250.00**

Father Time, aluminum, figure of Father Time
dressed in grey robe, holding a sickle & an
hour glass, rarity B, 4³/₄" h., N-599 (Fig. 3-26,
right) . . . . **75.00 to 150.00**

Flying fish, aluminum, model of a trout atop
a wave, rarity B, 4³/₄" h., N-656 (Fig. 3-26,
left) . . . . **75.00 to 150.00**

Freddie Frosh, cast iron, model of young man
w/his hands in his pockets wearing a beanie-

Fig. 3-24

Fig. 3-25

Fig. 3-26

Fig. 3-27

style cap, sweater w/Greek letter across the front, standing on a green base, rarity D, 4" h., F-37 (Fig. 3-27) . . . . **250.00 to 350.00**

Goat, cast iron, model of seated goat, rarity A, 4⁵⁄₁₆" h., F-71 (Fig. 3-9, left) . . . . . **50.00 to 75.00**

Gobbler, aluminum, model of gold-painted turkey w/stern look on his face, wearing suit w/arms crossed, 3" h., N-625 (Fig. 3-28, center) . . . . **75.00 to 150.00**

Good luck, aluminum, model of a hand in the form of a fist w/forefinger overlapping thumb, wrist marked "Good Luck," rarity A, 3³⁄₄" h., N-624 (Fig. 3-26, center) . . **50.00 to 75.00**

Grass skirt Greek, cast iron, figure of a black boy wearing a grass skirt, clutching a sign that reads "Phi Gamma Delta - Fiji Island Party - '53," rarity D, 5" h., F-43 (Fig. 3-29) . . . . **250.00 to 350.00**

Heart in hand, cast iron, model of an up-turned hand w/a cut-out heart in the palm, rarity E, 4¹⁄₄" h., F-203 (Fig. 3-19, left) . . . . **350.00 to 550.00**

Hunting dogs, aluminum, model of two dogs, one chocolate brown & one light brown, 2" h., N-587 (Fig. 3-8, right) . . . . . **50.00 to 75.00**

Fig. 3-28

Fig. 3-29

Fig. 3-30

Indian chief, aluminum, figure of Chief wearing full headdress, standing w/legs spread & hands on hips, 5" h., N-598 (Fig. 3-28, left) . . . . **50.00 to 75.00**

Iroquois Indian, cast iron, figural, aluminum, rarity A, 4³/₄" (F-197) . . . . **50.00 to 75.00**

Key (large), stainless steel, marked "Powell - White - Star Valves - are - Closers," rare, 9" l. (Fig. 3-30) . . . . **550.00 and up**

Lady in kimono, cast iron, stylized figure of woman wearing a kimono, entire figure is black except for the red sash & light brown hat, rarity D, 3⁷/₈" h., N-580 (Fig. 3-17, left) . . . . **250.00 to 350.00**

Lady in the wind, aluminum, figure of woman wearing royal blue dress & hat, she is leaning into the wind clutching her hat, 4" h., N-598 (Fig. 3-28, right) . . . . **50.00 to 75.00**

Lamp post drunks, cast iron, figural, common, 4¹/₈" (F-1, 2, 11) . . . . . . **10.00 to 25.00**

Lion hoop, cast iron, model of a lion jumping through hoop, 3⁵/₈" l., N-576 (Fig. 3-31, right) . . . . **250.00 to 350.00**

Mademoiselle lamp/sign, cast iron, rarity A, 4¹/₂" (F-10) . . . . **50.00 to 75.00**

Male nude w/garment, brass, rarity E 2⁷/₈" h., F-24 (Fig. 3-32, right) . . . . **350.00 to 550.00**

Mexican w/cactus, cast iron, figural group of Mexican wearing sombrero sitting beside cactus, rarity E, 2⁷/₈" h., F-24 (Fig. 3-18, left) . . . . **350.00 to 550.00**

Mighty Musky, cast iron, rarity B, 6¹/₈" l., N-659 (Fig. 3-14, bottom) . . . . **75.00 to 150.00**

Miner, FBOC '95, cast iron, figure of miner wearing blue pants, yellow shirt & brown hat holding pan & pick on base marked "FBOC 1995," rarity A, 4¹/₈", N-670 (Fig. 3-23, center) . . . . **50.00 to 75.00**

Missouri mule, bronze, model of stylized kicking mule, rarity A, 2⁷/₈" h., N-551 (Fig. 3-33, center) . . . . **50.00 to 75.00**

Monkey, cast iron, model of seated monkey, 2⁵/₈" h., F-89 (Fig. 3-12, center) . . . . **150.00 to 250.00**

Mother goose, aluminum, figure of woman in a green dress & white apron holding a goose, rarity A, 3³/₄" h., N-573 (Fig. 3-10, right) . . . . **50.00 to 75.00**

Motorcycle rider, aluminum, figural group of man riding motorcycle wearing a red helmet, goggles, white shirt & brown pants, rarity B, 2³/₄" h., N-588 (Fig. 3-3, center) . . . . **75.00 to 150.00**

Fig. 3-31

Fig. 3-32

Fig. 3-33

New Year baby, aluminum, figure of Baby New Year holding a parrot & wearing a black top hat, diaper & sash marked "1989," 4⅝" h., N-567 (Fig. 3-36, center) . . . .**75.00 to 150.00**

Nude on swan iron, brass, rarity B, 6⅝" h. (Fig. 3-32, left) . . . .**75.00 to 150.00**

Nude w/wreath, chrome, female nude w/raised arms & spread wings, rarity B, 5³⁄₁₆" h., F-173 (Fig. 3-32, center) . .**75.00 to 150.00**

Old pal, aluminum, model of a dog w/head turned & paw raised, rarity B, 2¾" h., N-570 (Fig. 3-3, right) . . . .**75.00 to 150.00**

Oriental clown, aluminum, figure of Oriental man w/hands in pockets dressed in brown, black & red clown suit, rarity C, 4³⁄₈" h., N-559 (Fig. 3-25, right) . . . . .**150.00 to 250.00**

Owl, bronze, model of a stylized owl sitting on a branch, rarity A, 2⅞" h., N-552 (Fig. 3-33, right) . . . .**50.00 to 75.00**

Owl, cast iron, rarity E, 2" (F-127) . .**350.00 to 550.00**

Paddy the Pledgemaster, cast iron, figure of a young man wearing a blue sweater & white pants holding a paddle marked "Phi Kappa Pi," standing on a base marked "Dinner Dance '57," 3⅞" h. (F-41) . . . . .**150.00 to 250.00**

Fig. 3-34

Fig. 3-36

Fig. 3-35

Palm tree, cast iron, rarity B, 4⁹/₁₆"
(F-21) . . . . **75.00 to 150.00**

Parrot, large, cast iron, rarity A, 5¹/₂"
(F-108) . . . . **50.00 to 75.00**

Parrot, FBOC, 1987, cast iron, model of a
colorful parrot on black perch, rarity A,
5¹/₂" h., F-108c (Fig. 3-34, right) . . **50.00 to 75.00**

Parrot on perch, cast iron, figure of yellow,
blue, green & red parrot on elaborate
perch, rarity E, 4⁵/₈" h., F-114 (Fig. 3-21,
right) . . . . **350.00 to 550.00**

Patty Pep, cast iron, figure of young woman
wearing a red cap & coat & a brown skirt,
buttons of coat marked w/Greek letters, on
a base marked "Pledge Dance '57," rarity E,
4" h., F-36 (Fig. 3-13, left) . . . . **350.00 to 550.00**

Pelican, cast iron, model of a pelican
w/orange eyes, 3³/₈" h., F-131 (Fig. 3-15,
right) . . . . **250.00 to 350.00**

Pelican, cast iron, model of a pelican w/up-
turned orange beak, 4" h., F-130 (Fig. 3-15,
left) . . . . **75.00 to 150.00**

Pelican w/flat head, cast iron, model of
pelican w/black head, colorful body &
yellow beak, rare, 3⁷/₁₆" h., like F-129
(Fig. 3-21, center) . . . . **550.00 and up**

Polar bear, aluminum, model of polar bear
standing on its hind legs holding a brown
stick, rarity C, 3³/₄" h., N-557 (Fig. 3-25,
left) . . . . **250.00 to 350.00**

Pretzel, cast iron or aluminum, rarity A,
3³/₈" w., F-230 (Fig. 3-35, left) . . . . **50.00 to 75.00**

Pretzel, cast iron, black, marked "Hauenstein
Beer," rarity D 2⁷/₈" w., F-231 (Fig. 3-35,
right) . . . . **250.00 to 350.00**

Pumpkin head, aluminum, figure of a person
w/pumpkin head wearing black robe, rarity B,
4¹/₄" h., N-565 (Fig. 3-20, right) . . . **75.00 to 150.00**

Fig. 3-37

Fig. 3-38

Red Riding Hood, aluminum, figure of Red
  Riding Hood holding a basket w/the wolf
  at her feet, 4" h., N-568 (Fig. 3-36,
  left) . . . . **50.00 to 75.00**

Rhino, cast iron, rarity E, 4"
  (F-76) . . . . **350.00 to 550.00**

Rooster, cast iron, 4" h., F-100
  (Fig. 3-31, left) . . . . **75.00 to 100.00**

Rooster, cast iron, rarity A, 3¹/₈" h., F-97
  (Fig. 3-37, left) . . . . **50.00 to 75.00**

Rooster (large), cast iron, tail down, rarity B,
  3³/₄" h., F-98 (Fig. 3-37, right) . . . **75.00 to 150.00**

Rooster (tail down), cast iron, rarity B, 3³/₄" h.,
  F-99 (Fig. 3-37, center) . . . . **550.00 and up**

Sailor, aluminum, cast iron, painted, rarity D,
  5⁷/₈" (F-18) . . . . **250.00 to 350.00**

Sammy Somoa, cast iron, figure of a native
  wearing leaves, rare, 4⁵/₁₆" h., F-39
  (Fig. 3-13, center) . . . . **550.00 and up**

Sawfish, cast iron, 5" l., F-157
  (Fig. 3-38, center) . . . . **250.00 to 350.00**

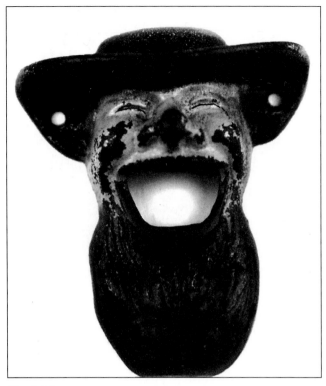

Fig. 3-39

Fig. 3-40

Sea gull, cast iron, model of a sea gull on a brown perch, 3" h., F-123 (Fig. 3-38, left) . . . . **50.00 to 75.00**

Sea horse, cast iron, 4" h., F-140 (Fig. 3-38, right) . . . . **75.00 to 150.00**

Setter dog, cast iron, model of a dog w/front paw raised & straight tail, rarity A, 2½" h., F-79 (Fig. 3-16, left) . . . . **50.00 to 75.00**

Shoe, aluminum, rarity C, 3¾" (F-209) . . . . **150.00 to 250.00**

Skeleton, aluminum, rarity B, 4⅞" h., N-566 (Fig. 3-20, center) . . . . **75.00 to 150.00**

Skunk, cast iron, 2" h., F-92c (Fig. 3-12, right) . . . . **150.00 to 250.00**

Steering wheel, brass, rarity A, 2⅞" (F-225) . . . . **50.00 to 75.00**

Straw hat/sign, FBOC 15th, cast iron, figural group of man clutching sign post that reads "F.B.O.C. 15th Conv.," rarity A, 3⅞" h., N-618 (Fig. 3-34, left) . . . . **50.00 to 75.00**

Swimmer, aluminum, rare, 3¼" (F-195) . . . . **550.00 and up**

Teen girl, cast iron, figure of a teen-aged girl lying on her stomach w/her chin in her hands & her feet in the air, wearing black pants, white shirt & a red ribbon in her blond hair, 2" l., N-577 (Fig. 3-31, center) . . . **250.00 to 350.00**

Top hatter, bronze, model of stylized bird wearing a top hat, rarity A, 2½" h., N-606 (Fig. 3-33, left) . . . . **50.00 to 75.00**

Totem pole, aluminum, rarity B, 3¾" h., N-573 (Fig. 3-10, center) . . . . **75.00 to 150.00**

Uncle Sam, figural group of Uncle Sam clutching sign post w/sign that reads "Uncle Sam," 1 of 13, rarity D, 3⅞" h., N-580 (Fig. 3-17, center) . . . . **250.00 to 350.00**

WALL MOUNT

◆ Type 1

Amish man, cast iron, w/long beard wearing Amish-style hat, rare, 4⅛" h., F-422 (Fig. 3-39) . . . . **550.00 and up**

Bear head, cast iron, 3" h., F-426 . . **150.00 to 250.00**

Beer drinker, cast iron, model of older man wearing cap, white shirt & orange vest holding a mug of beer, surrounded by cast-iron frame w/banner at the bottom marked "Spencer Brewing Co. - Lancaster, Pa.," rarity E, 6⅜" h., F-406 (Fig. 3-40) . . . . **350.00 to 550.00**

Fig. 3-41

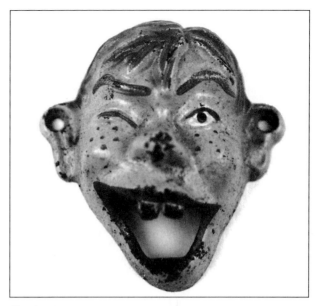

Fig. 3-42

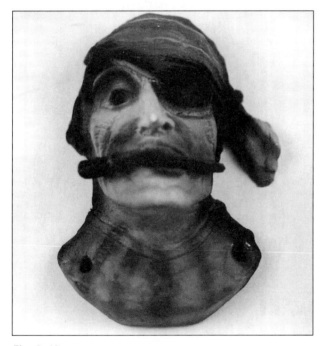

Fig. 3-43

Fig. 3-44

Black face, aluminum, black face wearing
bow tie w/mouth open to reveal
white teeth, rare, 5" h., F-401
(Fig. 3-41) . . . . **550.00 and up**

Black face, cast iron, black face w/red mouth
& hole in the ears, marked "Crowley," 4" h.
(F-404) . . . . **350.00 to 550.00**

Boy winking, cast iron, freckle-faced winking
boy w/two large front teeth, rare, 3⅞" h.,
F-418 (Fig. 3-42) . . . . **550.00 and up**

Bronze pirate, pirate head wearing a red
scarf on his head, an eye patch & holding
a knife between his teeth, 5" h., N-512
(Fig. 3-43) . . . . **75.00 to 150.00**

Bulldog, cast iron, rarity B, 4" h., F-425
(Fig. 3-44) . . . . **75.00 to 150.00**

Clown head, cast iron, model of a clown head
w/orange hair, red nose & mouth wearing
red polka-dotted tie, 4½" h., F-417
(Fig. 3-45) . . . . **75.00 to 150.00**

Fig. 3-45   Fig. 3-46   Fig. 3-47

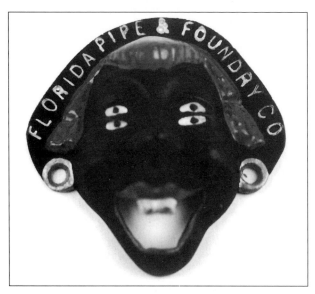

Fig. 3-48   Fig. 3-49

Coyote, cast iron, gold-painted, rare, 3¹/₂" h.,
F-429 (Fig. 3-46) . . . . **550.00 and up**

Double-eye, cast iron, four-eyed bald-
headed man, rarity A, 3⁷/₈" h., F-414
(Fig. 3-47) . . . . **50.00 to 75.00**

Florida Pipe & Foundry, cast iron, four-eyed
black woman w/red hair & lips, wearing
bonnet that reads "Florida Pipe & Foundry,"
rare, 4¹/₈" h., F-410 (Fig. 3-48) . . . . **550.00 and up**

Four-eyes man, cast iron, four-eyed man
w/mustache, rarity B, 3¹⁵/₁₆" h., F-413
(Fig. 3-49) . . . . **75.00 to 150.00**

Hanging drunk, cast iron, figure of a man
dressed in a black tuxedo & top hat,
holding bottle in left hand w/right hand
outstretched, rarity B, 5" h., F-415
(Fig. 3-50) . . . . **75.00 to 150.00**

Fig. 3-50

Fig. 3-51

Fig. 3-52

Fig. 3-53

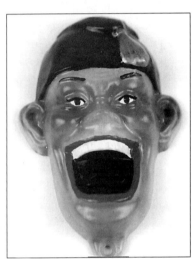

Fig. 3-54

Miss Four Eyes, cast iron, four-eyed woman
w/brown hair, red lips & gold earrings, rarity
B, 3³/₄" h., F-408 (Fig. 3-51) . . . . . . **50.00 to 75.00**

Miss Two Eyes, zinc, two-eyed woman w/short
hair & hoop earrings, rarity C, 3³/₈" h., F-409
(Fig. 3-52) . . . . **150.00 to 250.00**

Moon, aluminum, smiling & winking black
painted moon face w/silver painted
eyebrows, eyes, nose, cheeks, teeth &
chin, rarity B, 3¹/₂" h., N-664 (Fig. 3-53,
right) . . . . **75.00 to 150.00**

Norwegian, cast iron, man wearing blue cap
w/gold tassel, rarity D, 5³/₄" h., N-579
(Fig. 3-54) . . . . **250.00 to 350.00**

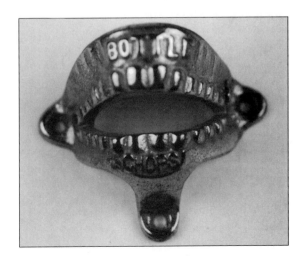

Fig. 3-55

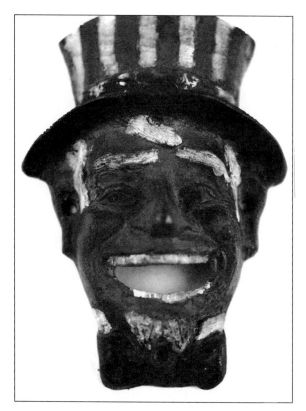

Fig. 3-56

Fig. 3-57

Sun, aluminum, orangish red-painted smiling
   sun w/black eyebrows, rarity B, 4" h., N-663
   (Fig. 3-53, left) . . . . **75.00 to 150.00**

Teeth, brass, model of teeth & gums marked
   "Bottle Chops," rarity B, 3¼" w., F-420B
   (Fig. 3-55) . . . . **75.00 to 150.00**

Uncle Sam, cast iron, head of Uncle
   Sam w/red & white painted top hat
   & white painted hair, eyebrows,
   teeth & bow tie, rarity B, 6⅛" h., N-537
   (Fig. 3-56) . . . . **75.00 to 150.00**

◆ Type 2

Old Snifter, zinc, turns head & corkscrew
   comes out (Fig. 3-57, left) **125.00**

Old Snifter, zinc, w/lighter & corkscrew
   (Fig. 3-57, right) **200.00**

◆ Type 3

Dachshund, Wilton Flats, cast iron, three-
   dimensional but does not stand (Fig. 3-58,
   bottom) . . . . **50.00 to 100.00**

Donkey, Wilton Flats, cast iron, three-
   dimensional but does not stand (Fig. 3-58,
   top) . . . . **50.00 to 100.00**

Elephant, Wilton Flats, cast iron, three-
   dimensional but does not stand (Fig. 3-58,
   left) . . . . **50.00 to 100.00**

Fish, Wilton Flats, cast iron, three-dimensional
   but does not stand (Fig. 3-58,
   center) . . . . **50.00 to 100.00**

Scottie Dog, Wilton Flats, cast iron, three-
   dimensional but does not stand (Fig. 3-58,
   right) . . . . **50.00 to 100.00**

◆ Type 4

Drunk, Wilton, cast iron, three-dimensional
   drunk wearing black top hat & suit, w/loop
   top (Fig. 3-59, left) **50.00**

Mermaid, cast iron, three-dimensional, marked
   "Chiquita," loop tail (Fig. 3-59, right) **90.00**

◆ Type 8

Gemini, zinc, flat back (Fig. 3-60, bottom left) . . **20.00**

Lobster, cast iron, flat back, red, claws serve
   as loop (Fig. 3-60, top left) **35.00**

Mad Man, zinc, flat back, depicts man
   bending at the knees w/hands clasped, legs
   serve as loop (Fig. 3-60, right) **45.00**

Fig. 3-58

Fig. 3-59

Fig. 3-60

◆ Type 9

Mermaid, lead & steel, depicts mermaid w/tail
curled under, her upraised arms holding
loop, loop inserted in casting process
(Fig. 3-61, right) **45.00**

Pretzel, large, lead & steel, top of pretzel
holds loop, loop inserted in casting process
(Fig. 3-61, center) **100.00**

Winston Churchill, aluminum & steel, shows
Churchill in front of hand giving a victory

sign, fingers of hand hold loop, loop
inserted in casting process (Fig. 3-61, left) . . **65.00**

◆ Type 11

Coin in holder, stainless steel & bronze,
bronze coin in rectangular holder, loop
cut-out at top (Fig. 3-62, left) **20.00**

Coins, cast iron, three Oriental coins joined
together w/loop cut-out of top coin
(Fig. 3-62, right) **15.00**

Fig. 3-61

Fig. 3-62

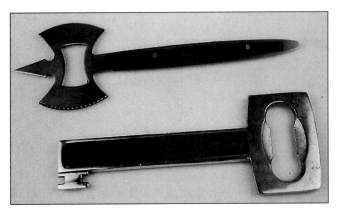

Fig. 3-63

Fig. 3-65

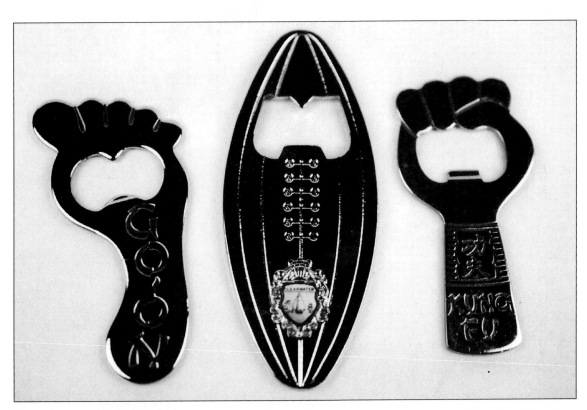

Fig. 3-64

Medallion, bronze, two-sided, w/loop at top
(Fig. 3-62, center) **10.00**

◆ Type 12

Ax, stamped steel & wood, rectangular wood
handle, opener cut-out of blade (Fig. 3-63,
bottom) **10.00**

Ax, stamped steel & wood, thin rounded wood
handle, opener cut-out of blade (Fig. 3-63,
top) **10.00**

Fist, stamped steel, w/opener cut-out of palm,
wrist reads "Kung - Fu" (Fig. 3-64, right) **8.00**

Foot, stamped steel, w/opener cut-out of the
ball of the foot, marked "Goon" (Fig. 3-64,
left) **8.00**

Football, stamped steel, w/opener cut-out of
top, small medallion at bottom reads
"Clearwater" (Fig. 3-64, center) **8.00**

◆ Type 13

Shark, aluminum, mouth serves as opener,
marked "Ocean City, MD," attached to key
ring (Fig. 3-65) **3.00**

◆ Type 14

Bar & patrons, bar holds two figural openers shaped as patrons (Fig. 3-66, center) . . . . **50.00 to 75.00**

Golf bag & caddie, golf bag holder holds figural caddie opener (Fig. 3-66, left) . . . . **50.00 to 75.00**

Shield & knight, shield holds figural knight opener (Fig. 3-66, right) . . . . **50.00 to 75.00**

Johnny Guitars, figures of old people w/magnets that hold Type 12 openers (Fig. 3-67 of group) each . . . . **6.00 to 10.00**

Fig. 3-66

◆ Type 15

Cat, attached to church key-type opener, depicts green cat w/crossed arms (Fig. 3-68, far right) **20.00**

Girl, attached to church key-type opener, girl w/long hair & large red bow on top of head (Fig. 3-68, center left) **20.00**

Violin case, attached to church key-type opener, case marked "Beethoven's Fifth" (Fig. 3-68, far left) **20.00**

Woman in bikini, attached to church key-type opener, woman wearing red & white polka-dotted cap & bikini (Fig. 3-68, center right) **20.00**

Fig. 3-67

◆ Type 17

Church keys & wire-type, w/scrolls, medallions & decorations (Fig. 3-69 of group) each . . . . **15.00 to 20.00**

◆ Type 18

Boar's head, nickel silver, full-figured, opener in bottom (Fig. 3-70, right) **85.00**

Bull's head, bronze, full-figured, opener in bottom (Fig. 3-70, left) **35.00**

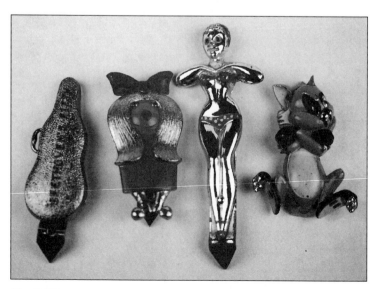

Fig. 3-68

Fig. 3-69

Fig. 3-70

Fig. 3-71

◆ Type 19

Hats, bronze, opener soldered in
bottom (Fig. 3-71 of group)
each **30.00**

◆ Type 20

Dog's head, Syroco, base plate opener
screwed in bottom (Fig. 3-72,
right) **55.00**

Horse's head, zinc, base plate opener
screwed in bottom (Fig. 3-72,
left) **35.00**

◆ Type 21

Butler, Syroco, wearing black suit &
white apron, holding green bottle,
metal opener attached to head
inside body (Fig. 3-73, right) **45.00**

Clown, Syroco, wearing white outfit
w/blue collar, metal opener attached
to head inside body (Fig. 3-73,
center) **150.00**

Man in tuxedo, Syroco, wearing top
hat, metal opener attached to head
inside body (Fig. 3-73, left) **65.00**

Fig. 3-72

Fig. 3-73

Fig. 3-74

Fig. 3-75

Man by lamppost, wooden, carved, figure of
man w/suitcase standing next to
lamppost, music box in suitcase, metal
opener attached to head inside body
(Fig. 3-74) **150.00**

Figure, wooden w/metal lifter on face, figure
wearing green scarf & hat, Danish (Fig. 3-75,
far left) . . . . **10.00 to 30.00**

Figure, wooden, figure of bird, Danish
(Fig. 3-75, far right) . . . . **10.00 to 30.00**

Figure, wooden, figure of golfer w/wooden golf
club serving as opener, Danish (Fig. 3-75,
center left) . . . . **10.00 to 30.00**

Figure, wooden, figure of Viking w/beard
& holding shield, horned hat serves
as opener, Danish (Fig. 3-75, center
right) . . . . **10.00 to 30.00**

Fig. 3-76

Wooden, metal opener attached, marked "War-
time Bottle Opener - With nail-head under
cap, pull up...your bottle is open!," World
War II era (Fig. 3-76) **45.00**

CHAPTER
4

BUTTER MOLDS & STAMPS

In early American kitchens, when butter was hand-churned, it was often the custom to mold or stamp the fresh butter with decorative designs. Most often round molds with design-carved plungers were used, but rectangular box-form molds were also made as well as flattened round "stamps" which often had a carved design on one side and an inserted handle on the other. Some stamps, referred to as "lollipop"-style, were flattened round double-sided types with a carved handle extending from one side giving them the appearance of a candy lollipop.

By the late 19th century many wooden molds were mass-produced with machine-stamped decorations and some were even made in clear pressed glass. It is the earliest, hand-carved examples, representing choice examples of American folk art, which bring the highest prices today.

Fig. 4-1

Cow with tree stamp, carved poplar, a standing horned animal amid tall grass & below a tree w/two long, leafy arching branches, zipper-cut border band, one-piece turned handle, old patina, 19th c., 4³/₈" d. **$358.00**

Eagle stamp, carved poplar, semi-circular, a stylized spread-winged bird w/long leafy wings flanked by long slender leaf clusters & leafy branches, notch-cut rim, old patina, 19th c., 7" l. **660.00**

Eagle stamp, carved poplar, a deeply carved spread-winged bird framed by a star & long, leafy sprigs within a zipper-cut border band, Pennsylvania, 1800-20, 4¹/₂" d. (Fig. 4-1, top left) **345.00**

Eagle & Acorn stamp, carved wood, a thin rectangular block divided into two halves, one half carved w/a spread-winged eagle,

Fig. 4-2

the other w/a large stylized acorn framed by
long leaves, 19th c., 2⅞ × 4½" **303.00**

Eagle "lollipop" stamp, carved pine, double-
sided, the front nicely carved w/a spread-
winged American eagle w/shield above the
reverse-incised words "Cedar Hill" all within
a serrated border, the back carved w/a
stylized tulip blossom & leafage, the head
continuing to a long turned handle,
Virginia, early 19th c., 4¼" d., overall 10¼" l.
(Fig. 4-2, right) **1,955.00**

Floral stamp, carved wood, a small deeply-
carved daisy-like flower below a fanned
cluster of leaves & flanked by large, long
serrated leaves, one-piece turned handle,
scrubbed finish, age cracks, 3⅛" d. **61.00**

Floral stamp, carved wood, decorated w/a
large oval cross-hatched blossom head
framed by small clusters of leaves over two
pairs of long, slender rounded leaves, notch-
cut border band, one-piece turned handle,
scrubbed finish, age cracks, 3⅞" d. **61.00**

Flower basket stamp, carved poplar, a large
ribbed, urn-form vase issuing large serrated
leaves centering a large central tulip
blossom & small star-like blossoms,
Pennsylvania, 1800-20, 4" d. (Fig. 4-1, lower
right) **748.00**

Heart & Distlefinks "lollipop" stamp, carved
poplar, double-sided, one side carved w/an
upside-down potted heart flanked by
distlefinks, the other side carved w/a central
radial design & concentric borders of
geometric carving, long side handle marked
"EF," dated "1792," Pennsylvania, stamp
3½" d. (Fig. 4-3) **1,380.00**

Fig. 4-3

Heart & Foliage stamp, carved poplar
w/chestnut handle, a large central cross-
hatched heart topped by a cluster of fanned
leaves & framed by long curved & pointed
leaves, zipper-cut border, old patina, relief-
carved "B" on back, age crack, 19th c.,
4⅜" d. **275.00**

Hearts & Waffle stamp, carved wood, slender
pointed almond-shaped, narrow deeply
carved hearts at each end flanking a central
reserve of deep waffle design w/a scalloped
border, notch-cut rim, dark patina, curved
top handle, 19th c., 8⅞" l. **358.00**

Leaves & Scrolls stamp, carved hardwood, a
central double-waisted stem flanked by two
pairs of large upturned serrated leaves &
slender scrolls w/dot-carved tips, one-piece
w/turned handle carved at the tip w/a
miniature print, scrubbed finish, 19th c.,
4¼" d. **402.00**

Pineapple stamp, carved wood, a large
stylized fruit w/a wide, fanned cluster of
leaves at the top & flanked by small clusters

Fig. 4-4

Fig. 4-5

of leaves above two pairs of long pointed leaves, narrow leaf band border, one-piece turned handle, scrubbed finish, 3⁷/₈" d. . . . **83.00**

Pineapple stamp, carved poplar, semi-circular form w/a rounded pineapple topped by feathered leaves & framed by pairs of short fanned & long serrated leaves, notch-cut border, worn surface, some edge wear, handle missing, 19th c., 7" l. **209.00**

Pine Cone stamp, carved poplar, oval, a large pine cone atop a notched stem flanked by pairs of serrated leaves, notch-cut borders, the top marked "S.E.G. - 1833," Lititz, Lancaster County, Pennsylvania, 3¹/₃ × 4¹/₈", 2" h. (Fig. 4-5, right) **863.00**

Pinwheel mold, carved poplar, two-part, two rectangular blocks, the top part carved w/a swirled, four-petal pinwheel with a dotted border band, Pennsylvania, ca. 1800, 8⁷/₈ × 9¹/₈", 2⁷/₈" h. (Fig. 4-4) **575.00**

Pinwheel stamp, carved poplar, a deeply carved five-arm pinwheel w/rounded petals within an incised border, w/handle, probably Schoenck, Lancaster County, Pennsylvania, 1800-20, 4" d. (Fig. 4-1, center bottom) **2,070.00**

Rooster stamp, carved poplar, a large stylized bird standing amid tall grasses & below an arched, leafy branch, zipper-cut border band, Pennsylvania, 1800-20, 4¹/₂" d. (Fig. 4-1, lower left) **690.00**

Sheaf of Wheat & Foliage stamp, carved wood, semi-circular, a large central sheaf of wheat framed by large leafy stems w/wheat heads, turned inserted handle, 19th c., 7" l. **440.00**

Star "lollipop" stamp, carved wood, a six-point star within a notched border surrounded w/a large six-sided star within a bold serrated outer border, short flaring side handle, 19th c., 4⁷/₈" d. stamp plus 2" l. handle **440.00**

Tulip stamp, carved pine, a large stylized tulip blossom flanked by deeply carved serrated leaves & scattered small stars, notch-cut border, turned maple shaped handle, Virginia, early 19th c., 5¹/₈" d. (Fig. 4-2, left) **920.00**

Tulip stamp, carved walnut, a triangular narrow board w/a rounded top deeply carved w/a long stylized tulip blossom design continuing into a long rounded "lollipop"-style handle, old patina, 19th c., 6⁷/₈" l. **363.00**

Tulip & Hearts stamp, carved wood, a rectangular block deeply carved on the bottom w/a central design of paired tulips & hearts surrounded by incised squares & w/rows of hearts at each end, Pennsylvania, 1800-30, 2⁷/₈ × 4³/₄" l. (Fig. 4-5, left) **633.00**

Tulip atop Star stamp, carved poplar, a large stylized serrated two-petal blossom above a large five-point star framed by bands of diamond-carving & a notched rim band, w/handle, Pennsylvania, ca. 1820, 4⁵/₈" d. (Fig. 4-1, upper right) **748.00**

Tulip with Stars stamp, carved wood, a rectangular head carved w/a large stylized tulip blossom framed by small stars, notch-cut border band, a tapering, arched natural growth side handle, 3¹/₈ × 3³/₄", 8¹/₂" l. **149.00**

C H A P T E R
5

CASH REGISTERS

The prices quoted are a guide to the antiques dealer or antiques buyer. These are fair retail prices that one might expect to find on a cash register at an antiques shop or show. One must understand that these are not cast in stone, and are subject to desire and availability.

Prices given are for the basic model cash register, properly operating and in good to excellent condition, with no missing or broken parts. Added features such as original top sign, clock, lights, electric motor, multiple drawers, documentation, or other uncommon factory options can significantly add to the value of the cash register. As with any antique, a missing or broken part on a cash register dramatically reduces the value of the machine. On the other hand, cash registers that are in superior pristine condition or are meticulously restored will be of much higher value.

Because National Cash Register Company of Dayton, Ohio, was the major manufacturer of cash registers, most of the prices listed in this guide are for National Registers. Registers manufactured by other companies are listed, but not specific models numbers. Prices for these machines are noted within a wide price range. Certain cash registers are quoted only as "rare." These machines are known to exist in such small quantities that it is difficult to assign a specific dollar value.

—William J. Heuring

NATIONAL COUNTER-TOP CASH REGISTERS

Model No. 0, wide-scroll case	**$6,500.00**
Model No. 0, narrow-scroll case	5,000.00
Model No. 1, extended base	4,000.00
Model No. 2, narrow-scroll case	1,000.00
Model No. 2, inlaid wood case	3,000.00
Model No. 3, wide-scroll case	1,200.00
Model No. 3, narrow-scroll case	1,000.00
Model No. 3, inlaid-scroll case	3,000.00
Model No. 4, fine-scroll case	1,800.00
Model No. 4, inlaid wood case	3,500.00
Model No. 5, fine-scroll case	2,000.00
Model No. 6, extended base, fine-scroll case	2,500.00
Model No. 6, extended base, fleur-de-lis case	3,500.00
Model No. 7, fleur-de-lis case	900.00
Model No. 8, fine-scroll case	1,200.00
Model No. 8, fleur-de-lis case	900.00
Model No. 9, fine-scroll case	1,200.00
Model No. 9, fleur-de-lis case	900.00
Model No. 11, cast-iron case	1,600.00
Model No. 13, cast-iron case	1,600.00
Model No. 14, cast-iron case	1,600.00
Model No. 30, inlaid wood case	**RARE**

Fig. 5-1

Fig. 5-3

Fig. 5-2

Model No. 35 through 49, fine-scroll
 case **1,200.00**
Model No. 35 through 49, Renaissance
 case **700.00**
Model No. 35 through 49, dolphin case . . . **500.00**
Model No. 50, Renaissance case **1,600.00**
Model No. 50, dolphin case **900.00**
Model No. 52, dolphin case **1,500.00**
Model No. 63, early combination ring-up . . **3,000.00**
Model No. 63, cast-iron case, w/top sign
 (Fig. 5-1) **800.00**
Model No. 64, early combination ring-up . . **3,000.00**
Model No. 64, cast-iron case **800.00**
Model No. 78, scroll case **1,200.00**
Model No. 79, scroll case **1,200.00**
Model No. 79, empire case **700.00**
Model No. 87, empire case **700.00**
Model No. 94, scroll case **1,200.00**
Models No. 210 or 211 . . . . **1,300.00**
Models No. 225 or 226 . . . . **700.00**
Model No. 310 . . . . **1,000.00**
Model No. 311 . . . . **1,000.00**
Model No. 313 (Fig. 5-2) **800.00**

Fig. 5-4

Fig. 5-5

Model No. 314 . . . . 800.00

Model No. 316 or No. 317 . . . . 800.00

Models No. 322, 323, 326 or 327 . . . . . . 1,400.00

Model No. 324 . . . . 700.00

Models No. 332, 333, 334, 336, 342, 343, 346, 347, 348, 349, 356, & 359,
each 600.00

Models No. 410, 415, 416, & 420,
each 800.00

Models No. 441, 442, & 451 (Fig. 5-3 of Model 442) each 800.00

Models No. 500 through 599, counter top-style, multi-drawer 1,600.00

Models No. 500 through 599, single drawer 1,000.00

Models No. 711 & 717, steel case 200.00

Models No. 1054 & 1064 . . . . 600.00

NATIONAL FLOOR MODELS

Models No. 500 through 599, floor model, metal case atop set of wood drawers (Fig. 5-4 of Model 572) each **2,000.00**

OTHER MANUFACTURERS:

American Cash registers (Fig. 5-5 of Model 50) . . . . **1,000.00 to 3,000.00**

Hallwood Cash registers . . . . **1,000.00 and up**

Michigan Cash registers . . . . 200.00 to 700.00

St. Louis Cash registers . . . . 200.00 to 700.00

Ideal Cash registers . . . . **RARE**

Chicago Cash registers . . . . **RARE**

Weller Cash registers . . . . 300.00 to 800.00

Dial Cash registers . . . . **RARE**

Basketweave & Morning Glory canisters.

CHAPTER

6

CERAMICS

BLUE & WHITE STONEWARE

From roughly 1900 to the late 1930s, embossed Blue and White Stoneware pottery was an extremely common commodity found in many American households. Stoneware was found in many American households and was a popular commodity essential to the way of life during that era. Huge numbers of inexpensive stoneware items were manufactured by a variety of potteries to fill a wide range of utilitarian purposes mostly for kitchen use and personal hygiene needs. Most of this stoneware was painted in various colors including Blue and White, yellow, brown, green, cream, and various combinations thereof. Most paint was applied with an airbrush, occasionally some specific features were detailed with a hand brush. "Spongeware" is the result of dabbing a piece with a sponge dipped in paint.

To collectors of antique embossed stoneware pottery, Blue and White has historically been the most collectible, although the other colors seem more difficult to find. Many stoneware pieces were highly decorated with an embossed design or

A group of Blue & White pieces.

decals or stencils in a very successful attempt to bring a bit of attractiveness and beauty into the lives of the owners. Embossed designs were the most common patterns and include various birds, animals, trees, flowers, people, woven willow canes, and abstract designs.

Manufacturers targeted this stoneware for "everyday folk" and most pieces were intended for hard daily use. The variety of pieces is almost endless and includes pitchers, ewers and basins, bowls, salt and butter tubs, kitchen canisters, preserving crocks, water coolers, sand jars, coffee and teapots, umbrella stands, spittoons, chamber pots (thunder mugs), slop jars (combinets), jardinieres and pedestals, birdbaths, and on and on.

Several large scale retailers, such as Sears Roebuck, usually carried several lines of conveniently priced stoneware in their sales catalogs. However, much of the stoneware was purchased directly from the local general store and several lines were available as "giveaways;" buy a bag of

Fig. 6-1

flour and a piece of stoneware (pitcher, bowl, salt or butter crock, etc.) was included. Sometimes the piece had advertising on it extolling the economic virtues of that store. Advertising pieces are now very collectible.

Blue and White Stoneware was not a product line unique to any one pottery. It was made by a number of potteries principally in the Ohio Valley region where good clay was available. Some potteries were in business for only a few years, others, such as Brush-McCoy, Nelson McCoy, Burley-Winter, Robinson-Ransbottom, Uhl, and Logan potteries were in business for decades. Many of the products, especially Blue and White Stoneware, from these potteries are lovely art designs in their own right; most such pieces are now quite popular and cherished objects to many collectors. Because of this popularity, a number of books and other publications have been written on Blue and White Stoneware. Two of the most recent publications are *Stoneware in the Blue and White* by M.H. Alexander, (1993 reprint), Image Graphics, Inc. Paducah, KY, and *Blue & White Stoneware* by Kathryn McNerney (1995 reprint), Collector Books, Paducah, KY

Prices quoted reflect the presently appraised values for Blue and White pieces in mint condition with good color and with lids and bails in originally furnished condition. Lidded pieces include some bowls (including milk crocks), butter tubs, slop jars, and batter crocks. Prices are meant as a guide only and may vary from region to region. Dimensions are given for each piece where known. The reference after each piece cites a popular publication where an illustration may be found.

—Stephen E. Stone

Baking dish, Peacock patt., 9" d., Joseph & Harbin, 1973, plate 15, row 1, no. 2 (Fig. 6-1, center) **$750.00**

Basin, Apple Blossom patt., 9" d. **185.00**

Batter jar, cov., Wildflower patt., 7" d., 8" h. (McNerney, 1991, pg. 43) **300.00**

Bean pot, cov., marked "Boston Bean Pot," 10" d., 9" h. (Alexander, 1993, pg. 88) **450.00**

Beer cooler, cov., Elves patt., includes spigot, 14" d., 18" h. (McNerney, 1991, pg. 35) . . . **725.00**

Bowl, Apricot with Honeycomb patt., 7½" d., 2¾" h. (McNerney, 1991, pg. 17) **135.00**

Bowl, Beaded Rose patt., 7" d. (Harbin, 1977, pg. 48, row 1, no. 1) **150.00**

Bowl, berry/cereal, 4" d., 2" h. (McNerney, 1991, pg. 16) **55.00**

Bowl, Daisy Roaster patt., 9" d., 4" h. (Alexander, 1993, pg. 41) **235.00**

Bowl, Diamond Point patt., 10½" d., 5½" h. (McNerney, 1991, pg. 14) **170.00**

Bowl, embossed Pineapple patt., ten sizes ranging from 4½" to 14" (McNerney, 1991, pg. 14) . . . . **174.00 and up**

Bowl, Flying Bird patt., 4" d., 2" h., w/advertising (Harbin, 1977, pg. 18) **300.00**

Bowl, Gadroon Arches or Pedal Panels patt., 9½" d., 4½" h. (McNerney, 1991, pg. 14) . . **175.00**

Bowl, Greek Key patt., sizes range from 6" to 12" d. (Harbin, 1977, pg. 46, row 1, no. 2) . . . . **85.00 to 170.00**

Bowl, Heart Banded patt., 10" d., 5" h. (Alexander, 1993, pg. 43) **135.00**

Fig. 6-2

Bowl, miniature, 4" d., 2" h. (McNerney, 1991, pg. 46) **50.00**

Bowl, Plain, 3" d. (Habin, 1977, pg., 48, row 1, no. 2) **40.00**

Bowl, Reverse Pyramid patt., 4¹/₂" d., 2¹/₂" h. (McNerney, 1991, pg. 16) . . . . **65.00 to 75.00**

Bowl, Reverse Pyramid patt., 7¹/₂" d., 5" h. (McNerney, 1991, pg. 16) . . . . . **90.00 to 100.00**

Bowl, Wildflower patt. (Fig. 6-11, top left) . . . .**135.00 & up**

Bowls, Cosmos patt., nesting-type (McNerney, 1991, pg. 16) the set . . . . **200.00 to 275.00**

Bowls, Ringsaround (Wedding Ring) patt., six sizes (McNerney, 1991, pg. 12 & 13) . . . . **85.00 to 225.00**

Bowls, Scallop patt., 6" d., 3¹/₂" h., 8" d., 3¹/₂" h., 9¹/₂" d., 5" h., nesting-type, (Alexander, 1993, pg. 43) the set . . **85.00 to 125.00**

Bowls, Wildflower patt., 4" to 14" d., nesting-type (Alexander, 1993, pg. 46) the set **250.00**

Brush vase, Bowtie (Our Lucile) patt., w/rose decal, 5¹/₂" h. (Sanford, 1992, pg. 10) **115.00**

Butter crock, cov., Cow and Fence patt., 7¹/₄" d., 5" h. (McNerney, 1991, pg. 105) . . . **625.00**

Butter crock, cov., Cows and Columns patt., range from 2 lbs. to 10 lbs., McNerney, 1991, pg. 106 (ILLUS. w/introduction, center w/pitchers) . . . . **425.00 to 650.00**

Butter crock, cov., Daisy & Basketweave patt., 7" d., 6³/₄" h. (Harbin, 1977, pg. 44, row 2, no. 1) **275.00**

Butter crock, cov., Daisy and Trellis patt., 6¹/₂" d., 4¹/₂" h. (Alexander, pg. 55, bottom) . . **225.00**

Butter crock, cov., Diffused Blue with Blocks patt., w/cov., 7¹/₂" d., 5¹/₂" h. (Harbin, 1972, pg. 7, row 3, no. 2) **125.00**

Butter crock, cov., Diffused Blue with Inverted Pyramid Bands patt., 6" d., 4" h. (Harbin, 1973, plate 7, row 3, no. 2) **125.00**

Butter crock, cov., Dragonfly and Flower patt., small, rare, McNerney, 1991, pg. 108 (Fig. 6-2, left) **500.00**

Butter crock, cov., Dragonfly and Flower patt., large, 8" d., 5" h., McNerney, 1991, pg. 108 (Fig. 6-2, right) **345.00**

Butter crock, cov., Grape and Leaves Low patt., 6" d., 5" h. (McNerney, 1991, pg. 103) **250.00**

Butter crock, cov., Greek Column or Draped Window patt., available in 2 lbs., 3 lbs., 4 lbs., & 5 lbs. (McNerney, 1991, pg. 22) . . . . **225.00 to 295.00**

Butter crock, cov. (Harbin, 1977, pg. 22) . . . **125.00**

Fig. 6-3

Butter crock, cov., Indian patt., 2 lbs. (Harbin, 1977, pg. 42, row 3, no. 1) **650.00**

Butter crock, cov., Lovebird patt., 6" d., 5" h., Alexander, 1993, pg. 59 (Fig. 6-3, right) . . . **700.00**

Butter crock, cov., Peacock patt., w/bail handle, 1 lb., 4" h. (Harbin, 1977, pg. 44) **1,000.00**

Butter crock, cov., Plain (Harbin, 1977, pg. 44, row 2, no. 2) **195.00**

Butter crock, cov., Printed Cows patt., 6½" d., 5" h. (McNerney, 1991, pg. 106) **195.00**

Butter crock, cov., Rose and Waffle patt., 5" d., 4½" h. (Harbin, 1977, pg. 44, row 3, no. 3) . **300.00**

Butter crock, cov., stenciled, 2 lbs. (McNerney, 1991, pg. 110) **245.00**

Butter crock, cov., stenciled, 3 lbs. (McNerney, 1991, pg. 110) **275.00**

Butter crock, Indian patt., without cov., 2 lbs. **600.00**

Butter crock, Indian patt., without cov., 3 lbs. (Harbin, 1977, pg. 42 row 3, no. 1) . . **750.00**

Butter pot, cov., Wildflower patt., four sizes available (Alexander, 1993, pg. 64) **150.00**

Canister, cov., Basketweave & Morning Glory (Willow) patt., "Beans," average 5½" to 6½" h. (Alexander, 1993, pg. 77) **325.00**

Fig. 6-4

Fig. 6-6

Fig. 6-5

Canister, cov., Basketweave & Morning Glory
(Willow) patt., "Coffee," average 5¹/₂" to
6¹/₂" h., Alexander, 1993, pg. 77 (Fig. 6-4, top
left) **325.00**

Canister, cov., Basketweave & Morning Glory
(Willow) patt., "Crackers," average 5¹/₂" to
6¹/₂" h. (Alexander, 1993, pg. 77) **600.00**

Canister, cov., Basketweave & Morning Glory
(Willow) patt., "Salt," average 5¹/₂" to 6¹/₂" h.,
Alexander, 1993, pg. 77 (Fig. 6-4, top
right) **475.00**

Canister, cov., Basketweave & Morning Glory
(Willow) patt., "Sugar," average 5¹/₂" to
6¹/₂" h., Alexander, 1993, pg. 77 (Fig. 6-4,
bottom) **325.00**

Canister, cov., Basketweave & Morning Glory
(Willow) patt., "Tea," average 5¹/₂" to 6¹/₂" h.
(Alexander, 1993) **325.00**

Canister, cov., Snowflake patt., 5³/₄" d., 6¹/₂" h.
(Alexander, 1993, pg. 80) **235.00**

Chamber pot, cov., Wildflower patt., 11" d.,
6" h. (McNerney, 1991, pg. 117) **250.00**

Chamber pot, Beaded Rose patt., 9¹/₂" d.,
6" h., McNerney, 1991, pg. 116 (Fig. 6-5) . . **250.00**

Chamber pot, Open Rose and Spear Point
Panels patt., 9¹/₂" d., 6" h **300.00**

Chamber pot, cov., Willow patt., 9¹/₂" d., 8" h.,
Joseph & Harbin, 1973, pg. 15, row 1
(Fig. 6-6, left) **325.00**

Cider cooler, cov., w/spigot, 13" d., 15" h.,
(Alexander, 1993, pg. 103) **425.00**

Fig. 6-7

Fig. 6-8

Fig. 6-9

Coffeepot, cov., molded vertical bands of bull's-eyes, Harbin, 1977, pg. 20, row 2, no. 3 (Fig. 6-7, right) **1,000.00**

Coffeepot, cov., Diffused Blue patt., oval body, 11" h., McNerney, 1991, pgs. 25, 26 (Fig. 6-7, left) **1,700.00**

Coffeepot, cov., Swirl patt., 11" h., McNerney, 1991, pgs. 25, 26 (Fig. 6-8) . . . . **1,000.00 or more**

Cold fudge crock, w/tin lid & ladle, marked "Johnson Cold Fudge Crock," 12" d., 13" h. (McNerney, 1991, pg. 39) **300.00**

Cookie jar, cov., Flying Bird patt., 6¾" d., 9" h., Alexander, 1993, pg. 81 (Fig. 6-9) **1,050.00**

Cookie jar, cov., Basketweave & Morning Glory (Willow) patt., marked "Put Your Fist In," 7½" h. (Alexander, 1993, pg. 77) **625.00**

Cuspidor, Snowflowers patt., 9¾" d., 9" h. (McNerney, 1991, pg. 125) **200.00**

Custard cup, Fishscale patt., 2½" d., 5" h. (McNerney, 1991, pg. 41) **100.00**

Custard cup, Peacock patt., 2⅞" h., Harbin, 1977, pg. 34 (Fig. 6-1, right) **245.00**

Fig. 6-10

Ewer & basin, Apple Blossom patt. (Alexander, 1993, pg. 122) the set . . **575.00**

Ewer & basin, Feather & Swirl patt., ewer 8½" d., 12" h., basin 14" d., 5" h. (McNerney, 1991, pg. 126) the set **550.00**

Ewer, Apple Blossom patt., 12" h., Harbin, 1977, pg. 12, row 1, no. 3 (Fig. 6-10, bottom right) **350.00**

Ewer, Banded Scroll patt., 7" h. (Harbin, 1977, pg. 12, row 1, no. 1) **275.00**

Ewer, Bowtie (Our Lucile) patt., w/rose decal, 11" h. (Sanford, 1992, pg. 10) **175.00**

Ewer, Small Floral Decal (Memphis Pattern), 7" h. (Harbin, 1977, pg. 54) **365.00**

Ewer, Wildflower patt., 7½" h., McNerney, 1991, pg. 67 (Fig. 6-11, bottom center) **300.00**

Fig. 6-11

Fig. 6-12

Foot warmer, signed Logan Pottery
  Co. (Harbin, pg. 26, row 3) **250.00**

Iced tea cooler, cov., w/spigot,
  Maxwell House, 13" d., 15" h.
  (McNerney, 1991, pg. 36) **325.00**

Jardiniere & pedestal base, Tulip
  patt., Jardiniere 7½" h., pedestal
  7" h. (Harbin, 1977, pg. 62, row 1,
  no. 1) **1,100.00**

Jardiniere, 6" h. (Harbin, 1977, pg. 24,
  row 3, no. 3) **325.00**

Match holder, model of a duck, 5½" d.,
  5" h. (McNerney 1991, pg. 48) **250.00**

Measuring cup, Spearpoint and
  Flower Panels, 6¾" d., 6" h.,
  McNerney, 1991, pg. 47, 48
  (Fig. 6-12, top) **450.00**

Meat Tenderizer, Wildflower patt.,
  3½" at the face, Alexander, 1993, pg.
  90 (Fig. 6-11, bottom right) **370.00**

Fig. 6-13

Fig. 6-14

Fig. 6-15

Fig. 6-16

Milk crock, cov., Lovebird patt., 9" d., 5¹/₂" h. (McNerney, 1991, pg. 21) . . **575.00**

Mixing bowl, Flying Bird patt., 8" d. (Alexander, 1993, pg. 44) **340.00**

Mouth ewer, Bowtie (Our Lucile) patt., 8" h. (Sanford, 1992, pg. 10) **275.00**

Mug, Cattail patt., 3" d., 4" h. (McNerney, 1991, pg. 73) **130.00**

Mug, Columns and Arches patt., 4¹/₂" h., rare, McNerney, 1991, pg. 80 (Fig. 6-13, right) **350.00**

Mug, banded design, Diffused Blue, w/advertising (ILLUS. bottom center, w/introduction) . . . . **300.00 and up**

Mug, Flying Bird patt., 3" d., 5" h. (Alexander, 1993, pg. 15) **225.00**

Mug, Grape Cluster in Shield patt., 12 oz. (McNerney, 1991, pg. 66) . . . **195.00**

Mug, Wildflower patt., 4¹/₂" h., Joseph & Harbin, 1973, plate 13, row 1, no. 4 (Fig. 6-11, bottom left) **150.00**

Mustard jar, cov., 3" d., 4" h. (McNerney, 1991, pg. 45) **200.00**

Pitcher, 8" h., Acorn patt., stenciled design (Fig. 6-10, top center) **300.00**

Pitcher, American Beauty Rose patt., 10" h., 7" d., Alexander, 1993, pg. 30 (Fig. 6-14, right) **425.00**

Pitcher, Apricot patt., 8" h., 5 pt. capacity, McNerney, 1991, pg. 61 (Fig. 6-15, right) **265.00**

Pitcher, Bands and Rivets patt., 1 pt. (McNerney, 1991, pg. 82) **285.00**

Pitcher, Bands and Rivets patt., 1 gal., McNerney, 1991, pg. 82 (ILLUS. bottom right w/introduction) **275.00**

Pitcher, Capt. John Smith & Pocahontas patt., 6¹/₄" h., 6³/₄" d., Alexander, 1993, pg. 21 (Fig. 6-16, right) **350.00**

Pitcher, Castle patt., 8" h., Alexander, 1993, pg. 25 (Fig. 6-16, left) **325.00**

Pitcher, Cherry Band patt., w/advertising, Alexander, 1993, pg. 6 (ILLUS. bottom left w/introduction) **300.00**

Pitcher, Cherry Cluster with Basketweave Pitcher patt., 10" h., 8¹/₂" d., McNerney, 1991, pg. 61 (Fig. 6-17, bottom left) **325.00**

Fig. 6-17

Pitcher, Columns and Arches patt., 9" h.,
McNerney, 1991, pg. 80 (Fig. 6-13, left) ... **600.00**

Pitcher, Cosmos patt., 9" h., 6¹/₂" d., Alexander,
1993, pg. 31 (Fig. 6-14, left) **415.00**

Pitcher, Daisy Cluster patt., 8" h., 8" d.,
McNerney, 1991, pg. 80 (Fig. 6-18) **675.00**

Pitcher, Dutch Farm patt., 9" h., 8" d., printed
(Alexander 1993, pg. 11) **250.00**

Pitcher, Eagle patt., 8" h., Alexander, 1993,
pg. 12 (Fig. 6-19, right) **600.00**

Pitcher, Grape Cluster in Shield patt., 4 pt.
(McNerney, 1991, pg. 66) **450.00**

Pitcher, Grape Cluster in Shield patt., 5 pt.
(McNerney, 1991, pg. 66) **475.00**

Pitcher, Grape Cluster on Trellis patt., 7" h.,
squat body, McNerney, 1991, pg. 65
(Fig. 6-17, top) **200.00**

Pitcher, Grape Leaf Band patt., 9¹/₂" h.
(McNerney, 1991, pg. 64) **250.00**

Pitcher, Grape with Rickrack patt., large size,
Alexander, 1993, pg. 16 (Fig. 6-17, bottom
right) **195.00**

Fig. 6-18

Fig. 6-19

Fig. 6-20

Fig. 6-21

Pitcher, Grape with Rickrack patt., middle size (Alexander, 1993, pg. 16) **235.00**

Pitcher, Grape with Rickrack patt., small size, Alexander, 1993, pg. 16 (Fig. 6-17, bottom center) **325.00**

Pitcher, Iris patt., 9" h., 5½" d., McNerney, 1991, pg. 69 (Fig. 6-12, right) **400.00**

Pitcher, Leaping Deer patt., 8½" h., 6" d., Alexander, 1993, pg. 22 (Fig. 6-20, left) **400.00**

Pitcher, Lovebird patt., 8½" h., 5½" d., Alexander, 1993, 23 & 97 (Fig. 6-19, left) **450.00**

Pitcher, Old Fashioned Garden Rose patt., 7" h., 7" d., McNerney, 1991, pg. 69 (Fig. 6-21, left) **400.00**

Pitcher, Pine Cone patt., 9½" h., 5¾" d. (Fig. 6-21, right) **625.00**

Pitcher, Plume patt. (Fig. 6-10, left) . .**350.00**

Pitcher, Shield patt., 8½" h., 6" d., Alexander 1993, pg. 32 (Fig. 6-16, center) **475.00**

Pitcher, Standing Deer patt., 8½" h., 6" d., Alexander, 1993, pg. 10 (Fig. 6-20, right) **275.00**

Pitcher, Swan patt., 8½" h., 5½" d., McNerney, 1991, pg. 58 (Fig. 6-15, left) **450.00**

Fig. 6-22

Fig. 6-24

Fig. 6-23

Pitcher, Tulip patt., 8" h., 4" d., Alexander,
1993, pg. 32 (Fig. 6-12, left) **350.00**

Pitcher, Wildflower patt., 7½" h., 4" d.
(Alexander, 1993, pg. 35) **275.00**

Pitcher, tankard, 9" h., 6½" d., Willow patt.,
Alexander, 1993, pg. 3 (Fig. 6-22) **245.00**

Pitcher, Windmill and Bush patt., 9" h.
(Harbin, 1977, pg. 10, row 2 no. 3) **400.00**

Ramekin, Peacock patt., 4", Sanford, 1992,
pg. 26 (Fig. 6-1, left) **300.00**

Rolling pin, Wildflower patt., large (Alexander,
1993, pg. 90) **300.00**

Rolling pin, Wildflower patt., small, Alexander,
1993, pg. 90 (Fig. 6-23) **375.00**

Salt box, Wildflower patt., w/hinged wooden
lid, 4½" h., 6" d., Alexander, 1993, pg. 74
(Fig. 6-11, top right) **170.00**

Salt, cov., Blue Band patt., 5" d., 6" h.
(McNerney, 1991, pg. 102) **130.00**

Salt, cov., Daisy patt., 6" d., 6½" h. (Alexander,
1993, pg. 69) **235.00**

Salt, cov., Diffused Blue patt., 6" d., 4" h.
(Alexander, 1993, pg. 70) **130.00**

Salt, cov., Flying Bird patt., 6½" d., 6" h.,
McNerney, 1991, pg. 99 (Fig. 6-3, left) . . **450.00**

Salt, cov., Plain (Harbin, 1977, pg. 38, row 1,
no. 1) **100.00**

Salt, cov., Raspberry patt., 5½" d., 5½" h.
(McNerney, 1991, pg. 101) **200.00**

Salt, cov., Waffleweave patt. (Harbin, 1977,
pg. 38, row 1, no. 2) **230.00**

Sand jar, Polar patt., 11" d., 13½" h.
(McNerney, 1991, pg. 123) **750.00**

Soap dish, Wildflower patt., 3⅝" w., 5¼" l.
(Alexander, 1993, pgs. 188 & 199) **225.00**

Spice jar, cov., "Cloves," Wildflower patt.
(Fig. 6-11, top center) **200.00**

Stein, Grape Leaf Band patt., 5" h. (McNerney,
1991, pg. 64) **125.00**

Stewer, cov., Wildflower patt., 4 qt. (Alexander,
1993, pg. 35) **285.00**

Stewer, cov., Willow patt., 4 qt. (McNerney,
1991, pg. 44) **275.00**

Teapot, cov., Swirl patt., 6" d., 6" h., Alexander,
1993, pg. 89 (Fig. 6-24) **800.00**

Tobacco jar, cov., Berry Scrolls patt., 5" d.,
6½" h. (McNerney, 1991, pg. 46) **300.00**

Umbrella Stand, Two Stags patt., solid blue,
21" h. (Harbin, 1977, pg. 60) **1,000.00**

Waste jar, cov., Willow patt., Joseph & Harbin,
1973, pg. 15, row 3 (Fig. 6-6, right) **325.00**

Water cooler, cov., Apple Blossom patt.,
w/spigot, 13" h., McNerney, 1991, pg. 30
(Fig. 6-25) **850.00**

Water cooler, cov., Polar patt., w/spigot, 6 gal.
(Alexander, 1993, pg. 104, 105) **850.00**

Water cooler, cov., Polar patt., w/spigot, 8 gal.
(Alexander, 1993, pg. 104, 105) **975.00**

Water cooler, cov., Polar patt., w/spigot, 10
gal. (Alexander, 1993, pg. 104, 105) **1,250.00**

HISTORICAL &
COMMEMORATIVE WARES

Numerous potteries, especially in England and
the United States, made various porcelain and
earthenware pieces to commemorate people,
places, and events. Scarce English historical wares
with American views command the highest prices.
Objects are listed here alphabetically by title of view.

Most pieces listed here will date between about
1820 and 1850. The maker's name is noted in paren-
thesis at the end of each entry.

Almshouse, Boston vase, handled, flowers
within medallions border, dark blue, 7½" h.,
7¼" d., Ridgway (handles, base, & rim
restored) **$1,100.00**

**American Scenery—View of Newburgh
platter,** long-stemmed roses border,
scalloped edge, brown, 18" l., Jackson
(hairline off the rim (1" l.) & mellowed
w/crazing) **358.00**

Arms of Delaware platter, flowers & vines
border, dark blue, ca. 1830, 17" l., Mayer
(Fig. 6-26) **4,025.00**

Fig. 6-25

Fig. 6-26

Fig. 6-27

Fig. 6-28

Arms of Georgia platter, flowers & vines border, spoked wheels equidistant around border, dark blue, ca. 1830, 12³/₄" l., Mayer (surface abrasions) **5,175.00**

Arms of New York plate, flowers & vines border w/spoked wheels equidistant around, dark blue, minute chips, ca. 1830, 10" d., Mayer (Fig. 6-27) **1,150.00**

Arms of Pennsylvania platter, flowers & vines border w/spoked wheels equidistant around, dark blue, ca. 1830, 21" l., Mayer (minor scratches) **7,475.00**

Baltimore Exchange plate, fruits, flowers, & leaves border, dark blue, 10" d. (Henshall, Williamson & Co.) **431.00**

Bank of the United States, Philadelphia plate, spread eagles amid flowers & scrolls border, dark blue, light mellowing, 10" d., Stubbs (Fig. 6-28) **479.00**

Boston Athenaeum (Lawrence Mansion,) wash bowl, vine border, dark blue, 12¹/₂" d., Ralph Stevenson & Williams (staple repair) **633.00**

Boston Harbor cup plate, flowers, foliage & scrolls border, spread eagle w/shield in foreground, city (Boston?) in far background, dark blue, 4" d. (Rogers) .. **1,870.00**

Boston State House pitcher, reverse, New York City Hall, fully opened roses w/leaves border, dark blue, 6³/₄" h. Stubbs (light re-

glazing to sides of body, restoration to internal hairlines) **440.00**

Boston State House platter, floral border, dark blue, 11¹/₄" l., Rogers (professional repair to chip on rim) **715.00**

Boston State House platter, floral border, dark blue, 14⁵/₈", Rogers (minute flake on inner rim & several short facial scratches) **605.00**

Boston State House sugar bowl, w/matching cov., embossed floral handles, floral border, dark blue, 5¹/₂" h., Rogers (rim chips restored on cover & chip restored on side of base) **495.00**

Boston State House toddy plate, floral border, dark blue, 5¹/₂" d. (Rogers) **154.00**

Boston State House vegetable dish, cov., decorated in stippled blue, lion finial, fully opened roses w/leaves border, dark blue, 9" sq., 5¹/₂" h., Rogers (restoration to a rim chip on base & rim chips on cover) **1,540.00**

British America—Montreal platter, floral border, scalloped edge, pink, 18¹/₄" l. (Davenport) **880.00**

British Views platter, large flowers & leaves border, dark blue, 19¹/₄" (few minor facial scratches) **715.00**

Cadmus plate, shell border w/irregular center, dark blue, 10" d., Wood (speckling on center transfer) **330.00**

Fig. 6-29

Cadmus toddy plate, Diorama border, dark blue, 7" d. (trace of staining) **209.00**

Capitol, Washington platter strainer, pierced, flowers within medallions border, dark blue, 13¼" oval, Ridgway (good restoration to rim chips & surface wear) **825.00**

Catskill Mountain House, U.S. plate, flowers, shells & scrolls border, maroon, 10¼" d. (W. Adams & Sons) **173.00**

Chesapeake & Shannon Naval Battle scene platter, shell & seaweed border, medium blue, ca. 1815-35, 19½" l. John Rogers & Sons (minor small pits) **1,495.00**

Chief Justice Marshall, Troy line plate, shell border, irregular opening to center giving "grotto" effect, dark blue, 8⅛" d. (Enoch Wood & Sons) **726.00**

City Hall, New York plate, fully opened roses, w/leaves border, dark blue, 7¼" d. (Stubbs) **248.00**

Fig. 6-30

City Hall, New York plate, flowers within medallions border, dark blue, light scratching, 10" d., Ridgway (Fig. 6-29) **149.00**

Columbus - Boat Scene tankard, handled, red, 3⅞" h. (Adams) **66.00**

Commodore MacDonnough's Victory dish, leaf-shaped, shell border, irregular center, dark blue, 6¼" w., Wood (pinpoint flake on handle) **2,750.00**

Commodore MacDonnough's Victory plate, shell border, dark blue, 6½" d., Enoch Wood & Sons (knife scratches) **201.00**

Commodore MacDonnough's Victory soup plate, w/flanged rim, shell border, irregular opening to the center gives a "grotto" effect, dark blue, 10⅛" d., Wood (some facial wear) **550.00**

Commodore MacDonnough's Victory sugar bowl, cov., shell border, irregular opening to center giving "grotto" effect, dark blue, 7" h., Wood (light mellowing, finial may have been re-attached) **413.00**

Court House, Baltimore plate, fruits, flowers & leaves border, dark blue, 8½" d., Henshall, Williamson & Company (internal spider on reverse, faint facial wear on inner rim) **330.00**

Doctor Syntax Amused with Pat in the Pond platter, flower & scroll border, dark blue, 19" l., Clews (professional restoration) ... **660.00**

Dorney Court, Buckinghamshire (England) openwork undertray, Grapevine border series, dark blue (Wood) **935.00**

English Country Scene soup tureen ladle, light blue bowl w/dark blue figural eagle head handle, Wood (mellowing & a chip on bowl) **468.00**

Erie Canal Inscription...DeWitt Clinton Eulogy plate, views of the canalboats & locks border, dark blue, 10¼" d. (mellowed) **440.00**

Esholt House, Yorkshire (England) plate, Grape Border series, dark blue, 10¼" d. (Wood) **187.00**

Esplanade & Castle Garden, New York coffeepot, cov., Boston Almshouse on reverse, Fort Gansevoort, New York on cover, vine border, dark blue, Ralph Stevenson & Williams (professional restoration to cover, spout & base) **8,800.00**

Esplanade & Castle Garden, New York oval platter, vine border, dark blue, 16⅝" l., Stevenson (Fig. 6-30) **1,955.00**

Esplanade & Castle Garden, New York platter, vine border, dark blue, R. Stevenson & Williams (facial paint mark & glaze crazing) **2,200.00**

Exchange, Baltimore plate, fruits, flowers & leaves border, dark blue, 9⅞" d. (Henshall) **880.00**

Fair Mount Near Philadelphia plate, spread eagles amid flowers & scrolls border, medium blue, 10" d., Stubbs (Fig. 6-31, right) .... **225.00 to 325.00**

Fort Edward, Hudson River toddy plate, birds, flowers & scrolls border, brown, 5½" d., Clews (minute glaze flake on rim) .. **33.00**

Franklin's Tomb creamer, floral border, dark blue, 6" h., Wood (heavy mellowing) **660.00**

Franklin's Tomb cup & saucer, floral border, dark blue, Wood (cup has rim restoration) **330.00**

Franklin's Tomb teapot, cov., floral border, dark blue, 7" h., Wood (restoration to tip of spout, mellowing) **2,310.00**

Franklin's Tomb teapot, cov., floral border, dark blue, 8¾" h., Wood (large crack) **690.00**

Franklin's Tomb waste bowl, floral border, dark blue, 6½" d., 3¼" h. (Wood) **495.00**

Harvard College fruit basket, medium blue, 11" (darkened, crack) **690.00**

Harvard College (four buildings) plate, acorn & oak leaves border, dark blue, 10" d., Stevenson & Williams (Fig. 6-31, left) **358.00**

Harvard College plate, fruit & flowers border, medium blue, 10⅛" d., Enoch Wood & Sons (minor darkening) **230.00**

Hospital, New York—City Hall, New York pitcher, vine border, dark blue, 6¼" h., Ralph Stevenson & Williams (restoration to rim & handle) **660.00**

Hope Mill, Catskill, State of New York soup tureen undertray, shell border, circular center w/trailing vine around outer edge of center, dark blue, 14¼" w., Wood (hairline off the rim) **2,090.00**

Iron Works at Saugerties platter, long-stemmed roses border, brown, 13¼" l., Jackson (short faint hairline off the rim, large faint internal spider crack on the back) ... **275.00**

Kirkstal Abbey, Yorkshire (England) plate, grapevine border, dark blue, 6½" d. (Wood) .. **171.00**

Lafayette at Washington's Tomb soup plate, w/flanged rim, floral border, dark blue, 10" d. (Wood) **1,100.00**

Fig. 6-31

Courtesy of Sotheby's

Lakes of Kilarney plate, flowers & leaves border, dark blue, 8³⁄₄" d. (light mellowing & trace of an internal spider crack on reverse) **44.00**

Landing of General Lafayette at Castle Garden, New York, 16 August, 1824, bowl, footed, flowers & leaves border, dark blue, 9³⁄₄" sq., 3³⁄₄" h. Clews (three unseen chips & light re-glazing in interior) **880.00**

Landing of General Lafayette at Castle Garden, New York, 16 August, 1824 cup plate, groups of large & small flowers w/vine leaves full border, 4⁷⁄₁₆" d. (Clews) **248.00**

Landing of General Lafayette at Castle Garden, New York, 16 August, 1824 hot water dish, deep handled w/liner & domed cover, groups of large & small flowers w/vine leaves border, dark blue, 15¹⁄₂" w., 9" h. Clews (invisible restoration to rim/shoulder of liner & dish, small flake on underside of dish) **3,520.00**

Landing of General Lafayette at Castle Garden, New York, 16 August, 1824 plate, floral & vine border, dark blue, 9" d., Clews (flake on foot rim & minute glaze rubs on edge of rim) **220.00**

Landing of General Lafayette at Castle Garden, New York, 16 August, 1824 platter, floral & vine border, dark blue, ca. 1830-35, 15¹⁄₄" l., Clews (minor scratches) **1,380.00**

Landing of General Lafayette at Castle Garden, New York, 16 August, 1824 soup tureen base, floral & vine border, dark blue, 15¹⁄₄" w., 7¹⁄₂" h., Clews (restoration to base & handles, cover missing) **605.00**

Landing of the Fathers at Plymouth, Dec. 22, 1620 plate, pairs of birds & scrolls & four medallions w/ships & inscriptions border, dark blue, 10¹⁄₈" d. (Enoch Wood & Sons) **230.00**

Anthony Abbey, Monmouthshire (England) tea set: 12" w., 7¹⁄₄" h.. cov. teapot, 11" w., 6¹⁄₂" h. cov. teapot, 7¹⁄₂" w., 5¹⁄₂" h. cov. sugar bowl, creamer & 7" d. oversized saucer (waste bowl?); dark blue, Wood (large teapot has small rim chip, smaller teapot has under-spout chip, base chip & meandering base hairline, sugar bowl has one re-glued handle & several small glaze flakes on rim, saucer has hairline) **990.00**

Louisville, Kentucky soup tureen base, groups of flowers & scrolls border, dark blue, 15" d., 6¹⁄₂" h., Davenport (cover missing) **1,760.00**

Marine Hospital, Louisville, Kentucky plate, shell border, irregular opening to the center gives a "grotto" effect, dark blue, 9¹/₂" d. Wood (some mellowing on back, unseen chip on foot rim) **248.00**

Near Fishkill, Hudson River plate, birds, flowers & scrolls border, black, light overall mellowing & small area of inner rim wear, 10¹/₂" d., Clews (Fig. 6-32) **88.00**

Near Hudson, Hudson River vegetable dish, open, birds, flowers & scrolls border, brown, 8⁵/₈" d. (Clews) **248.00**

Newburg, Hudson River platter, birds, flowers & scrolls border, brown, 19³/₄" l. (Clews) **413.00**

New Haven, Connecticut platter, long-stemmed roses border, mulberry, 11" l., Jackson (glaze wear to scalloped rim) **288.00**

Octagon Church, Boston openwork undertray, pierced rim, flowers within medallions border, dark blue, 10³/₈" d., Ridgway (invisible restoration to rim, reglazed) **715.00**

Park Theatre, New York plate, acorn & oak leaves border, dark blue, 10" d., Stevenson (glazed-over chip on reverse) **248.00**

Peace & Plenty gravy tureen undertray, wide band of fruit & flowers border, dark blue, 8¹/₂" w., Clews (glaze rubbing on edge of rim, unseen chip on back) **605.00**

Peace & Plenty plate, wide band of fruit & flowers border, dark blue, 9" d., Clews (rim chip, glaze wear) **201.00**

Penitentiary in Allegheny, Near Pittsburgh, Pa. platter, birds, flowers & scrolls border, brown, 15³/₄" l. (Clews) **275.00**

Pennsylvania Hospital, Philadelphia platter, flowers within medallions border, dark blue, 18¹/₂" l., Ridgway (professionally restored) **825.00**

Pittsburgh—Steamboats Home, Lark & Nile soup plate, birds, flowers & scrolls border, black, 10¹/₂" d., Clews (light mellowing, a short hairline on shoulder) **303.00**

The Race Bridge, Philadelphia plate, long-stemmed roses border, red, 9" d. (Jackson) **132.00**

Sandusky platter, groups of flowers & scrolls border, dark blue, 16¹/₂" (Davenport) . . . **3,520.00**

State House, Boston gravy boat, flowers within medallions border, dark blue, 3¹/₂" h., 7" w. (J & W. Ridgway) **303.00**

Fig. 6-32

State House, Boston plate, long-stemmed roses border, dark blue 6³/₈" d. (Wood) **193.00**

States series pitcher, mansion, winding drive, names of fifteen states in festoons on border, separated by five- or eight-point stars, dark blue, 6¹/₈" h., Clews (restored hairline near spout) **660.00**

States series plate, building, sheep on lawn, names of fifteen states in festoons on border, separated by five- or eight-point stars, dark blue, 8³/₄" d., Clews (unseen flake on reverse & several glaze rubs on extreme edge of rim) **215.00**

States series wash pitcher, castle w/flags, names of states in festoons separated by stars border, dark blue, 10" h., Clews (shallow flake on rim, another on base & one on foot rim) **880.00**

State series platter, dock w/large building & ships, names of fifteen states in festoons on border, separated by five- or eight-point stars, dark blue, 18³/₄" l., Clews (professional restoration to rim chips & a hairline, reglazed) **935.00**

Table Rock, Niagara—Catskill Mountains, Hudson River bowl, shallow, beaded rim, shell border, circular center w/trailing vines around outer edge of center, dark blue, 11¹/₄" d., Wood (internal hairline in exterior shoulder) **1,650.00**

Fig. 6-33

Texian Campaigne—Battle of Chapultepec plate, symbols of war & a "goddess-type" seated border, light purple, 9½" d., Shaw (¾" d. chip on facial rim) **165.00**

Trinity College, Oxford (England) platter, College series, scalloped border, medium dark blue, 9⅛" d., Ridgway (has been in four pieces, poor restoration) **275.00**

Union Line plate, shell border, dark blue, 10⅛" d., Wood (Fig. 6-33) **413.00**

Upper Ferry Bridge over River Schuylkill ladle, spread eagle amid flowers & scrolls border, dark blue, 10" l. (Stubbs) **1,093.00**

Upper Ferry Bridge over River Schuylkill wash pitcher, spread eagle amid flowers & scrolls border, medium dark blue, 9¾" h. (Stubbs) **990.00**

Vevay, Indiana(?) plate, fruits, flowers & leaves border, dark blue, 6⅝" d. (Henshall) **468.00**

View of the Capitol at Washington platter, American Scenery series, floral border, light blue, 21¼" l. (Ridgway) **715.00**

View of New York from Weehawk—Troy from Mt. Ida soup tureen base, flowers between leafy scrolls border, dark blue, 16¼" w., 6¼" h., Andrew Stevenson (cover missing, restored handle & rim) **1,870.00**

Vue du Chateau Ermenonville soup tureen undertray, flowers, grapes & leaves border, dark blue, 14¼" w. (Enoch Wood & Sons) . . **605.00**

Washington standing at his Tomb, Scroll in Hand, cup & saucer, floral border, dark blue (Enoch Wood) **330.00**

White Sulphur Springs, Town of Delaware, Ohio, 22 Miles From City of Columbus plate, alternating scenic medallions border, light blue, 9¼" d., Jackson (unseen chips on foot rim) **358.00**

Winter View of Pittsfield, Mass. (A) plate, floral w/medallions of center view border, dark blue, 10½" d. (Clews) **374.00**

Yarmouth Isle of Wright fruit basket, shell border, irregular opening to center gives a "grotto" effect, dark blue, 10¼", Enoch Wood & Sons (lacks undertray) **1,150.00**

PENNSBURY POTTERY

In 1990, when Lucile Henzke wrote the first complete book on Pennsbury Pottery, only a small group of collectors had been amassing items from this company. Today, just a few years later, pottery enthusiasts have come to realize what a wonderful piece of Country Americana the Pennsbury owners, Henry and Lee Below (pronounced "Bello") created.

Pennsbury invoices from 1963 show that a cookie jar could be purchased for $14.00 and a bowl in the Dutch Talk pattern was selling for $4.00. Today, those same items would cost about $210.00 and $125.00, respectively.

Begun in 1950, Pennsbury Pottery was established in Morrisville, Pennsylvania. The Belows named the company Pennsbury for the nearby home of William Penn. Lee had been connected with the Stangl Pottery Company of Trenton, New Jersey and was considered a talented artist-designer. She designed most of Pensbury's folk art, the various rooster patterns and the hand-painted Pennsylvania German blue and white dinnerware. Henry, who studied pottery-making in Germany and was considered a professional in ceramic engineering and mold making, designed many of the Pennsbury shapes and managed the day-to-day office operations. Mr. Below had also been an employee at Stangl Pottery and when he decided to establish his own business, several employees at Stangl joined in his new enterprise. This probably accounts for the Pennsbury birds resembling those of Stangl. Birds were the first items produced at Pennsbury and even though they are not plentiful,

Fig. 6-35

they are popular with collectors today. The birds are usually marked by hand with "Pennsbury Pottery" and often the name of the bird. Many times the artist's initials or name were also included.

The most prominent and successful Pennsbury coloring was accomplished by the sgraffito technique followed with a smear-type glaze of light brown.

The bird line, dinnerware, art pieces, ashtrays, mugs, teapots, canisters, and cookie jars with finials of animals and birds, commemoratives (especially trays for railroad companies which were used as gifts for passengers), and the scarce blue and white pieces, have all found their place in the Country Americana setting for collectors today.

Pennsbury was in business seventeen years and at one time almost fifty people were working there. Mr. Below died unexpectedly in 1959 and Mrs. Below, following a long illness, died in 1968. Bankruptcy was filed in late 1970 and in April 1971 fire destroyed the pottery.

—Susan Cox

Ashtray, Amish patt., "What giffs? What ouches you?," three cigarette rests, 5" d. (Fig. 6-34) $20.00

Ashtray, Black Rooster patt., three cigarette rests 5" d. 30.00

Bowl, pretzel, 12" l., 8" w., Barber Shop Quartet patt. w/Luigi, Olson, Schultz & Horowitz 85.00

Bread plate, round, "Give us this day our daily bread," sheaf of wheat in center, 8" d. 65.00

Bread plate, rectangular, sheaf of wheat in center, border reads "Give us this day our daily bread," 9" l., 6" w. (Fig. 6-35) 60.00

Candleholder, Tulip patt., w/finger hold, 5" d. (Fig. 6-36) 55.00

Candlestick, white high gloss, hummingbird w/beak raised, wings back, on irregular oval base, model no. 117, 5" h. 15.00

Canister, cov., Black Rooster patt., w/black rooster finial, front reads "Flour," 9" h. 185.00

Fig. 6-34

Fig. 6-37

Fig. 6-36

Cup & saucer, Black Rooster patt., cup 2½" h., saucer 4" d. (Fig. 6-37) **45.00**

Desk basket, Two Women Under Tree patt., 5" h. **75.00**

Model of chickadee, head down, on irregular base, model no. 111, signed R.B., 3½" h. . . **140.00**

Mug, beer, Amish patt., dark brown rim & bottom w/dark brown applied handle, 5" h. (Fig. 6-38) **38.00**

Pie plate, Dutch Haven commemorative, birds & heart in center, inscribed around the rim "When it comes to Shoo-Fly Pie - Grandma sure knew how - t'is the Kind of Dish she used - Dutch Haven does it now," 9" d. (Fig. 6-39) **125.00**

Pitcher, 5" h., Delft Toleware patt., fruit & leaves, white body w/fruit & leaves outlined in blue, blue inside **85.00**

Fig. 6-38

Fig. 6-39

Fig. 6-40

Fig. 6-41

Pitcher, 7¼" h., Amish patt. w/interlocked
pretzels on reverse (Fig. 6-40) **105.00**

Plaque, commemorative, "What Giffs, what
ouches you?," reverse marked "NFBPWC
Philadelphia, PA 1960," drilled for hanging,
4" d. (Fig. 6-41) **30.00**

Plaque, shows woman holding Pennsbury
cookie jar, marked "It is Whole Empty,"
drilled for hanging, 4" d. (Fig. 6-42) **35.00**

Plaque, Rooster patt., "When the cock crows
the night is all," drilled for hanging, 4" d.
(Fig. 6-43) **38.00**

Plaque, Amish man & woman kissing
over cow, drilled for hanging, 8" d.
(Fig. 6-44) **75.00**

Plate, 6" d., Black Rooster patt.
(Fig. 6-45) **25.00**

Fig. 6-42

Fig. 6-43

Fig. 6-44

Fig. 6-45

Fig. 6-46

Fig. 6-47

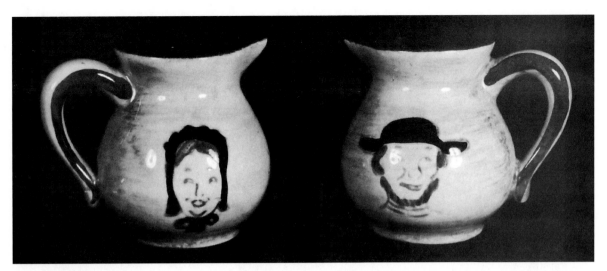

Fig. 6-48

Fig. 6-49

Plate, 8" d., Courting Buggy patt. (Fig. 6-46) . . **75.00**

Plate, 10" d., Red Rooster patt. (Fig. 6-47) . . . **48.00**

Relish tray, Black Rooster patt., five-section
each w/different scene, 14½" l., 11" w. **195.00**

Salt & Pepper shakers, shaped as small
pitchers w/image of Amish man & woman,
2½" h., pr. (Fig. 6-48) **45.00**

Tile, Black Rooster patt., 6" sq. **40.00**

Tray, high-relief design of train, reads
"Baltimore & Ohio R.R. 1837 - Lafayette,"
7½" l., 5½" w. (Fig. 6-49) **60.00**

Tray, shows image of gun above "Remington
.50 Caliber Single Shot Pistol, Model 1871,"
7½" l., 5" w. (Fig. 6-50) **40.00**

Fig. 6-50

Fig. 6-51

Wall pocket, donkey & clown w/dark green
  border, ivory center, 6½" sq. (Fig. 6-51) . . **105.00**

REDWARE

Red earthenware pottery was made in the
American colonies from the late 1600s. Bowls,
crocks and all types of utilitarian wares were turned
out in great abundance to supplement the pewter
and handmade treenware. The ready availability of
the clay, the same used in making bricks and roof
tiles, accounted for the vast production. The lead-
glazed redware retained its reddish color though a
variety of colors could be obtained by adding various metals to the glaze. Interesting effects occurred
accidentally through unsuspected impurities in the
clay or uneven temperatures in the firing kiln which
sometimes resulted in streaks or mottled splotches.

Redware pottery was seldom marked by the
maker.

Apple basket, flaring cylindrical body
  w/pierced sides, yellow slip glaze w/sgraffito
  decoration on the interior in the form of
  birds perched on a leafy vine, the base w/an
  incised & stylized tree, the exterior w/bands
  of incised circles & flowering vines,
  inscribed "Sarah Dunn," some wear & losses
  to glaze, Pennsylvania, ca. 1820, 11" d.,
  4½" h. (Fig. 6-52) **$9,200.00**

Bank, miniature Empire chest of drawers form
  w/overall scroddle yellow & brown
  decoration, probably Philadelphia, ca. 1840,
  1⅝ × 3¾", 3" h. (Fig. 6-53, left) **575.00**

Bank, globular jug-form w/ring-turned finial
  pierced w/a coin slot, yellow & brown glaze,
  decorated w/incised bird, flowers, bust
  portrait of a man & leafy vines, inscribed on
  front "William Mount Joy is a very good boy
  mad (sic) the 29th May 1839," Pennsylvania,
  5¾" h. (Fig. 6-54) **4,025.00**

Fig. 6-52

Fig. 6-53

Fig. 6-54

Fig. 6-55

Fig. 6-56

Bank, miniature chest of drawers form w/overall yellow & brown scroddle decoration, probably Philadelphia, ca. 1840, 3½ × 7", 6½" h. (Fig. 6-53, right) **460.00**

Basket, divided w/overhead handle, applied dark brown figures of cherubs, impressed "Wedgwood Z," & paper label w/"1984 Hammond Museum," 3¾" h. **187.00**

Bean pot, flattened bulbous form w/pulled handles & short cylindrical neck, mottled olive-green & orange glaze, Pennsylvania or New England, mid-19th c., 8¾" h. (some old chips & imperfections) **690.00**

Bottle, standing squirrel cast in a two-piece mold w/incised eye, tail & paw detail, covered in a mottled & streaky orange &

brown glaze, Moravian Potteries, Salem, North Carolina, early 19th c., base restored, 8¼" h. (Fig. 6-55) **1,725.00**

Bowl, cov., 4½" d., 4¾" h., cylindrical body w/domed lid, yellow glaze, decorated w/applied solid compass star medallion designs w/yellow, orange, brown & green glaze, the double-walled body decorated w/zigzag everted rim & pierced compass stars & geometric perforations over a solid glazed redware bowl, small chip to rim & lid, possibly Henry Grady, Shanksville, Somerset County, Pennsylvania, ca. 1843-80 (Fig. 6-56) **12,650.00**

Coffeepot, cov., cylindrical body w/fine manganese "tortoiseshell" decoration on a

Fig. 6-57

Courtesy of Christie's

red body w/clear lead glaze, domed lid w/flattened finial & applied molded spout & handle, stamped "John Bell, 1800-1880, Waynesboro, Franklin County, Pennsylvania, 1850-1880," 9" h. (Fig. 6-57, center) **7,475.00**

Creamer, jug-form, ovoid body w/flat rim & small rim spout, loop handle, applied relief decoration of a Chinaman w/parasol & an East Indian w/parrot in a hoop, basketweave molded handle & spout, impressed pseudo-Chinese mark, Staffordshire, England, ca. 1755, 3" h. (spout chips) **748.00**

Creamer, baluster-form on a short pedestal & circular foot, applied long S-scroll handle, red body daubed w/manganese, clear lead glaze, Pennsylvania, 19th c., 3½" h. (Fig. 6-57, left) **1,093.00**

Cuspidor, waisted form w/crimped edge, decorated w/impressed stellate devices, leaves, hearts & flowers w/mottled olive-green & orange ground, Pennsylvania, ca. 1820, some age chips & minor losses, 8" d., 5" h. (Fig. 6-58) **920.00**

Dish, flattened edge decorated w/sgraffito tulips & leafage climbing from a double-handled diamond patterned pot, yellowish white glaze daubed w/green copper oxide, incised meandering border, possibly Jacob Medinger, Pennsylvania, early 20th c., 9⅞" d. **2,070.00**

Dish, incised & coggled edge, yellowish white glaze w/drippings of copper oxide & orange sgraffito decorated w/a spread-winged American eagle & shield beneath a spray of flowers, the borders inscribed in ornamental German calligraphy, initialed "S.T." & dated "1825," Pennsylvania, 11¼" d. (exfoliation, old chips & cracks) **5,175.00**

Dish, yellowish white slip w/sgraffito decoration in the form of a double eagle w/large central heart & two pendant tulip blossoms, the sides inscribed in ornamental German calligraphy, everted edge, signed "Gemacht von Samuel Paul Im Jahr 1798 vor Maria Helbard," Limerick Township, Montgomery County, 12½" d. (some chips, wear & minor imperfections) **36,800.00**

Fig. 6-58

Fig. 6-59

Dough tray, deep-sided oblong shape w/crimped edge, interior decorated w/bands of comb-trailed slip & sprays of stylized leaves, orangish brown ground, Pennsylvania, mid-19th c., 15 × 23¼", 5" h. **16,100.00**

Figure of a boy, wearing a peaked cap & holding a basket of fruit, standing on a shaped circular base, light & dark manganese glaze, attributed to John Bell, Waynesboro, Pennsylvania, mid-19th c., 6½" h. **3,737.00**

Flowerpot, footed, inverted bell form w/banded neck, molded lip & applied strap handles, covered w/mottled green, white & brown glaze & decorated w/sgraffito birds perched in flowering branches, gouge-work flowers & initialed "M.M." & dated "1783" on both sides, probably Chester County, Pennsylvania, ca. 1783, some exfoliation & rim chips & hairline crack, 7¼" h. (Fig. 6-59) **2,875.00**

Flowerpot w/attached saucer, baluster-shaped w/ruffled rim & midband, applied saucer base w/ruffled rim, overall dappled manganese glaze, Pennsylvania, 19th c., 8" d., 8¼" h. (Fig. 6-60, left) **1,495.00**

Flowerpot w/saucer, tapering cylindrical form w/double ruffled rim, midband & saucer,

Fig. 6-60

Courtesy of Christie's

Fig. 6-61

Fig. 6-62

applied green glazed foliate designs, the body glazed w/streaks of manganese glaze, Pennsylvania, 19th c., 8¼" d., 9" h., 2 pcs. (Fig. 6-60, center) **1,725.00**

Flowerpot w/saucer, urn-shaped w/double ruffled rim above inscription "Earl Pell L. C. Leah Connell/5th moth, 18th dy, 1827," decorated w/foliate sprigs embellished w/daubs of green, brown & yellow on red ground w/clear lead glaze, resting on a double ruffled saucer, attributed to Enos Smedley, Washington Township, Chester County, Pennsylvania, ca. 1827, 8½" d., 9¾" h. (Fig. 6-61) **18,400.00**

Flowerpot w/saucer, tapering cylindrical form w/ruffled rim & saucer & pressed ruffled bands w/applied foliate floral decorations, dark brown & black manganese glaze, attributed to Henry Fahr, Mt. Aetna, Tulpehocken Township, Berks County, Pennsylvania, ca. 1867-85, 8¾" d., 8¼" h. 2 pcs. (Fig. 6-60, right) **250.00**

Jar, cov., wide ovoid body w/narrow molded rim, eared shoulder handles, slip glaze w/dark splotches, early 19th c., New England, chips, 9" h. (Fig. 6-62) **2,990.00**

Jug, bulbous ovoid tapering to small rolled neck, applied handle, variegated green glaze w/dripped brown lines, possibly New England, 19th c., 10" h. (Fig. 6-63, left) .. **8,625.00**

Jug, ovoid body w/applied top handle & short cylindrical top spout, dripped manganese glaze, Pennsylvania, 19th c., 11" h. (Fig. 6-63, right) **403.00**

Model of a bird, stylized crested long-necked bird w/incised wings covered in a dark brown glaze & mounted on an oval base, 4" l., 3¼" h. **690.00**

Model of a bird, full-bodied hawk perched on a tree trunk w/incised feather detail, dark brown manganese glaze, attributed to John Bell, Waynesboro, Pennsylvania, third quarter 19th c., 6¼" h. (restorations to base) **1,725.00**

Model of a dog, hand-formed stylized seated long-necked dog, Pennsylvania or Virginia, mid-19th c., 5" l., 3¼" h. **345.00**

Model of a dog, brown glaze ground w/white spots, seated on a shaped thick base, inscribed on bottom "Right (?) Feuzle fecit" & dated "1796," 6" l., 5½" h. (Fig. 6-64) .. **517.00**

Model of a dog, recumbent Whippet w/crossed forepaws, rectangular base, black glaze w/"Solomon Bell Winchester" inscribed in script on verso, Virginia, mid-19th c., 10" l., 6½" h. (Fig. 6-65) **13,800.00**

Model of a lamb, recumbent sleeping lamb w/incised fur covered in a yellowish white glaze w/daubings of manganese brown & green copper oxide, attributed to S. Bell &

Fig. 6-63

Courtesy of Christie's

Fig. 6-64

Fig. 6-65

Fig. 6-66

Fig. 6-67

Fig. 6-68

Fig. 6-69

Son, Strasburg, Virginia, late 19th c., some wear & exfoliation of glaze, 12" l., 3½" h. (Fig. 6-66) **20,700.00**

Model of a goat, stylized seated goat w/impressive horns, rectangular base stamped three times "Baecher Winchester," covered in lead & manganese glazed over slip wash redware, Virginia, ca. 1880, repair to the tail, 6½" l., 7" h. (Fig. 6-67) **82,250.00**

Mold, food, Turk's turban-style, yellow glaze, rim decorated w/alternating brown & white slip polka dots, Pennsylvania, 19th c., 8" d., 3" h. (Fig. 6-68, left) **345.00**

Mold, food, Turk's turban-style, yellow glaze w/manganese decorated brim, stamped "J.BELL" on exterior, Waynesboro, Pennsylvania, 1830-80, 8¼" d., 3¼" h. (Fig. 6-68, right) **920.00**

Mug, child's, enameled decoration of flowers, shaded pink, black & green w/black rim, 2¼" h. **94.00**

Mug, ovoid w/tapering shoulder, applied strap handle, beige glaze w/vertical bands alternating in green, black & red, possibly Pennsylvania, 19th c., 6¼" h. (Fig 6-63, center) **115.00**

Mug, tapering cylindrical form w/applied molded handle w/German inscriptions & decorated w/a distlefink, glazed in yellow daubed w/green & brown, signed "W. Roth - 1821" under handle, possibly Berks or Montgomery County, Pennsylvania, 4¾" d., 5" h. (Fig 6-69, left) **4,025.00**

Mug, tapering cylindrical form w/applied molded handle, glazed yellow w/green daubs & stamped "SOLOMON BELL" on exterior, Winchester or Strausburg, Virginia, 1843-82, 4¼" d., 5" h. (Fig. 6-69, right) . . **2,990.00**

Mug, bulbous ovoid form w/applied strap handle, yellow slip w/daubings of brown manganese & copper-green oxide, decorated w/sgraffito tulips & featherleaf motifs, Pennsylvania, early 19th c., some old rim chips & imperfections, 5¾" h. (Fig. 6-70) **4,025.00**

Pie plate, yellowish white slip w/sgraffito decoration of a gentleman & lady both wearing top hats, her dress embellished w/flowers, his coat w/a long line of buttons, the figures flanked by climbing flowering vines below a group of four small birds, coggled edge, probably Medinger, Pennsylvania, early 20th c., 9" d. (Fig. 6-71) **5,750.00**

Fig. 6-70

Fig. 6-71

Fig. 6-72

Courtesy of Sotheby's

Pipe holder, cov., three-footed, cylindrical form w/perforated lid & four pipe stands, daubed w/manganese on red body w/clear lead glaze, ca. 1875-96, George A. Wagner Pottery, Weissport, Carbon County, Pennsylvania, 4" h. (Fig. 6-57, right) **2,760.00**

Pitcher, 3¾" h., footed bulbous body w/flaring neck, pinched spout & applied strap handle, mottled cream, orange & green glaze, attributed to S. Bell & Son, Strasburg, Virginia, late 19th c. (Fig. 6-72, left) **1,610.00**

Pitcher, 7" h., footed ovoid body, cylindrical neck, applied strap handle & incised collar bands, mottled brown & white glaze w/traces of green, some minor rim chips & imperfections, attributed to the Bell family, Virginia, late 19th c. (Fig. 6-73) **1,037.00**

Pitcher, water, 10" h., elongated baluster-form on a tooled circular foot w/applied & incised strap handle & wide flaring spout, mottled olive-green & brown manganese glaze, decorated w/relief-molded blossoms

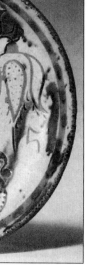

Fig. 6-73   Fig. 6-74   Fig. 6-75

Fig. 6-76   Fig. 6-77

& leaves, signed "Anthony Bacher" on
base, Winchester, Virginia, late 19th c.
(Fig. 6-74) **5,462.00**

Plate, 8³/₄" d., incised Hessian soldier design
w/coggled edge, decorated w/sgraffito
figures of a fife player & drummer flanked
by tulips on a yellow slip ground
w/daubings of green, Jacob Medinger,
Montgomery County, Pennsylvania, early
20th c. (Fig. 6-75) **2,875.00**

Plate, 9⁷/₈" d., coggled edge, sgraffito
decoration of three tulip blossoms climbing
from a double-handled pot within a dotted

glaze border, white slip ground daubed
w/green, dated "1815" & indistinctly signed
"John M." on the reverse, attributed to John
Monday, Haycock Township, Bucks County,
Pennsylvania (Fig. 6-76) **11,500.00**

Plate, 11⁵/₈" d., coggled edge w/sgraffito
decoration in the form of three tulip
blossoms & wide leaves on white slip
ground w/daubings of green, wear &
exfoliation, attributed to Conrad
Mumbouer, Haycock Township, Bucks
County, Pennsylvania, early 19th c.
(Fig. 6-77) **2,875.00**

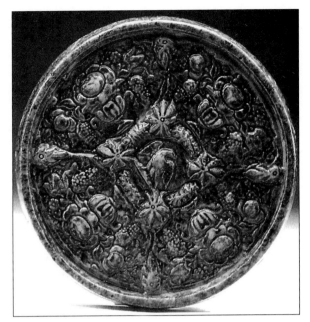

Fig. 6-78

Fig. 6-81

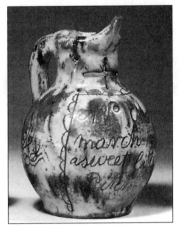

Fig. 6-79

Fig. 6-80

Courtesy of Sotheby's

Plate, 12" d., coggled edge, yellowish white slip ground w/sgraffito "blowing" tulips & asters, w/daubings of green, attributed to Jacob Medinger, Montgomery County, Pennsylvania, early 20th c. **1,725.00**

Plate, 12½" d., coggled edge, yellow slip w/sgraffito checkered tulips & asters climbing from a checkered pot within an incised line border, daubed w/brown & green, attributed to Jacob Medinger, Montgomery County, Pennsylvania, early 20th c. (rim chips) **805.00**

Pot stand w/rolled molded edge, turned & scored feet, center decoration of relief-molded spread-winged American Eagle within a frame of four blossoms, surrounded by relief-molded intricate & elaborate clusters of fruits, leaves & flowers in footed urns, mottled glaze of brown & yellow w/yellow glaze on reverse, stamped "John Bell Waynesboro," Pennsylvania, 1850-80, some wear to glaze, 7¼" d., 1½" h. (Fig. 6-78) **2,587.00**

Puzzle jug, bulbous body tapering to wide cylindrical neck, elongated upturned pour spout & drawn handle, the neck pierced w/a cross, decorated w/sgraffito tulips, the figure of a standing bird & the inscription "W.M. March 10, 1841, a sweet little pitcher," variegated green, yellow & brown glaze, Pennsylvania, some minor exfoliation & wear, 7" h. (Fig. 6-79) **2,070.00**

Slip cup, bulbous body w/cylindrical lip, one flattened side, orange glaze, probably Pennsylvania, late 19th c., 3¼" l., 2¼" h. (Fig. 6-80, right) . . . **345.00**

Slip cup, bulbous body w/cylindrical lip, one flattened side & two compressed finger hold sides, mottled orange & brown glaze, John Schweinfurt, New Market, Virginia, ca. 1880, 3½" l., 2¼" h. (Fig. 6-80, center) **1,495.00**

Slip cup, bulbous body w/short cylindrical lip, impressed sides & three-holed channel for pouring, inscribed "Jake 1821" on front, Pennsylvania, some old chips, 2⅝" h. (Fig. 6-80, left) **1,610.00**

Teapot, cov., Astbury-type, spherical body on three short feet, the molded rim w/a domed cover, an angled spout & D-form handle, decorated w/cream trim & florals & berries in relief, Staffordshire, England, ca. 1735, 3¾" h. (rim nicks on body, inner lid collar restored) **920.00**

Vase, 6¼" h., baluster-form body tapering to a wide domed circular foot, wide slightly flared cylindrical neck flanked by applied reeded handles, applied "coleslaw" & floral decoration, streaky brown & cream glaze, incised "A.W. Bacher 1887" on base, some chips & loss of glaze, A. W. Bacher (Baecher), Winchester, Virginia (Fig. 6-81) **8,050.00**

Vases, 12¼" h., footed baluster-form body w/tall cylindrical neck flaring to flat rim, large applied strap handles, elaborately decorated w/applied & incised flowers & "coleslaw" details on front & back, painted red, yellow, blue & green on mottled cream, brown & green glaze, each stamped "Baecher Winchester," old repair on lip of one vase, Virginia, late 19th c., pr. (Fig. 6-82) **21,850.00**

Wall pocket, cylindrical form, coggled rim w/relief-molded figure of a bird perched on two stylized blossoms & incised decorations, mottled white, green & manganese glaze, attributed to S. Bell & Son, Strasburg, Virginia, late 19th c., restoration to bird's head, some exfoliation to coggled rim, 5¾" h. (Fig. 6-72, right) . . **920.00**

Fig. 6-82

Fig. 6-83

Wall pocket, cylindrical form w/scalloped rim & back rim loop handle, decorated w/relief-molded applied bird perched on two floral blossoms, mottled green, white & manganese brown glaze, attributed to S. Bell & Son, Strasburg, Virginia, late 19th c., chip to bird's beak, 7½" h. (Fig. 6-72, center) **3,105.00**

Washbowl & pitcher, baluster-form pitcher w/applied & spurred strap handle, the matching bowl w/pierced soap dish, scrolled crest & mock screws, both w/creamy white slip glaze w/daubings of green & red, attributed to J. Eberly & Co., Strasburg, Virginia, ca. 1880, some wear, scratches & old chips, bowl 13½" d., pitcher 11½" h., the set (Fig. 6-83) **5,462.00**

RED WING

The Stoneware industry came to Red Wing, Minnesota because the right conditions existed—Glaciers had deposited perfect clay in the area; capital and manpower existed in town; and there was a functional need for stoneware at that time in history.

Red Wing Stoneware Company began producing stoneware on a large scale in 1878. Due to the success of this company, a new company was formed in 1883 known as the Minnesota Stoneware Company. Both of these companies prospered and in 1892 another stoneware company, the North Star Stoneware Company, was formed.

A short time after the North Star Company began, the stoneware industry developed some economic difficulties. In order to end the competition among the three companies, they consolidated under the name Union Stoneware Company in 1894. By 1896, the North Star Company ceased production and was bought out by the other two companies.

The two remaining companies merged in 1906, forming the Red Wing Union Stoneware Company. They continued production under this name until 1936, when their name changed to Red Wing Potteries. Following a union strike in the mid-1960s, Red Wing Potteries ceased operations in 1967.

Even today, the Red Wing Potteries is remembered as a long and proud tradition of Red Wing, Minnesota.

—Charles W. Casad

SUMMARY OF THE RED WING STONEWARE COMPANIES

1877-1906	Red Wing Stoneware Company
1883-1906	Minnesota Stoneware Company
1892-1896	North Star Stoneware Company
1896-1906	Union Stoneware Company
1906-1936	Red Wing Union Stoneware Company
1936-1967	Red Wing Potteries

◆ Art Pottery

Ash receiver, figure of a pelican, marked "Red Wing, USA, #880" **$85.00**

Casserole dish, cov., green rooster-shape, marked "Red Wing USA, #249," 9¼" l. **95.00**

Cookie jar, cov., Labriego design, brown or white, incised peanuts, no markings **55.00**

Cookie jar, cov., yellow Dutch girl w/brown trim, signed "Red Wing USA" (Fig. 6-84, right) **85.00**

Planter, canoe-shaped, white birch pottery, marked "Red Wing USA," 9¾" l. **145.00**

Planter, 'The Muse,' green, figure of woman w/harp & deer, marked "Red Wing USA #B-2507," 13¾" l. **105.00**

Planter, swan-shaped, green, marked "Red Wing USA #259," 5⅛" l. **28.00**

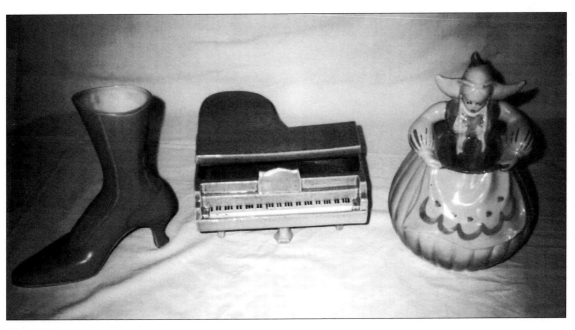

Fig. 6-84

Fig. 6-85

Fig. 6-86

Fig. 6-87

Planter, cov., piano-shaped, blue, marked
"Red Wing USA #M-1525" (Fig. 6-84,
center) **225.00**

Trivet, Minnesota Centennial, 1858-1958,
signed "Red Wing Potteries, Red Wing
Minn.," 6⅝" d. **75.00**

Vase, 7⅜" h., brushed-ware vase w/cattails,
green, rose & white, stamped "Red Wing
Union Stoneware" **55.00**

Vase, 9" h., in the shape of a ladies high-top
shoe, pink & cream, marked "Red Wing USA
#638" (Fig. 6-84, left) **60.00**

Vase, 10" h., brushed ware cemetery vase,
green & white, unmarked (Fig. 6-85) **40.00**

◆ Commemoratives

Ashtray, wing-shaped, 1987 Red Wing
Collectors Society Commemorative **75.00**

Butter churn, 1979 Red Wing Collectors
Society Commemorative **900.00**

Butter crock, 20 lbs., 1994 Red Wing
Collectors Society Commemorative **75.00**

Canning jar, 1983 Red Wing Collectors Society
Commemorative **475.00**

Jug, North Star, 1992 Red Wing Collectors
Society Commemorative **100.00**

Pitcher, Gray Line, 1989 Red Wing Collectors
Society Commemorative **225.00**

Plate, Pompeii design, 1988 Red Wing
Collectors Society Commemorative **60.00**

Water cooler, 1985 Red Wing Collectors
Society Commemorative **250.00**

Water cooler, Birch Water, 1984 Red Wing
Collectors Society Commemorative **375.00**

◆ Stoneware

Note: Beater jars had inside round bottoms for
convenient household necessities & were issued by
different stores for their advertising.

Bean pot, white & brown glazed stoneware,
advertising marked "Compliments of D.
Theophilus Grain-Coal Howard S.D.,"
(Fig. 6-86) **75.00**

Bean pot, white & brown glazed stoneware,
wire handles, signed "Red Wing Union
Stoneware" **80.00**

Beater jar, white glazed stoneware w/blue
bands, advertising Semon's Fair Store,
Athens, Wisc. **150.00**

Beater jar, white glazed stoneware w/blue
bands, advertising Raoke & Strueber,
Juneau, Wisc. (Fig. 6-87) **145.00**

Bowl, 4" d., spongeware, paneled stoneware,
rare (Fig. 6-88, left) **350.00**

Bowl, 7" d., spongeware, paneled stoneware
(Fig. 6-88, right) **145.00**

Bowl, 11" d., spongeware, paneled
stoneware **235.00**

Bowl/milk pan, white glaze stoneware, base
signed "Red Wing USA," 13" d. **55.00**

Butter crock, white glazed stoneware, 4"
wings, "20 lbs.," rare (Fig. 6-89) **675.00**

Fig. 6-88

Fig. 6-89

Fig. 6-90

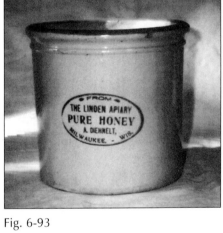

Fig. 6-93

Fig. 6-92

Fig. 6-94

Fig. 6-91

Fig. 6-95

Fig. 6-96

Fig. 6-97

Christmas tree holder, white-glazed
(Fig. 6-90) **650.00**

Churn, white glazed stoneware, large wing, red
oval wing stamp below wing, 2 gal. **250.00**

Churn, white glazed stoneware, large wing, red
oval wing stamp above wing, 3 gal. **225.00**

Churn, white glaze stoneware, large wing, red
oval wing stamp above wing, 6 gal. **350.00**

Churn, Union Stoneware Co., Red Wing,
Minn., 20" h. (Fig. 6-91) **295.00**

Churn, cov., white glazed stoneware w/blue
birch leaves & oval, 2 gal. (Fig. 6-92) **365.00**

Cooler, iced tea, white glazed stoneware,
bailed handles, no wing, 11¾" d., 5 gal. . . **385.00**

Crock, white glazed stoneware, "From The
Linden Apiary Pure Honey A. Diehnelt,
Milwaukee - Wis.," signed "Red Wing
Stoneware" on base, 8" d., 1 gal.
(Fig. 6-93) **225.00**

Crock, white glazed stoneware, two birch
leaves, oval "Red Wing Union Stoneware"
stamp, 9¾" d., 2 gal. (Fig. 6-94) **65.00**

Crock, cov., white glazed stoneware, Nebraska
advertising, 3 gal. **525.00**

Crock, white glazed stoneware, two "elephant
ears," Union oval stamp, 10¾" d., 3 gal. . . . **85.00**

Crock, hand-decorated leaf, salt glaze,
sidewall stamp, 5 gal. (Fig. 6-95) **425.00**

Crock, white glazed stoneware, two birch
leaves, eared handles, Union oval stamp,
12¼" d., 5 gal. **75.00**

Crock, white glazed stoneware, 4" wing, bailed
handles, Red Wing oval stamp, 17" d.,
12 gal. **110.00**

Crock, white glazed stoneware, 4" wing, eared
handles, Red Wing oval stamp, 13" d.,
6 gal. **55.00**

Crock, cobalt blue markings, salt glazed,
eared handles, 18½" d., 15 gal. **875.00**

Crock, white glazed stoneware, eared handles,
four birch leaves, Union oval stamp,
19½" d., 20 gal. **95.00**

Filter, cov., white glazed stoneware w/blue
bands, blue or black stamp reads "Sucess -
Filter Manufactured by - Union Stoneware
Co. - Red Wing, Minn.," w/spigot, 4 gal.,
3 pcs. (Fig. 6-96) **725.00**

Fruit jar., cov., white glazed stoneware, blue or
black stamp reads "Stone - Mason Fruit Jar -
Union Stoneware Co. - Red Wing, Minn.,"
½ gal. (Fig. 6-97, left) **235.00**

Fruit jar, cov., white glazed stoneware, blue or
black stamp reads "Stone - Mason Fruit Jar -
Union Stoneware Co. - Red Wing, Minn.,"
1 qt. (Fig. 6-97, right) **185.00**

Note: The following are self-sealing jars also
known as applesauce jars.

Jar, cov., white glazed stoneware, 4" wing,
Red Wing oval stamp, ball lock, 3 gal.
(Fig. 6-98) **210.00**

Jar, cov., white glazed stoneware, 4" wing, Red
Wing oval stamp, ball lock, 5 gal. **175.00**

Jug, white shoulder, advertising, "John Baum,
Wholesale Liquors, Stillings, Mo.," ½ gal.
(Fig. 6-99) **145.00**

Jug, Albany slip North Star Stoneware, beehive-
shaped, star on base, rare, 1 qt. **230.00**

Fig. 6-98

Fig. 6-99

Fig. 6-100

Fig. 6-101

Fig. 6-102

Fig. 6-103

Jug, brown top, white bottom, advertising "Red Wing Liquor Co.," ½" gal. (Fig. 6-100) **278.00**

Jug, vinegar, white glazed stoneware, wire handle, signed Red Wing Stoneware Co., 1 gal. **95.00**

Jug, wide mouth, Albany slip brown glaze, Minn., bottom marking, 1 gal. (Fig. 6-101) . . **85.00**

Jug, white glazed shoulder, 4" wing, Red Wing Oval stamp, 3 gal. **95.00**

Jug, white glazed stoneware, beehive-shaped, two birch leaves, Union oval stamp, 3 gal. (Fig. 6-102) **315.00**

Jug, beehive-shaped, wing & oval on domed portion, after 1918, 15" h., 4 gal. **575.00**

Jug, white glazed shoulder, 4" wing, Red Wing oval stamp, 5 gal. **85.00**

Note: The Koverwate was placed inside of the crock to keep the contents submerged under the preserving liquid, bottom and side holes allowed the brine to come to the top.

Koverwate, white glazed stoneware, stamped, 12" d., 10 gal. (Fig. 6-103) **175.00**

Pantry jar, cov., white glazed stoneware w/red ring & blue bands, 5 lbs. (Fig. 6-104) **435.00**

Pitcher, 7½" h., molded iris & water lilies, chocolate glaze, impressed "Red Wing USA" on bottom, ca. 1930 (Fig. 6-105) **165.00**

Fig. 6-104

Fig. 6-105

Fig. 6-106

Fig. 6-108

Fig. 6-109

Plate, pie, 9¾" d., white glazed
stoneware, signed "Minnesota
Stoneware Co. Red Wing," rare . . . **110.00**

Poultry drinking fount, "Eureka"-style,
"Patd. April 7, 1885," Red Wing
bottom marking, rare (Fig. 6-106) . . **245.00**

Poultry waterer, vacuum-type, white
glazed stoneware, no wing, stamped
"Made by the Red Wing Potteries,
Red Wing, Minn.," 5 gal.
(Fig. 6-107) **225.00**

Refrigerator jar, stacking-type, white
glazed stoneware w/blue bands,
"Red Wing Refrigerator Jar," 5½" d.
(Fig. 6-108) **165.00**

Roaster, bisque, signed "Minnesota
Stoneware Co. Red Wing, Minn,"
2 pcs. **135.00**

Fig. 6-107

Fig. 6-110

Wash bowl & pitcher, embossed lily,
blue & white glaze (Fig. 6-109) **795.00**

Water cooler, cov., white glazed, w/spigot,
5" red wing, no oval stamp, was used in the
office or school room; a hose ran into the
hole near the top right side; it could hold
up to 100 lbs. of ice. 18¹/₂" d., 15 gal., rare
(Fig. 6-110) **410.00**

ROCKINGHAM WARES

The Marquis of Rockingham established an earthenware pottery on his estate in the Yorkshire district of England in about 1745 and in its earliest years it was operated by a succession of potters. Around 1788 the Brameld Brothers, working at this pottery, developed a mottled brown glaze, somewhat resembling tortoiseshell, which became extremely popular. By the 1820s porcelain manufacture had been introduced at the pottery and a fine quality of this type of china was produced until the pottery finally closed in 1842. English potters introduced the popular "Rockingham" glaze to this country and it was being produced by a number of American firms by the mid-19th century, probably the best known being those located in Bennington, Vermont. A special variation of the Rockingham glaze, called "Flint Enamel" was patented by a Bennington pottery, but keep in mind that not all "Rockingham-glazed" wares were produced in that small city. Potteries in Ohio and other regions produced closely related wares. The following listing includes a selection of Rockingham-glazed utilitarian and decorative wares and those pieces known to have been produced in Bennington are so noted.

Bank, model of a chest of drawers, mottled
dark brown glaze, mid-19th c., small chip to
front top edge, 3¹/₄" h., 3³/₄" w. (Fig. 6-113,
No. 7) **$144.00**

Bank, squatty bulbous body w/wide finely
beaded center band below coin slot, topped
w/tall ringed finial & raised on pedestal
base w/wide disc foot, flint enamel glaze,
ca. 1850-60, Bennington, Vermont,
6¹/₂" h. **863.00**

Bowl, 6¹/₄" d., tub-shaped w/ring handles,
mottled brown glaze (Fig. 6-111, No. 3) . . . **303.00**

Bowl, 7¹/₈" d., shallow, mottled brown & yellow
Rockingham glaze, Bennington, Vermont,
Fenton's "1849" mark (Fig. 6-112, No. 5) . . **770.00**

Candlestick, ringed columnar shape w/flaring
foot, Flint Enamel glaze, Bennington,
Vermont, 6³/₄" h. (Fig. 6-112, No. 3) **798.00**

Fig. 6-111

Courtesy of Garth's Auctions

Fig. 6-112   *Courtesy of Garth's Auctions*

Candlestick, ringed columnar shape w/flaring foot, Flint Enamel glaze, Bennington, Vermont, chip on flange at base of socket, 6⁷/₈" h. (Fig. 6-112, No. 4) **385.00**

Candlestick, flaring base w/large knobbed feet tapering up to a ringed ovoid stem below a tall slender tulip-shaped socket w/bulbous lobed rim, Flint Enamel glaze, ca. 1849-58, Bennington, Vermont, 8" h. (repair to petal of rim & chip to base) **920.00**

Candlestick, ringed columnar shape w/flaring foot, Flint Enamel glaze, Bennington, Vermont, 8¹/₄" h. (Fig. 6-112, No. 7) **880.00**

Candlestick, ringed columnar shape w/flaring foot, Flint Enamel glaze, Bennington, Vermont, 9¹/₂" h. (Fig. 6-112, No. 6) **715.00**

Candlestick, ringed columnar shape w/flaring foot, Flint Enamel glaze, Bennington, Vermont, 9⁵/₈" h. (Fig. 6-112, No. 9) **935.00**

Candlestick, ringed columnar shape w/flaring foot, Flint Enamel glaze, Bennington, Vermont, 9⁵/₈" h. (Fig. 6-112, No. 10) . . . **1,430.00**

Coachman bottle, figure of standing coachman wrapped in a cloak & wearing a top hat, mottled brown glaze, Bennington, Vermont, "1849-58" mark on base, hairline crack, 10¹/₄" h. (Fig. 6-113, No. 3) . . . . . **500.00 to 700.00**

Creamer, cov., figural cow, standing on oval base, tail draped over back, opening in center of back, mouth serves as spout, dark brown slightly mottled glaze, mid-19th c., repairs, chipped cover, attributed to Bennington, 6³/₄" l., 5¹/₂" h. (Fig. 6-113, No. 5) **115.00**

Creamer, Alternate Rib patt., footed bulbous waisted shape, arched rim spout, applied C-scroll handle, Bennington, Vermont, Fenton's "1849" mark, pinpoint flakes & short rim hairline at handle, 5¹/₂" h (Fig. 6-111, No. 2) **1,100.00**

Crock, footed cylindrical body w/incurved panels to the rolled rim, applied cherub head handles, mottled brown glaze, 6³/₄" d., 5" h. (Fig. 6-111, No. 4) **72.00**

Fig. 6-113

Courtesy of Skinner, Inc.

Curtain tiebacks, pointed star-shaped head, dark brown slightly mottled glaze, ca. 1849-58, Bennington, Vermont, one chipped, 4" d., 4½" l., pr. (Fig. 6-113, No. 4, one) . . **173.00**

Flask, model of a book, titled on the spine, Flint Enamel glaze, Bennington, Vermont, ca. 1849-58, 5¾" h. **460.00**

Flask, model of a book, mottled brown glaze, "Bennington Battle" impressed on spine, ca. 1849-58, Bennington, Vermont, 5¾" h. . . . **748.00**

Flask, model of a book, Flint Enamel glaze, "Ned Buntline's Bible" impressed on the spine, Bennington, Vermont, Fenton's "1849" mark, 6" h. (Fig. 6-112, No. 2) . . . **2,530.00**

Flask, model of a book, Flint Enamel glaze, "Hermit's Life & Suffering" impressed on the spine, Bennington, Vermont, ca. 1849-58, 6" h. **978.00**

Flask, model of a book, Flint Enamel glaze, "Battle of Bennington" impressed on the spine, Bennington, Vermont, lip chips, 6⅞" h. (Fig. 6-112, No. 1) **440.00**

Flask, model of a book, mottled brown glaze, "Bennington Companion G" impressed on the spine, Bennington, Vermont, ca. 1849-58, 8" h. **748.00**

Foot warmer, bell-shaped w/one side flattened w/impressed foot rests, opening at center of top, dark brown slightly mottled glaze, ca. 1847-58, Bennington, Vermont, large repaired crack, 9½" h. (Fig. 6-113, No. 2) . . . . **300.00 to 400.00**

Model of a lion, standing & facing left, "coleslaw" mane & tongue up, tail draped over its back, one forepaw raised on a globe, no base, Flint Enamel glaze, Bennington, Vermont, 10" l., 7½" h. (minor repair to tail & repaired chip on base of back left paw) **4,313.00**

Models of lions, head turned slightly to one side, "coleslaw" mane, tongue up, one forepaw raised on a globe, tail draped over its back, standing on a rectangular plinth (appear to be re-attached to bases), covered in a mottled green, rust & cream Flint Enamel glaze, Bennington, Vermont, 1849-58, one w/hind legs repaired & minor chip to base, break & repairs, 11" l., 9½" h., facing pr. (Fig. 6-114) **7,475.00**

Pie plate, wide flat bottom w/low sloping sides, mottled brown & yellow glaze,

Fig. 6-114   *Courtesy of Sotheby's*

Bennington, Vermont, Fenton's "1849" mark,
9" d. (minor scratches & a little glaze wear
on one edge) **935.00**

Pie plate, wide flat bottom w/flaring sides,
mottled brown & yellow glaze, Bennington,
Vermont, Fenton's "1849" mark, minor wear,
11³/₄" d. **825.00**

Pipkin, bulbous body w/molded rim & applied
curved handle, mottled brown glaze,
Bennington, Vermont, minor wear & short
hairlines in rim, 5¹/₂" h., plus handle
(Fig. 6-111, No. 5) **358.00**

Pitcher, 6¹/₄" h., footed bulbous base tapering
to cylindrical sides, rim spout & applied
C-scroll handle (minor wear & small
flakes) **50.00**

Pitcher, 7" h., footed bulbous body tapering to
high arched spout, applied C-scroll handle,
mottled dark brown glaze, decorated
w/relief-molded tulips (Fig. 6-111,
No. 1) **110.00**

Pitcher, 7¹/₄" h., footed cylindrical body
w/wide shoulder below a wide waisted
neck, rim spout & applied C-scroll handle,
Flint Enamel glaze, small flake on
spout, Bennington, Vermont (Fig. 6-112,
No. 8) **275.00**

Pitcher, 8¹/₄" h., footed ovoid body w/arched
spout & loop handle, yellowware w/mottled
brown glaze **193.00**

Pitcher, 9" h., wide paneled baluster-form
body w/a wide mask spout & angled loop
handle, mottled brown & green glaze (kiln
adhesion chips on bottom) **193.00**

Pitcher, 9" h., footed bulbous body w/arched
spout & C-scroll handle, light mottled
brown glaze, relief-molded scene of hunter
& dog w/hanging game **50.00**

Pitcher, 9¹/₂" h., Swirled Alternate Rib patt.,
bulbous double-gourd shape, rim spout
w/molded scrolls & high C-scroll handle,
Flint Enamel glaze, chip at end of handle,
Bennington, Vermont, impressed 1849 mark
A (Fig. 6-111, No. 7) **1,815.00**

Pitcher, 11" h., footed bulbous ovoid body
w/arched rim spout & applied C-scroll
handle, mottled dark brown glaze, relief-
molded hanging game (small flakes on base
& filled-in chip on spout) **50.00**

Snuff jar, cov., seated figural Mr. Toby holding
mug in his hand, hat serves as cover, 1849
mark on base, Bennington, Vermont,
mismatched cover, base chips, 4¹/₄" h.
(Fig. 6-113, No. 6) . . . . **500.00 to 700.00**

Fig. 6-115 *Courtesy of Skinner, Inc.*

Fig. 6-116 *Courtesy of Sotheby's*

Tobacco jar, cov., cylindrical sides w/a flaring, ringed foot & rim, the sides w/a continuous molded grapevine design, flattened domed cover w/button finial, mottled dark brown glaze, small chips, 7½" h. **220.00**

Toby bottle, seated Mr. Toby, wearing jacket & top hat, straddling barrel & holding a beer mug in his hand, dark brown slightly mottled glaze, mid-19th c., possibly English, rim & base chips, 9" h. (Fig. 6-113, No. 1) . . **173.00**

Vegetable dish, open, octagonal w/wide flanged rim, mottled brown & yellow glaze, Bennington, Vermont, Fenton's "1849" mark, minor glaze wear on rim, 12⅞" l. (Fig. 6-111, No. 6) **1,265.00**

Washbowl & pitcher, washbowl w/wide paneled sides, footed pitcher w/tapering octagonal sides w/wide flaring spout & angled handle, Flint Enamel glaze, each w/1849 mark on base, Bennington, Vermont, ca. 1849-58, bowl 13½" d., pitcher 13" h., the set (glaze wear to interior of bowl, mold crack to pitcher handle) **1,093.00**

Water cooler, octagonal w/embossed brick base & Doric columns, Flint Enamel glaze, "Fenton's Enamel pat. 1849, Lyman Fenton Co. Bennington Vermont" impressed in block letters on frieze of entablature, ca. 1848-53, Bennington, Vermont, cracks, lacks cover, 15¾" h. (Fig. 6-115, left) . . . . **1,700.00 to 2,000.00**

Water cooler, octagonal w/embossed brick base & Gothic-arched sides, Flint Enamel glaze, Bennington, Vermont, ca. 1848-53, cracks, lacks cover, 16¾" h. (Fig. 6-115, right) . . . . **1,500.00 to 2,000.00**

SLIPWARE

"Slip" is the term used to describe liquefied, colored clay. Slip has long been used to add decoration to pottery pieces, most often redware. Such "slipware" has been produced in England and the Continent for centuries and was especially popular in Germany. Early potters who settled in America, especially in Pennsylvania Dutch and other German-dominated areas, continued to use slip to highlight even the most utilitarian redware pieces. Some of these unique pieces, produced from the 18th century right through to the 20th century, feature slip-trailed figural scenes and inscriptions and are now considered rare examples of folk art. The finest examples bring very high prices in today's market.

Baking Dish, circular, redware w/interior decorated in cream slip w/a series of double bands combed & dissected by a spiraling arrangement of brown bands against a dark brown ground, piecrust rim, England, ca. 1800, two rim chips, 13⅛" d. (Fig. 6-116, right) **$1,495.00**

Bowl, 6⅛" d., 2" h., wide shallow sides w/molded edge, redware slip-decorated w/bird perched in a tree trunk surrounded by dots & squiggles of dark manganese brown & thick white lead, possibly Moravian, early 19th ca. (Fig. 6-117, right) **690.00**

Bowl, 10¼" d., 3¼" h., molded lip & incised banding, orangish brown glazed redware, decorated in yellow slip alternating w/wavy line in bright green, some wear &

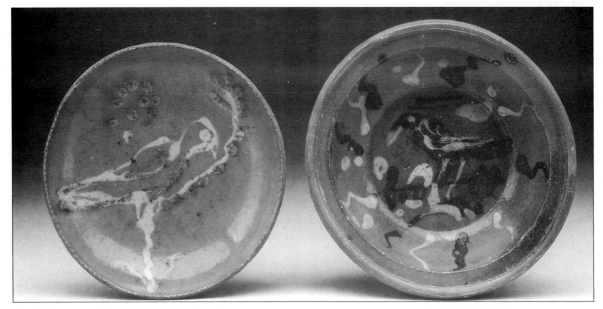

Fig. 6-117   *Courtesy of Sotheby's*

Fig. 6-118

Fig. 6-119

exfoliation, possibly Pennsylvania, early
19th c. (Fig. 6-118) **632.00**

Bowl, 13" d., circular, "Moravian" redware,
the everted rim w/white slip squiggle
decoration, bowl decorated w/alternating
bands of green & brown glaze, some
minor rim chips, Pennsylvania, 19th c.
(Fig. 6-119) **978.00**

Bowl, 13⅝" d., 3¼" h., wide shallow sides
w/molded lip & foot, redware, slip-
decorated w/center floral & leaf motif
w/borders of concentric circles & scallops in
yellow, green & brown glaze, some

exfoliation & wear, possibly Pennsylvania,
19th ca. (Fig. 6-120) **6,325.00**

Dish, redware w/crimped edge, center figure
of a bird in a stylized tree in yellow, white
& green slip decoration, probably
Pennsylvania, early 19th c., some minor
rim chips, 5¾" d. (Fig. 6-117, left) **3,450.00**

Dish, circular, drape-molded redware
w/center decoration of tulip w/yellow &
brown slip, John Drey, Dryville, Rockland
Township, Berks County, Pennsylvania,
1806-47, minor chips to rim, 7" d.
(Fig. 6-121, right) **1,380.00**

Fig. 6-121

Courtesy of Christie's

Fig. 6-120

Fig. 6-122

Dish, molded redware w/coggled edge decorated w/the figure of a large bird surrounded by scrolling pea pods & bud clusters in thick white slip on dark manganese brown ground, Pennsylvania, early 19th c., old repairs, 13⅝" d., 3" h. (Fig. 6-122) **4,025.00**

Dish, molded edge, slip-decorated w/a green, white & black bird perched above flowers & leafage outlined w/a series of black dots surrounded by a border enclosing a wavy line & inscription in ornamental German calligraphy which reads "I am a bird, of course, whose bread I eat his song I

sing" & "1772" on orangish brown ground, reverse incised w/the Roman numeral "VI," possibly John Neis, Upper Salford Township, Montgomery County, Pennsylvania, 14⅜" d. (Fig. 6-123) **6,900.00**

Dish, redware w/molded edge, center decorated w/a cross-hatched flower surrounded by trailings & rings, the borders w/stylized leaf motifs in green oxide, brown manganese & white lead slip, label attached to back inscribed "From C. Heffner Reading, 1938," Pennsylvania, late 18th c., large (Fig. 6-124) **6,037.00**

Fig. 6-123

Fig. 6-124

Loaf Dish, rectangular w/coggle wheel rim, redware w/yellow four-quill slip decoration, Pennsylvania, 19th c., 12 × 15³/₄" (Fig. 6-125, bottom) **1,725.00**

Loaf Dish, rectangular w/coggle wheel rim, redware, w/yellow triple-quill zigzag slip decoration, Pennsylvania, 19th c., 11¹/₂ × 16" (Fig. 6-125, top) **2,185.00**

Plate, 7¹/₈" d., circular, w/everted brim, redware w/center slip-decorated distlefink resting on a branch w/the initials "HB," yellow, green & brown slip, chip to rim, probably Lancaster County, Pennsylvania, early 19th c. (Fig. 6-121, left) **2,185.00**

Plate, 8¹/₈" d., molded redware w/worn coggled edge decorated w/sgraffito zigzags highlighted w/manganese, copper oxide & white lead lines & dots, some wear & old age chips, Pennsylvania, early 19th c. (Fig. 6-126, right) **920.00**

Plate, 8⁵/₈" d., molded redware w/coggled edge w/sgraffito decoration of a large tulip blossom heightened w/manganese & thick lead glaze, some wear & old rim chips, Pennsylvania, early 19th c. (Fig. 6-126, left) **2,185.00**

Plate, 11¹/₄" d., circular, drape-molded w/coggle-wheel rim, redware w/central large flowering plant decorated w/yellow, green & brown slip, some chips to rim & overall crazing, Pennsylvania, 19th c. (Fig. 6-121, center) **2,185.00**

Fig. 6-125 *Courtesy of Christie's*

Tobacco jar, cov., redware, baluster-form w/stand-up incised lip, incised & gouged horizontal & vertical bands w/yellow, white & green slip, the shoulder w/sawtooth design filled in w/yellow, white & green slip decoration, the lid w/horizontal bands of

Fig. 6-126   *Courtesy of Sotheby's*   Fig. 6-127

Fig. 6-128   Fig. 6-129   *Courtesy of Sotheby's*

green, yellow & black gouging finished w/a turned finial, probably Pennsylvania, mid-19th c., repair to lid, overall 11" h. (Fig. 6-127) **10,350.00**

Umbrella stand, bulbous ovoid w/flared rim & double-crimped edge w/lion's head handles, redware, slip-decorated w/glaze forming floral decoration in green & brown on a white ground, stamped "Solomon Bell, Strasburg, Virginia," ca. 1850, old chips to rim & foot, 14" d., 15³/₈" h. (Fig. 6-128) . . **2,875.00**

Whistle, redware, stylized model of a porcupine on a raised circular foot w/scored bristle & slip decoration, Pennsylvania, late 19th c., 4" l., 2" h. (Fig. 6-129, right) **2,185.00**

Whistle, redware w/orangish brown glaze, stylized bird on a raised circular foot w/incised feather & wing detail heightened w/slip decoration, Pennsylvania, late 19th c., restoration to tail, 4¹/₄" h. (Fig. 6-129, left) **920.00**

Whistle, red earthenware model of a large bird perched on a horizontal bar, flanked by a smaller bird (one missing), another smaller horizontal bar w/two birds below, protruding from the sides of an inverted conical base molded w/raised florets, covered in cream slip & mottled w/runny brown glaze, Staffordshire, England, 19th c., some minor chips & abrasions, 10" h. (Fig. 6-116, left) . . **402.00**

STAFFORDSHIRE TRANSFER WARES

The process of transfer-printing designs on earthenwares developed in England in the late 18th century and by the mid-19th century most common ceramic wares were decorated in this manner, most often with romantic European or Oriental landscape scenes, animals, or flowers. The earliest such wares were printed in dark blue but a little later light blue, pink, purple, red, black, green, and brown were used. A majority of these wares were produced at various English potteries right up until the turn-of-the-century. French and other European firms also made similar

Fig. 6-130

pieces and all are quite collectible. The best reference on this area is Petra Williams' book *Staffordshire Romantic Transfer Patterns—Cup Plates and Early Victorian China* (Fountain House, East, 1978). Also see: HISTORICAL & COMMEMORATIVE WARES.

Bowl, shallow, 8" d., 1⅛" h., scene of Chinese family, dark blue **$77.00**

Charger, creamware, round dished form w/flanged rim, decorated in the center w/a large black transfer scene of a lady & anchor representing "Hope" on shore w/a sailing ship at sea to the side, the rim w/a lovebird printed design, trimmed w/polychrome enamel, probably Liverpool, ca. 1800, 10" d. (rim chip repairs) **173.00**

Cup plate, Lady of the Lake patt., medium blue, Careys, 3⅞" d. **143.00**

Cup plate, Fakeer's Rock patt., Oriental Scenery series, dark blue, second quarter 19th c., John Hall & Sons, 4¼" d. **86.00**

Custard cup, w/flared rim, handled, game birds depicted (deceased), dark blue, Stubbs (unseen, blued in chip under the rim) **66.00**

Gravy boat, scene w/elk in foreground w/another elk pulling a sleigh in background, Zoological series, dark blue, Wood, 4½" h. **385.00**

Gravy tureen & attached underplate, cov., overall groupings of variety of sea shells, applied olive-ochre enamel line on rims & finial, medium dark blue, Spode, Wedgwood or possibly Davenport, 6¾" h. (small portion of lid broken off & staple-repaired back on) **220.00**

Pitcher, 4½" h., applied green enamel band enclosing black transfer-prints, "The Enterprise and Boxer," reverse w/"The United States and Macedonian," applied pink lustre band around neck (restoration & reglazing) **1,210.00**

Pitcher, 5" h., black transfer-print "Arms of the United States" & "Free Trade and Sailor's Rights" on reverse, white w/applied brown, tan, black, red, yellow, blue & green enamel trim (chip on rim, the rim has been repainted & reglazed) **1,650.00**

Plate, 6¼" d., Beehive patt., dark blue, underglaze mark, Ralph Stevenson & Williams **138.00**

Plate, 7" d., Palestine patt., Bethlehem scene, mulberry **40.00**

Plate, 7⅛" d., brownish black transfer-printed center bust of bewigged gentleman titled "Brougham," highly embossed rim & four red transfer-printed floral vignettes around border (traces of two faint hairlines off the rim) **94.00**

Plate, 7⅝" d., Chinoisere patt., dark blue, Stubbs, impressed propeller mark **55.00**

Plate, 10¼" d., center scene of hunter & spaniel w/ducks, dark blue, Wood, impressed mark (in the making pit in center of plate) **330.00**

Plates, 10" d., English Scenery patt., blue, Enoch Wood, set of 4 . . . . **72.00**

Platter, well & tree, 10⅝" l., rectangular, blue transfer-printed river scene w/boats, bridge, cottage & grazing animals, trees, Wild Rose border, medium dark blue, unknown maker **660.00**

Platter, 18½" l., Grecian Scenery patt., dark blue w/white embossed border, Wood (trace of a 10" l. meandering hairline on reverse) **413.00**

Platter, 19½" l., University patt., greyish black, Ridgway (Fig. 6-130) **110.00**

Platter strainer, oval, Far Eastern center scene of buildings near a river, man in a boat & animals on opposite grassy bank, Morning Glory border, medium blue, maker unknown, 12⅞" w. (faint 3" l. hairline off the center hole) **330.00**

Platter strainer, oval, river scene w/boats & bridge w/cottage, trees, grazing animals, medium blue, unknown maker, 12⅞" w. (unseen flake on underside) **358.00**

Soup plate, Pastoral patt., medium light blue w/embossed white border, W. Stevenson, 10½" d. (unseen chipping on foot rim) **55.00**

Vegetable dish, footed w/domed cover, blue transfer-printed scene of castle w/fruit & flower border, dark blue, second quarter 19th c., 12⅛" w. (chips) **748.00**

Vegetable dish, open, rectangular, carmine central transfer w/scene of hunters jumping a hedge, w/one rider & horse falling, 10⅜" w. **77.00**

STONEWARE

Stoneware is essentially a vitreous pottery, impervious to water even in its unglazed state, that has been produced by potteries all over the world for centuries. Utilitarian wares such as crocks, jugs, churns, and the like, were the most common productions in the numerous potteries that sprang into existence in the United States during the 19th cen-

tury. These items were often enhanced by the application of a cobalt blue oxide decoration. In addition to the coarse, primarily salt-glazed stonewares, there are other categories of stoneware known by such special names as basalt, jasper, and others. Also see: RED WING.

Batter jug, bulbous ovoid body tapering to short wide molded rim, cobalt blue brushed accents at ears, handle & spout, impressed "Binghamton, N.Y.," wire bail handle w/wooden handgrip, ca. 1870, 4 qt., minor chips at spout from use, 9" h. (Fig. 6-131, left) **$275.00**

Batter jug, bulbous ovoid body tapering to short wide molded rim, cobalt blue slip-quilled long-tailed running bird, unsigned, attributed to Whites, Utica, New York, original wire bail handle w/wooden handgrip, ca. 1870, 1 gal., 9" h. (few minor surface chips) **1,210.00**

Batter jug, bulbous ovoid body tapering to short wide molded rim, cobalt blue slip-quilled "4" above pine tree design beneath spout unsigned, attributed to Whites, Utica, New York, w/original bail handle & wooden handgrip, ca. 1870, 4 qt., 10" h. (a few insignificant surface chips at spout & rim) **635.00**

Bowl, 11½" d., 5½" h., brushed cobalt blue squiggle design & "1½," unsigned, possibly N. Clark Lyons, ca. 1830, 1½ gal. **484.00**

Bowl, 15" d., 7½" h., impressed "Mason & Carnes Cortland," New York, blue accents at handles, ca. 1830, 3 gal. (minor age line in base on side) **523.00**

Butter churn, table top-type, pitcher-shaped, squatty bulbous body tapering to a slightly flared molded rim w/pinched spout, applied strap handle, hand-fitted wooden dasher insert, cobalt blue slip-quilled basket of flowers, impressed "J. & E. Norton & Co. Bennington, VT.," ca. 1859, 2 gal, 12" h. (tight, full length, stabilized through line in front & interior rim chip, from use) **2,239.00**

Butter churn, slightly tapering cylindrical body w/molded rim & applied eared handles, cobalt blue slip-quilled pair of love birds & "3" above a squiggle, impressed "S. Hart Fulton," ca. 1870, 3 gal., 14" h. (very minor surface chip & spider lines in back) **1,029.00**

Fig. 6-131

Fig. 6-132

Butter churn, slightly swelled cylindrical sides tapering to ring-necked molded rim cobalt blue slip-quilled bird sitting on plowed field, flanked by "3" above squiggle design, impressed "W.H. Farrar Geddes, N.Y.," ca. 1860, 3 gal., 14½" h. (professional restoration to line throughout) **2,420.00**

Butter churn, slightly swelled cylindrical sides tapering to ring-neck wide molded rim & applied eared handles, brushed cobalt blue floral decoration below "4" w/impressed "N. Clark & Co. Lyons," ca. 1840, 4 gal., 18" h. (kiln imperfection on side, design fry) **275.00**

Butter churn, slightly swelled cylindrical sides tapering to molded rim, applied eared handles, cobalt blue slip-quilled detailed peacock & tree decoration, impressed "J. Norton & Co. Bennington, VT." & "5," two year mark (when the factory was under the direction of Julius Norton until his death in 1861), 5 gal., 18" h. (professional restoration to horizontal Y-shaped tight through line in front) **2,420.00**

Butter churn, original dasher guide, slightly swelled cylindrical sides tapering to wide, slightly flared molded rim, applied eared handles, cobalt blue slip-quilled large orchid decoration, impressed "N.A. White & Son, Utica, N.Y.," ca. 1885, 5 gal., 18½" h. (minor surface chip at rim) **990.00**

Butter churn w/original dasher guide, slightly swelled cylindrical sides tapering to molded rim, applied eared handles, detailed thick cobalt blue slip-quilled compote of flowers, impressed "J. & E. Norton Bennington VT," ca. 1859, 6 gal, 19" h. (Fig. 6-132) **4,510.00**

Butter churn w/original dasher guide, slightly swelled cylindrical sides tapering to wide slightly flared molded rim, applied eared handles, large slip-quilled cobalt blue top-to-bottom floral decoration, impressed "W.H. Farrar Geddes, N.Y.," ca. 1850, 6 gal., 19½" h. (large chip missing from dasher guide, stabilized horizontal crack on back side) **1,320.00**

Butter churn, cov. w/dasher guide, slightly swelled cylindrical sides tapering to wide slightly flared molded rim, applied eared handles, thick cobalt blue slip-quilled eight-point star w/face in center, impressed "T. Harrington Lyons," Lyons, New York, ca. 1860, 6 gal., 19½" h. (one repaired rim chip above ear, one minor rim chip on opposite side) **4,235.00**

Butter crock, bulbous ovoid body tapering to wide molded rim, flanked by eared handles, cobalt blue script slip-quilled "Butter" on one side & "Lard" on reverse, unsigned, ca. 1840, 11¼" h. (one handle professionally restored, minor glaze wear) **660.00**

Fig. 6-133   Fig. 6-134   Fig. 6-135

Cake crock, cylindrical body w/molded rim & applied eared handles, cobalt blue slip-quilled "Cake 1866" in script, impressed "A. O. Whittemore, Havana, N.Y.," ca. 1866, 2 gal., 5³/₄" h. **990.00**

Cake crock, slightly waisted cylindrical body w/rolled molded rim & applied eared handles, cobalt blue slip-quilled stylized design, impressed "J. & E. Norton Bennington VT." & "2," ca. 1859, 2 gal., 7¹/₂" h. (stabilized line in front extending through blue) **165.00**

Cream crock, cov., baluster form body w/molded rim & applied eared handles, cobalt slip-quilled floral decoration beneath "2," unsigned, attributed to M. Woodruff, Cortland, N.Y., ca. 1870, 2 gal., 12¹/₂" h. (very minor stone ping in the making, surface chip in lid) **393.00**

Crock, cylindrical w/molded rim, applied eared handles, cobalt blue slip-quilled flower & leaves, impressed "John Burger Rochester," New York, ca. 1855, 1 gal., 6" h. **1,705.00**

Crock, cylindrical w/molded rim & applied eared handles, cobalt blue slip-quilled dotted fantail bird, impressed label "W. Roberts Binghamton, N.Y.," ca. 1860, 1 gal., 7" h. (professional restoration to age line on side) **514.00**

Crock, cylindrical w/rolled molded rim & applied eared handles, cobalt blue brushed floral decoration, impressed "Taft & Co. Keene N.H.," ca. 1870, 1 gal., 7¹/₂" h. (two rim chips & tight through line above right ear) **145.00**

Crock, cylindrical w/molded rim & applied eared handles, cobalt blue slip-quilled Smiley-face flower & "2," impressed "J. Burger Rochester, N.Y.," ca. 1880, 2 gal, few minor glaze flake spots, 8¹/₂" h. (Fig. 6-133) **1,271.00**

Crock, cylindrical w/molded rim & applied eared handles, cobalt blue slip-quilled geometric decoration, unsigned, ca. 1870, 2 gal., 9" h. (large rim chip on back side) . . **121.00**

Crock, cylindrical w/molded rim & applied eared handles, cobalt blue slip-quilled leaf decoration beneath "2," impressed " J. Fisher & Lyons, N.Y.," ca. 1880, 2 gal., 9" h. **157.00**

Crock, cylindrical w/rolled molded rim & applied eared handles, cobalt blue slip-quilled bird on twig & "2," impressed "W. Roberts Binghamton, N.Y.," ca. 1860, 2 gal., 9" h. (professional restoration to line in front, just touching the blue & two rim chips) **278.00**

Crock, cylindrical w/rolled molded rim, applied eared handles, very thick cobalt blue slip-quilled dotted bird perched on branch w/squiggly leaves & bullseye flowers, flanked w/ribbed leaf motif, impressed "Edmunds & Co.," ca. 1865, 2 gal., 9¹/₂" h. (professional restoration to rim chip & tight line in back) **936.00**

Crock, cylindrical w/molded, slightly flared rim, applied eared handles, cobalt blue slip-quilled detailed chicken pecking corn decoration, impressed "J. Fisher & Lyons, N.Y.," Ft. Edward, N.Y., ca. 1880, 3 gal., 15¹/₂" h. (some glaze flaking & age line at base, on back & minor surface chips around rim) . . . **787.00**

Crock, cylindrical w/molded rim & applied eared handles, cobalt blue slip-quilled bullseye, squiggle, impressed "F.T. Wright & Son Taunton, Mass.," ca. 1860, 3 gal., 10" h. (minor surface rim chip in back & staining) **182.00**

Crock, cylindrical w/molded rim & applied eared handles, incised "3" above cobalt blue slip-quilled large bird on fence decoration, unsigned, attributed to Brady & Ryan, Ellenville, New York, ca. 1885, 3 gal., two separation lines in the making, on back & side, 10" h. (Fig. 6-134) **1,089.00**

Crock, semi-ovoid w/rolled molded rim & applied eared handles, cobalt blue brushed double hops w/blue accents at ears, impressed "T. Harrington Lyons," New York, ca. 1860, 3 gal., 12" h. **666.00**

Crock, wide ovoid body w/rolled molded rim & applied eared handles, cobalt blue slip-quilled decoration of reclining deer near fence & tree, house in background, impressed "J. & E. Norton & Co. Bennington, VT.," ca. 1859, 3 gal., 12½" h. (professional restoration to rim chip & line towards front, not through blue, also restoration to tight through lines in back) **4,477.00**

Crock, ovoid body w/wide cylindrical rim flanked by eared handles, cobalt blue brushed flower decoration, impressed "I. Seymour Troy," ca. 1830, approx. 3 gal., 13" h. (professional restoration to right ear, stone pings in the making, three 5" tight age lines around rim) **121.00**

Crock, cylindrical w/molded rim & applied eared handles, cobalt blue slip-quilled large bird on stump w/arrow in his beak, impressed "Whites Utica, N.Y.," ca. 1870, 4 gal., 11" h. (professional restoration to tight line on side) **1,271.00**

Crock, cylindrical w/molded rim & applied eared handles, cobalt blue brushed waterfall-like design, impressed "M. Woodruff Cortland," New York, ca. 1870, 4 gal., 11" h. (professional restoration to through lines on side & back) **495.00**

Crock, cylindrical w/rolled molded rim & applied eared handles, cobalt blue slip-quilled stag standing, extensive ground cover, tree & flowers, impressed "Fort Edward Pottery Co.," New York above "4," ca. 1860, 4 gal., 11½" h. (professional restoration to 6" tight line on one side, not through the blue) **3,850.00**

Crock, cylindrical w/molded rim & applied eared handles, cobalt blue slip-quilled very large bird on twig decoration, unsigned, attributed to Brady & Ryan, Ellenville, New York ca. 1885, 4 gal., 11½" h. (professional restorations to 4" tight line & rim chips in front & back) **545.00**

Crock, cylindrical w/molded rim & applied eared handles, cobalt blue slip-quilled pair of birds on leafy branch decoration, impressed "Ottman Bro's & Co. Fort Edward, N.Y.," ca. 1880, 5 gal., 14" tight through line in back, 12" h. (Fig. 6-135) . . **1,876.00**

Crock, cylindrical w/molded rim & applied eared handles, cobalt blue slip-quilled detailed winged banner surrounding "S & M," impressed "New York Stoneware Co. Fort Edward, N.Y.," ca. 1870, 5 gal., 12½" h. (insignificant glaze spider in front) **877.00**

Crock, cylindrical w/molded rim & applied eared handles, cobalt blue slip-quilled fan-tailed bird on floral branch, impressed "W. Roberts Binghamton, N.Y.," ca. 1860, 6 gal., 13½" h. (glaze flake spots & 5" tight line on back) **545.00**

Crock, cylindrical w/ring molded rim, applied eared handles, cobalt blue slip-quilled large daisy & leaves, impressed "Burger & Lang Rochester, N.Y." & "6," ca. 1870, 6 gal., 14½" h. **468.00**

Crock, cylindrical w/molded rim, applied eared handles, cobalt blue slip-quilled double flower & leaves decoration, impressed "Harrington & Burger Rochester," New York & "6," ca. 1851, 6 gal., 14½" h. (4" tight through line in front, stabilized freeze line at base extending around side, back, & through bottom, minor glaze flakes around back) **3,850.00**

Jar, ovoid body w/molded rim & applied eared handles, cinnamon clay w/incised swag design front & back, highlighted w/blue, unsigned, attributed to John Remmey III New York City, ca. 1800, ½ gal., 8" h. (insignificant surface chips at rim) **1,430.00**

Jar, slightly ovoid body w/molded rim & applied eared handles, cobalt blue slip-quilled deer standing on grass, impressed "Edmunds & Co.," ca. 1870, 2 gal., 12" h. (professional restoration to glaze blemish just touching chest of deer, 6" tight through line in back, minor age spider & stack mark on back) **1,650.00**

Jar, bulbous ovoid body w/ringed molded rim & applied eared handles, cobalt blue brushed floral decoration surrounding jar, accents at handles, unsigned, ca. 1850, 2 gal., 12" h. (staining, Y-shaped through line near base) **218.00**

Jug, semi-ovoid, tapering to a wide flared rim, applied strap handle, cobalt blue brushed double flower on stem w/leaves decoration, unsigned, attributed to Cortland factory, ca. 1870, ¹/₂ gal., 9" h. (professional restoration to tight line in handle) **182.00**

Jug, grotesque face-type, ash glazed, cylindrical neck & strap handle above a double-bellied form, the front centering a human face w/inset porcelain teeth flanked on each side by articulated ears, signed "Lanier Meaders," 9¹/₂" h. **483.00**

Jug, ovoid w/molded lip & applied handles, brushed cobalt blue large stylized blossom & leaves, impressed maker's mark for P. Mugler & Co., Buffalo, N.Y., ca. 1850, 1 gal., 11" h. (Fig. 6-131, right) **578.00**

Jug, semi-ovoid, tapering to a short cylindrical neck, applied strap handle, cobalt blue slip-quilled orchid decoration, impressed "Whites Utica," New York, ca. 1870, 1 gal, 11" h. (Fig. 6-136) **351.00**

Jug, face-type, comprising a head of a man w/protruding eyes, nose & open mouth, fitted w/the remains of porcelain teeth, Southern U.S., 19th c., lacks handle & other losses, 11¹/₄" h. **1,725.00**

Jug, semi-ovoid, tapering to a short cylindrical neck, applied strap handle, cobalt blue slip-quilled bird on a twig decoration, impressed "F.T. Wright & Son Taunton, Mass.," ca. 1860, 1 gal., 11¹/₂" h. (3" separation line in the making & 6" tight through line in back) **278.00**

Jug, bulbous ovoid w/molded rim, applied strap handle, impressed "I. Seymour & Co. Troy," New York, ca. 1827, 2 gal., 13" h. **165.00**

Jug, semi-ovoid w/molded rim, applied strap handle, cobalt blue slip-quilled dotted bird on branch decoration, impressed "Whites Binghamton," New York, ca. 1860, 2 gal., 13" h. (professional restoration to spout & handle) **453.00**

Jug, semi-ovoid w/molded rim, applied strap handle, cobalt blue slip-quilled large dotted

bird sitting on branch, holding a worm in its beak, impressed "J.&E. Norton & Co. Bennington, VT.," ca. 1859, 2 gal, 13¹/₂" h. (professional restoration to handle) . . . **2,000.00**

Jug, ovoid w/molded rim, applied strap handle, brushed cobalt blue floral decoration, impressed mark "N. & A. Seymour Rose," ca. 1830, approx. 2 gal., 13¹/₂" h. (freeze line at base in back, two insignificant glaze drips on back) **290.00**

Jug, semi-ovoid w/molded rim & applied strap handle, cobalt blue slip-quilled cherries on leafy branch, blue accents at handle, impressed "Cowden & Wilcox Harrisburg, PA.," ca. 1870, 2 gal., 14" h. (professional restoration to tight line through the name) **605.00**

Jug, tall cylindrical tapering to molded rim, applied strap handle, large cobalt blue slip-quilled tornado design, impressed "W.H. Farrar Geddes, N.Y.," ca. 1850, 2 gal., 14" h. (very minor staining) **297.00**

Jug, semi-ovoid w/molded rim, applied strap handle, thick cobalt blue slip-quilled landing hawk or eagle design, impressed "J. & E. Norton Bennington VT." & "3," ca. 1859, 3 gal., 15¹/₂" h. (Fig. 6-137) **7,425.00**

Jug, semi-ovoid w/molded rim, applied strap handle, cobalt blue slip-quilled double flower decoration beneath "3" & impressed "Harrington & Burger Rochester," ca. 1852, 3 gal., 16" h. **696.00**

Jug, semi-ovoid w/ring-molded rim, applied strap handle, slip-quilled cobalt blue bird on berry branch, unsigned, attributed to Fulper Bros. Flemington, New Jersey, ca. 1880, 4 gal., 18" h. **635.00**

Jug, semi-ovoid w/ring-molded rim, applied strap handle, slip-quilled cobalt blue floral & leaf design, signed "Jordan" in blue script, ca. 1850, 4 gal., 18" h. **1,089.00**

Pitcher, 10" h., bulbous ovoid body tapering to a flat rim w/pinched spout, applied strap handle, slip-quilled cobalt blue plume decoration w/blue highlighting around incised lines, unsigned, 1 gal. (minor surface chip in back, 2" through line on side) **206.00**

Pitcher, 10" h., bulbous ovoid body tapering to a wide, slightly flared molded rim

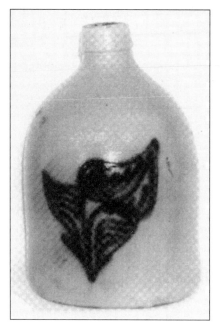

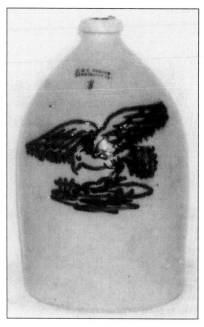

Fig. 6-136   Fig. 6-137   Fig. 6-138

w/pinched spout, applied strap handle, dark brown Albany slip accent against a light brown ground, impressed "Wm. E. Warner West Troy," ca. 1850, approx. 1 gal. (a few filled-in surface chips at rim) **121.00**

Preserving jar, slightly tapering cylindrical body w/wide, slightly flared rim, cobalt blue slip-quilled elaborate floral design front & back, top to bottom, blue accents at ears, impressed "B.C. Milburn Alex VA," ca. 1870, 1½ gal., 11" h. (stack marks, in the making, otherwise excellent) **786.00**

Preserving jar, cylindrical w/slightly flared molded rim, cobalt blue slip-quilled basket w/flowers forming heart shape around "1878," & impressed "2" above decoration, unsigned, possible Whites Utica, New York, ca. 1878, 2 gal., 11" h. (professional repair to rim & ear chips on one side) **605.00**

Preserving jar, slightly tapering cylindrical body w/rolled molded rim, applied eared handles, cobalt blue slip-quilled stylized bullseye decoration, impressed "F. Laufersweiler Empire City Pottery 517 & 519 W 27 St. N," ca. 1880, 2 gal., 11" h. (clay discoloration in the making) **817.00**

Preserving jar, slightly tapering cylindrical body w/molded rim & applied eared handles, cobalt blue slip-quilled bird peacock-type bird on leafy branch,

impressed "Whites Utica," ca. 1870, 2 gal., 11" h. (professional restorations to chips & minor hairlines in back) **242.00**

Preserving jar, slightly tapering cylindrical body w/rolled molded rim & applied eared handles, cobalt blue slip-quilled bird on a twig decoration, impressed "Wm Dornet Albany, N.Y.," ca. 1870, 2 gal., 11½" h. (Fig. 6-138) **696.00**

Preserving jar, cylindrical w/molded rim & applied eared handles, cobalt blue slip-quilled flower, impressed "C.W. Braun Buffalo, N.Y.," ca. 1870, 2 gal., 11½" h. (minor, tight glaze line at back) **194.00**

Preserving jar, cylindrical w/slightly flared molded rim, applied eared handles, cobalt blue slip-quilled pair of love birds decoration, unsigned, attributed to Brady & Ryan, Ellenville, New York, ca. 1885, 3 gal., 12½" h. (1" hairline at base, professional restoration to tight line & rim chip, both on back) **484.00**

Preserving jar, slightly tapering cylindrical body w/molded slightly flared rim & applied eared handles, cobalt blue slip-quilled decoration of artistic flower encompassing the entire front canvas, impressed "N. Clark & Co. Lyons," Lyons, New York, ca. 1850, 3 gal., 13" h. (glaze line, minor surface chips) **2,662.00**

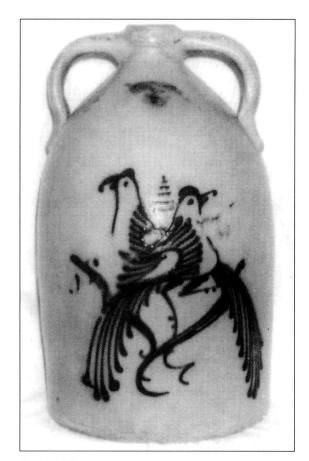

Fig. 6-139

Preserving jar, slightly tapering cylindrical
  body w/molded rim, applied eared handles,
  cobalt blue slip-quilled large bird on stump
  & floral decoration, unsigned, attributed to
  Brady & Ryan, Ellenville, New York, ca. 1885,
  5 gal., 15½" h. (two minor surface rim chips
  in back) **847.00**

Water cooler, barrel-shaped, cinnamon clay
  ground w/"Ice Water" incised in script,
  flanked by cobalt blue leaf & flower
  decoration, lower front has molded facial
  design around circular spigot w/cork serving
  as mouth, unsigned, attributed to
  Wingender Factory, Haddonfield, N.J.,
  original family owner registry penned on
  bottom, ca. 1885, 3 gal, 13" h. (minor
  surface interior chips) **660.00**

Water cooler, semi-ovoid w/large loop
  handles, cobalt blue slip-quilled pair of
  crossed love birds on branch, impressed
  "Whites Utica," ca. 1870, 5 gal., separation
  stack mark on back done in making, 19" h.
  (Fig. 6-139) **2,057.00**

WATT POTTERY

In July, 1922 the Watt Pottery was incorporated on the site of the old Burley Pottery in Crooksville, Ohio where it was owned and operated by the Watt family of Perry County, Ohio. It remained in business until a fire halted production in 1965.

Through the 1920s and early 1930s the Watt Pottery manufactured stoneware crocks, churns, and jars. These are marked with an eagle or acorn in blue, with gallonage marked in a circle.

In 1935, the pottery dropped its stoneware line in favor of more modern ovenwares. The lightweight clay body gave the wares the necessary resilience to go from icebox to oven. In 1949, the Watt Pottery began hand-decorating its wares. The pieces were decorated by teams of three decorators and the patterns were simple in nature, with as few brush strokes as possible to allow low production costs. The bright colors against the deep cream clay give Watt Pottery its unique country appeal.

The first hand-decorated patterns are called the "Classic Patterns" and were produced from 1949 until about 1953. They are: Rio Rose, Moonflower, Dogwood, and Daisy and Crosshatch.

The patterns most sought after by today's collectors and their introduction dates are as follows: Starflower —1951; Apple—1952; Cherry—1952; Silhouette— 1953; Rooster—1955; Dutch Tulip—1956; American Red Bud (Tear Drop)—1957; Morning Glory—1958; Autumn Foliage—1959; Double Apple—1959; and Tulip—1961.

Most pieces of Watt ware are well marked. The marks are large, often covering the entire bottom of the piece. They usually consist of one or more concentric rings deeply impressed into the bottom. The words "Watt" and "Oven Ware U.S.A." are impressed as well, although some pieces have only one phrase, not both. Earlier marks featured a script "Watt" without circles. Most pieces also have the mold number impressed in the center, making identification easy. The most significant pieces which were not marked are the ice bucket (all patterns) and Apple dinner plates.

—Dennis M. Thompson

Baker, Apple patt., rectangular, No. 85,
  9" w. **$1,000.00**
Baker, cov., Apple patt., No. 67, 8¼" d. **125.00**
Baker, cov., Apple patt., No. 601, 8" d. **120.00**

Fig. 6-140

Baker, cov., Autumn Foliage patt., No. 110,
8¹/₂" d. **90.00**

Baker, cov., Cherry patt., No. 53, 7¹/₂" d. **110.00**

Baker, cov., Cherry patt., No. 54, 8¹/₂" d. **110.00**

Baker, cov., Open Apple patt., No. 110,
8¹/₂" d. **350.00**

Bean pot, cov., Apple patt., No. 76, 6¹/₂" h. . **175.00**

Bean pot, cov., Autumn Foliage patt., No. 76,
6¹/₂" h. **150.00**

Bean pot, cov., bisque, No. 76, 6¹/₂" h. **15.00**

Bean pot, cov., Dutch Tulip patt., No. 76,
6¹/₂" h. **275.00**

Bean pot, cov., Rooster patt., No. 76, 6¹/₂" h. . **350.00**

Bean cup, Tear Drop patt., No. 75, 3¹/₂" d.
2¹/₄" h. **15.00**

Bowl, 4" d., 1¹/₂" d., Apple patt., No. 602
(Fig. 6-140, far left) **125.00**

Bowl, 4¹/₄" d., 2" h., Apple patt., No. 04 . . . . . **60.00**

Bowl, 5" d., 2" h., Apple patt., No. 603
(Fig. 6-140, center left) **100.00**

Bowl, 6" d., 2¹/₂" h., Apple patt., No. 604
(Fig. 6-140, center) **90.00**

Bowl, 7" d., 3" h., Apple patt., No. 600
(Fig. 6-140, center right) **65.00**

Bowl, 7¹/₄" d., 3" h., Apple patt., No. 07 . . . . . **50.00**

Bowl, 8" d., 3¹/₂" h., Apple patt., No. 601
(Fig. 6-140, far right) **65.00**

Bowl, 8¹/₄" d., 3¹/₂" h., Apple patt., No. 67 . . . . **50.00**

Bowl, 10" d., 3" h., Autumn Foliage patt.,
No. 106 . . . . **85.00**

Bowl, 13" d., 3¹/₂" h., Autumn Foliage patt.,
No. 39 . . . . **135.00**

Bowl, 6¹/₄" d., 2¹/₄" h., Cherry patt., No. 52 . . . **25.00**

Fig. 6-141

Bowl, spaghetti, 13" d., 3¹/₂" h,. Dogwood patt.,
No. 39 (Fig. 6-141, back) **135.00**

Bowl, 4¹/₄" d., 2" h., Double Apple patt.,
No. 04 . . . . **100.00**

Bowl, 7¹/₄" d., 3" h., Double Apple patt.,
No. 07 . . . . **70.00**

Bowl, spaghetti, 13" d., 3¹/₂" h., Dutch Tulip
patt., No. 39 (Fig. 6-142) **400.00**

Bowl, 9¹/₂" d., 4" h., Open Apple patt.,
No. 73 . . . . **250.00**

Fig. 6-142

Fig. 6-143

Bowl, spaghetti, 13" d., 3¹/₂" h., Open Apple
patt., No. 39 . . . . **1,100.00**

Bowl, 15" d., 3¹/₂" h., Rio Rose patt. **100.00**

Bowl, 5¹/₂" d., 2" h., Reduced Apple patt.,
No. 74 . . . . **45.00**

Bowl, 8¹/₄" d., 3¹/₂" h., Rooster patt., No. 67 . . **90.00**

Bowl, spaghetti, 13" d., 3¹/₂" h., Rooster patt.,
No. 39 . . . . **375.00**

Bowl, 8¹/₄" d., 3¹/₄" h., Starflower patt., No. 54 . . **40.00**

Bowl, 11" d., 4" h., Starflower patt., No. 55 . . . **75.00**

Bowl, spaghetti, 13" d., 3¹/₂" h., Starflower
patt., No. 39 . . . . **110.00**

Bowl, 5¹/₄" d., 2¹/₂" h., Tear Drop patt., No. 05 . . **40.00**

Bowl, 6" d., 2¹/₂" h. Tulip patt., No. 604 . . . . . **150.00**

Bowl, 7" d., 3" h., Tulip patt., No. 600 . . . . . . **125.00**

Bowl, 8" d., 3¹/₂" h., Tulip patt., No. 601 . . . . **125.00**

Canister, cov., Apple patt., No. 82, 5" d. **450.00**

Canister, cov., Apple patt., No. 80, 8¹/₂" d. . **1,300.00**

Canister, cov., Dutch Tulip patt., No. 81,
6¹/₂" d. **500.00**

Canister, cov., Rio Rose patt., No. 72, 7¹/₄" d.
(Fig. 6-143) **350.00**

Canister, cov., Rooster patt., No. 80, 8¹/₂" d. . **650.00**

Canister, cov., Starflower patt., No. 82, 5" d. . . **325.00**

Carafe, cov., Autumn Foliage patt., No. 115,
9¹/₂" h. (Fig. 6-150, far left) **175.00**

Carafe, cov., Brown banded, No. 115, 10¹/₂" h. . **450.00**

Casserole, cov., Apple patt., No. 18, 5" d. . . . **175.00**

Casserole, cov., Apple patt., w/French handle,
No. 18, 5" d. **225.00**

Casserole, cov., Dogwood patt., No. 18, 5" d.
(Fig. 6-141, front) **150.00**

Casserole, cov., Rooster patt., w/French
handle, No. 18, 5" d. **225.00**

Casserole, cov., Silhouette patt., No. 18, 5" d. . **35.00**

Casserole, cov., Starflower patt., No. 18,
5" d. **125.00**

Chip-n-Dip set, Autumn Foliage patt., No. 110
& 120 bowls, the set (Fig. 6-144, center) . . **175.00**

Chip-n-Dip set, Double Apple patt., No. 96 &
120 bowls, the set **350.00**

Churns, stoneware, Eagle or Acorn patt.,
various sizes . . . . **100.00 to 150.00**

Cookie jar, cov., Apple patt., No. 21, 7¹/₂" h. . . **375.00**

Cookie jar, cov., Cherry patt., No. 21, 7¹/₂" h. . . **250.00**

Cookie jar, cov., "Cookie Barrel," wood grain,
10¹/₂" h. **75.00**

Cookie jar, cov., "Goodies," No. 76, 6¹/₂" h. . . . **150.00**

Cookie jar, cov., happy/sad face, wooden lid,
No. 34, 8" h. **175.00**

Cookie jar, cov., Morning Glory patt., cream,
No. 95, 10" h. **750.00**

Cookie jar, cov., figural, Policeman, 10¹/₂" h.,
rare (Fig. 6-145) **1,500.00**

Cookie jar, cov., Rio Rose patt., No. 21,
7¹/₂" h. **150.00**

Cookie jar, cov., Starflower patt., No. 503,
8" h. **400.00**

Fig. 6-144

Cookie jar, cov., Tulip patt., No. 503, 8" h. . . . **375.00**

Creamer, Apple (two-leaf) patt., No. 62,
4¹/₄" h. **150.00**

Creamer, Apple (three-leaf) patt., No. 62,
4¹/₄" h. **90.00**

Creamer, Autumn Foliage patt., No. 62,
4¹/₄" h. (Fig. 6-144, left) **250.00**

Creamer, Dutch Tulip patt., No. 62,
4¹/₄" h. **275.00**

Creamer, Morning Glory patt., cream, No. 97,
4¹/₄" h. **500.00**

Creamer, Starflower patt., four-petal, No. 62,
4¹/₄" h. (Fig. 6-152, second from left) **250.00**

Creamer, Starflower patt., five-petal, No. 62,
4¹/₄" h. (Fig. 6-154, far right) **225.00**

Creamer, Tulip patt., No. 62, 4¹/₄" h. **225.00**

Crocks, stoneware, Eagle or Acorn patt.,
various sizes (Fig. 6-146, of two) . . **50.00 to 100.00**

Cruet set, cov., Apple patt., 7¹/₂" h. **1,800.00**

Cruet set, cov., Autumn Foliage patt., 7¹/₂" h. . **500.00**

Grease jar, cov., Apple patt., No. 47, 5" h. . . . **400.00**

Grease jar, cov., Autumn Foliage patt., No. 01,
5" h. **200.00**

Grease jar, cov., Starflower patt., No. 01,
5" h. **275.00**

Ice bucket, cov., Autumn Foliage patt., No. 59,
7" h. **200.00**

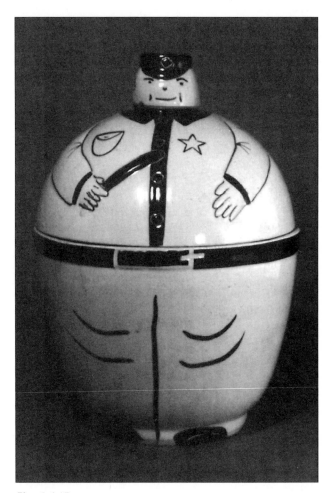

Fig. 6-145

Fig. 6-148

Fig. 6-149

Fig. 6-146

Fig. 6-147

Ice bucket, cov., Dutch Tulip patt.,
No. 59, 7" h. **400.00**

Ice tea keg, cov., plain, 11" h.
(Fig. 6-147) **125.00**

Ice tea keg, cov., brand name, 11" h.
(Fig. 6-147) **125.00**

Mixing bowl, Morning Glory patt.,
5" d. **125.00**

Mixing bowl, Reduced Apple patt.,
deep, No. 61 . . . . **125.00**

Mixing bowls, nesting, Apple patt.,
Nos. 5, 6, 7, & 9, 5" to 9" d.,
each **50.00**

Mixing bowls, nesting, Apple patt.,
ribbed, Nos. 5, 6, 7, & 9, 5" to 9" d.,
each **60.00**

Mixing bowls, nesting, Morning Glory
patt., Nos. 6, 7, 8, & 9, 6" to 9" d.,
each **80.00**

Mixing bowls, nesting, Open Apple
patt., Nos. 5, 6, 7, & 8, 5" to 8" d.,
each (Fig. 6-148, of three) **125.00**

Mixing bowls, nesting, Starflower patt.,
Nos. 5, 6, 7, 8, & 9, 5" to 9" d.,
each **35.00**

Mixing bowls, nesting, Tulip patt.,
deep, Nos. 63, 64, & 65, 6½" d.,
7½" d. & 8½" d. (Fig. 6-149) each . . **90.00**

Mug, Apple patt., No. 121, 3" h. **175.00**

Mug, Apple patt., No. 501, 4½" h. . . . **300.00**

Fig. 6-150

Fig. 6-152

Fig. 6-151

Fig. 6-153

Fig. 6-154

Fig. 6-155

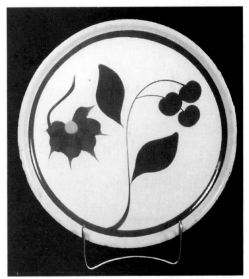

Fig. 6-156

Mug, Autumn Foliage patt., No. 501, 4¹/₂" h. . **135.00**

Pie plate, Apple patt., No. 33, 9¹/₄" d. **125.00**

Pie plate, Rooster patt., No. 33, 9¹/₄" d. **400.00**

Pie plate, Starflower patt., five-petal, No. 33,
9¹/₄" d. (Fig. 6-151) **200.00**

Pitcher, 5¹/₄" h., Apple patt., No. 15 . . . . **65.00**

Pitcher, 8" h., Apple patt., w/ice lip, No. 17 . . **225.00**

Pitcher, refrigerator, 8" h., Apple patt.,
No. 69 . . . . **450.00**

Pitcher, 5¹/₄" h., Autumn Foliage patt.,
No. 15 (Fig. 6-150, far right) **60.00**

Pitcher, 6¹/₂" h., Autumn Foliage patt.,
No. 16 (Fig. 6-150, second from right) **75.00**

Pitcher, 8" h., Autumn Foliage patt.,
No. 17 (Fig. 6-150, second from left) **60.00**

Pitcher, 6¹/₂" h., Cherry patt., No. 16 . . . . . . **135.00**

Pitcher, 5¹/₄" h., Cross Hatch patt., No. 15 . . **250.00**

Pitcher, 6¹/₂" h., Double Apple patt., No. 16 . . **250.00**

Pitcher, 5¹/₄" h., Dutch Tulip patt., No. 15 . . . **300.00**

Pitcher, 8" h., Eagle patt., No. 17 . . . . **400.00**

Pitcher, 8" h., Morning Glory patt., No. 96 . . **325.00**

Pitcher, 6¹/₂" h., Rio Rose patt., No. 16 . . . . . **200.00**

Pitcher, 8" h., Rio Rose patt., No. 17 . . . . **175.00**

Pitcher, old style, 7" h., Raised Rose patt.
(Fig. 6-153, right) **225.00**

Fig. 6-157

Pitcher, old style, 7" h., Rio Rose (Fig. 6-153, left) **150.00**

Pitcher, 5¼" h., Silhouette patt., No. 15 . . . . **200.00**

Pitcher, 6½" h., Silhouette patt., No. 16 . . . . **100.00**

Pitcher, 5¼" h., Starflower patt., four-petal, No. 15 (Fig. 6-152, center) **150.00**

Pitcher, 6½" h., Starflower patt., four-petal, No. 16 (Fig. 6-152, second from right) **85.00**

Pitcher, 8" h., Starflower patt., four-petal, No. 17 (Fig. 6-152, far right) **150.00**

Pitcher, refrigerator, 8" h., Starflower patt., No. 69 (Fig. 6-152, far left) **550.00**

Pitcher, 5¼" h., Starflower patt., five-petal, No. 15 (Fig. 6-154, second from right) **65.00**

Pitcher, 6½" h., Starflower patt., five-petal, No. 16 (Fig. 6-154, second from left) **85.00**

Pitcher, 8" h., Starflower, five-petal, No. 17 (Fig. 6-154, far left) **160.00**

Pitcher, refrigerator, 8" h., Tear Drop patt., four-petal, No. 69 . . . . **500.00**

Pitcher, 5¼" h., Tulip patt., No. 15 . . . . **500.00**

Plate, 10" d., Moonflower patt. (Fig. 6-155, right) **75.00**

Plate, 6½" d., Rio Rose patt. **25.00**

Platter, 15" d., Apple patt., No. 31 . . . . **350.00**

Platter, 15" d., Autumn Foliage patt., No. 31 . . **110.00**

Platter, 12" d., Cherry patt., No. 49 (Fig. 6-156) **150.00**

Platter, 15" d, Moonflower patt., No. 31 (Fig. 6-155, left) **100.00**

Platter, 12" d., Rio Rose patt., No. 49 . . . . **75.00**

Platter, 15" d., Starflower patt., No. 31 . . . . . **110.00**

Salt shaker, barrel-shaped, Cherry patt., 4" h. **85.00**

Salt & pepper shakers, hourglass-shaped, Autumn Foliage patt., 4" h., the set (Fig. 6-144, far right) **160.00**

Salt & pepper shakers, barrel-shaped, Starflower patt., five-petal, 4" h., the set **160.00**

Salt & pepper shakers, hourglass-shaped, 6-petal Starflower patt., 4" h., the set . . . **250.00**

Salt & pepper shakers, hourglass-shaped, Rooster patt., 4" h., the set **375.00**

Salt & pepper shakers, barrel-shaped, Tear Drop patt., 4" h., the set **325.00**

Sugar bowl, cov., Autumn Foliage patt., No. 98, 4½" h. (Fig. 6-144, far left) **300.00**

Sugar bowl, Morning Glory patt., No. 98, 4¼" h. **250.00**

Teapot, cov., Apple patt., No. 505, 5" h. (Fig. 6-157, left) **3,000.00**

Teapot, cov., Apple (three-leaf) patt., No. 112, 6" h. (Fig. 6-157, right) **1,800.00**

Teapot, cov., Autumn Foliage patt., No. 112, 6" h. **1,500.00**

CHAPTER 7

CHALKWARE

This decorative ware, which became especially popular in the first half of the 19th century, is actually made of molded plaster of Paris. Early pieces are often associated with the Pennsylvania German region and many pieces were probably produced in Pennsylvania but marketed throughout the country. The earliest examples were most often made in the forms of busts, animal figures, and mantel ornaments, often highlighted by brightly painted details. In the early 20th century larger and finer quality pieces were being produced and the chalkware tradition continued in the form of cheap carnival souvenirs right through the first half of this century. All chalkware is collectible but the early 19th century "folksy" examples in top condition bring the highest prices today.

Mantel garniture, hollow-molded figure depicting a tall, fanned stylized group of fruit, vegetables & foliage on a flaring pedestal base, decorated in yellow, red & brown, Pennsylvania, 19th c., 13¼" h. (Fig. 7-1, top center) **$1,093.00**

Mantel garniture, hollow-molded figure depicting a tall, fanned stylized group of fruit & foliage w/original bright polychrome paint in green, yellow, orange & black, on a short pedestal w/square foot, 19th c., 14" h. (minor chip on base) **1,760.00**

Fig. 7-1

Courtesy of Christie's

Fig. 7-2

Fig. 7-3   *Courtesy of Skinner, Inc.*

Model of a cat, hollow-molded seated animal w/tail curled around the body, worn painted spots of detailing, on rectangular foot, 19th c., 7¼" h. (Fig. 7-3, left) **920.00**

Model of a cat, hollow-molded seated animal w/tail curled around the body, on a stepped oblong base, painted dark yellow w/black spots & red details, Pennsylvania, 19th c., 7½" h. (Fig. 7-1, center left) . . . . **600.00 to 900.00**

Model of a cat, hollow-molded seated Cheshire cat w/a gold-painted body & smoke-decorated stripes, red & black highlights, on a round base, Pennsylvania, 19th c., 14¾" h. (Fig. 7-2) **10,925.00**

Model of 'Love Doves,' hollow-molded figure group of two kissing doves mounted on a circular plinth, decorated w/yellow, red, green & black trim, Pennsylvania, 19th c., 5⅝" h. (Fig. 7-1, bottom center) **1,265.00**

Model of a parrot, hollow-molded bird perched atop an orb on a plinth base, the bird in yellow w/green wings & orange beak, orange orb on white base, black trim, 7¼" h. (Fig. 7-1, center right) **920.00**

Model of a rooster, hollow-molded figure of a stylized bird w/high arched tail & conical base, original red, yellow & black paint w/some wear, 19th c., 5¼" h. **484.00**

Model of a stag, the recumbent animal w/one leg forward, conjoined antlers & flaring large ears, dark paint decoration, 19th c., repaired, imperfections, 15" l., 16" h. (Fig. 7-3, right) **173.00**

Models of birds, each hollow-molded bird perched on a group of molded eggs in a striped basket resting on a thick rectangular foot, decorated in green, red & black w/a yellow base, Pennsylvania, 19th c., 4¾" h., facing pr. (Fig. 7-1, bottom left & right) **4,600.00**

Models of dogs, hollow-molded seated Spaniels on oval bases, decorated w/black spots on white & w/red collars & yellow bases, wear & damage, 19th c., 5¼" h., facing pr. **220.00**

CHAPTER
8

CHILDREN'S DISHES

A tin tea set featuring Sunbonnet Babies valued in the $300.00 to $475.00 range.

The children of today play an increasingly important role in nearly every aspect of life. It is clearly evident in marketing. Toy stores world-wide are enjoying the fruits of the demand of the little people. Although the world did not gravitate around the children of the past, they had many wonderful toys which were cared for and kept for today's adults to collect, display, and to organize clubs which celebrate their importance.

Nearly everything made for mother was made for the daughters of the house. The function of these toys was many-faceted. They were bought to teach social graces, for fun, and for the hard road to the kitchen which many would travel before and after marriage.

America's famous glass factories paid tribute to children with fabulous glass such as sets for berries, sets for beverages, table accessories, and decorative items such as epergnes, candlesticks, and cake stands.

Great Britain gave us many wonderful china sets, the end of which is still to be discovered. France favored children with dolls and accessories as well as lovely porcelain tea, dinner and dessert sets. Germany produced china sets, too, but they delved more deeply into interesting room settings, doll houses, butcher shops, grocery shops, and common, but now expensive kitchen accessories.

—Doris Anderson Lechler

Fig. 8-1

GLASSWARE

*These items have been reproduced.

Berry set, Colonial Flute patt.: main berry bowl & six small berry bowls; pressed glass, clear, set of 7 . . . . **$50.00 to 100.00**

Berry set, Fine Cut patt., No. 379: 1³/₄" main berry bowl & six ⁷/₈" berry bowls; pressed glass, Co-Operative Flint Glass Company, clear, set of 7 . . . . **125.00 to 175.00**

***Berry set,** Lacy Daisy patt.: 1⁵/₈" main berry bowl & six 1" berry bowls; pressed glass, United States Glass Company, clear, set of 7 . . . . **75.00 to 100.00**

Berry set, Nursery Rhyme patt.: 1³/₄ × 4¹/₂" main berry bowl & six 1¹/₄ × 2¹/₂" berry bowls; pressed glass, clear, set of 7 . . . . **225.00 to 325.00**

Berry set, Wheat Sheaf patt.: 2¹/₄" main berry bowl & six 1" berry bowls; pressed glass, Cambridge, clear, set of 7 . . . . . **100.00 to 175.00**

Ice cream set, ABC patt.: 4¹/₂ × 5³/₄" oval platter & six 2³/₄" d. round plates; pressed glass, Wabash Series, Federal Glass Company, Columbus, Ohio, set of 7 . . . . . **475.00 to 550.00**

Lemonade or water set, Colonial Flute patt.: 3¹/₂" pitcher & six 2" tumblers; pressed glass, clear, common, set of 7 . . **75.00 to 150.00**

***Lemonade or water set,** Galloway patt.: 3⁷/₈" pitcher & six 2" tumblers; colored pressed glass, set of 7 . . . . **300.00 to 390.00**

Lemonade or water set, enameled ruffled design, 1³/₄" pitcher & two 1¹/₂" tumblers; emerald glass decorated w/heavy enameled flowers, Europe, set of 3 . . . . . **400.00 to 700.00**

Lemonade or water set, Hobbs patt.: pitcher & six tumblers; pressed glass, clear, set of 7 . . . . **300.00 to 500.00**

Lemonade or water set, Mary Gregory decoration on colored glass: 4¹/₂" pitcher & six 2¹/₂" tumblers; rare, set of 7 . . . . **500.00 to 1000.00**

Lemonade or water set, Nursery Rhyme patt.: 4¹/₄" pitcher & six 2" tumblers; pressed glass, United States Glass Company, clear, set of 7 . . . . **250.00 to 390.00**

Lemonade or water set, Oval Star patt., No. 300: 4¹/₄" pitcher & six 2³/₈" tumblers; pressed glass, Indiana Glass Co., clear, without tray, set of 7 (Fig. 8-1) . . . . **125.00 to 200.00**

Lemonade or water set, Pattee Cross patt.: 4¹/₂" pitcher & six 1³/₄" tumblers; pressed glass, clear, set of 7 . . . . **175.00 to 275.00**

Lemonade or water set, Petite Hobnail patt.: 4³/₄" pitcher & six 2³/₁₃" tumblers w/tray; pressed glass, clear, set of 8 . . . . **700.00 to 900.00**

Fig. 8-2

Lemonade or water set, Portland patt.: 4" pitcher & six 2¹/₈" tumblers; pressed glass, clear or clear w/gold, set of 7 . . . **75.00 to 190.00**

Stein set, Grape patt., Wabash series: main stein & six or four 1¹/₂" steins; pressed glass, Federal Glass Company, Columbus, Ohio, rare, clear, the set . . . . . . **500.00 to 800.00**

Stein set, Michigan patt.: 2⁷/₈" stein & six or four 2" steins; pressed glass, clear, the set . . . . **100.00 to 175.00**

Table set, Acorn patt.: 4" cov. butter, 4³/₄" cov. sugar, 3³/₈" creamer & 3¹/₈" spooner; pressed glass, possibly Crystal Glass Company, frosted clear, rare, 4 pcs. . . . . **1,000.00 to 1,500.00**

Table set, Amazon or Sawtooth Variation patt.: 4¹/₄" cov. butter, 5" cov. sugar, 3³/₄" creamer & 2⁷/₈" spooner; pressed glass, clear, 4 pcs. . . . . **300.00 to 350.00**

Table set, Austrian patt.: 4" cov. butter, 4³/₄" cov. sugar, 3³/₈" creamer & 3¹/₈" spooner; pressed glass, Greentown, chocolate glass, 4 pcs. . . . . **2,500.00 to 3,500.00**

Table set, Bead & Scroll patt.: 4" cov. butter, 4" cov. sugar, 3" creamer & 2¹/₂" spooner; colored pressed glass, 4 pcs. . . **900.00 to 1200.00**

Table set, Beaded Swirl patt.: 2¹/₂" cov. butter, 3³/₄" cov. sugar, 2⁵/₈" creamer & 2³/₈" spooner; pressed glass, clear, 4 pcs. . . . . **125.00 to 175.00**

Table set, Block (Large) patt.: 2¹/₂" cov. butter, 3³/₄" cov. sugar, 2⁵/₈" creamer & 2³/₈" spooner; pressed glass, clear, 4 pcs. . . . . **400.00 to 500.00**

Table set, Block (Large) patt.: 3" cov. butter, 4¹/₂" cov. sugar, 3" creamer & 3" spooner; pressed glass, color or milk glass, 4 pcs. **500.00 to 700.00**

Table set, Bucket patt.: 2⁵/₈" cov. butter, 3³/₄" cov. sugar, 2⁵/₈" creamer & 2¹/₂" spooner; pressed glass, Bryce Brothers, rare when complete, clear, 4 pcs. . . . . . . **900.00 to 1,200.00**

Table set, Button Panel patt., D. & M. No. 44: 4" cov. butter, 4⁵/₈" cov. sugar, 2⁵/₈" creamer & 2⁵/₈" spooner; pressed glass, Duncan and Miller, clear or clear w/gold, 4 pcs. . . . . **300.00 to 400.00**

Table set, Cambridge Colonial patt., No. 2630: 2¹/₈" cov. butter, 3" cov. sugar, 2³/₈" creamer & 2¹/₈" spooner; pressed glass, cobalt blue or two shades of green, 4 pcs., each . . . . **175.00 to 275.00**

Table set, Chateau patt., No. 714: 5¹/₄" d., 4¹/₂" h. cov. butter, cov. sugar, 3" creamer & 2¹/₄" spooner; pressed glass, New Martinsville, clear, rare, 4 pcs. . . . . **500.00 to 800.00**

Table set, Clambroth Scenery patt.: 2³/₈" cov. butter, 2¹/₈" cov. sugar, 2" creamer & 2¹/₈" spooner; pressed glass, w/various scenes & writings, rare, 4 pcs. (Fig. 8-2) . . . . **800.00 to 1,000.00**

Table set, Clear and Diamond Panels patt.: 2⁷/₈" cov. butter, 3¹/₂" cov. sugar, 2³/₄" creamer & 2³/₈" spooner; pressed glass, clear, 4 pcs. **100.00 to 200.00**

Table set, Dewdrop or Dot patt.: 2⁵/₈" cov. butter, 4" cov. sugar, 3" creamer & 2⁵/₈" spooner; pressed glass, Columbia Glass Company, clear, 4 pcs. . . . . . . **375.00 to 475.00**

Table set, Doyle No. 500 patt.: 2¹/₄" cov. butter, 3⁵/₈" cov. sugar, 2¹/₂" creamer, 2³/₈" spooner & tray; pressed glass, Doyle and Company, amber, blue or canary, 5 pcs., each . . . . **450.00 to 575.00**

Table set, Drum patt.: 2¹/₄" cov. butter, 3¹/₄" cov. sugar, 3³/₄" creamer & 2⁵/₈" spooner; pressed glass, clear, 4 pcs. . . . . **475.00 to 600.00**

Table set, Fernland patt., No. 2635: 2³/₄" cov. butter, 3" cov. sugar, 2³/₈" creamer & 2³/₈" spooner; pressed glass, Cambridge, clear, 4 pcs. . . . . **125.00 to 175.00**

Table set, Fernland patt., No. 2635: 2³/₄" cov. butter, 3" cov. sugar, 2³/₈" creamer & 2³/₈" spooner; colored pressed glass, Cambridge, 4 pcs. . . . . **175.00 to 275.00**

Table set, Grape Vine with Ovals patt.: 1³/₄" cov. butter, 2⁷/₈" cov. sugar, 2¹/₈" creamer & 2" spooner; pressed glass, clear, 4 pcs. . . . . **375.00 to 500.00**

*****Table set,** Hawaiian Lei patt.: 2¹/₄" cov. butter, 3" cov. sugar, 2³/₄" creamer & 2¹/₄" spooner; pressed glass, Higbee Company, reproduced in color, clear, 4 pcs. . . . **75.00 to 150.00**

Table set, Hobnail with Thumbprint Base patt., No. 150: 2" cov. butter, 4" cov. sugar, 3³/₈" creamer & 2⁷/₈" spooner, 7³/₈" tray; pressed glass, Doyle and Company, amber or blue, 5 pcs. . . . . **475.00 to 575.00**

Table set, Horizontal Threads patt.: 2" cov. butter, 3³/₈" cov. sugar, 2¹/₄" creamer & 2¹/₈" spooner; pressed glass, clear, 4 pcs. . . . . **225.00 to 350.00**

Table set, Horizontal Threads patt.: 2" cov. butter, 3³/₈" cov. sugar, 2¹/₄" creamer & 2¹/₈" spooner; colored pressed glass, 4 pcs. . . . . **600.00 to 900.00**

*****Table set,** Lamb patt.: 3¹/₈" cov. butter, 4³/₈" cov. sugar, 2⁷/₈" creamer & 2³/₄" spooner; pressed glass, reproduced in color, old milk glass, 4 pcs. . . . . **700.00 to 800.00**

Table set, Liberty Bell patt.: ¹/₄" cov. butter, 3⁵/₈" cov. sugar, 2¹/₂" creamer & 2³/₈" spooner; pressed glass, clear, 4 pcs. . . . . **700.00 to 900.00**

Table set, Lion patt.: 2³/₄" cov. butter, 4⁵/₈" cov. sugar, 3³/₈" creamer & 3¹/₈" spooner; pressed glass, some old frosted sets but some are being frosted today to make them more

Fig. 8-3

desirable, clear, 4 pcs. (Fig. 8-3, of sugar bowl) . . . . **400.00 to 600.00**

Table set, Menagerie patt.: 2³/₈" cov. turtle-shaped butter, 4¹/₄" cov. bear-shaped sugar, 3³/₄" owl-shaped creamer & 2⁵/₈" fish-shaped spooner; pressed glass, Bryce Higbee, clear, 4 pcs. . . . . **2,000.00 to 3,000.00**

Table set, Michigan patt., No. 15077: 3³/₄" cov. butter, 4³/₄" cov. sugar, 2⁷/₈" creamer & 3" spooner; pressed glass, overall red stain, rare, 4 pcs. . . . . **900.00 to 1,200.00**

Table set, Michigan patt., No. 15077: 3³/₄" cov. butter, 4³/₄" cov. sugar, 2⁷/₈" creamer & 3" spooner; pressed glass, clear or clear w/gold trim, 4 pcs. . . . . **225.00 to 300.00**

Table set, Oval Star patt., No. 300: 3¹/₂" cov. butter, 4¹/₄" cov. sugar, 2⁵/₈" creamer & 2¹/₂" spooner; pressed glass, Indiana Glass Company, clear, 4 pcs. . . . . **100.00 to 175.00**

Table set, Pennsylvania patt., No. 15048: 3½" cov. butter, 4" cov. sugar, 2½" creamer & 2½" spooner; pressed glass, United States Glass Company, green, 4 pcs. . . **475.00 to 600.00**

Table set, Pert patt.: 2⅞" cov. butter, 5⅛" cov. sugar, 3⅝" creamer & 3½" spooner; pressed glass, clear, 4 pcs. . . . . **375.00 to 475.00**

Table set, Plain Pattern No. 13: 2⅛" cov. butter, 3⅜" cov. sugar, 2½" creamer & 2¼" spooner; pressed glass, King Glass Company, clear, 4 pcs. . . . . **400.00 to 600.00**

Table set, Plain Pattern No. 13: 2⅛" cov. butter, 3⅜" cov. sugar, 2½" creamer & 2¼" spooner; pressed glass, King Glass Company, cobalt blue, 4 pcs. . . . . **800.00 to 1,000.00**

Table set, Pointed Jewel (Long Diamond) patt.: 2" cov. butter, 3⅞" cov. sugar, 3⅞" creamer & 2½" spooner; pressed glass, Factory J of United States Glass Co., clear, complete set rare, 4 pcs. . . . . . **500.00 to 700.00**

Table set, Rex or Fancy Cut patt.: 2⅜" cov. butter, 3⅛" cov. sugar, 2¼" creamer & 2¼" spooner; pressed glass, Co-Operative Glass Company, cobalt blue, rare, 4 pcs. . . . . **700.00 to 900.00**

Table set, Sawtooth patt., No. 1225: 4" cov. butter, 4⅛" cov. sugar, 2¾" creamer & 2½" spooner; pressed glass, clear, 4 pcs. . . . . **475.00 to 600.00**

Table set, Standing Lamb patt.: 3¾" cov. butter, 5⅛" cov. sugar, 3¼" creamer & 3½" spooner; pressed glass, possibly Crystal Glass Company, clear or frosted clear, rare, 4 pcs. . . . . **5,000.00 to 6,000.00**

Table set, Stippled Diamond patt.: 2¼" cov. butter, 3⅛" cov. sugar, 2¼" creamer & 2⅛" spooner; colored pressed glass, 4 pcs. . . . . **900.00 to 1,200.00**

Table set, Stippled Raindrop and Dewdrop patt :2" cov. butter, 3⅛" cov. sugar, 2¼" creamer & 2⅛" spooner; pressed glass, clear, 4 pcs. . . . . **400.00 to 500.00**

Table set, Stippled Vine and Beads patt.: 2½" cov. butter, 3⅛" cov. sugar, 2½" creamer & 2⅛" spooner; colored pressed glass, 4 pcs. . . . . **600.00 to 900.00**

Table set, Sultan patt.: 3¾" cov. butter, 4½" cov. sugar, 2½" creamer & 2½" spooner; pressed glass, McKee Glass Company, transparent green, 4 pcs. . . . . . **700.00 to 800.00**

Table set, Sultan patt.: 3¾" cov. butter, 4½" cov. sugar, 2½" creamer & 2½" spooner; pressed glass, McKee Glass Company, chocolate glass, 4 pcs. . . . . . **2,200.00 to 2,700.00**

Table set, Sunbeam Patt. No., 15139 (or Twin Horseshoes): 2" cov. butter, 3⅛" cov. sugar, 2¾" creamer & 2¼" spooner; pressed glass, McKee, ca. 1894-1908, clear, 4 pcs. . . . . **450.00 to 600.00**

*Table set, Thumbleina (or Flattened Diamond) patt.: 2½" cov. butter, 2¼" cov. sugar, 2⅜" creamer & 2¼" spooner; colored pressed glass, 4 pcs. . . . . **375.00 to 475.00**

Table set, Twist patt., No. 137: 2½" cov. butter, 3⅞" cov. sugar, 2⅞" creamer & 2½" spooner; pressed glass, Albany Glass Company, clear, 4 pcs. . . . . **125.00 to 175.00**

Table set, Twist patt., No. 137: 2½" cov. butter, 3⅞" cov. sugar, 2⅞" creamer & 2½" spooner; pressed glass, Albany Glass Company, frosted color, 4 pcs. . . . . **800.00 to 1,200.00**

Table set, Two Band patt.: 2" cov. butter, 3⅞" cov. sugar, 2¾" creamer & 2¾" spooner; pressed glass, LaBelle Glass Co., 4 pcs. **350.00 to 475.00**

Table set, Wee Branches patt.: 2" cov. butter, 3" cov. sugar, 2¼" creamer & 2⅜" spooner; pressed glass, clear, 4 pcs. . . . **500.00 to 700.00**

Table set, Wild Rose patt.: 3⅞" cov. butter, 1⅞" sugar, 2" creamer & 1⅞" spooner; pressed glass, milk glass with or without decoration, 4 pcs. . . . . **225.00 to 375.00**

FOREIGN TOY DISHES

Prices for English Tea, dinner and dessert sets vary with the number of pieces and the condition of the ware. For this guide, the prices are based on the following: Tea sets should contain a teapot, sugar bowl, creamer, and at least four cups and saucers; a dinner service should include six main pieces such as tureens, a nest of platters, a sauceboat, a salad bowl, a pie dish or covered vegetable, along with six dinner plates, six soups, and a few other odds and ends if possible. Remember, a dinner service can have as many as eighty pieces, but that is only if you are lucky. Rarely is a dinner service sold with a matching tea set or dessert set, but if you find one, it is a good thing. A dessert set should have at least one compote, four serving dishes and six individual plates. Dessert sets can have several compotes, several serving dishes, strawberry or cress strainers with underplates and twelve individual round plates.

Britain produced most of the tea, dinner, and dessert sets and that will be the main thrust of this guide. The French, on the other hand, loved to box china, mixing it with glass decanters and goblets, menus, napkins, and flatware. They produced tea, dinner, and dessert sets and many times they mixed their categories. These boxed beauties range from $175.00 to $3,000.00 depending on the porcelain, condition, and complexity of the combination of the ware.

The Germans produced whimsical porcelain sets with animals, children, and botanical explosions mainly in tea or coffee ware. There are, however, some dinner service examples on large blanks, suitable for nursery use. R.S. Prussia and Royal Bayreuth ware demands the highest prices in the German category. Normally, the R.S. Prussia pieces will not be marked in toy ware, but if the set is marked it will be on the three main pieces. R.S. Prussia sets range from $300.00 to $8,000.00, depending on the number of pieces, blank, condition and decoration. Royal Bayreuth sets will range from $400.00 to $2,000.00 with the same qualifications.

◆ French Toy Ware

Basket sets, porcelain, tied in original
    containers w/all pieces . . . . **2,800.00 to 3,800.00**

Dinner service, earthenware, Chain of
    Morning Glories decoration, the
    set . . . . **1,000.00 to 1,800.00**

Dinner service, porcelain, Red Riding Hood
    decoration, the set . . . . **1,800.00 to 2,000.00**

Pan set: four graduated pans; enamelware, set
    of four (Fig. 8-4) . . . . **200.00 to 275.00**

Knife rest set, porcelain, dinner service,
    Old Paris, in original box, rare, the
    set . . . . **1,800.00 to 2,800.00**

Pots de Créme **(cream pot):** cup, cover &
    underplate; white porcelain w/gold trim,
    Old Paris, set of 12 . . . . **400.00 to 700.00**

    with matching dinner service . . **800.00 to 1,000.00**

Tea set, porcelain, floral decoration w/twist
    handles, rare, the set . . . . . **2,000.00 to 2,500.00**

Tea set, earthenware, Kate Greenaway
    decoration, Sarreguemines, the
    set . . . . **1,000.00 to 1,800.00**

Washstand set: divided bowl, pitcher & other
    pieces; earthenware, Kate Greenaway-style
    decoration, Sarregueimines, in stand,
    the set (Fig. 8-5) . . . . **2,500.00 to 3,000.00**

◆ British Ware

Dessert set, earthenware, Dresden Flowers
    patt., possibly Spode or Copeland, marked
    "Improved Stone China," rare, the
    set . . . . **1,400.00 to 1,800.00**

Dessert set: two $1^{1}/_{2} \times 4^{1}/_{2}$" & two $2^{1}/_{2} \times 4^{1}/_{2}$"
    compotes, $4^{1}/_{2}$" plates; earthenware,

Fig. 8-4

Fig. 8-5

Fig. 8-6

Humphrey's Clock patt., marked "Humphrey's Clock" on banner & "England" under banner, Ridgway, ca. 1890-1908, the set . . . . **800.00 to 1,000.00**

Dessert set, 3¼ × 5½" dessert compote, 3¾" plates, 4½" server, 4⅝" handled plate; earthenware, Blue Marble patt., ca. 1850, the set . . . . **1,000.00 to 1,400.00**

Dessert set: 3½ × 5½" compote, 5" oval dish, 4¼" square dish, 4 × 4½" server, 4" plates; earthenware w/blue transfer decorations, some marked by Edge Malkin, ca. 1873, the set . . . . **1,400.00 to 1,800.00**

Dessert set: 3½ × 5½" compote, 5" oval dish, 4¼" square dish, 4 × 4½" server, 4" plates; earthenware, green majolica w/a leafy scroll design, some marked by Edge Malkin, ca. 1873, the set (Fig. 8-6) . . . . **500.00 to 800.00**

Dinner service, earthenware, Amherst Japan patt., multi-colored transfer-printed Imari-style design, Minton, ca. 1854, rare, the set . . . . **2,800.00 to 3,400.00**

Dinner service, earthenware, Clover Leaf variant, the set . . . . **400.00 to 800.00**

Dinner service, earthenware, Eva patt., ca. 1830, the set . . . . **1,200.00 to 1,800.00**

Dinner service, earthenware, Mandarin patt., Blue Willow style decoration, Copeland, ca. 1860-1875, the set . . . . . . **800.00 to 1,200.00**

Dinner service: platters, tureens, two cov. vegetables, sauces, salads, soups, plates; earthenware, Tower patt., Copeland and Garrett, the set . . . . **2,000.00 to 2,800.00**

Dinner service: 3½", 4" & 4½" nest of platters, 2½" & 3½" tureens, 2" cov. vegetable, 3¼" open vegetable, 1½" sauceboat, 2¾" ladle, 1 × 2½" salad bowls, 3¼" soups, 2½", 2¾" & 3" plates; earthenware, decorated w/Blue Willow design, Hackwood, ca. 1827-1843, the set . . . . **2,800.00 to 3,800.00**

Dinner service: 3½", 4" & 4¼" nest of platters, 2½" & 3½" tureens, 3¼" cov. vegetable, 2" oval open vegetable, 3¼" sauceboat, 1 × 2½" salad bowls, 2¾" ladle, 2½", 2¾" & 2" plates; earthenware, Institution (Monastery Hill) patt., tall straight building on a hill w/shorter counterparts, series of trees to the left, animal & person stand near the foremost tree, to the right is a house, surrounded by a border of flowers & leaves, Hackwood, ca. 1827-1843, the set (Fig. 8-7, a plate) . . . . **1,800.00 to 2,800.00**

Fig. 8-7

Dinner service: 3", 3½", 4¼", 5", 5¾" & 6" platters, 2½" open compote, 3¾" soups, 2¼", 2½" & 3½" plates; Fishers patt., marked "C. E. & M., Cork," Edge, Malkin, earthenware, Newport Pottery, Burslem, Staffordshire Potteries, ca. 1860-1871, the set . . . . **1,500.00 to 2,000.00**

Dinner service: 4½" & 5½" platters, 4½", 5½" & 6⅓" tureens, 2½" sauce, 4½" soup, 2½" & 4¼" ladles, 3⅝", 4¼" & 4½" plates, 4½" cov. teapot, 3¼" open sugar, 3¼" creamer, 2½" cups, 4¼" plates, 2⅛ × 4" waste bowl; earthenware, Penny Dolls patt., Bishop and Stonier, ca. 1887, the set . . . . . **400.00 to 600.00**

Dinner service: 4½" & 5" platters, 3¾" × 4½" & 3 × 3" tureens, 3½" open oval vegetable, 2 × 3½" cov. oval vegetable, 2½" sauce boat, 2½" & 3" plates; earthenware, Monopteros patt., attributed to Rogers, ca. 1820-1830, the set . . . . **3,000.00 to 3,800.00**

Dinner service: 4¼", 4½" & 5½" platter, 3¼", 3½" & 4¼" tureens, 4¼", 4½", 5½" & 5¾" tureen underplate, 2½" & 2¾" cov. vegetables, 3, 3½ & 4½" ladles, 4½" wine cooler, 3", 2", 3¼" & 3¾" plates; earthenware, Flow Blue, decorated w/two people w/one kneeling & Chinese bells, Davenport, ca. 1840-1850, the set . . . . **1,500.00 to 3,500.00**

Dinner service: 4$\frac{1}{4}$", 4$\frac{1}{2}$" & 5$\frac{1}{2}$" platters, 3$\frac{1}{4}$", 3$\frac{1}{2}$" & 4$\frac{1}{4}$" tureens, 4$\frac{1}{4}$", 4$\frac{1}{2}$", 5$\frac{1}{2}$" & 5$\frac{3}{4}$" tureen underplates, 2$\frac{1}{2}$" & 2$\frac{3}{4}$" cov. vegetables, 3$\frac{1}{2}$" soups, two 1$\frac{3}{4}$" sauces, 3", 3$\frac{1}{2}$" & 4$\frac{1}{2}$" ladles; 4$\frac{1}{2}$" wine cooler, 2$\frac{1}{4}$", 3", 3$\frac{1}{4}$", 3$\frac{3}{4}$" plates; earthenware, Floral Flow, impressed anchor mark, Davenport, ca. 1840-1850, the set . . . . **1,800.00 to 2,000.00**

Dinner service: 4$\frac{1}{4}$", 4$\frac{1}{2}$" & 5" platters, 3$\frac{1}{2}$", 3$\frac{1}{4}$", 3$\frac{1}{2}$" & 4$\frac{1}{4}$" tureens, 4$\frac{1}{4}$", 4$\frac{1}{2}$" & 5$\frac{3}{4}$" tureen underplates, 1$\frac{3}{4}$" open vegetable, 2$\frac{1}{2}$" & 2$\frac{3}{4}$" cov. dishes, two 1$\frac{3}{4}$" sauces, 3$\frac{1}{2}$" soups, 3", 3$\frac{1}{2}$" & 4$\frac{1}{2}$" ladles, 2$\frac{1}{2}$", 3", 3$\frac{1}{4}$" & 3$\frac{3}{4}$" plates; earthenware, Chinese Bells patt., Flow Blue, ca. 1835, the set . . . . **2,000.00 to 3,000.00**

Dinner service: 4$\frac{1}{4}$", 4$\frac{1}{2}$" & 5" platters, 3$\frac{1}{4}$", 3$\frac{1}{2}$" & 4$\frac{1}{4}$" tureens, 3$\frac{1}{2}$", 4$\frac{1}{4}$", 4$\frac{1}{2}$" & 5$\frac{3}{4}$" tureen underplates, 4$\frac{1}{2}$" open vegetable, 2$\frac{1}{2}$" & 3$\frac{1}{2}$" cov. dishes, two 1$\frac{3}{4}$" sauces, 3$\frac{1}{2}$" soups, 3", 3$\frac{1}{2}$" & 4$\frac{1}{2}$" ladles, 2$\frac{1}{2}$", 3", 3$\frac{1}{4}$" & 3$\frac{3}{4}$" plates; earthenware, Asiatic Birds patt., Flow Blue, Charles Meigh, ca. 1838-1849, the set . . . . **3,000.00 to 4,000.00**

Dinner service: 4$\frac{1}{4}$", 5$\frac{1}{4}$", 5$\frac{3}{4}$" & 6$\frac{1}{2}$" platters, 4$\frac{5}{8}$ × 5$\frac{7}{8}$" tureen, 3$\frac{5}{8}$ × 4" cov. tureen, 3" cov. vegetable, 2 × 3$\frac{1}{2}$" serving bowl; earthenware, Lea Flower patt., ca. 1840, the set . . . . **1,800.00 to 2,200.00**

Dinner service: 4$\frac{3}{4}$" & 5$\frac{3}{4}$" platters, 4$\frac{1}{4}$" cov. tureen, 3" cov. footed tureen, 2$\frac{1}{2}$" cov. vegetable w/5" underplate, 3$\frac{1}{4}$ × 5$\frac{1}{2}$" compote, 2$\frac{3}{4}$", 3" & 5" oval servers, 4$\frac{1}{2}$" server, 4" soup, 2$\frac{1}{2}$" & 3$\frac{1}{4}$" & 4" plates, 4$\frac{5}{8}$" plate w/scalloped handles; earthenware, Pearl patt., decorated w/aqua, yellow, orange, green, blue & red flowers, possibly Alcock or Burgess & Leigh, ca. 1850, the set . . . . **1,500.00 to 1,800.00**

Dinner service: 4$\frac{3}{4}$" & two 6" nest of platters, two 4$\frac{1}{4}$" & one 4$\frac{3}{4}$" scroll-handled platters, two 3" open vegetables, 1$\frac{3}{4}$ × 3$\frac{1}{2}$" footed crimped-rim server, 2" sauce boat, 4$\frac{1}{4}$" soup, 2$\frac{3}{4}$", 3$\frac{1}{2}$" & 4$\frac{1}{8}$" plates; earthenware, Garden Sports patt., ca. 1842, the set . . . . **1,800.00 to 2,500.00**

Dinner service: 4" & 4$\frac{3}{4}$" platters, 2$\frac{1}{4}$ × 4" & 3$\frac{1}{4}$ × 5$\frac{1}{2}$" tureens, 1 × 3$\frac{1}{4}$" sauce, 3" & 4" plates; earthenware, Ferns & Flowers patt., marked w/applied "C.K." impressed on raised pad, attributed to Charles Keeling, ca. 1822-1825, the set . . . . . **1,000.00 to 1,500.00**

Dinner service: 5" & 5$\frac{1}{4}$" platters, 5$\frac{3}{4}$" meat platter w/dripping well, 2$\frac{3}{4}$" tureen, 4$\frac{1}{4}$" cov. vegetable, 5$\frac{1}{4}$" vegetable, 4$\frac{1}{4}$" chop plate, 3$\frac{1}{4}$" & 3$\frac{3}{4}$" plates; earthenware, Servants patt., Flow Blue transfer of gardener watering plants & a servant drawing water from a well, ca. 1830-1850, the set . . . . **2,000.00 to 2,800.00**

Dinner service: 6$\frac{1}{4}$", 7" & 8" platters, 2$\frac{1}{2}$" & 3$\frac{1}{2}$" cov. servers, 4$\frac{1}{2}$ × 6$\frac{1}{2}$" tureen, 3$\frac{1}{2}$", 3$\frac{3}{4}$" soup, 4" & 5" ladles, 3$\frac{1}{4}$" & 4$\frac{1}{4}$" plates; earthenware, Humphrey's Clock patt., marked "Humphrey's Clock" on banner & "England" under banner, Ridgway, ca. 1890-1908, the set . . . . **700.00 to 900.00**

Dresser set: pair of 3" candlesticks, 1 × 1$\frac{3}{4}$" ring tree, 1$\frac{3}{4}$ × 2$\frac{1}{2}$" & 1$\frac{1}{2}$ × 2" cov. pomades, 7" tray; earthenware, Humphrey's Clock patt., marked "Humphrey's Clock" on banner & "England" under banner, Ridgway, ca. 1890-1908, the set . . . . . . **800.00 to 1,200.00**

Tea set: cov. teapot, cov. sugar, creamer, cups, saucers, plates, waste bowl; earthenware, Eva patt., the set . . . . **800.00 to 1,000.00**

Tea set, earthenware, Souvenir (Friendship) patt., ca. 1830-1840, the set . . **1,000.00 to 1,200.00**

Tea set, earthenware, Asiatic Birds patt., Flow Blue, Charles Meigh, ca. 1838-1849, the set . . . . **2,000.00 to 2,800.00**

Tea set: cov. teapot, cov. sugar, creamer, handleless cup, saucers, plates, waste bowl; earthenware, decorated w/castle scene & floral border, Staffordshire (Fig. 8-8) . . . . **1,000.00 to 1,800.00**

Tea set, earthenware, Athens patt., blue Roman key-type decorations, elongated cov. teapot, marked "J.M. & Sons," ca. 1840, the set . . . . **400.00 to 800.00**

Tea set, earthenware, Clover Leaf variant, the set . . . . **400.00 to 800.00**

Tea set, earthenware, Flow Blue, decorated w/two people w/one kneeling & Chinese bells, Davenport, ca. 1840-1850, the set . . . . **2,000.00 to 3,000.00**

Tea set: 2$\frac{3}{4}$" cov. teapot, 2$\frac{3}{4}$" cov. sugar, 1$\frac{3}{4}$" creamer, 1$\frac{3}{4}$" cups, 4$\frac{1}{4}$" saucers, 2$\frac{1}{4}$ × 4$\frac{1}{4}$" waste bowl, earthenware, Pink Lustre Blossoms patt., melon-shaped set, marked "Davenport" in an arc over an anchor, ca. 1836, the set . . . . **1,200.00 to 2.800.00**

Fig. 8-8

Tea set: 2⅝" cov. teapot, 2⅝" cov. sugar, 2" creamer, 1½" cups, 4½" saucers, 4¼" plates, 2 × 3½" waste bowl; earthenware, Wind Flower patt., ca. 1830, the set . . . . **2,500.00 to 2,800.00**

Tea set: 3¼" cov. teapot, 2½" cov. sugar, 2" creamer, 1½" cups, 4" saucers, 4¾" plates, 5½" serving plates, 2½ × 4½" waste bowl; earthenware, gold lustre Pomegranate patt., the set . . . . **150.00 to 350.00**

Tea set: 3¼" cov. teapot, 2¾" cov. sugar, 2" creamer, 2" cups, 4½" saucers, 2 × 3½" waste bowl; earthenware, Gazebo patt., marked "Imperial D. M. & Sons," David Methven & Sons, Kirkcaldy Pottery, Fife, Scotland, ca. 1840-1930, the set . . . . **400.00 to 600.00**

Tea set: 3½" cov. teapot, 1¾" open, footed sugar, 1½" creamer, 1¾" cups, 4" d. saucers; earthenware, Anemone patt., handleless cups, twist loop finials, Charles Meigh & Sons, ca. 1850-1860, the set . . . . **2,500.00 to 3,000.00**

Tea set: 3¾" cov. teapot, 1⅜" open sugar, 2⅛" cups, 4⅜" saucers, 4⅞" plates; earthenware, Kate Greenaway designs, early 1900s, the set . . . . **400.00 to 600.00**

Tea set: 3¾" cov. teapot, 3¾" cov. sugar, 2¼" creamer, 2¼" cups, 4½" saucers, 2¾ × 4¼" waste bowl; earthenware, Garden Sports patt., ca. 1842, the set . . . . . . **500.00 to 800.00**

Tea set: 3¾" cov. teapot, 3" cov. sugar, 2" creamer, 2¼" cups, 4¾" saucers, 5" plates, 2½" waste bowl; earthenware, Chang patt., Edge, Malkin & Co., ca. 1873-1903, the set . . . . **400.00 to 600.00**

Tea set: 3⅞" cov. teapot, 3⅝" cov. sugar, 2½" creamer, 2¾" & 2⅝" cups, 4" d. & 4½" d. saucers, 2⅝" d. & 4⅜" d. plates, 2⅝ × 4⅜" waste bowl; earthenware, Amusements patt., ca. 1842, the set . . . . **700.00 to 900.00**

Tea set: 4" cov. teapot, 3¾" cov. sugar, 2" creamer, 2" cups, 1¾" handleless cups, 4½" saucers, 5" plates, 2¾ × 4½" waste bowl; earthenware, Flow Blue Hopberry patt., Charles Meigh & Sons, ca. 1838-1849, the set . . . . **1,800.00 to 2,200.00**

Tea set: 4" cov. teapot, 3½" cov. sugar, 2½" creamer, 1⅞" cups, 4½" saucers; earthenware, Goat patt., marked "J & G," & "Goat," John and Robert Godwin, ca. 1834-1866, the set . . . . **500.00 to 900.00**

Tea set: 4" cov. teapot, 3½" cov. sugar, 2" creamer, 1¾" h. handleless cups, 4⅝" saucers, 4½" plates; earthenware, "Gaudy" Flow (Pinwheel) patt., gaudy red flowers flowing into blue, probably Davenport, ca. 1830, the set . . . . **2,500.00 to 3,000.00**

Tea set: 4" cov. teapot, 3½" cov. sugar, 4½" saucers, 5¼" plates; earthenware, Chinese patt., blue & white, marked "Davenport" on bottom of teapot, ca. 1844, the set . . . . **900.00 to 1,200.00**

Tea set: 4" cov. teapot, 3³/₄" cov. sugar, 1⁷/₈" cups, 4³/₈" saucers; earthenware, Juvenile patt., pink transfer, some pieces marked "Juvenile," ca. 1850s, the set . . . **700.00 to 900.00**

Tea set: 4" cov. teapot, 3³/₄" cov. sugar, 2" creamer, 2" cups, 4¹/₂" saucers, 5" plates, 1³/₄" handless cups, 1³/₄ × 4¹/₂" waste bowl; earthenware, Chinese Bells patt., flow blue, ca. 1850, the set . . . .**2,000.00 to 3,000.00**

Tea set: 4" cov. teapot, 3³/₄" cov. sugar, 3" creamer, 1⁷/₈" cup, 2" cup, two saucers, 2⁷/₈ × 4¹/₂" waste bowl, 6" plates; earthenware, Alhambra patt., grey honeysuckle border, ornate handles & King of Prussia-type finials, Ridgway, ca. 1850-1860, the set . . . . **500.00 to 1,000.00**

Tea set: 4" cov. teapot, 3³/₄" cov. sugar, 3" creamer, 1⁷/₈" cup, 2" cup, two saucers, 2⁷/₈ × 4¹/₂" waste bowl, 6" plates; earthenware, Flow Blue w/dogwood flowers, w/King of Prussia-type finials, Ridgway, ca. 1850-1860, the set . . . .**2,000.00 to 2,800.00**

Tea set: 4" cov. teapot, 3" creamer, 2¹/₄" cups, 4¹/₂" saucers, 4¹/₂" individual plates, 6¹/₄" serving plate, 2¹/₄ × 4¹/₄" waste bowl; earthenware, Tea Leaf patt., American, East End Pottery, ca. 1894-1901, the set . . . .**2,000.00 to 2,400.00**

Tea set: 4" cov. teapot, 3" creamer, 2¹/₄" cups, 4¹/₂" saucers, 4³/₄" plates, 4³/₄" serving plates, 2¹/₄ × 4¹/₄" waste bowl; earthenware, old Tea Leaf, the set (incorrect teapot cover) . . . . **150.00 to 350.00**

Tea set: 4¹/₄" cov. teapot, 3³/₄" cov. sugar, 2¹/₂" creamer, 1³/₄" cups, 4¹/₂" saucers, 5" plates, 2¹/₂ × 4¹/₂" waste bowl; earthenware, Fruit Girl patt., blue transfer, J&R Godwin, ca. 1845, the set . . . . **500.00 to 800.00**

Tea set: 4¹/₄" cov. teapot, 4¹/₄" cov. sugar, 4" creamer, 2¹/₂" cups, 5" saucers, 5¹/₄" plates, 2¹/₂" waste bowl; earthenware, House that Jack Built patt., ca. 1870-1890, the set . . . . **400.00 to 500.00**

Tea set: 4¹/₄" cov. teapot, 3³/₄" cov. sugar, 3¹/₃" creamer, 2" cups, 2" saucers, 3" plates; earthenware, Hey! Diddle Diddle patt., solid color, ca. 1888, the set . . . . . **800.00 to 1,000.00**

Tea set: 4¹/₄" cov. teapot, 3⁷/₈" cov. sugar, 1¹/₂" cups, 1³/₄" saucers, 4³/₄", 4¹/₄" & 5" saucers,

4" & 5" plates; earthenware, Basket patt., probably Cork, Edge & Malkin, Newport Pottery, Burslem, Staffordshire Potteries, ca. 1850-1871, the set . . . . . **2,000.00 to 3,000.00**

Tea set: 4¹/₄" cov. teapot, 2¹/₂" open sugar, 2³/₄" creamer, 2" cups, 4¹/₂" saucers, 4¹/₄" plates, 2¹/₂ × 4" waste bowl; earthenware, Cinderella patt., comes in multi-colored version, Ridgway, ca. 1889-1900, the set . . . .**1,500.00 to 2,000.00**

Tea set: 4¹/₄" cov. teapot, 4" cov. sugar, 2³/₄" creamer, 1³/₄" handleless cups, 4" saucers; earthenware, Columbia Star patt., John Ridgway, ca. 1840, the set . . .**1,800.00 to 2,000.00**

Tea set: 4¹/₂" cov. teapot, 1¹/₂" open sugar, 1¹/₂" creamer, 1³/₄" cups, 4" saucers, 2¹/₈ × 3¹/₂" waste bowl; earthenware, Humphrey's Clock patt., marked "Humphrey's Clock" on banner & "England" under banner, Ridgway, ca. 1890-1908, the set . . . . **500.00 to 600.00**

Tea set: 4¹/₂" cov. teapot, 4¹/₄" cov. sugar w/scroll cut handles, 2¹/₂" creamer, 1³/₄" cups, 4¹/₄" saucers, 6" serving plate, 2¹/₂ × 4³/₄" waste bowl; earthenware, Poonah patt., marked "GFB" on some pieces, ca. 1842-1858, the set . . . .**1,000.00 to 1,500.00**

Tea set: 4¹/₂" cov. teapot, 4¹/₈" cov. sugar, 1¹/₂" cups, 4⁵/₈" saucers, 4⁵/₈" plates, 2¹/₈ × 2¹/₈" waste bowl; earthenware, sponge-decorated Flow Blue, bases marked w/impressed crown & ★, ca. 1850, the set . . . . .**2,000.00 to 2,800.00**

Tea set: 4³/₄" cov. teapot, 3³/₈" cov. sugar, 2¹/₄" creamer, 1³/₄" cups, 4¹/₂" saucers, 5" plates, 2³/₄" h. waste bowl; earthenware, Chelsea (Minerva) patt., white w/powder blue design & rust trim, Minton, ca. 1854, the set . . . . **500.00 to 1,000.00**

Tea set: 5" cov. teapot, 4¹/₂" cov. sugar, 3¹/₄" creamer, 2" cups, 4¹/₄" saucers, 5" plates; earthenware, Child and Dog patt., set comes in brown, rose, green & blue, ca. 1870-1880, the set . . . . **175.00 to 250.00**

Tea set: 5" cov. teapot, 4¹/₂" cov. sugar, 3¹/₄" creamer, 2" cups, 4¹/₄" saucers, 5" plates; earthenware, May patt., multi-colored, ca. 1870-1880, rare, the set . . . .**1,800.00 to 2,000.00**

Tea set: 5" cov. teapot, 4¹/₂" cov. sugar, 3¹/₄" creamer, 2" cups, 4¹/₄" saucers, 5" plates; earthenware, Persian patt., decorated w/Oriental design of fans & fish, ca. 1870-1880 . . . . **400.00 to 600.00**

Tea set: 5" cov. teapot, 4$^{1}/_{2}$" cov. sugar, 3$^{1}/_{4}$" creamer, 2" cups, 4$^{1}/_{4}$" saucers, 5" plates; earthenware, Octagon Blue Willow patt., ca. 1870-1880, the set . . . . **600.00 to 800.00**

Tea set: 5" cov. teapot, 4$^{1}/_{2}$" cov. sugar, 3" creamer, 2$^{1}/_{8}$" cups, 4$^{1}/_{4}$" saucers, 2$^{3}/_{4}$ × 3$^{1}/_{2}$" waste bowl, 7" underplates; earthenware, Birds & Holly patt., mid-Victorian, the set . . . . **500.00 to 900.00**

Tea set: 5" cov. teapot, 4$^{1}/_{4}$" cov. sugar, 3$^{1}/_{2}$" creamer, 2" cups, 4$^{3}/_{4}$" saucers; earthenware, Mason's Willow, Blue Willow patt., marked "Mason's Patent Ironstone China," Ashbury, ca. 1891, the set . . . . **1,800.00 to 2,800.00**

Tea set: 5" teapot, 4" cov. sugars, 3" creamer, 1$^{3}/_{4}$" cups, 4" saucers, 5$^{1}/_{2}$" plates, 2$^{1}/_{8}$" h. waste bowl; earthenware, Horse Drawn Cart patt., octagonal shape, blue transfer of horse drawn cart, Brown Westhead, Moore and Company, ca. 1862, the set . . . . **1,000.00 to 1,500.00**

Tea set: 5$^{1}/_{4}$" cov. teapot, 5" creamer, 3$^{1}/_{4}$" creamer, 2" cups, 4$^{1}/_{4}$" saucers, 4$^{1}/_{2}$" plates, 3" h. waste bowl; earthenware, "Indian Ironstone," soft green w/hand-painted flower & foliage motif, ca. 1860-1890, the set . . . . **800.00 to 1,500.00**

Tea set: 5$^{5}/_{8}$" cov. teapot, 5$^{1}/_{4}$" cov. sugar, 3$^{1}/_{2}$" creamer, 2$^{1}/_{4}$" cups, 4$^{1}/_{2}$" saucers, 5" plates, 2 × 3" waste bowl; earthenware, gold lustre Tea Leaf decoration, Mellor, Taylor & Co., ca. 1880-1904, the set . . . . . **1,800.00 to 2,800.00**

Tea set: 6" cov. teapot, 5$^{1}/_{4}$" cov. sugar, 3$^{1}/_{2}$" creamer, 2" cups, 4$^{3}/_{4}$" saucers, 5$^{1}/_{4}$" plates; earthenware, At The Well patt., teapot has ring handles & bent bud finials, ca. 1840-1860, the set . . . . **500.00 to 900.00**

◆ German Toy Ware

Chamber set, porcelain, Blue Onion patt., ca. 1920, the set . . . . **375.00 to 775.00**

***Cheese board,** porcelain, Blue Onion patt, ca. 1920 . . . . **300.00 to 400.00**

Chocolate set: 5" cov. chocolate pot, six 2" cups, six 4$^{1}/_{4}$" saucers; porcelain, decorated w/swags of white flowers & chained together w/green foliage, unmarked, turn-of-the-century, set of 13 . . . . . . **600.00 to 1,200.00**

Dinner set, porcelain, Cherubs patt., marked "Prov. Saxe. E.S. Germany," E.S. Prussia, ca. 1900-1920, the set . . . . . **1,200.00 to 1,800.00**

Funnel, porcelain, Blue Onion patt., ca. 1920 . . . . **300.00 to 475.00**

***Rolling pin,** porcelain, Blue Onion patt, ca. 1920 . . . . **300.00 to 400.00**

Strainer, porcelain, Blue Onion patt., ca. 1920 . . . . **300.00 to 475.00**

Tea set, porcelain, Buster Brown decoration, the set . . . . **800.00 to 1,500.00**

Tea set, porcelain, decorated w/golden pheasant motif, R.S. Prussia, ca. 1920, rare, the set . . . . **1,800.00 to 2,000.00**

Tea set, porcelain, decorated w/scenes of sledding children, boxed sets will range from two to twelve settings, Royal Bayreuth, ca. 1919-1930, the set . . . . . **900.00 to 1,500.00**

Tea set, porcelain, Petite Roses patt. w/butterscotch trim, R.S. Prussia, ca. 1890-1900, the set . . . . **700.00 to 900.00**

Tea set, porcelain, Rose Swag patt., vertical swags of peach, cream & pink roses surrounded by vertical gold runners, unmarked, R.S. Prussia, ca. 1900-1915, the set . . . . **400.00 to 700.00**

Tea set, porcelain, Sweet Pea patt., R.S. Prussia, ca. 1918-1925, w/original box, the set . . . . **400.00 to 1,000.00**

Tea set: 3$^{1}/_{4}$" cov. teapot, 2$^{1}/_{4}$" cov. sugar, 1$^{1}/_{2}$" cups, 3$^{3}/_{4}$" saucer, 3$^{1}/_{4}$" plates; porcelain, Cherubs patt., marked "Prov. Saxe. E.S. Germany," E.S. Prussia, ca. 1900-1920, the set . . . . **800.00 to 1,600.00**

Tea set: 3$^{1}/_{2}$" cov. teapot, 2$^{1}/_{8}$" cov. sugar, 2$^{1}/_{4}$" creamer, 1$^{1}/_{8}$" cups, 2$^{7}/_{8}$" saucer, 3$^{1}/_{8}$" plates; porcelain, decorated w/Indian runner motif, R.S. Prussia, turn-of-the-century, very rare, the set . . . . **3,800.00 to 6,000.00**

Tea set: 4" cov. melon-shaped teapot, 2" cov. squatty sugar, 2" cups, 4" saucer; porcelain, portraits of ladies & gentlemen surrounded by gold leaves & flowers, R.S. Prussia, ca. 1900, the set . . . . **400.00 to 800.00**

Tea set: 4" cov. teapot, 2$^{3}/_{4}$" cov. sugar, 2$^{1}/_{2}$" creamer, 1$^{1}/_{8}$" cups, 3" saucer, 3" plates; porcelain, decorated w/baby red roses, unmarked, R.S. Prussia, turn-of-the-century, the set . . . . **400.00 to 700.00**

A grouping of R.S. Prussia children's teapots.

Tea set: 4¹/₂" cov. teapot, 2⁵/₈" cov. sugar, 2" creamer, 1¹/₂" cups, 3" saucer; porcelain, Hanging Basket patt., R.S. Prussia, three main pieces w/R.S. Prussia red mark, ca. 1890-1920, the set . . . . **2,500.00 to 3,000.00**

Tea set: 5" cov. teapot, 3" cov. sugar, 2¹/₄" creamer, 1³/₄" cups, 5¹/₂" cake plate; porcelain, Tea Roses patt., R.S. Prussia, ca. 1890-1900, the set . . . . **700.00 to 900.00**

Tea set: 5" cov. teapot, 3" cov. sugar, 2¹/₄" creamer, 2" cups, 4¹/₂" saucer, 4³/₄ × 6¹/₄" pierced cake plate; porcelain, decorated w/fruit motif, R.S. Prussia, ca. 1920, the set . . . . **1,500.00 to 1,850.00**

Tea set: 5³/₈" cov. teapot, 3" cov. sugar, 3" creamer, 2¹/₄" cups, 4¹/₂" saucer, 5¹/₄" plates; porcelain, Santa on the Move patt., shows Father Christmas in old car & in hot air balloon, ca. 1890-1900, the set . . . . **1,200.00 to 1,800.00**

Tea set: 6¹/₂" cov. teapot, 3¹/₂" cov. sugar, 2¹/₂" creamer, 4¹/₄" saucer, 6" plates; porcelain, decorated w/castle, mill or cottage, R.S. Prussia, late 19th c., the set . . . . **2,000.00 to 2,800.00**

Tea set: 7" cov. teapot, 3¹/₂" cov. sugar, 2¹/₂" creamer, 2" cups, 4¹/₂" saucer, 6" plates; porcelain, Stippled Floral Mould patt., R.S. Prussia, ca. 1880-1890, the set . . . . **1,800.00 to 2,000.00**

An early Christmas postcard.

CHAPTER
9

CHRISTMAS COLLECTIBLES

Today, much excitement ripples through the air whenever anything Christmas comes up for sale, be it at an auction, estate sale, antique show or flea market. For increasing numbers of collectors join the ranks of those who are attempting to recapture the spirit of Christmas past through their collecting. Record prices have been set for Santas, Dresden ornaments, and rare glass figurals, but beginning collectors will find multitudes of items at very inexpensive to moderate prices. Christmas collecting has a wide range of interests and prices. The past few years have seen accelerated prices in the rarer areas, stabilized in the medium to low end items, and even a reduction in price when very common items come up for sale.

Even though Christmas has been celebrated for years, its celebration as a national holiday is as recent as 1891 and its unusual appeal as a collectible is, of course, much newer than that. It is in recent years that Americans have become enamored with many different collecting interests in Christmas. Christmas collecting is a vast field and a collector may amass a collection of many different things, but there are certain areas of Christmas that attract more interest than others, such as: feather trees, candy containers, paper ornaments, Dresden paper figures, wax decorations, pressed cotton creations, glass ornaments, early lighting devices, and electric bulbs.

—Robert Brenner

ARTIFICIAL & FEATHER TREES

As far back as the last third of the 19th century, artificial trees have been in existence. From what can be determined, feather tree manufacturing was a cottage industry similar to the manufacture of glass tree ornaments. However, it was different in several respects. The parts for the tree—wire, wood, and berries—were factory made & the heavy wire branches were sent to cottages for wrapping. Turkey and goose feathers were the most commonly used feathers, but swan feathers also were used.

Sheared trees, as we know them today, did not exist at that time and feather trees accurately reflected the neutral appearence of live white pines. These trees are a relatively expensive collectors item, they can command prices ranging from $50.00 to $1,200.00 or more, depending on age and size. It seems to be a rule of thumb that trees are priced about $100.00 to $125.00 per foot.

In addition to feather trees, visca trees made in America and even brush trees from the 1960s are seeing an increase in price. But aluminum trees, which appeal to the younger generation of collectors, are dramatically rising in price. Produced as early as the mid-1950s and into the late 1960s, these trees are snapped up almost as fast as they placed on sale.

Tree, blue w/candleholders, square white
   base, 46" **$425.00**

Tree, green w/red berries, in round white
   base, 12" **125.00**

Tree, green w/candleholders, square white
   base, 24" (Fig. 9-1) **250.00**

Tree, white w/red berries, round red base,
   24" **200.00**

CANDY CONTAINERS

Some of the earliest decorations for the
Christmas tree were edibles and the containers that
held these "goodies" were often used as decorations
for the tree. Many cornucopias and candy containers
found today are small and their appearance on the
tree seems quite obvious. Candy containers in the
shape of Father Christmas command the highest
prices and those containers made in Germany easily command over $100.00 each. In fact, the composi-
tion and papier-mâché containers are becoming
increasingly difficult to find as collectors scramble
to add them to collections.

Basket, paper, w/tinsel handle & Santa scrap
   on front **120.00**

Boot, papier-mâché, German **30.00**

Child, cotton, w/bisque head pushing papier-
   mâché snow ball **425.00**

Cornucopia, paper, gold foiled cone **85.00**

Egg, silk over pressed cardboard **150.00**

Elf, composition, sitting on candy container
   log **275.00**

Santa in car, celluloid head, cardboard car
   w/wheels **200.00**

Santa on Donkey, candy box (Fig. 9-2) **175.00**

Santa on bombshell, composition
   (Fig. 9-3) **500.00**

Santa, celluloid head, mesh body **95.00**

Snow ball, cotton covered w/red cotton Santa
   on top, Japan, 4" **100.00**

PAPER ORNAMENTS

Of all the early decorations, perhaps the most
revered are the "paper and tinsel" ornaments that

Fig. 9-1

hung on almost everyone's Christmas tree. Today,
these paper ornaments are known as "scraps,"
"diecuts," or "chromos." From the Civil War to the
late 1900s, a scrapbook craze swept across America.
Almost every woman or child kept a scrapbook. By
the late 1800s, the Germans with their perfection of
the printing process, provided these keepers of
memorabilia with a vast array of paper for their
scrapbooks. By World War I, the craze for keeping a
scrapbook had all but died. The Germans, needing
to find a new use for all these scraps, began producing Christmas ornaments and they quickly became
fashionable. By the late 1920s, the popularity of
papers decreased sharply and paper ornaments were
advertised less and less in mail order catalogs. The
majority of these ornaments found today date from
1880 to the mid-1920s. Paper ornaments range in
price from $5.00 to over $300.00, depending on size
and subject material, with Father Christmas ornaments attracting the highest prices.

Fig. 9-2

Fig. 9-3

Fig. 9-4

Angels, w/tinsel holder, 3" **15.00**

Angels, w/cellophane & tinsel, 7" (Fig. 9-4) . . . **75.00**

Miss Liberty, tinsel & cellophane **125.00**

Santa, full-bodied, w/tree & toys, 15" w/tinsel . . **25.00**

Santa, full-bodied, riding sled (Fig. 9-5, right) . . **60.00**

Santa head, w/tinsel holder, 4" **15.00**

Star w/a scrap angel, tinsel trim , 6" (Fig. 9-5, left) **40.00**

Victorian children, in car w/Santa, cellophane & tinsel trim, 6" **125.00**

DRESDEN PAPER ORNAMENTS

Of all the Christmas ornaments, none capture the interest of collectors more than those made primarily from cardboard called "Dresden" ornaments because they originated in or near Dresden, Germany between 1880 and 1910.

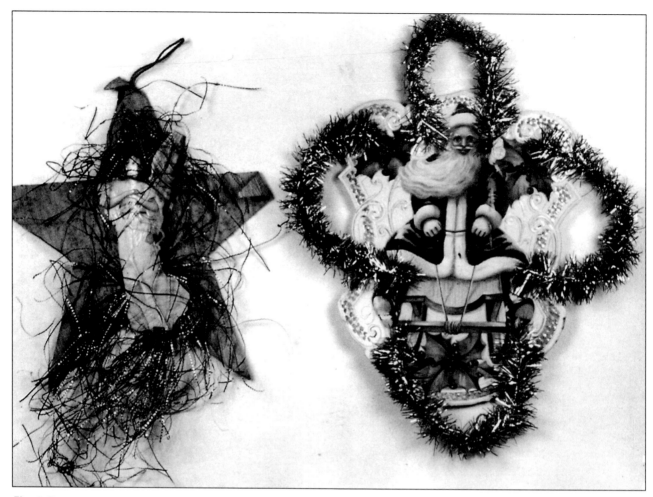

Fig. 9-5

Three-dimensional Dresdens command the attention of collectors of antique Christmas memorabillia. These heavily embossed cardstock (cardboard) items were part of the *Luxus-papier* industry in Germany from ca. 1850 to the present. In order to give them the appearence of sheet metal, they were constructed from two or more separately prepared pieces of cardboard and then heavily embossed. The most desirable are made of unusual material, such as the pig with the sacks of money on his back and a four-leaf clover in his mouth. A Dresden in good condition can easily bring over $400.00.

Banjo, three-dimensional, 3" **160.00**

Elf, holding money bag, three-dimensional, 3" **650.00**

Elephant, three-dimensional, 4" (Fig. 9-6, bottom right) **425.00**

Elk, brown, three-dimensional, 2" (Fig. 9-6, top left) **150.00**

Face in quarter moon, three-dimensional (Fig. 9-6, bottom left) **425.00**

Fox, brown & tan, three-dimensional, 2" . . . **350.00**

Goat, black & white, three-dimensional, 2" **295.00**

Heart, gold, three-dimensional, 3" **85.00**

Jockey on horse, three-dimensional, 3" **525.00**

Lion, three-dimensional, 2" (Fig. 9-6, top right) **175.00**

Lobster, orange, three-dimensional, 4" **375.00**

Monkey on branches, flat, 4" **150.00**

Parrot, gold, three-dimensional (Fig. 9-6, far left) **120.00**

Owl, tan & black, three-dimensional, 2" **375.00**

Pig, gold, three-dimensional, 2" **500.00**

Rabbit, silver, three-dimensional, 3" **275.00**

Santa, gold, three-dimensional, 4" **170.00**

Star, gold, flat, 3" **65.00**

Fig. 9-6

SPUN-GLASS ORNAMENTS

These are actually "glass thread" ornaments consisting of strands of glass manufactured by the glass blowers of Laushau. While white is the most common color found, red, blue, green, and gold were also used. The spun glass is usually combined with paper "scraps" picturing Santas, angels, and people. The larger colored spun-glass ornaments are the most desirable. Spun-glass ornaments are extremely collectible, with prices ranging anywhere from $15.00 to $250.00 depending on desirability and condition.

Angel, in circle, 4" 55.00

Angel, paper on clip, w/spun glass wings . . . 275.00

Peacock, flat, elaborately painted, 5" 175.00

Sailboat, double sided, in circle, 5" 30.00

Santa, in circle w/comet tail, 8" 110.00

Victorian boy, in circle, 5" (Fig. 9-7) 40.00

Fig. 9-7

Fig. 9-8

WAX & WAXED ORNAMENTS

Many photographs of decorated trees from the turn-of-the-century show wax angels and wax children ornaments hanging on the tree. For purposes of easier identification, the angel ornaments must be divided into two categories: "waxed angels" and "wax angels." Waxed angels have a firm core of papier-mâché or composition and had only a very thin coating of wax; wax angels were solid wax. Small, common waxed angels go for between $50.00 and $70.00 while wax angels easily fetch over $150.00. It seems that these angels become more expensive every year and they are becoming as rare as, and as desirable as, Dresden ornaments.

Angel, American, ca. 1940s, 4" **15.00**

Angel, waxed, 4" (Fig. 9-8, left) **95.00**

Angel, waxed, 5" (Fig. 9-8, right) **165.00**

Angel, waxed, 6" (Fig. 9-8, middle) **175.00**

Angel, wax, 6" **175.00**

Bird, in metal circle, 5" **220.00**

Soldier, American, ca. 1940s, 4" **15.00**

PRESSED COTTON ORNAMENTS

The most non-destructive ornaments are those manufactured of pressed cotton (sometimes wrongly called wool). These were primarily manufactured in Breslau. Human figures are probably the most sought-after of cotton ornaments. The endless variety of cotton wool people is simply astounding, including clowns, farmers, glass blowers, children, a plant seller, and many others.

Every imaginable animal can also be found—exotic animals such as elephants, tigers, leopards, and giraffes; and common animals such as squirrels, dogs, cats, and rabbits. Most cotton ornaments bring over $150.00 on today's market.

Angel, paper face, Dresden wings, 3" **175.00**

Bell, blue, 3" **25.00**

Cow, brass bell, 4" **170.00**

Cucumber, green & yellow, 4" **75.00**

Girl, paper face, 4" (Fig. 9-9, far left) **150.00**

Fig. 9-9

Girl, bisque head/wool coat, w/lead ice skates,
4" (Fig. 9-9, left center) **150.00**

Jockey, w/horse head, 4" **450.00**

Man, paper crown on head, 4" (Fig. 9-9, center
right) **225.00**

Orange, 3" **65.00**

Peddler, cotton fruit in pack, 4" **285.00**

Sailor, w/cap, 4" **300.00**

Santa, school girl, bisque, 4" **250.00**

Victorian lady, 3" (Fig. 9-9, far right) **170.00**

GLASS ORNAMENTS

The first glass ornaments were heavy glass creations that are known to collectors today as Kugels. It is a German term meaning "a round or ball shape." Kugels have become quite popular, especially those of rarer colors including red, amethyst, and cobalt blue. Because of the over use of the word, many people now call any old, heavy blown-glass ornament a kugel.

Of most interest to collectors in glass ornaments today are the thin glass figural ornaments blown into the shapes of many different objects. From their first early appearence, figural ornaments proved to be exceptionally popular.

Before 1918, the most common glass tree ornaments were the indent, ball-, melon-, and pear-shaped ornaments. Among the outstanding examples of glass ornaments from this period are the unsilvered, Victorian wire-wrapped ornaments produced in profusion before World War I.

The number and variety of glass figurals made from the beginning of production through World War II (1939) have been conservatively estimated at at least 10,000. Glass ornaments are sometimes worth hundreds of dollars, but only those rarer ones command such prices. Santas, birds, and other common figurals go for much less.

Many fine ornaments are once again being manufactured in Europe and collectors should educate themselves in order to know the difference between old and new. Kugels have been reproduced as well. However, some of these newer ornaments are quite desirable, as prices for the original items have risen. Most intriguing is the secondary market for Old World Christmas, Christopher Radko, and Pat Breen as collectors scramble to amass these collectible ornaments.

Fig. 9-10

Fig. 9-11

Al Jolson head, 3¼" **375.00**
Amelia Earhart, 4" **245.00**
Automobile, red & silver, 3" (Fig. 9-10, top) . . **85.00**
Baby, head, glass eyes, 2" (Fig. 9-11, left) . . . **125.00**
Baby, w/pacifier, in crib, 2" **325.00**
Bacchas, head, 2" (Fig. 9-11, right) **375.00**
Bear, 3" **175.00**
Beetle, red & gold, 2" **95.00**
Bird, spun glass tail, 5" **25.00**
Bird, owl, standing on clip, 4" **115.00**
Bird, owl, on clip, glass eyes, 5" **75.00**
Bird, game pheasent, 4" **250.00**
Bird, peacock, on clip, fanned spun glass, 4" . . **50.00**
Bird, w/berry in beak, 5" **120.00**
Boy, whistling, w/hat & scarf, 4" **95.00**
Cat in shoe, 4" **145.00**
Cat, w/fiddle & cap, 3" **225.00**
Charlie Chaplin head, 3" **320.00**
Christ Child head, 3" **165.00**
Clown, "My Darling," 4" **70.00**
Clown, circus, 4" **35.00**
Carrot, 4" (Fig. 9-12, right center) **95.00**
Corn, 4" (Fig. 9-12, right) **75.00**
Devil head, gold, 4" **425.00**
Dog, blowing horn, 4" **195.00**
Elephant, 4" **75.00**

Fig. 9-12

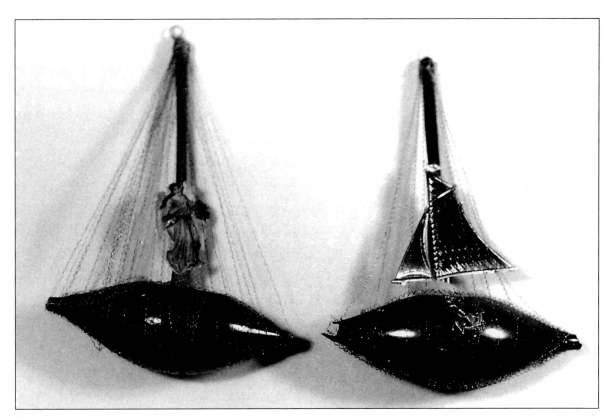

Fig. 9-14

Elephant, on ball, 3" 280.00
Fantasy ornament, bells 85.00
Father Christmas, early, 5" 125.00
Fish, w/paper fins & tail, 4" 155.00
Flower, on clip, venetian dew, 3" 90.00
Frog, on toadstool, 3" 65.00
Grape cluster, individual grapes, 4" 40.00
Happy Hooligan, extended legs, 5" 500.00
Hot air balloon, angel, 4" (Fig. 9-13, left) 95.00
Hot air balloon, angel, 6" (Fig. 9-13, right) . . . 120.00
Hot air balloon, Santa, 7" (Fig. 9-13,
    center) 270.00
Horn, silver w/flowers, 4" 15.00
Indian bust, painted feathers, 4" 295.00
Indian head, on clip, 2" 195.00
Keystone Cop, extended legs, 5" 500.00
Kite, chenille string, 3" 450.00
Kugel, grape cluster, green, 4" 250.00
Kugel, pear shaped, silver, 3" 200.00
Kugel, round, gold, 2" 15.00
Los Angeles zeppelin, paper label, 4"
    (Fig. 9-10, bottom) 295.00
Mermaid, red & flesh face, 4" 225.00

Fig. 9-13

Mrs. Santa Claus, 4" 445.00
Mushroom, cluster of three on clip, 4" 60.00
Pear, matte finish, 4" 45.00
Pickle, curved, 4" (Fig. 9-12, left center) . . . 120.00
Pine cone, silver, 4" 5.00

Potato, 4" (Fig. 9-12, left) **160.00**
Rabbit, w/carrot, 4" **45.00**
Rose, white w/venetian dew, on clip **85.00**
Sailboat, angel scrap, 5" (Fig. 9-14, left) **170.00**
Sailboat, Dresden sail, 5" (Fig. 9-14, right) . . **175.00**
Santa, red w/tree, 4" (Fig. 9-15, left) **35.00**
Santa, blue w/tree, 4" **30.00**
Santa, in basket, 4" **65.00**
Santa, on clip, 4" (Fig. 9-15, right) **55.00**
Santa, below ball, 5" (Fig. 9-15, center) **65.00**
Snowman, w/broom, 4" **25.00**
Songbird, on clip, 3" **5.00**

Storks, mother & baby, on clip, 5" **185.00**
Uncle Sam, full-figure, 3" **450.00**
Walnut, gold, 2" **10.00**
Witch, w/cat & broom, 4" **525.00**
Zeppelin, wire-wrapped, w/glass gondola,
    5" (Fig. 9-16, left) **450.00**
Zeppelin, wire-wrapped, 5" (Fig. 9-16,
    right) **270.00**

Fig. 9-15

ITALIAN GLASS ORNAMENTS

Manufactured in northern Italy following World War II, these free-blown glass figurals are attracting collector interest. The art of blowing glass Christmas ornaments was taught to the Italians by Germans who fled their war-ravaged homeland. These are still being produced today, but the one-of-a-kind 1950s fanciful free-blown glass ornaments are the most desirable. Prices seem to rise every year.

Alpine man, w/rope, 5" **100.00**
Cat head, 3" (Fig. 9-17, no. 2) **50.00**
Elf, seated, 6" (Fig. 9-17, no. 8) **50.00**
Lamp, 5" (Fig. 9-17, no. 1) **45.00**
Man in Moon, 4" (Fig. 9-17, no. 6) **75.00**
Mouse, playing saxaphone, 6" (Fig. 9-17,
    no. 5) **75.00**
Robin Hood, 6" (Fig. 9-17, no. 9) **85.00**
Wizard, 6" (Fig. 9-17, no. 4) **75.00**

(**Note:** No.'s 3 & 7 not listed but of similar value.)

Fig. 9-16

Fig. 9-17

EARLY LIGHTING DEVICES

Candles were the most popular and widely used method for illuminating the tree. Due to the fact that many fires were caused by tipping candles, balanced weight candleholders were invented. These would keep the candle standing upright, avoiding its tipping over into a branch or another ornament. The earliest and most economical were those with clay or wooden balls at the bottom. Also used as counter-balances were lead figures, heavy glass ornaments, and soft metal ornaments.

Some of the rarest Christmas candleholders include thin, fragile glass lanterns that clip onto the tree. First manufactured just before the turn-of-the-century, they were introduced as being novel alternatives to plain metal candleholders. The counter balance holders many times bring $50.00 or more with the simple clip-ons in the $1.00 to $5.00 range.

Candleholder, counterbalance, tin & lead
geometric figure at end, several varieties
(Fig. 9-18, of four) **60.00**
Candleholder, counterbalance, w/clay ball at
bottom **15.00**
Candleholder, pinch-on, lithographed
w/Father Christmas **150.00**

Fig. 9-18

Christmas light, quilted blue **50.00**

Christmas light, quilted milk glass **65.00**

Christmas light, glass, cranberry **225.00**

Lantern, glass, in shape of aviator w/candle
    insert, clip-on **400.00**

Lantern, metal w/glass panels, six-sided **65.00**

Reflector, tin, American **3.00**

ELECTRIC LIGHT BULBS

When Christmas trees began to be lit with electricity, a whole new area of collectibles was opened. One type of electric lamp used was the "Festoon Lamp" (sometimes referred to as "Stringer"), produced around 1895. A Festoon Lamp was a round glass globe with a carbon filament running lengthwise attached to brass connectors on either end with loops for wiring them together in a series.

Around 1908, fancy figural lamps started being imported from Germany, Austria, and Hungary. They were similar to clip-on ornaments and some had an exhaust tip at the top; in the case of many birds, the tip was their beak. The glass had detailed molding, soft shades of paint and expressive faces making them comparable to the early European ornaments.

After World War I, Japan began to manufacture glass figural light bulbs and soon the milk glass figural light was commonplace on American trees. Regardless of whether the lights work or not, they can easily bring more than $30.00, with the European lights being worth over $100.00.

Bubble lights, Italian miniature light sets, and matchless stars continue to set price records. The different types appeal to the younger generation of collectors.

Andy Gump, milk glass **75.00**

Aviator, milk glass, boy w/airplane **40.00**

Ball, milk glass, red w/stars **15.00**

Bird, brown, early European **35.00**

Bubble light, oil, working **50.00**

Bubble light, shooting stars **100.00**

Bulbs, C-6, Detecto **3.00**

Fig. 9-19 – A grouping of various old figural light bulbs.

Clown head, milk glass 25.00
Cottage, milk glass, six-sided 10.00
Dick Tracy, milk glass 85.00
Dog in basket, milk glass 50.00
Dresden, dog, 5" 185.00
Dresden, flowers, 3" 70.00
Grapes, milk glass 15.00
Humpty Dumpty, milk glass, large head 35.00
Jack-O' Lantern, milk glass 40.00
Lion, w/tennis racket, milk glass 40.00
Matchless star, single row points 35.00
Pig, w/bowtie, milk glass 65.00
Rose, clear glass, Dresden 50.00
Rose, clear glass, small, Japan 10.00
Santa head, large, milk glass, 4" 25.00
St. Nicholas, clear glass, early European 90.00
Smitty, milk glass 70.00
Woman in shoe, milk glass 45.00
Zeppelin, milk glass 60.00
Boxed set, Disney Silly Symphony 220.00
Boxed set, glass, Mother Goose characters . . 190.00

SANTA FIGURES

The most valuable Santa figures are the Victorian papier-mâché items. Papier-mâché (the combination of pulp paper, glue or paste, oil, and rosin) was pressed into two half-molds and once dry, pieces were removed, glued together, and smoothed with sandpaper. They were then sealed with varnish and painted in realistic colors. Many times beards of rabbit fur were glued on for added realism. Originally called Pelze-Nicols, they became known as Belsnickles.

Another popular version of the Santa figure used composition. These papier-mâché-type figures were dipped into liquid plaster, which dried in a very thin coat. These figures were realistically painted, paying close attention to the face and hands. They were dressed in authentic clothing and many carried branches or trees made of goose feathers. The candy containers were hidden beneath the flowing cloth skirt. There were numerous other materials also used, including: wood, wax, cotton, plaster, chalk, and metal. All of the earliest European-types command extremely high prices on the market today.

Somewhat neglected, even though they are quickly gaining in popularity, are the later cardboard

Fig. 9-20

Santas, made from material resembling old egg-cartons. These were copies of a more robust Santa, like those seen in Coca-Cola ads. Most had an opening in which candy or small presents could be inserted. They were excellent representations of our jolly American Santa Claus.

Belsnickel, red, w/feather branch, 7" (Fig. 9-20, center) 350.00
Belsnickel, white, w/feather branch, 11" (Fig. 9-20, right) 650.00
Belsnickel, blue, w/feather branch, 12" (Fig. 9-20, left) 725.00
Bisque, miniature, pulling sleigh 145.00
Bisque, miniature, on cardboard 65.00
Celluloid, standing, w/black doll, Japan, 4" (Fig. 9-21, left) 95.00
Celluloid, standing, w/pack, Japan, 4" (Fig. 9-21, right) 75.00
Celluloid, Painted details, Irwin, 12" 250.00
Cotton, w/paper face, 6" 150.00
Japan, standing, paper, 4" 45.00
Japan, chenille body over cardboard, composition face, 9" 350.00
Plaster, bank, standing, American, 10" (Fig. 9-22) 150.00
Plaster, in chimney, American, 10" 185.00

Fig. 9-21

Fig. 9-22

POSTCARDS

Santa and Christmas-related themes have always been incorporated on postcards. The rarest of these include the hold-to-light, silk, mechanical and full-figured European cards. The hold-to-lights are especially of value to collectors because they are composed of multiple layers of cardboard, with the top layer cut-out in strategic places, letting the light shine through. Some cards used pieces of silk fabric to make Santa's clothes and the rarest of these cards are those that use colors other than the traditional red.

Hold-to-light, Santa w/child **200.00**

Mechanical, Santa w/children **75.00**

Real photo, Santa w/children **60.00**

Santa riding in train w/children **30.00**

Silk, Santa leaning over child in chair
(ILLUS. w/introduction) **40.00**

Silk, Santa standing w/sack of toys **45.00**

CHRISTMAS ADVERTISING

During Victorian times, small lithographed prints known as trade cards were the primary form of written advertisements. These advertising cards were used for products ranging from coffee to farm machinery. Lion Brothers and McLaughins advertised their coffee with some of the most beautiful of cards, many of which used the figure of St. Nicholas as their central theme. Along with the increased use of color in magazines, came numerous new advertisements at Christmas employing Santa Claus and other Christmas-related themes.

Biscuit tin, Kennedy w/Santa **375.00**

Button, celluloid, Santa w/stocking **70.00**

Button, celluloid, TB, 1936 . . . . **25.00**

Calendar top, blue Santa w/children **95.00**

Candy pail, Santa, early **325.00**

Cigar box, Santa w/toys inside cover **95.00**

Coca-Cola, standing Santa, ca. 1930s **175.00**

CHRISTMAS COLLECTIBLES ✤ 149

Fig. 9-23

Lion Coffee, Santa w/children chromo **185.00**
Snow King, stand-up Santa w/sleigh **750.00**
Soap box, Fairbank's **400.00**
Trade card, Santa w/sleigh, Snow King baking
    powder **85.00**

GREETING CARDS

Although greeting cards originated as early as 1846 in England, they did not become popular in the United States until the late 1870s. The earliest of these cards were illustrated with flowers, birds, and other such non-Christmas themes. It wasn't until the beginning of the 1920s that Santa was widely used on greeting cards. St. Nick was depicted in every conceivable style of dress and would appear in cars, airplanes, train cars, and engines and even with polar bears. His fine details of color and accessories was interpreted individually by the whims of countless artists. Since his appearance was not standardized, it is fairly simple for a collector to find unusual and interesting cards.

Fold-out, two-layer, Angels w/nativity **40.00**
Fold-out, two-layer, Father Christmas
    (Fig. 9-23) **70.00**
Fold-out, five-layer, nativity scene **95.00**
Fold-over, airbrush, "Xmas," 1908 . . . . **10.00**
Walt Disney, Mickey Mouse **75.00**

COOKIE MOLDS, CANDY MOLDS, & COOKIE CUTTERS

Molds and cookie cutters were often fashioned in the shape of Father Christmas. Some of the earliest of molds were created by the gingerbread bakers and lebküchen creators who were also chandlers (or wax workers). After the mid-1600s, molds were made from carved wood or molded plaster, unlike the earlier molds made of fired, unglazed clay. Candy molds were made of heavy metal and have surprisingly good detail. Even ice cream and cake molds in various Santa shapes have been found. Eppelsheimer and Co. produced pewter ice cream molds in the shape of Father Christmas in the late 1800s.

Cookie cutters were at first made at home from tin and these examples of folk art are highly sought after by today's collectors. Many of these were quite large, up to 13" in length. The first ones were without handles and were awkward to use. Cutters from the 1940s and 1950s are quite interesting as many of them had quite defined shapes. Many of these molds and cutters can make interesting wall displays during the Christmas season

Bell, candy mold **50.00**
Christmas tree, candy mold **45.00**
Santas, candy mold, two rolls of 14 . . . . **100.00**
Santa on Donkey, candy mold, two-part . . . **225.00**

GAMES, PUZZLES, & TOYS

Toy collectors cross with Christmas collectors in vying for some very expensive items. With the Victorian fascination with parlor games came the inevitable manufacturing of many Christmas and Santa-related games. These were not manufactured in huge quantities since their use only seemed appropriate during a short period of the year. Wooden puzzles are also of interest to collectors because of the beautiful lithographed images of Father Christmas and later Santa Claus.

Among some of the finest old toys available include cast-iron toys made by Hubley, manufactured in the early 1900s. Toys made of pressed tin were made in the Nurnberg area of Germany as early as the late 1700s. Nodders and clockwork Santas were absolutely beautiful and very few of these were saved. Paper lithography enabled the manufacturers to decorate even the most inexpensive toy with color. Especially desirable are the tin German toys such as those made after World War I because many of these survived and are available to collectors today. Those toys depicting Santa riding in mechanical cars, sleighs and airplanes are highly collectible. The tin mechanical toys manufactured in Japan from the 1930s through the 1950s have seen some dramatic price increases.

Fig. 9-25

Fig. 9-24

Battery-operated, Santa w/drum, eyes light
up, Japan **280.00**

Santa on top of house, 9" **300.00**

Jigsaw puzzle, lantern, Santa head,
American **200.00**

Mechanical, skating Santa, Japan **425.00**

Rolly polly, Santa, Schoenhut, 7" **850.00**

Wind-up, Santa w/book, Japan (Fig. 9-24) . . . **125.00**

Wind-up, celluloid Santa, Japan **95.00**

Church, cardboard, large, Japan (Fig. 9-25,
front **35.00**

Deer, celluloid, Japan, 6" **25.00**

Figures, human, celluloid, Japan **35.00**

House, cardboard, medium, Japan (Fig. 9-25,
top left) **20.00**

House, cardboard, large, Japan (Fig. 9-25, top
right) **25.00**

Sheep, composition head, wool body, 4" **85.00**

Trees, brush, small, Japan **5.00**

Trees, sponge, large, Japan **12.00**

PUTZ (NATIVITY) RELATED MATERIALS

Animals, composition, assorted, German **20.00**

Animals, wood, assorted, German **45.00**

MISCELLANEOUS CHRISTMAS ITEMS

Beaded chains, glass, German, 12" **15.00**

Fence, cast iron, painted, four-sections **345.00**

Fig. 9-26

Fence, feather w/red berries, 6 pcs. 450.00

Handkerchief, family decorating tree 225.00

Handkerchief, Nast Santa 450.00

Mask, papier-mâché, early 1900s,
 German 350.00

Nativity set, Sunday school fold-out
 (Fig. 9-26) 35.00

Snow Baby figure, china, riding polar bear . . 225.00

Snow Babies figures, china, sliding down
 roof, each 250.00

Tinsel, lead, National Tinsel 15.00

Tree stand, cast iron, Santa molded on both
 sides, Germany 225.00

Tree stand, lithographed tin, American 50.00

Tree stand, wind-up, revolving, musical, early
 1900s, German 550.00

COOKBOOKS

Cookbook collectors are usually good cooks and will buy important new cookbooks as well as seek out notable older ones. Many early cookbooks were published and given away as advertising premiums for various products used extensively in cooking. While some rare, scarce first edition cookbooks can be very expensive, most collectible cookbooks are reasonably priced.

Advertising, "Delicious Milk Dishes," Van Camps, paper covers, ca. 1929, 31 pp. (Fig. 10-1) . . . . **$5.00 to 8.00**

Advertising, "Dainty Deserts for Dainty People," Knox Geletin, New York, 1924 . . . . . **6.00**

Advertising, "E.R. Durkee & Co. Cook Book," Washington, fair cond. **10.00**

Advertising, "Elsie's Cook Book," Borden Co., New York, 1952, excellent cond. **12.00**

Advertising, "Gone With the Wind Cookbook," Pebco Toothpaste **25.00**

Advertising, "Good Things to Eat and How to Prepare Them," Larkin Co., New York, New York **12.00**

Advertising, "Making Biscuits," Royal Baking Powder Co., 1927, paper covers, 14 pp. (Fig. 10-2) . . . . **8.00 to 10.00**

"Alice B. Toklas Cookbook," A.B. Toklas, New York, 1954, w/dust jacket, very good cond. **50.00**

"The Art of Eating," M.F.K. Fisher, New York, 1954, excellent cond. **40.00**

"At Home on the Range," M.Y. Potter, 1947, w/dust jacket, very good cond. **6.00**

Fig. 10-1

Fig. 10-2

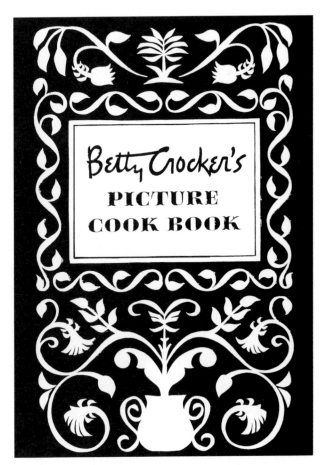

Fig. 10-3

"A Treatise on Bean and Bread-making,"
S. Graham, Boston, 1937, very good cond. . . . **750.00**

"Betty Crocker's Picture Cook Book,"
B. Crocker, Minnesota, 1950, first edition
hard cover, excellent cond. (Fig. 10-3) **50.00**

"Cookery for Beginners," Marion Harland,
Boston, 1893, excellent cond. **75.00**

**"The Cosmos Girls' Guide to New
Etiquette,"** H.G. Brown, New York, 1971,
w/dust jacket, excellent cond. **12.00**

"Dinnerology (Our Experiments in Diet),"
Pan, Chicago, 1889, very good cond. **35.00**

"The Enterprising Housekeeper," H.L.
Johnson, Philadelphia, 1897, excellent
cond. **25.00**

"Glow of Candlelight," P. Murphy, New Jersey,
1961, illus. in dust jacket, excellent cond. . . **12.00**

"The Golden Age Cook-Book,"vegetarian,
H.L. Dwoght, New York, 1898, very good
cond. **75.00**

"Harvest of American Cooking," M.M. Mc
Brides, New York, 1957, w/dust jacket, very
good cond. **20.00**

"I Hate to Cook Book," P. Bracken, New York,
1961, w/dust jacket, very good cond. **14.00**

"The International Cookbook," Heywood,
Boston, 1929, excellent cond. **30.00**

"Jewish Cookery Book," Tattersall, London,
1895, good cond. **150.00**

"The Kitchen and Fruit Gardener," bound
w/"The Complete Florist," Philadelphia, 1844,
first American edition, very good cond. **200.00**

"Martha Deane's Cooking for Compliments,"
M.Y. Potter, Philadelphia, New York, 1947,
w/dust jacket, very good cond. **12.00**

"My Cookery Books," Elizabeth Pennell,
Boston/New York, 1903, limited to 300
copies, excellent cond. **500.00**

"New England Cook Book," M. Harland
(et al), Boston, 1905, very good condition . **50.00**

"Trader Vic's Book of Food & Drink," Trader
Vic, New York, 1946, autographed copy . . . **25.00**

"The White House Cookbook," Mrs. Fanny L.
Gillet, Chicago, 1889, Werner, very good
cond. **65.00**

THE BEAUTY OF THE PACIFIC.

A typical Victorian bust portrait of a lovely lady by Currier & Ives. Similar examples still can be found for under $100.00.

CHAPTER
11

CURRIER & IVES PRINTS

This lithographic firm was founded in 1835 by Nathaniel Currier with James M. Ives becoming a partner in 1857. Current events of the day were portrayed in the early days and the prints were hand-colored. Landscapes, vessels, sport and hunting scenes of the West all became popular subjects. The firm was in existence until 1906. All prints listed are hand-colored unless otherwise noted.

Values for many of the following original Currier & Ives prints were compiled by Robert L. Searjeant in concert with four other leading authorities on original Currier & Ives prints. The numbers at the end of each listing refer to those assigned by Frederick Conningham in his book *Currier & Ives Prints, An Illustrated Checklist* (Crown Publishers, 1982). All quoted prices are for prints in very good condition.

Actress (The), small folio, full-length portrait, N. Currier, undated (34) **$119.00**

American Country Life, Pleasures of Winter, after F. F. Palmer, large folio, N. Currier, 1855 (123) **2,375.00**

American Country Life, Summer's Evening, after F. F. Palmer, large folio, N. Currier, 1855 (124) **2,350.00**

American Fireman (The), Always Ready, medium folio, 1858 (152) **1,325.00**

American Homestead—Autumn, small folio, 1869 (168) **500.00**

American Homestead—Summer, small folio, 1868 (171) **400.00**

American Homestead—Winter, small folio, 1868 (172) **400.00**

American National Game of Baseball (The), large folio, 1861, 180 (Fig. 11-1) **31,900.00**

American Whaler, small folio, N. Currier, undated (204) **1,349.00**

Ann Maria, small folio, three-quarters portrait of woman on balcony, N. Currier, 1849 (236) **95.00**

Arkansas Traveller (The), small folio, 1870 (270) **280.00**

Autumn on Lake George, small folio, highly colored foliage, deer & young in center w/deer & doe at side, undated (324) **195.00**

Barefoot Girl (The), small folio, full-length portrait of girl at the seashore w/pail & shovel, undated (370) **159.00**

Battle of Gettysburg, PA, July 3rd, 1863, (The), small folio, undated (407) **255.00**

Battle of New Orleans, Jany. 8th, 1815, 1842, (The), small folio, N. Currier, 1842 (416) . . **210.00**

Bear Hunting—Close Quarters (summer scene), small folio, undated (447) **720.00**

Beauty of Virginia, small folio, upright, vignette, undated (473) **65.00**

Benjamin Franklin—The Statesman and Philosopher, small folio, N. Currier, 1847, minor mend in red curtain (499) **495.00**

Best Likeness (The), medium folio, girl looking through empty frame w/dog beside her, 1858 (505) **135.00**

Fig. 11-1

Between Two Fires, small folio, fisherman on tree stump, dog on one bank, irate farmer on other, 1879 (511) **89.00**

Boquet (sic) of Roses, small folio, 1862 (611) **115.00**

Burial of the Bird, small folio, five children burying bird, undated (736) **80.00**

Burning of the New York Crystal Palace, on Tuesday Oct. 5th, 1858, small folio, undated (744) **440.00**

Burning of the Steamship "Austria," Sept. 13th 1858, small folio, undated (748) **265.00**

California Scenery, small folio, moonlight scene, carriages, horsemen in foreground, undated (768) **365.00**

Camping in the Woods—"A Good Time Coming," after A. F. Tait, large folio, 1863, 773 (Fig. 11-2) **4,100.00**

Capture of Atlanta, Georgia (The)—Sept. 20, 1864, small folio, undated (807) **325.00**

Capturing the Whale, small folio, N. Currier, undated (812) **1,500.00**

Carrier Dove—The Departure, small folio, undated (832) **50.00**

Catterskil Falls, small folio, Falls in center, stream to right, undated (858) **235.00**

Celebrated Horse "Lexington," large folio, undated (888) **2,500.00**

Central Park—The Bridge, small folio, undated (949) **370.00**

Chatham Square, New York, small folio, N. Currier, undated (1020) **850.00**

Children in the Wood (The), unlisted, undated **95.00**

City Hall, New York, small folio, view from southeast, N. Currier, undated (1086) **470.00**

Clipper Ship "Comet" of New York, large folio, N. Currier, 1855 (1140) **3,475.00**

Clipper Ship "Cosmos" (The), medium folio, undated (1142) **1,320.00**

Clipper Ship "Dreadnought"—Off Tuskar Light, Large folio, N. Currier, 1856 (1144) **2,995.00**

Fig. 11-2

Clipper Ship "Great Republic," small folio, N. Currier, undated (1148) **415.00**

Clipper Ship "Queen of Clippers," small folio, N. Currier, undated (1163) **495.00**

Col. Elmer E. Ellsworth, small folio, undated (1188) **95.00**

Cooling Stream (The), medium folio, undated (1246) **440.00**

Cornelia, small folio, three-quarters length portrait of woman wearing red dress under tree on balcony, N. Currier, 1846 (1256) . . . **75.00**

Daniel Webster, small folio, half-length portrait, N. Currier, 1851 (1363) **190.00**

Darktown Fire Brigade (The)—A Prize Squirt, small folio, black comic scene, 1885 (1386) **255.00**

Day Before Marriage (The), small folio, full-length portrait of bride trying on jewelry, seated before mirror, N. Currier, 1847 (1459) **110.00**

Death of Harrison, April 4, A.D. 1841, small folio, N. Currier, 1841 (1487) **85.00**

Death of President Lincoln, small folio, 1865 (1501) **100.00**

Defiance!, small folio, undated (1541) **195.00**

Drive Through the Highlands (The), medium folio, after F. F. Palmer, undated (1627) . . . **225.00**

Easter Flowers, small folio, 1847 (1656) **25.00**

Emma, small folio, N. Currier, 1849 (1727) . . . **95.00**

Enoch Arden—The Lonely Isle, large folio, 1869 (1749) **275.00**

Express Train (The), small folio, engine, tender, baggage car & six coaches passing under bridge at left, 1870, 1792 (Fig. 11-3) . . **1,900.00**

Fall of Richmond, Va. (The)—On the Night of April 2nd, 1865, small folio, 1865 (1823) **270.00**

Fruits of the Season, small folio, baskets of currants, peaches, pears, apples, strawberries & blackberries, undated (2199) **155.00**

General Grant, small folio, 1884 (2269) **90.00**

General Grant—The Nation's Choice for President of the U.S., small folio, undated (2316) **80.00**

General Shields at the Battle of Winchester, Va., 1862, small folio, 1862 (2294) **190.00**

Great Fire at Boston (The)—November 9th & 10th, 1872, small folio, 1872 (2614) . . . **315.00**

Gold Mining in California, small folio, 1871, 2412 (Fig. 11-4) **1,575.00**

Hannah, small folio, undated (2701) **60.00**

Hiawatha's Wooing, large folio, 1860 (2809) . . **395.00**

High Brigade at Harlem, N.Y. (The), small folio, horse & buggy in foreground, N. Currier, 1849 (2810) **625.00**

Home in the Wilderness (A), small folio, 1870 (2861) **725.00**

Home of the Deer (The), medium folio, undated (2867) **565.00**

Home, Sweet Home (motto), small folio, 1874 (2878) **210.00**

Horticultural Hall—Grand United States Centennial Exhibition 1876—Fairmount Park, Philadelphia, small folio, undated (2950) **165.00**

Hudson Highlands (The), small folio, 1871 (2975) **420.00**

Hungry Little Kitties, small folio, undated (2991) **80.00**

Idlewild—On The Hudson—The Glen, small folio, undated (3026) **145.00**

In Full Bloom, small folio, 1870 (3048) **70.00**

In the Mountains, medium folio, undated (3072) **420.00**

In the Woods, small folio, group of people on bank of stream & children wading, undated (3075) **160.00**

Jane, small folio, three-quarters length portrait of woman holding fan in hand, N. Currier, undated (3175) **80.00**

Jesus Blessing the Children, small folio, 1866 (3216) **20.00**

John Quincy Adams, small folio, N. Currier, 1848 (3278) **175.00**

Landscape and Ruins, medium folio, undated (3437) **195.00**

Laugh No. 1 (The)—The Butt of the Joker, small folio, 1879 (3459) **240.00**

Life and Age of Man (The)—Stages of Man's Life From the Cradle to the Grave, small folio, undated (3498) **170.00**

Life of a Fireman (The)—The Fire, large folio, N. Currier, 1854 (3515) **2,475.00**

Little Favorite (The), small folio, N. Currier, undated (3621) **70.00**

Little Manly, small folio, three-quarter length portrait, seated, undated (3663) **85.00**

Looking Down the Yo-Semite, small folio, undated (3767) **350.00**

Maiden's Rock—Mississippi River, small folio, undated (3891) **450.00**

Moss Rose (The), small folio, undated (4217) **100.00**

Mountain Ramble (A), small folio, undated (4244) **170.00**

My Little White Kittens—Learning Their ABC's, small folio, undated (4333) **140.00**

Narrows, New York Bay (The)—From Staten Island, small folio, undated (4381) **265.00**

Niagara Falls—From the Canada Side, small folio, undated (4461) **150.00**

Old Bradford Church (The), Petersburg, Virginia, after F. F. Palmer, small folio, undated, grey tinge to margins (4549) . . . **129.00**

Partridge Shooting, small folio, undated (4719) **390.00**

Patriot of 1776 Defending His Homestead (A), small folio, 1876 (4725) **175.00**

Presidents of the United State (The), small folio, N. Currier, 1844 (4893) **155.00**

"Sleepy Hollow" Church—Near Tarrytown, N.Y., after F. F. Palmer, medium folio, 1867 (5551) **575.00**

Soldier's Return (The), small folio, N. Currier, 1847 (5608) **100.00**

Squall off Cape Horn (A), small folio, undated (5680) **650.00**

Three Little White Kittens—Fishing, small folio, 1870 (6042) **145.00**

Through to the Pacific, small folio, 1870, 6051 (Fig. 11-5) **925.00**

To The Memory of. . ., small folio, woman kneeling to left of tomb along w/two children, tree at left, river in background, N. Currier, 1845 (6069) **45.00**

Tomb of Washington, (The), Mount Vernon, Virginia, medium folio, undated (6110) . . **165.00**

Trotting Gelding Frank with J.O. Nay, His Running Mate (The), large folio, 1884 (6174) **1,400.00**

Trotting on the Road—Swill against Swell, small folio, 1873 (6195) **195.00**

Trotting Stallion "Nelson," small folio, 1889 (6215) **290.00**

THE EXPRESS TRAIN.

Fig. 11-3

GOLD MINING IN CALIFORNIA.

Fig. 11-4

Fig. 11-5

Trout Brook (The), after F. F. Palmer, medium folio, 1862 (6227) **1,200.00**

Two Little Fraid Cats, small folio, mouse & two kittens, undated (6263) **140.00**

U.S. Frigate "Constitution," small folio, N. Currier, undated (6303) **535.00**

Vase of Flowers (The), small folio, 1870 (6362) **115.00**

View of Chicago, small folio, also published as "Chicago As It Was," undated (6393) . . **660.00**

View of Harper's Ferry, Va.—From the Potomac Side, large folio, undated (6395) **995.00**

View on St. Lawrence—Indian Encampment, small folio, undated (6452) **249.00**

Washington (President), small folio, N. Currier, undated (6502) **160.00**

Washington Family (The)—George and Martha Washington, small folio, undated (6527) **85.00**

Water Fowl Shooting, small folio, undated (6562) **625.00**

Water Rail Shooting, small folio, 1870 (6568) **690.00**

Wedding Day (The), small folio, full-length portrait of couple about to enter church, N. Currier, undated (6596) **95.00**

Whale Fishery (The)—Cutting In, small folio, undated (6624) **1,425.00**

Whale Fishery (The)—Laying On, small folio, N. Currier, 1852 (6626) **1,125.00**

Wild Duck Shooting, small folio (6666) **540.00**

Windsor Castle and Park, medium folio, undated (6720) **185.00**

Winter in the Country—Getting Ice, large folio, 1864 (6737) **11,000.00**

Winter Pastime, after F. F. Palmer, medium folio, N. Currier, 1855 (6743) **2,500.00**

Wonderful Albino Family (The), small folio, undated (6763) **95.00**

Wonderful Mare "Maud S," small folio, 1880 (6765) **290.00**

Woodcock Shooting, small folio, 1870 (6775) . . **565.00**

"Wooding Up" on the Mississippi, after F. F. Palmer, large folio, 1863 (6776) **4,995.00**

Woodlands in Summer (The), small folio, undated (6778) **240.00**

Wreck of the "Atlantic" (The), small folio, 1873 (6787) **295.00**

Yacht "Dauntless" of N.Y., small folio, undated (6796) **380.00**

Yacht "Puritan" of Boston, large folio, 1885 (6810) **1,400.00**

Yacht "Sappho" of New York, 310 Tons, small folio, undated (6814) **230.00**

Yosemite Falls, California, small folio, undated (6829) **380.00**

Young Housekeeper (The), small folio, full-length portraits, N. Currier, undated (6856) . . **89.00**

CHAPTER

12

DECOYS

The use of bird decoys to attract wild game birds has a long history in North America. It has been discovered that Native Americans had used hand-made decoys in prehistoric times and when European settlers arrived they continued to use this craft, eventually hand-carving decoys to represent various game birds and water fowl. Throughout most of the 19th century decoys were individually hand-carved by individuals for their own use or

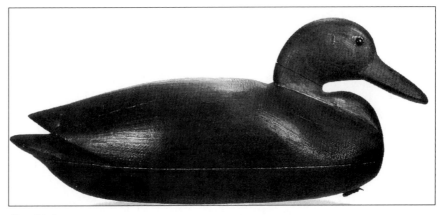

Fig. 12-1

local sale. It was not until the late 19th century that carved decoys were produced on a commercial scale by factories such as the Mason Decoy Factory in Detroit, Michigan. Throughout this century carvers in different regions of the United States have carved by hand a wide variety of decoys and today decoy carving continues among talented artisans.

Early decoys and those produced by noted carvers with careful hand-detailing are still readily available today and there is a strong market for the finest examples in top condition.

Photos courtesy of Gary Guyette & Frank Schmidt, W. Farmington, Maine

Black-bellied Plover, by Dave "Umbrella" Watson, Chincoteague, Virginia, carved wood w/good original paint w/minor wear, one tack eye partially rusted away, few shot scars, ca. 1900-10 . . . . **$7,150.00**

Black Duck, by Nathan Cobb, Cobb's Island, Virginia, hollow-carved wood, worn original paint, some thin cracks, old brass tack in top of head, ca. 1880 (Fig. 12-1) **23,100.00**

Black Duck, by Captain Wilbur Corwin, Bellport, Long Island, New York, carved wood w/early worn & weathered working paint, several small body gouges, old & crude bill repair, tight cracks in head, few shot scars, ca. 1873 (Fig. 12-2, left) **3,520.00**

Black Duck, by Albert Terry, Riverhead, Long Island, New York, carved wood w/probably old working repaint w/average wear, professional bill repair, some tight age cracks in body, old neck crack repair, serified initials "AT" in bottom, ca. 1870s (Fig. 12-2, right) **1,320.00**

Fig. 12-2

Black Duck, by Daniel Lake Leeds, Pleasantville, New Jersey, hollow-carved body in swimming pose w/round-bottom style, turned head w/glass eyes, original paint w/minor flaking & wear, thin wash of overpaint on some worn areas .. **1,650.00**

Black Duck, by Doug Jester, Chincoteague, Virginia, carved wood w/fine original scratch paint w/minor wear, desirable sleek form, ca. 1930s **770.00**

Fig. 12-3

Black Duck, by the Mason Decoy Factory, Detroit, Michigan, Premier grade, carved solid wood body w/snakey head slightly turned, strong original paint w/minor wear, several tiny body dents, small professional tail chip repair, ca. 1905 . . . . **2,750.00**

Bluebill Drake, by Willard C. Baldwin, Stratford, Connecticut, carved wood w/original paint w/minor wear on combed area of back, the remainder w/old in-use repaint, several small dents, stamped "WC BALDWIN 1923 FOR KEN PECK" on bottom **330.00**

Fig. 12-4

Bluebill Drake, by Robert Elliston, Bureau, Illinois, carved wood w/original paint w/very minor wear & good patina, slight wear to bill edges, ca. 1890 . . . . **7,425.00**

Bluebill Drake, by Delbert Hudson, Chincoteague, Virginia, carved wood w/original paint in near mint condition, very thin crack in neck, ca. 1930s **330.00**

Bluebill Hen, by Mark Kears, Northfield, New Jersey, hollow-carved body w/original paint in average condition, tight crack on the back, small chip in tail & on side of bill, ca. 1910 . . . . . **440.00**

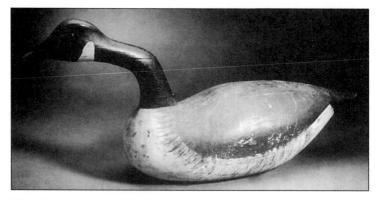

Fig. 12-5

Fig. 12-6

Fig. 12-7

Bluebill Hen, by the Ward Brothers, Crisfield, Maryland, solid carved wood in near mint condition, signed & dated "1970" **880.00**

Bluebill Hen & Drake, the Peterson Factory, Detroit, Michigan, carved wood w/tack eyes, outstanding original paint w/minor wear, drake w/thin age crack in bottom & neck filler gone, hen w/thin sliver missing on bill, ca. 1880, pr. **770.00**

Bluewing Teal Drake, by the Dodge Decoy Factory, Detroit, Michigan, carved wood w/original paint w/minor wear, some neck filler missing, some small dents, hairlines, slightly worn on tip of bill, ca. 1880 . . . . . **660.00**

Brant, by Ira Hudson, Chincoteague, Virginia, carved solid body w/original worn & weathered paint, narrow crack filled on back & under tail, thin neck crack, ca. 1920 . . . . **660.00**

Brant, by Henry Grant, Barnegat, New Jersey, carved wood w/original paint w/minor wear, old in-use touch-up on black area of tail, small chip missing from underside of bill, branded "LB" on underside & in weight, ca. 1900 (Fig. 12-3) **1,595.00**

Bufflehead Drake, by Mark English, Northfield, New Jersey, hollow-carved wood body w/early working repaint w/average wear, some nails at base of neck & back of head, ca. 1890 . . . . **770.00**

Bufflehead Drake, by Doug Jester, Chincoteague, Virginia, carved wood w/original paint w/moderate wear & some flaking, thin crack on back, some damage to top of head w/small nail holding chip in place, ca. 1920s **330.00**

Bufflehead Hen, by Harry V. Shourds, Tuckerton, New Jersey, hollow-carved wood, outstanding original paint w/minor wear & great patina, ca. 1890 (Fig. 12-4) **18,700.00**

Canada Goose, attributed to Joe Lincoln (1859-1938), carved wood w/original paint, extended neck pose, age cracks, 30" l., 12½" h. (Fig. 12-5) **9,775.00**

Canada Goose, Ward Brothers, Crisfield, Maryland, hollow-carved wood, original paint w/fine scratch feathering, all white & black areas w/old repaint, age split in back, several small rough areas in the bottom board, old repairs to neck, made for a hunting club on Deal Island, Virginia, ca. 1931 (Fig. 12-6) **2,475.00**

Canada Goose, by Levi Rhodes Truex, Atlantic City, New Jersey, hollow-carved wood, original paint w/minimal wear, tight age line on back, stamped w/collector's name & address, ca. 1920s (Fig. 12-7) **7,150.00**

Canvasback Hen, by Richard "Fresh-Air" Janson, San Pablo Bay, California, carved wood w/original paint w/minor wear & mellow finish, carved w/the skeg under the tail, ca. 1930 . . . . **1,925.00**

Canvasback Hen, by the Ward Brothers, Crisfield, Maryland, carved wood w/excellent original paint w/minor wear, thin neck crack, small gouges near tail, very minor roughness & couple of minor dents in bill, classic 1936 model **5,335.00**

Canvasback Hen & Drake, by John "Daddy" Holly, Havre de Grace, Maryland, carved wood w/several coats of old working repaint w/wear & flaking, early iron keels, drake w/some neck fractures, hen w/bill repair, ca. mid-to-late 19th c., pr. **715.00**

Crow, by the Mason Decoy Factory, Detroit, Michigan, carved wood w/glass eyes & original paint w/minor wear, crack in breast, small missing chip on one eye, hairline in bill **660.00**

Fig. 12-9

Dowitcher, carved wood w/long bill, original paint w/minor wear & mellow finish, original hardwood bill, holes drilled through body for stringing on the rig, from Cobb Island, Virginia, ca. 1890-1900 . . **2,475.00**

Eider Drake, oversized, carved wood, inlet head, old in-use repaint, several small cracks in neck reinforced w/small nails, light shot marks, slight roughness to tip of tail, Orrs Island, Maine, approximately 27½" l. (Fig. 12-8) **3,520.00**

Fig. 12-8

Goldeneye Hen, by Bill Hammel, Absecon, New Jersey, hollow-carved wood w/pegged construction & carved eyes, nice shoulder carving, old working repaint w/average wear, few shot scars, thin tight neck crack, ca. 1890 or earlier **743.00**

Greenwing Teal, by Emiel Garibaldi, Sacramento, California, so-called "Style No. 1," carved wood w/original paint w/minor wear & shrinkage, ca. 1928 . . . . **1,210.00**

Mallard Drake & Hen, by Hector Whittington, Oglesby, Illinois, hollow-carved wood, original paint w/minor wear, some minor blistering & flaking on hen, ca. 1947, pr. (Fig. 12-9) **1,870.00**

Merganser Drake & Hen, by the Mason Decoy Factory, Detroit, Michigan, Challenge grade, carved wood w/strong original paint w/minor wear & good patina, small defect in wood in hen's back, slight roughness on hen's bill & tip of tail, very slight roughness of edge of drake's bill, minor discoloration in white areas, pr. (Fig. 12-10) . . **11,550.00**

Fig. 12-10

Fig. 12-11

Fig. 12-13

Fig. 12-12

Fig. 12-14

Pintail Drake, by Robert Elliston, hollow-carved wood, cleaned down to original paint, well-carved head w/glass eyes & original lead weight marked "The Elliston Decoy," old damage to edge of bill, ca. 1925, 17" l. (Fig. 12-11) **440.00**

Pintail Drake, attributed to Walter Pelzer or possibly Earl Voelker, Milwaukee, Wisconsin, carved wood w/outstanding original paint w/mellowed finish, few dings & some minor damage at tip of bill, ca. mid-to-late 1940s (Fig. 12-12) **6,600.00**

Pintail Drake, by the Dodge Decoy Factory, Detroit, Michigan, carved wood w/original paint w/minor flaking & wear, small worn area on top of tail w/touch-up, crack & several small chips in neck filler, minor age lines, ca. 1880 . . . . **743.00**

Redbreasted Merganser Drake, attributed to Samuel Barton, Mathistown, New Jersey, carved wood w/mostly original paint w/some traces of very old & thin working overpaint, ca. 1900 or earlier **358.00**

Redhead Drake, by Harry V. Shourds, Tuckerton, New Jersey, carved wood w/old repaint in the Shourds style **440.00**

Ruddy Duck, carved wood w/old in-use repaint, end of bill worn off, numerous age lines & small dents, touch-up on white cheek patch, from Virginia **330.00**

Sandpiper, by Obediah Verity, Seaford, New York, carved wood w/relief wing carving & carved eyes, original paint w/good patina & minor wear, shot marks (Fig. 12-13, left) **1,870.00**

Sandpiper, attributed to William Southard, Seaford, New York, plump carved wood body w/carved wings & eyes, original paint w/minor wear, bill a professional replacement, several small dents in breast, hairline on one side (Fig. 12-13, right) **1,815.00**

Scoter Hen, by "Shang" Wheeler, Stratford, Connecticut, cork body w/finely carved wooden head, mint original paint w/good patina, several minor defects in the cork, ca. 1940 . . . . **3,575.00**

Wigeon Drake, by Joseph Lincoln, Accord, Massachusetts, carved wood, never rigged, fine original paint w/several slight scuffs, two paint drips on body, tip of bill broken & reattached (Fig. 12-14) **13,200.00**

Fig. 12-15

Fig. 12-16

Fig. 12-17

GROUP PHOTOGRAPHS

Black Duck, by Dan English, Florence, New Jersey, lowhead pose, hollow-carved wood w/fine incised feather carving & raised primaries, second coat of paint by English shows minimal wear, ca. 1940 (Fig. 12-15, left) **4,620.00**

Pintail Drake, by John Blair, Philadelphia, Pennsylvania, carved wood w/worn old paint w/traces of original, retains original weight, several small dents & small cracks, body halves joined by small wooden dowels, ca. 1870s (Fig. 12-15, right) **2,475.00**

Black Duck, by Samuel Smith, Tuckerton, New Jersey, well-carved wood w/original paint w/fine feather detail, good patina, very slight wear, tight crack in neck, several small holes where weight was attached, ca. 1920 (Fig. 12-16, left) **1,100.00**

Redhead Drake, by Chris Sprague, Beach Haven, New Jersey, carved wood w/original paint w/minor flaking & wear, signed at a later date (Fig. 12-16, right) **660.00**

Black Duck, by A.E. Crowell, E. Harwich, Massachusetts, carved wood w/original paint w/minor wear, minor wear around edges of tail, tip of bill slightly blunted, oval brand mark (Fig. 12-17, left) **1,485.00**

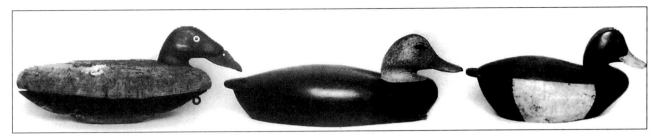

Fig. 12-18

Fig. 12-19

Fig. 12-20

Fig. 12-21

Redhead Hen, by Elmer Crowell, E. Harwich, Massachusetts, carved wood in early carving style w/carved crossed wing tips, fluted tail & slightly turned head, worn original paint, several minor age lines, light shot marks, pre-stamp mark (Fig. 12-17, right) **1,760.00**

Black Duck, by Reggie Culver, Stratford, Connecticut, hollow-carved wood, near mint, branded "R.I. Culver" (Fig. 12-18, center) . . . **485.00**

Bluebill Drake, by Reggie Culver, Stratford, Connecticut, hollow-carved wood, excellent original comb paint w/minor wear, branded "R.I. Culver" (Fig. 12-18, right) **413.00**

Scoter, by "Shang" Wheeler, Stratford, Connecticut, cork-bodied w/wooden head & keel, body attached to keel w/small wooden dowels, original paint w/moderate wear, speculums w/old in-use touch-up, moderate shrinkage & cracking to cork (Fig. 12-18, left) **605.00**

Bluebill Drake, by Wendell Smith, Chicago, Illinois, hollow-carved wood w/original paint & glass eyes, minor wear, ca. 1930, 13" l. (Fig. 12-19, left) **110.00**

Redhead Drake, by Frank Louis, Ogdensburg, New York, "Ogdensburg Humpback"-type, carved wood w/old working repaint w/original paint beneath, tack eyes, inlet head & hinged weight, edge wear & crack in neck, pre-1925, 13" l. (Fig. 12-19, right) **61.00**

Redbreasted Merganser Hen, by Sam Toothacher, Brunswick, Maine, carved wood w/worn paint, signed on base, split, losses to tail, 16¼" l. (Fig. 12-20, left) **489.00**

Fig. 12-22

Surf Scooter, attributed to Wendell Gilley, hollow-carved wood w/carved wing tips, paint wear, cracks, 20" l. (Fig. 12-20, right) **1,725.00**

American Eider, full-carved body of solid construction, retains old working paint, minor loss to front of bill, northern coast of Maine, 17" l. (Fig. 12-21, bottom row, center) **172.00**

American Eider, full-carved wooden body of solid construction, retains most of the original paint, cracks, northern coast of Maine, possibly Orrs Island, 20th c., 17³⁄₄" l. (Fig. 12-21, middle row, far right) **172.00**

Black Duck, full-carved wood of solid construction, original paint worn to a fine patina, minor loss to tip of bill, northern coast of Maine, possibly Orrs Island, early 20th c., 21¹⁄₂" l. (Fig. 12-21, top row, right) . . **115.00**

Canada Goose, full-carved wood body of solid construction, in a swimming position w/carved eyes, remnants of original paint, probably from the Annapolis Valley, Nova Scotia, 25" l. (Fig. 12-21, bottom row, left) **345.00**

Canvasback Drake, primitive full-carved solid body in high head position w/glass eyes, retains most of the original paint, branded w/an "E," crack down center of back, northeastern Wisconsin, ca. 1930, 17" l. (Fig. 12-21, middle row, center) **460.00**

Eider Drake, by John McCay, Little Harbor, Nova Scotia, full-carved solid body, retains some of the original paint, minor loss to bill, signed on base "John McCay, Little Harbor," ca. 1930, 16¹⁄₂" l. (Fig. 12-21, middle row, left) **172.00**

Fig. 12-23

Eider Hen, by John McCay, Little Harbor, Nova Scotia, full-carved solid body, retains worn original paint, loss to tip of bill, base signed "John McCay, Little Harbor, N.S.," 17" l. (Fig. 12-21, top row, left) **115.00**

Goldeneye Drake, attributed to R. Webber, northern coast of Maine, full-carved solid body w/an inlet bill, original paint, branded "R. Webber," 20th c., 16¼" l. (Fig. 12-21, top row, center) **287.00**

Surf Scoter, full-carved solid body in preening position, retains most of the original paint, carved initials "CENN," cracks & losses, northern coast of Maine, 20¾" l. (Fig. 12-21, bottom row, right) **402.00**

Bluebill Hen, Mason Decoy Factory, Challenge grade, carved wood w/extra wide round bill style, fine paint detail, minimal wear, short hairline crack in one side, tiny dent in head (Fig. 12-22, bottom row, left) **935.00**

Merganser Drake, Mason Decoy Factory, Premier grade, carved wood w/'snakey' head, original paint w/moderate wear & flaking, some shot scars, initials "H.C." on bottom (Fig. 12-22, bottom row, right) . . **1,403.00**

Scoters, Mason Decoy Factory, Standard grade, carved wood w/tack eyes, good original paint, hen w/age split in underside, drake w/crack in back & several small paint rubs, pr. (Fig. 12-22, center row) **3,850.00**

Wigeon Drake, Mason Decoy Factory, Standard grade, carved wood w/glass eyes, fine original paint w/minor wear, minor flaking on neck filler, gunner's name stenciled on the back in black (Fig. 12-22, top row, left) **1,595.00**

Wigeon Hen, Mason Decoy Factory, Standard grade, carved wood w/glass eyes, fine original paint w/minor wear, minor touch-up on neck filler, thin crack in bottom (Fig. 12-22, top row, right) **1,485.00**

Egret, roothead confidence-type, full-carved solid body, worn natural wood w/a fine patina, mounted on an iron rod & a black wood base, cracks, probably from New Jersey, 15½" l. (Fig. 12-23, center) **57.00**

Eider Drake, full-carved solid wood body w/a carved bill & head, retains some original paint w/fine worn patina, weighted by a large mule shoe secured by square nails, northern coast of Maine, 21" l. (Fig. 12-23, bottom row, left) **345.00**

Plover, full-carved solid body w/shoe button eyes, in an overlook position w/detailed

Fig. 12-24

wing carving, retains original spring plumage paint w/minor losses, signed on bottom "R. Birch," mounted on a wood rod & a naturalistic wood base, 7³/₄" l. (Fig. 12-23, top row, right) **287.00**

Shorebird, full-carved solid body in snakey-head feeding position, carved eyes & primary feathers, original paint w/minor losses, signed "R. Birch," mounted on a wood rod & a naturalistic wood base, 10¹/₂" l. (Fig. 12-23, top row, left) **690.00**

Surf Scoter, full-carved solid wood body w/glass eyes, finely carved w/raised wing tips, detailed nostril & nail at the bill, additional board added to the bottom for flotation, loss to tip of tail, northern coast of Maine, 22" l. (Fig. 12-23, bottom row, right) **575.00**

Black-Bellied Plover, by Daniel Lake Leeds, Pleasantville, New Jersey, carved wood w/fine original paint w/minor wear, bill may be later replacement, ca. 1900 (Fig. 12-24, bottom right) **3,020.00**

Curlew, by Daniel Lake Leeds, Pleasantville, New Jersey, carved wood in near mint condition, ca. 1890 (Fig. 12-24, top left) **14,300.00**

Curlew, by Harry V. Shourds, Tuckerton, New Jersey, carved full-body style, good original paint w/very slight wear & good patina, most of bill a professional replacement, lightly hit by shot (Fig. 12-24, top right) **2,750.00**

Robin Snipe, by H.V. Shourds, Tuckerton, New Jersey, carved wood w/original paint w/minor wear, bill appears to be a professional replacement, ca. 1900 (Fig. 12-24, bottom left) **2,970.00**

Sanderling, by Dan Lake Leeds, Pleasantville, New Jersey, carved wood w/dry original paint w/minor wear, original hardwood inserted bill, ca. 1890-1900 (Fig. 12-24, bottom center) **3,300.00**

Black-Bellied Plover, by William Bowman, Lawrence, Long Island, New York, good original paint in intermediate plumage

Fig. 12-25

w/some wear, front part of the bill
professionally restored, several shot scars,
some small tail chips, branded initials
"R.L." for owner, ca. 1890 (Fig. 12-25,
bottom row, right) **7,150.00**

Curlew, oversized, carved wood w/original
paint w/good patina, minor wear, age split
in lower side filled, several small dents &
shot marks, shoe button eyes, attributed by
some to Captain Al Ketchum (Long Island,
New York), Southport, Connecticut,
approximately 19" l. (Fig. 12-25, middle
center) **2,750.00**

Greater Yellowlegs, by Thomas Gelston,
Quogue, New York, carved wood in running

stance, head slightly cocked & relief wing
carving, original paint w/minor shrinkage &
wear, several small dents & hairline cracks,
small chip at stick hole, several tiny nail
holes on underside (Fig. 12-25, bottom
center) **3,300.00**

Robin Snipe, by John Dilley, Quogue, New
York, carved wood w/original paint w/good
detail, old bill touch-up, moderate shot
hits, short hairline in bottom, original bill,
ca. 1880 (Fig. 12-25, bottom left) **4,400.00**

Willet, by John Dilley, Quogue, New York,
carved wood w/good original paint w/fine
detail & good patina, some discoloration on
back (Fig. 12-25, top center) **10,450.00**

DOLL FURNITURE & ACCESSORIES

Fig. 13-1

Dry sink, hard wood w/bird's-eye maple
doors below small drawer & well
(Fig. 13-1) . . . . **$1,200.00 to 2,000.00**

Coffee grinder, "Little Tot," wood & iron
(Fig. 13-1, top left) . . . . **150.00 to 175.00**

Tea kettle, iron w/a slide lid & bail handle
w/wooden grip (Fig. 13-1, in well) . . **100.00 to 150.00**

Tea kettle, copper, rounded cylindrical shape
w/straight spout & bail handle w/wooden
grip (Fig. 13-1, bottom left) . . . **100.00 to 150.00**

Rocking chair w/arms, Lincoln-style, shaped &
pierced crestrail w/open scroll arms,
upholstered, tufted back, serpentine seatrail,
mid-19th c. (Fig. 13-2, left) . . . **900.00 to 1,500.00**

Fig. 13-2

Sewing table, Classical style, mahogany, rectangular top w/beaded edges above a round-fronted drawer over a drawer w/wooden knob, on a tapering square pedestal & cross-form base w/block feet, mid-19th c. (Fig. 13-2, right) . . . . **1,200.00 to 1,800.00**

Tea set, Staffordshire china decorated w/lustre-trimmed florals, ca. 1840, the set (Fig. 13-2, on sewing table) . . . . **1,200.00 to 1,800.00**

Secretary-bookcase, fruitwood, the rectangular top w/a stepped cornice above a pair of glazed cupboard doors opening to a shelf above a narrow slant-lid w/recessed oblong panels opening to a fitted interior above a pair of drawers w/small wooden knobs above a pair of recessed panel cupboard doors centered by roundels & flanked by half-round colonettes at the sides, flat molded base, last quarter 19th c. (Fig. 13-3) . . . . **2,000.00 to 2,800.00**

Fig. 13-3

FRAKTUR

Fig. 14-1

The word "fraktur" refers to a wide range of hand-painted or printed documents which were produced in the 18th and early 19th centuries in this country, mainly for the Pennsylvania German population. Colorful designs and German inscriptions highlight fraktur which often served as birth and baptism records, marriage records, book plates or simply decorative drawings. Stylized birds, flowers, angels, and hex signs can be found on the most desirable early fraktur examples and rare and unusual hand-drawn designs fetch very high prices today. Known as "fraktur" because the German inscrip-tions resembled a 16th century type face of that name, this unique folk art was often practiced by local ministers, schoolmasters or talented itinerant penmen.

Baptism record for Johannes Haeffner, pen & ink & water-color on paper, a central oblong reserve flanked by two pairs of colorful birds on flowering branches & two mermaids at the top, done in red, yellow & blue, signed & dated "Peter Bernhart 1804," Augusta County, Virgina, framed, 8¼ × 13" (Fig. 14-1) **$8,050.00**

Fig. 14-2

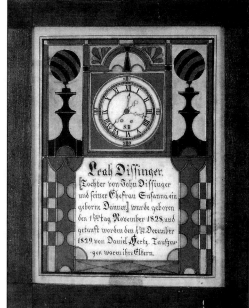

Fig. 14-3

Baptism record for Daniel Leithner, pen & ink & water-color on paper, a large heart-shaped central reserve filled w/a long inscription below a small spread-winged American eagle w/shield & framed by colorful tulips, hex signs & other flowers, two small heart-shaped reserves w/inscriptions at the bottom, done in bright red, yellow, blue & green, signed "Johannes Bard," dated "1838," York County, Pennsylvania, framed, 13 × 16¼" (Fig. 14-2) **11,500.00**

Birth record for Leah Dissinger, pen & ink & water-color on paper, decorated in maroon, pale olive-green, green & taupe & centering a Roman & Arabic chapter-ringed clock face initialed at the base "S.B." & flanked on either side by striped spheres on cyma-scrolled supports above gridded & alternatingly pigmented columns all enclosing the German inscription, by Samuel Bentz, the "Mount Pleasant artist," dated 1829, Lancaster County, Pennsylvania, framed, 7½ × 9⅝" (Fig. 14-3) **11,500.00**

Birth record for Elizabeth Ernst, pen & ink & water-color on paper, a large central oblong keystone filled w/a German inscription & flanked by stylized tulips & other flowers & leaves, done in red & blue, signed & dated "Peter Bernhart Keezletown Virginia 1803,"

Rockingham County, Virginia, framed, 8 × 13" (Fig. 14-4) **4,887.00**

Birth record for Frederick Krebs, printed paper decorated w/pen & ink & water-color, a large central heart filled w/a German inscription above two small hearts w/inscriptions all framed by undulating leafy vines w/stylized blossoms at the corners, decorated in red & green, dated "1797," Northampton County, Pennsylvania, framed, 16 × 19" (stains, creases, small hole) **495.00**

Birth record for Jacob Kuhn, pen & ink & water-color on paper, a large central heart filled w/a German inscription & framed by radiating tulips, berries & leafy tendrils, done in red, yellow & green, attributed to Daniel Otto, the "Flat Tulip artist," dated "1818," southeastern Pennsylvania, framed, 8 × 13" (Fig. 14-5) **3,220.00**

Birth record for Lidia Otto, pen & ink & water-color on paper, a large, elongated central heart filled w/the German inscription, flanked at the bottom outside by standing figures of ladies wearing striped dresses & flanking large flowering vines & facing birds, flowering leafy vines w/perched birds across the top of the heart, done in shades of red, yellow, green & blue, dated "1843," attributed to William Otto, Schuylkill County, Pennsylvania, framed, 12 × 15" (Fig. 14-6) **21,850.00**

Birth record for Jacob Rohland, pen & ink & water-color on paper, a large central heart in maroon & brown flanked above & below by red, green, blue & yellow parrots, tulips, vines, flowers & a smaller Angel Sofia-capped heart, Lebanon Township, Dauphin County, Pennsylvania, dated "1792," attributed to Christian Mertel, framed, 11³/₄ × 15¹/₄" (Fig. 14-7) **10,925.00**

Birth record for Anna Maria Trewer, pen & ink & water-color on a printed paper form, a central rectangular reserve w/the German inscription surrounded by a wide colorful continuous border of flowering vines & large birds, a winged angel-headed heart at the center bottom, dated "1764," Carores Township, York County, Pennsylvania, framed, 13¹/₄ × 16³/₈" (Fig. 14-8) **2,185.00**

Birth record for Johannes Weiss, pen & ink & water-color on laid paper, a large central ring filled w/a delicate flowering vine & enclosing the German inscription w/a heart at the bottom edge, the sides decorated w/tall stylized flowering vines, a pair of stylized flying angels at the top corners, done in red, green, yellow & black, dated "1806," Northampton County, Pennsylvania, attributed to the Flying Angel artist, framed, 16¹/₄ × 19⁷/₈" (wear, damaged fold lines, old repair, some color fading & bleeding) **990.00**

Birth record for Georg Zigler, pen & ink & water-color on paper, a large colored heading entwined w/flowers above the colored inscription flanked by tall stylized potted tulips & another tulip spray at the center bottom, dated "1814," Shenandoah Valley, Virginia, framed, 12⁵/₈ × 15" (Fig. 14-9) **8,625.00**

Birth records for Catarina & Elizabeth Westenberger, pen & ink & water-color on paper w/pin pricking, matching designs w/a large central tulip blossom above a small heart filled w/a German inscription above a small urn-form vase, the sides w/pairs of matching facing birds & large tulip blossoms, done

Fig. 14-4

Fig. 14-5

Fig. 14-6

Fig. 14-7

Fig. 14-8

Fig. 14-9

Fig. 14-11

Fig. 14-10

Courtesy of Sotheby's

in yellow, green, & red, each signed "Christian Bamberger," dated "1832," Lebanon County, Pennsylvania, framed, 10 × 12", pr. (Fig. 14-10) **25,300.00**

Birth & baptismal record for Anna Margreta Bishop, pen & ink & water-color on paper, a large central brown & gold heart filled w/a German inscription flanked on each side by a large rampant unicorn & crowned small animals & w/a pair of facing parrots flanking a smaller heart at the top, done in red, dark green, brown & gold, dated "1791," attributed to Christian Mertel, Lancaster County, Pennsylvania, framed, 12¼ × 15½" (Fig. 14-11) **32,200.00**

Birth & baptismal record for Henry Brider, pen & ink & water-color on paper, a central rectangular block filled w/a German inscription & topped by a tree-filled landscape w/a large red & small yellow house, two large starbursts at the top corners & large, tall scrolling potted flowers along the sides w/another pot of flowers across the bottom, done in red, yellow & green, dated "1823," attributed to Abraham Huth, Lebanon County, Pennsylvania, framed, 12¼ × 15¼" (Fig. 14-12) **12,650.00**

Birth & baptismal record for Peter Hansel, pen & ink & water-color on paper, the title & central German inscription flanked by a pair of facing ladies holding bouquets of flowers, a spread-winged eagle w/shield at the center bottom, done in shades of light brown & brown, foxing, paper tears, dated "1831," framed, 11¾ × 14¾" (Fig. 14-13) **1,035.00**

Birth & baptismal record for Elisabeth Schlosser, pen & ink & water-color on paper, a large colorful central heart w/a serrated edge frames the German inscription, flanked by a pair of large tulip blossoms atop long, curved flowering stems ending in small hearts w/further inscriptions, done in pale red, yellow, green & black, dated "1808," Lehigh (formerly Northampton) County, Pennsylvania, framed, 7⅝ × 13" (Fig. 14-14) **2,990.00**

Fig. 14-12

Fig. 14-13

Fig. 14-14

Fig. 14-15

Fig. 14-16

Fig. 14-17

Birth & death record for Johannes Lindemuth, pen & ink & water-color on paper, the name of the deceased in very large colored letters across the top above a graduated German inscription trimmed w/flowering vines, all within a double-banded border filled w/flowering vines & w/florette-decorated corner blocks, dated "1815," attributed to the Stony Creek artist, Shenandoah County, Virginia, framed, 13½ × 16½" (Fig. 14-15) **13,225.00**

Bookplate, pen & ink & water-color on paper, inscription in German "This testament belongs to Susanna Metz, 1819," all within a narrow wavy border, done in red, yellow, black & green, minor wear & damage, Pennsylvania, framed, 8¾ × 10¾" (Fig. 14-16) **440.00**

Drawing, pen & ink & water-color on paper, a dramatic picture of a lady on horseback, titled under the horse "Malley Quen of Sedburg," done in shades of brown, red, blue, gold & black, attributed to the Washington-Sussel artist, late 18th c., 6⅜ × 8" (Fig. 14-17) **54,625.00**

Drawing, pen & ink & water-color on paper, a large stylized parrot-like bird decorated w/bands of black, red & yellow, wavy &

Fig. 14-18   Fig. 14-19

straight corner bands in red & black & another band across the top, inscribed "Jacob Henley his - Quill 1819," possibly northern Lancaster or Huntington County, Pennsylvania, framed, 3½ × 5⅜" (Fig. 14-18) **10,925.00**

Drawing, pen & ink & water-color on paper, a tall bouquet of colorful flowers w/a central tulip flanked by flowering, scrolling leafy vines all issuing from a domed base w/feathered trim all within a narrow border band, done in red, yellow & green, early 19th c., framed, 13 × 15¾" (Fig. 14-19) . . **6,612.00**

Drawing, pen & ink & water-color on paper, a rectangular sheet w/a dividing band down the center, on the left side a large figure of a standing woman wearing a long brown dress, neckerchief & top hat framed by large stylized blossoms & standing above a script German inscription, on the right side a large figure of a standing man wearing a red swallow-tailed jacket, yellow pants, white vest & black top hat & also framed by large stylized blossoms & standing above a script German inscription, attributed to Frederick Krebs, Pennsylvania, late 18th c., framed, 12½ × 15¼" (Fig. 14-20) **33,350.00**

House blessing, printed paper decorated w/pen & ink & water-color, the vertical page centering a decorated heart enclosing a

printed house blessing, the whole surrounded by twelve individual printed & hand-colored blessings in small hearts, a pair of large facing parrots at the top & stylized flowers & starbursts down the sides, done in red, green, yellow & blue, attributed to Heinrich Otto, Lancaster & Northumberland Counties, Pennsylvania, dated "1785," framed, 12¾ × 16" (Fig. 14-21) **5,750.00**

Presentation fraktur, pen & ink & water-color on paper, large strapwork colored letters w/a presentation for Sara Jacckelin, trimmed w/delicate flowering vines & all within an entwined flowering vine border, done in red, yellow, blue & green, late 18th c., framed, 4⅜ × 7¼" (Fig. 14-22, top) **2,070.00**

Presentation fraktur, pen & ink & water-color on paper, a large, long-necked bird perched amid leafy vines w/large stylized flowers above the date "1817" & a lower register w/a German presentation inscription for Carel Gerhart, Pennsylvania, framed, 5½ × 7⅜" (Fig. 14-22, bottom) **2,300.00**

Valentine fraktur, pencil, crayon & pen & ink on ledger paper w/cut-out birds & hearts & a long German Valentine inscription w/sixteen verses, decorated in yellow, orange & blue, framed, 17" sq. (some damage at fold lines & corners) **1,760.00**

Fig. 14-20

Fig. 14-21

Fig. 14-22   *Courtesy of Sotheby's*

Chippendale curly maple tall chest of drawers, ca. 1780 (see Fig. 15-24).

C H A P T E R

15

FURNITURE

BEDS

**Classical country-style low poster child's
bed,** painted & decorated, the boldly
arched headboard w/incurved sides
mounted between baluster- and ring-turned
posts w/large knob finials, raised on
tapering baluster-turned legs w/knob ankles
& long peg feet, footboard w/slightly shorter
posts, original rosewood grain painting,
Maine, second quarter 19th c., some
surface imperfections, 32¼ × 72", 41" h.
(Fig. 15-1) **$633.00**

**Classical country-style tall poster canopy
bed,** hardwood, the headboard w/a wide
board w/scroll-cut terminals between
slightly tapering cylindrical posts topped by
ring turnings & tapering pointed finials
supporting the gently arched canopy frame,
matching footpost w/a simple rail, original
side rails now fitted w/iron brackets for box
springs, first half 19th c. (Fig. 15-2) . . . **1,430.00**

BENCHES

Dining bench, carved & painted pine, the
long, wide, flat-topped crestrail w/shaped
ends raised on flat shaped stiles flanking a
double-section back w/two scalloped & cut-
out splats flanking a center flat slat all on a
raised rail above the long plank seat

Fig. 15-1

w/rounded front corners, on slender square
tapering pointed & canted legs, old olive
brown paint w/black accents, Germany, mid-
19th c., imperfections, 62½" l., 37½" h.
(Fig. 15-3) **575.00**

Utility bench, painted, a long rectangular top
w/a low gallery overhanging one-board
supports w/bootjack feet joined by a medial
shelf w/a low backboard, original cranberry
red paint, minor surface imperfections, New
England, late 19th c., 13¼ × 49½", 35¼" h.
(Fig. 15-4) **748.00**

Fig. 15-2

Fig. 15-3

Fig. 15-4

CHAIRS

Chippendale side chair, carved mahogany, the ox-bow crestrail w/reeded ears & centered by a shell crest above an interlaced volute-carved splat & upholstered slip seat, on stop-fluted square legs joined by flat stretchers, repairs to crest, Goddard-Townsend School, Newport, Rhode Island, ca. 1775 (Fig. 15-5) **1,610.00**

Chippendale country-style side chair, carved birch, the ox-yoke crestrail w/incised ears & centering a shell carving above the pierced

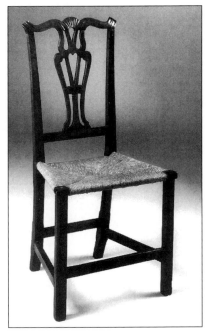

Fig. 15-5   Fig. 15-6   Fig. 15-7

Fig. 15-8

vase-form splat, the woven rush seat on molded square legs joined by flat box stretchers, New England, second half 18th c. (Fig. 15-6) **1,610.00**

Chippendale country-style side chair, carved cherry, an ox-yoke crestrail w/rounded ears on gently shaped stiles flanking the scroll-pierced back splat, upholstered seat on a flat seatrail & square legs joined by box stretchers, old refinish, minor imperfections, possibly by Eliphalet Chapin, East Windsor, Connecticut, ca. 1780, 38" h. (Fig. 15-7) **805.00**

Classical "fancy" side chairs, painted & decorated, a scalloped tablet crestrail centering a painted bouquet flanked by yellow-painted swags above a pierced urn-shaped splat painted in green & yellow centering three painted buds flanked by baluster-turned & painted stiles over a shaped plank seat, on tapering knob-turned front legs & plain turned rear legs, knob-turned front stretcher & plain turned side stretchers, Pennsylvania, 19th c., 33¾" h., pr. (Fig. 15-8) **1,035.00**

Classical side chairs, country-style, tiger stripe & bird's-eye maple, the rounded crestrail continuing to stiles flanking a lyre-form splat on a lower rail above the slightly concave rectangular caned seat, flat front sabre legs joined by a curved, flat stretcher, turned side & back stretchers, New England or New York State, ca. 1835, refinished, repairs, 33¼" h., set of 8 (Fig. 15-9) **2,185.00**

Country-style "balloon-back" side chairs, painted & decorated, the "balloon-back" w/a wide crestrail decorated w/polychrome florals curving in & flanking a wide vase-form splat decorated w/pinstriping above the shaped plank seat, on knob-turned front legs joined by a turned stretcher & plain turned rear legs & plain side & rear stretchers, original brown background paint w/pink & yellow striping, ca. 1850, 34½" h., set of 6 (Fig. 15-10 of one) **1,650.00**

Fig. 15-9

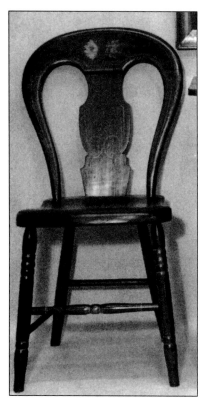

Fig. 15-10

Fig. 15-11

Fig. 15-12

Early American country-style highchair,
turned walnut, the back composed of three
baluster-turned rungs between simple
round stiles w/knob finials, low open rail
arms w/turned hand-holds & arm supports
continuing down to form front legs, a woven
splint seat, complete w/narrow footrest &
double set of box stretchers on the tall legs,
original dark surface, Pennsylvania, 34" h.
(Fig. 15-11) **546.00**

Federal country-style side chair, cherry, the
arched crestrail raised on gently flaring
stiles flanking the pierced baluster-form
splat centered by a small carved urn,
trapezoidal woven rush seat, on square
tapering molded front legs joined by an
H-stretcher & a rear stretcher, probably
Connecticut, ca. 1790, 39" h. (Fig. 15-12) . . **633.00**

Queen Anne country-style armchair, painted
& turned, the simple ox-yoke crestrail raised

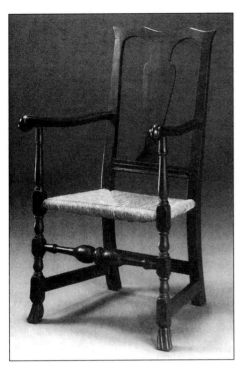

Fig. 15-13

Fig. 15-14

Fig. 15-15

on flat stiles flanking the plain vase-form splat on a lower molded rail, shaped open arms w/scrolled hand holds on baluster-turned arm supports over the woven rush seat, baluster- and block-turned front legs joined by a bulbous turned front stretcher, flat stretchers at the sides & back, front Spanish feet, painted reddish brown, appears to retain an old, possibly 19th c. or original finish, New England, 1740-70 (Fig. 15-13) **2,300.00**

Queen Anne country-style rocking chair w/arms, maple, the ox-yoke crest w/curved corners above baluster- and knob-turned stiles flanking the vase-form splat above flat half-arms on slender baluster- and ring-turned arm supports, woven rush seat, boldly turned ring- and rod-turned front legs joined by a baluster- and ring-turned front stretcher & plain turned side & back stretchers, added shaped rockers, old varnish-stained surface, Connecticut, late 18th - early 19th c., 42" h. (Fig. 15-14) **201.00**

William & Mary "banister-back" side chair, stained maple & ash, the C-scroll & foliate-carved arched crest above four turned split banisters & a scroll-carved stayrail flanked by turned stiles w/ball-turned

finials above a trapezoidal rush seat w/maple corner blocks, on block- and baluster-turned front legs ending in Spanish feet & joined by a double-knob-and-ring-turned stretcher, knob-turned stretchers at the sides & a plain turned stretcher at the rear, eastern Massachusetts, 1715-40, 45¾" h. (Fig. 15-15) **4,600.00**

Windsor "bow-back broken-arm" armchair, ash, the widely bowed crestrail over seven plain tall spindles flanked by flat curved arms raised on three canted plain spindles & extending beyond the crestrail, on a shaped saddle seat on canted baluster- and ring-turned legs joined by a swelled H-stretcher, possibly New England, ca. 1800, old refinish, 35" h. (Fig. 15-16) **2,070.00**

Windsor "bow-back" armchairs, pine, ash & mahogany, the arched crestrail continuing down to form shaped arms above nine bamboo-turned spindles, S-scroll arm supports, shaped saddle seat, raised on canted bamboo-turned legs joined by an unusual spoke-stretcher w/incurved front rail, branded "Seavers and Frost," Boston, Massachusetts, 1790-1810, old refinish, minor imperfections, 38" h., pr. (Fig. 15-17) **4,600.00**

Fig. 15-16

Fig. 15-17

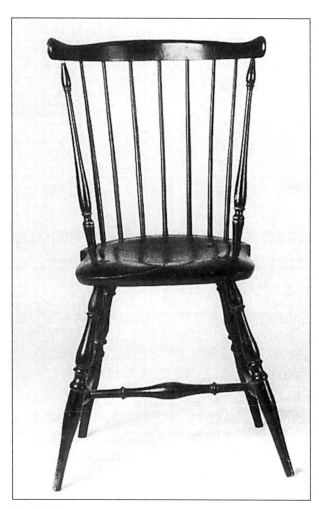

Fig. 15-18

Fig. 15-19

Fig. 15-20

Windsor "fan-back" side chair, painted, the slightly serpentine crestrail over seven nearly vertical slender spindles between nearly vertical baluster-turned stiles, on a shaped saddle seat raised on canted baluster- and ring-turned legs joined by a swelled H-stretcher, old black paint, New England, ca. 1790, 37" h. (Fig. 15-18) **920.00**

Windsor "sack-back" armchair, turned wood, the bowed crestrail above seven tall, plain spindles over a medial rail continuing to shaped arms above a plain spindle & a baluster- and ring-turned canted arm support, wide shaped seat, on canted baluster- and ring-turned legs joined by a swelled H-stretcher, old varnished & stained surface, Massachusetts, 18th c., imperfections, 39" h. (Fig. 15-19) **2,530.00**

CHESTS & CHESTS OF DRAWERS

Blanket chest, country-style, painted & decorated pine, six-board construction, rectangular hinged top w/molded edges opening to a deep well, on a flat, molded base, decorated overall w/a bold swirled & looped burnt sienna & tan wood-grained design, probably Pennsylvania, ca. 1830, ball feet missing, 18½ × 28", 19" h. (Fig. 15-20) **1,093.00**

Blanket chest, Federal country-style, painted & decorated, the rectangular hinged top w/molded edge opening to a well, a molded base on short ring-turned legs, the sides decorated w/overall grain painting imitating crotch grain mahogany & w/vertical forked branches, Pennsylvania, ca. 1820, 23 × 48", 25" h. (Fig. 15-21) **1,610.00**

Blanket chest, Pilgrim Century, painted yellow pine, the rectangular top w/molded edges opening to a deep well, the flaring stepped base molding raised on bun feet, vestiges of early painted decoration, possibly Milford, Connecticut, early 18th c., feet replaced, imperfections, 20 × 42½", 26½" h. (Fig. 15-22) **920.00**

Chippendale tall chest of drawers, curly maple, the rectangular top w/a molded cornice above a pair of short drawers above four long graduated drawers all w/simple bail pulls, some w/oval brass keyhole escutcheons, molded base on simple bracket feet, rich honey color, some damages at drawer edges, New England, ca. 1770, 21 × 38", 4' 1⅞" h. (Fig. 15-23) **4,025.00**

Fig. 15-21

Fig. 15-22

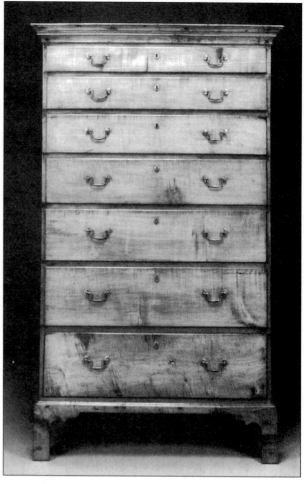

Fig. 15-24

Fig. 15-23

Chippendale tall chest of drawers, curly maple, rectangular top w/deep flaring molded cornice above a case w/seven long graduated drawers w/simple bail pulls & oval keyhole escutcheons, molded base on tall bracket feet, appears to retain original brasses, Rhode Island, ca. 1780, 20½ X 39½", 5' 4¾" h. (Fig. 15-24) **6,900.00**

Classical country-style chest of drawers, cherry & curly maple, the rectangular top w/rounded front edge above a pair of very deep drawers slightly overhanging a case of three long graduated drawers flanked by half-round ring- and rod-turned pilasters ending on blocks above short baluster-turned front legs w/knob feet, curly maple drawer fronts, replaced early clear pressed glass pulls, old worn finish, wear & some edge damage, ca. 1840, 22½ X 43", 4' 3" h. (Fig. 15-25) **990.00**

Fig. 15-25

Fig. 15-26

Fig. 15-27

Country-style multi-drawer chest, pine & poplar, the narrow rectangular top above a case w/a row of four small drawers over a row of four slightly deeper drawers over a row of three larger drawers w/a deep long drawer at the bottom, scalloped apron & bootjack ends, original graining on the top w/mahogany staining on the drawers, some original turned wood pulls, imperfections, New England, ca. 1840, 8½ × 23½", 23½" h. (Fig. 15-26) **1,380.00**

Mule chest (box chest w/one or more drawers below a storage compartment), William & Mary country-style, cherry, a rectangular hinged top w/molded edges opening to a deep well faced by two molded false drawers over two long working drawers, all w/brass butterfly pulls, molded base & short stile legs, dark stained finish, old replaced brasses, New England, early 18th c., imperfections, 18½ × 30¼", 41½" h. (Fig. 15-27) **1,035.00**

CUPBOARDS

Corner cupboard, Chippendale country-style, pine, one-piece construction, the flat top over a tall open section w/three scalloped shelves above a mid-molding over a tall raised-panel cupboard door in the base w/"H" hinges, flat base, refinished, shelves painted blue, Middle Atlantic States, 18th c., original doors missing, repairs, 16 × 45", 6' 10" h. (Fig. 15-28) **1,380.00**

Fig. 15-28

Fig. 15-29

Corner cupboard, Federal country-style, cherry, one-piece construction, the flat top w/a cove-molded cornice above a pair of tall eight-pane cupboard doors opening to three shelves above a narrow mid-molding over a pair of panelled cupboard doors w/wooden knobs & an oval keyhole escutcheon, wood thumb-latches, flat base, old mellow refinishing, some edge damage, minor repairs, early 19th c., 53¾" w., 6' 11" h. (Fig. 15-29) **1,320.00**

Pie safe, butternut & mixed woods, the rectangular top above a pair of drawers w/wooden knobs above a pair of tall three-panel cupboard doors, each panel w/punched tin inserts featuring a design of a large central star in a circle surrounded by diamonds & ovals, flat apron & tapering bracket feet, Ohio or western Pennsylvania, mid-19th c. (Fig. 15-30) **1,100.00**

Fig. 15-30

Fig. 15-31

15-33

Fig. 15-32

Wall cupboard, country-style, painted pine, rectangular top above a pair of flat cupboard doors w/wooden turn latches, flat apron & bootjack ends, four interior shelves, old green paint, New England, mid-19th c., imperfections, 14³/₄ × 28¹/₂", 35" h. (Fig. 15-31) **2,415.00**

Wall cupboard, country-style, one-piece construction, a narrow flat rectangular top above a tall case w/a narrow tall door w/small knob & thumb latch, wide front side boards notched to form cut-out feet, old blue paint, Pennsylvania, mid-19th c., imperfections, 16¹/₂ × 35¹/₂", 5' ³/₄" h. (Fig. 15-32) **920.00**

Wall cupboard, painted, one-piece construction, the rectangular top w/a narrow dentil-carved cornice above a pair of tall double raised-panel cupboard doors w/rattail hinges & one w/a knob & keyhole opening to a three-shelved interior, early blue paint, Canada, late 18th c., some paint loss, minor foot repairs, 17³/₄ × 48", 5' 3¹/₄" h. (Fig. 15-33) **3,335.00**

Wall cupboard, late Victorian, mixed woods, one-piece construction, the rectangular top w/a narrow stepped cornice above a pair of tall arch-topped glazed cupboard doors

Fig. 15-34

Fig. 15-35

opening to three shelves above a pair of chamfer-edged drawers decorated w/incised leaf bands & stamped brass pulls above a wide paneled door w/incised leaf designs beside a stack of four small square drawers beside a tall, narrow paneled door decorated w/incised roundels, corner brackets at front feet, ca. 1890-1910 (Fig. 15-34) **1,000.00**

DESKS

Fall-front desk, country-style, cherry, a flat rectangular top above a wide, tall double-paneled hinged fall-front opening to a two-shelved interior w/four small drawers, the

stepped-out lower section w/a long drawer, raised on slender tapering turned legs, old surface, New Hampshire, mid-19th c., no drawer pulls, imperfections, 18½ × 26½", 4' 7¾" h. (Fig. 15-35) **1,725.00**

Roll-top desk, oak, turn-of-the-century, a narrow rectangular top above the wide S-scroll roll top opening to a fitted interior above a case w/a long central drawer w/arched apron flanked on one side by a stack of four small drawers w/long wooden finger pulls & on the other side by two small drawers over a deeper bottom drawer w/a double-drawer false front, all w/wooden finger pulls, paneled sides on top & base, deep base molding, 30½ × 50", 46" h. (Fig. 15-36) . . . . **1,000.00 to 1,500.00**

Fig. 15-36

Fig. 15-37

Stand-up desk, painted pine, a high
three-quarters gallery on a narrow
rectangular shelf above the wide
slant-top w/molded edges & incised
pencil groove opening a well above a
case w/two long, graduated drawers
w/two small wooden knobs above a
narrow pull-out writing surface
w/knobs below, on tall square
tapering stile legs joined by a flat H-
stretcher, original red wash w/grained
pull-out writing surface, western
Massachusetts, early 19th c.,
imperfections including height loss &
old replaced pulls, 25½ × 31¼", 4'
7½" h. (Fig. 15-37) **1,380.00**

Fig. 15-38

DRY SINKS

Cherry & poplar, hutch-style, the tall back w/a
flat backrail on the rectangular top over a
row of three drawers w/porcelain knobs over
cut-out sides over the wide shallow well
w/evidence of removed metal liner
overhanging the lower case w/a pair of
paneled cupboard doors w/metal latches,
flat base, cleaned to old greyish patina,
found in Indiana, probably Amish, late
19th c., 23¾ × 45½", 44" h. **880.00**

Painted pine, the long rectangular well w/upright
sides overhanging a case w/a stack of three
short drawers at one end & a cupboard door
opening to a fitted interior near the other end,
flat base, painted brown, late 19th c., 21½ ×
61½", 33" h. (Fig. 15-38) **1,380.00**

Fig. 15-39

Pine, a rectangular well above a pair of paneled cupboard doors w/cast-iron thumb latches, flat apron & simple cut-out feet, old mellow finish, late 19th c., 18¼ × 46¼", 33" h. **825.00**

Pine, hutch-style, the high back w/a shelf across the top w/an applied three-quarter gallery over two small dovetailed drawers w/white porcelain knobs flanking a small open shelf area, the base w/double raised paneled doors on iron hinges & w/cast-iron latches w/porcelain knobs, two shelves in interior, solid plank sides w/squared arched cut-out base, nailed construction, refinished, late 19th c., 20½ × 52", 4' 11" h. **350.00**

Stained pine, the rectangular top w/enclosed sides above a conforming case fitted w/a pair of recessed-panel cupboard doors opening to a shelved interior, the case sides continuing to bracket feet, 19th c., 14½ × 35¾", 31¼" h. **345.00**

LOVE SEATS, SOFAS & SETTEES

Settee, Classical country-style, painted & decorated, a triple-back style w/three arched & shaped crestrails joined by simple turned stiles centering three wide lyre-form splats, long downswept S-scroll end arms on short turned spindles & arm supports, long, wide plank seat, raised on eight simple ring- and rod-turned legs joined by box stretchers, light brown ground w/black, gold & green striping & highlighted by painted peach clusters on the crestrails & splats, Pennsylvania, early 19th c., imperfections, 17 × 72", 36" h. (Fig. 15-39) **1,725.00**

Settee, Windsor, painted wood, a birdcage-form crestrail above multiple slender spindles w/a thicker turned center stile & canted end stiles w/ball finials above the outswept S-scroll end arms on bamboo-turned spindles & arm supports, long shaped plank seat, raised on six canted bamboo-turned legs joined by two long front rod stretchers & rod stretchers between front & back legs, early black paint, New England, 1790-1810, imperfections, 75" l., 35½" h. (Fig. 15-40) **5,570.00**

Settee, Windsor, painted wood, the long flat narrow rectangular crestrail above numerous plain turned spindles w/a thicker central spindle, heavy down-curved end arms over small spindles, thick plank seat on four pairs of plain turned legs joined by flat front stretchers & lower turned trestle-style stretchers, early mustard yellow paint & natural arms, paint wear & loss, New England, early 19th c., 98" l., 32" h. (Fig. 15-41) **1,265.00**

Fig. 15-40

Fig. 15-41

SHELVES

Floor shelves, painted, a serpentine three-quarter gallery w/shaped ends on the narrow rectangular top shelf raised on one-board sides w/undulating front edges flanking two lower open shelves, rounded bootjack legs, overall robin's-egg blue paint, 6 × 12¼", 25½" h. (Fig. 15-42) **2,645.00**

Hanging shelf, country-style, walnut, a half-round shelf above cut-out brackets w/fan carving against the arched backboard carved w/two pointed drops, old worn & alligatored varnish finish, found in Pennsylvania, 6 × 14", 6¾" h. **303.00**

Hanging shelves, country-style, painted poplar, the side boards w/tapering rounded tops & flat sides flanking three open shelves, bottom shelf dovetailed to sides,

Fig. 15-42

Fig. 15-44

Fig. 15-43

old worn green paint, 19th c., 9³⁄₄ × 38¹⁄₂",
33" h. (some edge damage, base end
moldings missing) **495.00**

Hanging shelves, country-style, pine, shaped
ends join three molded shelves, original
surface, possibly New Hampshire, 18th c.,
16 × 21¹⁄₂", 21¹⁄₂" h. **1,495.00**

Wall shelves, Classical style, mahogany, a
narrow rectangular top above three long
graduated open shelves flanked by scroll-
cut sides, old finish, New England, ca. 1825,
7¹⁄₂ × 31³⁄₄", 27¹⁄₂" h. (Fig. 15-43) **1,265.00**

Wall shelves, Classical 'pillar & scroll' style, an
arched broken-scroll crestrail on the top
above three narrow open shelves flanked by
ring- and rod-turned half-round pilaster
sides, old finish, New England, ca. 1825,
8¹⁄₂ × 33", 33¹⁄₂" h. (Fig. 15-44) **920.00**

Wall shelves, pine, a three-quarter low gallery
on the top narrow shelf above scalloped
sides flanking three graduated open shelves
w/incised plate rails, scalloped three-

quarter gallery at the base, 19th c.,
9¹⁄₂ × 38¹⁄₂", 40" h. (Fig. 15-45) **1,955.00**

STANDS

Candlestand, Chippendale, cherry, the
squared top w/serpentine sides & wide
rounded corners raised on a simple ring-
and baluster-turned pedestal on a tripod
base w/flattened cabriole legs ending in
snake feet, Connecticut River Valley, late
18th c., 16 × 16¹⁄₂", 26" h. (refinished) . . **2,415.00**

Fig. 15-45

Fig. 15-46

Fig. 15-47

Candlestand, Federal country-style, painted maple, a round dished top above a rod-, ring-, and baluster-turned standard on a tripod base w/spider legs, retains old reddish brown & brown painted decoration simulating mahogany, old surface, New England, ca. 1810, 15¾" d., 30" h. (imperfections) **3,450.00**

Candlestand, Federal, cherry, the square tray top above an elongated vase-form pedestal on a tripod base w/simple flattened cabriole legs ending in tapering slipper feet, appears to retain original finish, New England, possibly Shaker, ca. 1815, 16¼" sq., 27½" h. (repair to one leg & underside of top) . . **1,380.00**

Candlestand, Federal, cherry, the squared serpentine top above a baluster-, ring-, and urn-turned pedestal on a tripod base w/cabriole legs ending in snake feet, possibly Connecticut, 1790-1810, repair to one foot, 27½" h. (Fig. 15-46) **460.00**

Candlestand, Federal, inlaid cherry & maple, a round dished top above a tapered vase-form standard, on line-inlaid tripod spider legs ending in spade feet, New England, ca. 1805, 18¼" d., 29½" h. (Fig. 15-47) **2,875.00**

Fig. 15-48

Fig. 15-49

Candlestand, Federal, inlaid cherry, the long octagonal top w/a beaded rim inlaid w/bird's-eye maple, stringing & mahogany cross-banding, tilting above a ring- and baluster-turned standard on a tripod base w/spider legs ending in spade feet, old refinish, New Hampshire, ca. 1800, 14 × 19¼", 28½" h. (Fig. 15-48) **3,105.00**

Candlestand, Federal, mahogany veneer, the oblong octagonal top tilting above a baluster-turned standard on a tripod base w/spider legs ending in spade feet, New York State, ca. 1810, 17¼ × 23", 29¾" h. (Fig. 15-49) **1,725.00**

Candlestand, Federal, maple, wide octagonal top tilting above a swelled reeded pedestal w/chip-carved detail, old red varnish, possibly New Hampshire, ca. 1815-20, 15⅝ × 20", 29½" h. (minor imperfections) **920.00**

Washstand, Classical, mahogany & mahogany veneer, the flat three-quarter gallery w/reeded edges & rounded ends above the original grey veined rectangular marble top over a drawer w/an early pressed glass pull,

the top raised on four baluster- and ring-turned supports on a lower rectangular shelf above another drawer w/glass pull, on short ring-turned tapering legs, minor veneer loss, ca. 1830, 21½ × 26", 32¼" h. (Fig. 15-50) **605.00**

Washstand, Federal, inlaid cherry & tiger stripe maple, the rectangular top w/an oval-inlaid central reserve above a front apron in figured maple & banded inlay flanked by panel-inlaid supports to the scalloped-top medial section fitted w/a single drawer w/figured maple & banded inlay & a round brass pull, on delicate ring- and baluster-turned legs ending in peg feet, New England, probably Vermont, ca. 1815, 17⅞ × 18", 30¾" h. (Fig. 15-51) **2,875.00**

Federal country-style one-drawer stand, tiger stripe maple, the rectangular top widely overhanging a deep apron w/a single drawer w/a simple bail pull, on slender square tapering legs, old refinish, imperfections, New England, ca. 1810, 15 × 18½", 23¾" h. (Fig. 15-52) **1,265.00**

Fig. 15-50

Fig. 15-52

Fig. 15-51

Federal one-drawer stand, bird's-eye maple, a rectangular tray top above a single drawer on base, old red surface, old brass pulls, Canterbury, New Hampshire area, ca. 1830, 19¼ × 20¼", 26½" h. (very minor imperfections) **1,610.00**

Federal one-drawer stand, cherry, nearly square tray top above an apron w/a single flush-front drawer w/no knob, on square tapering legs, old cherry color, Connecticut River Valley, ca. 1800, 16 × 16½", 28¾" h. (very minor imperfections) **863.00**

Federal two-drawer stand, maple & bird's-eye maple veneer, square top w/molded edge above a case w/two drawers faced w/bird's-eye maple & each w/two turned knobs, on slender ring- and rod-turned tapering legs w/baluster-turned peg feet, cross-banded veneer outlining the veneered sides & rear, top w/a figured mahogany panel & bird's-eye maple border, original pulls, old refinish, Portsmouth, New Hampshire, early 19th c., 17" sq., 28¾" h. **8,050.00**

Federal country-style two-drawer stand, cherry & curly maple, the thin rectangular top above a deep apron framed w/curly maple w/two cherry drawers each w/two

Fig. 15-53

replaced glass knobs, on ring-, knob-, and rod-turned tapering legs ending in knob feet, refinished, top patch, small repair on front edge strip, early 19th c., 16¾ × 21¾", 28¼" h. (Fig. 15-53) **770.00**

TABLES

Chippendale drop-leaf table, cherry, rectangular top flanked by wide drop leaves above an apron w/scalloped ends & square molded legs w/two pulling out to form leaf supports, original surface, attributed to Samuel Sewall, York, Maine, 18th c., 17 × 48", 27½" h. (imperfections) **1,955.00**

Chippendale serving table, country-style, painted, the rectangular top w/deeply serpentine molded edges & canted front corners overhanging a deep green-painted apron w/thumb-molded skirt, on square molded legs, 21 × 40¾", 29" h. (Fig. 15-54) **1,150.00**

Fig. 15-54

Fig. 15-55

Chippendale country-style tilt-top tea table, cherry, the squared wide top w/serpetine edges tilting above a simple columnar pedestal on a tripod base w/cabriole legs ending in snake feet, Massachusetts, 1760-80, 31½ × 32", 27½" h. (refinished, imperfections) **1,380.00**

Classical country-style work table, inlaid walnut, a rectangular top w/rounded edges above a deep case w/two long drawers inlaid around the drawers w/large diamonds, diamond clusters & stars & inlaid on the drawer fronts w/pairs of stars centered by early pressed glass pulls & framed by small inlaid diamonds, the block- and ring-turned legs further inlaid w/long diamonds & pairs of hearts, baluster-turned feet ending in knobs, Ohio River Valley, ca. 1840, old finish, some loss of inlay, 16½ × 20", 29" h. (Fig. 15-55) **2,990.00**

Country-style work table, painted poplar & pine, rectangular removable top w/carved pins doweled through the supporting

Fig. 15-56

Fig. 15-57

battens, deep apron w/two thumb-molded
drawers w/original turned wood knobs,
original red paint, ring- and rod-turned legs,
Pennsylvania, 1780-1810, 26 × 30½",
27¾" h. **6,440.00**

Country-style work table, pine, a wide
rectangular scrubbed top w/a hinged drop
leaf along one side widely overhanging a
deep apron w/a long drawer w/a turned
wooden knob, square tapering legs, red-
painted base w/paint loss, imperfections,
Massachusetts, early 19th c., 26½ × 47",
28" h. (Fig. 15-56) **978.00**

Federal dining table, cherry, a rectangular
top flanked by deep drop-leaves w/rounded
& notched corners raised on six baluster-
and ring-turned legs, two serving as swing-
out leaf supports, New York State, early
19th c., old refinish, imperfections
(Fig. 15-57) **518.00**

Federal dressing table, painted & decorated,
a high scroll-cut splashboard above a
narrow shelf over a long narrow drawer
w/two wooden knobs on a stepped-out top
overhanging the apron w/a long drawer
w/two wooden knobs, raised on slender
ring- and rod-turned legs w/button feet,
painted on the upper section in mustard
yellow to resemble tiger stripe maple, the
legs decorated w/free-hand decoration of
diamonds & arrow heads in lemon yellow,
black & mustard yellow, New England, ca.
1830, minor imperfections, 17 × 31½",
33¾" h. (Fig. 15-58) **1,150.00**

Federal Pembroke table, cherry, rectangular
top flanked by two rectangular drop leaves,
on slender square, slightly tapering legs
joined by serpentine cross-stretchers, old
surface, imperfections, New England, early
19th c., 21¼ × 38", 28½" h. (Fig. 15-59) . . **1,150.00**

Fig. 15-58

"Harvest" table, walnut, the long narrow scrubbed top above four cross-slats on the deep putty-painted apron raised on double-baluster- and ring-turned supports to corner blocks & a long H-stretcher, on waisted turned feet, replaced feet & other repairs, northern New England, 18th c., 25½ × 72", 26¼" h. (Fig. 15-60) **2,300.00**

Hutch (or chair) table, maple, pine & birch, the round top hinged in the center above four baluster-turned supports over the square boxed base w/a single drawer w/turned wood knob, on ring- and baluster-turned feet, weathered surface w/traces of red paint, imperfections, probably New England, late 18th c., 52" d., 28" h. (Fig. 15-61) **4,313.00**

Hutch (or chair) table, painted, the rectangular top above two bootjack supports joined by a medial shelf w/straight apron, painted brown, New England, 19th c., 40¾ × 60", 28¾" h. **1,955.00**

Fig. 15-59

Fig. 15-60

Fig. 15-61

Tavern table, maple, the rectangular top widely overhanging an apron w/a single long drawer w/turned wood knob, rod- and block-turned legs joined by box stretchers, old red surface, minor imperfections, southeastern Massachusetts, late 18th c. (Fig. 15-62) **1,955.00**

Tavern table, painted pine & maple, a rectangular top w/breadboard ends widely overhanging the apron w/a single long drawer w/a small knob pull, on baluster- and ring-turned legs joined by low box stretchers, old brown paint, minor repairs &

surface imperfections, New England, late 18th c., 23 × 40¾", 24¼" h. (Fig. 15-63) . . **1,150.00**

Tavern table, tiger stripe maple & pine, the rectangular top above an apron w/a drawer, on vase- and ring-turned legs joined by stretchers, on turned feet, New England, late 18th c., 26 × 41", 25¾" h. (old refinish, restoration) **863.00**

William & Mary tavern table, walnut, rectangular top raised on turned legs joined by stretchers, possibly Boston, early 18th c., old finish, 19 × 31½", 24¼" h. (some imperfections) **8,050.00**

Fig. 15-62

Fig. 15-63

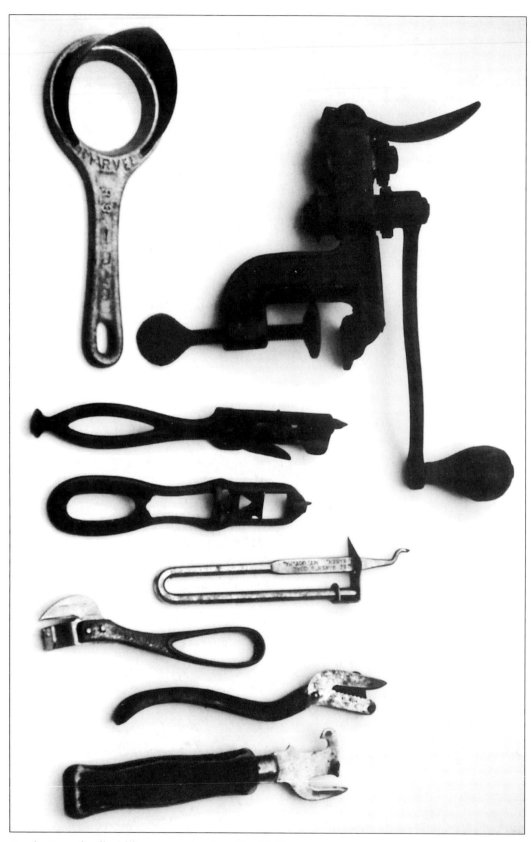

A selection of collectible can openers (see Fig. 16-5).

CHAPTER

16

KITCHENWARES & RELATED ITEMS

Antique kitchenware is very collectible and *still* afford-able. Its addictive power has lured many innocent collectors into the never-ending search and adventure. American inventors patented thousands of objects, many with only a slight variation in design and each with a unique function.

People collect kitchen objects for various reasons. Some like the decorating and simple aesthetic appeal, yet others collect kitchen-ware from a particular era. Many are intrigued with the form and function of pieces. Some purchase items for use which are reminiscent of those used in "grandmother's kitchen." Today, common kitchen gadgets command great respect in the field of collecting. Highly sought after are marked patent-dated pieces, particularly mechanical, of the Industrial Revolution-era. Rarity commands higher prices, however reasonably-priced items are still available.

—Carol Bohn

Note: Extended Egg Beaters, Graniteware, Irons & Juice Reamers sections are included at the end of general Kitchenwares section.

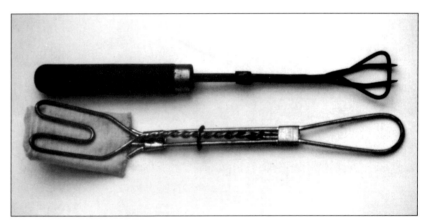

Fig. 16-1

GENERAL

Apple corer, tin, T-shaped, available **$18.00**

Apple parer, Reading "78" turntable,
  available **75.00**

Bacon (griddle) greasers, black wood handle,
  marked "SANITARY GREASER HOLDER,
  OBLOSSER MFG. CO., FEB 5, 1910,"
  available (Fig. 16-1, top) **20.00**

Bacon (griddle) greaser, cloth wrapped
  around bottom fingers, "'Fairy'" griddle
  greaser PAT Dec 1903," available (Fig. 16-1,
  bottom) **25.00**

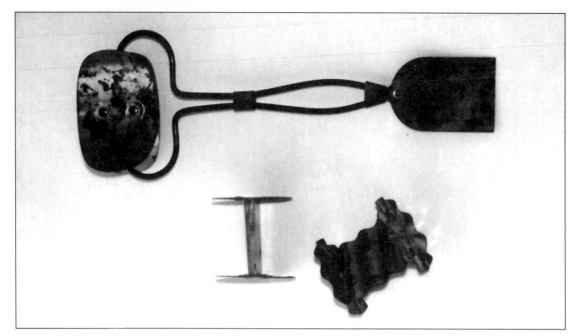

Fig. 16-2

Fig. 16-3

Fig. 16-4

Bake board, tin, S-curved bottom to hold pin, available **295.00**

Biscuit cutter, w/three interchangeable discs, marked "Patented Felds MFG Co. INC; Jamestown, NY," complete, available (Fig. 16-2) **85.00**

Bowl, blue painted rim w/white interior, exterior blue & white sponge-painted, w/short foot, unmarked, available (Fig. 16-3) **350.00**

Bowl, yellowware, 8", rim decorated w/blue band between two thin white bands, body decorated w/blue band between two thin white bands all above impressed vertical ridges, common (Fig. 16-4) **38.00**

Butter churn, wooden cylinder mounted on three wooden legs, marked "Union No. 1, American Woodenware Manf. Co.," iron wheel & shaft, 23" h. **195.00**

Can opener, aluminum w/steel blade, marked "MARVEL," hard to find (Fig. 16-5, No. 2) . . **65.00**

Can opener, cast iron, adjustable clamp-on style, Blue Streak, available (Fig. 16-5, No. 1) **85.00**

Can opener, cast iron, adjustable, unmarked, available (Fig. 16-5, No. 3) **60.00**

Can opener, cast iron, adjustable, marked "WORLD'S BEST, DILLSBURG, PA," available (Fig. 16-5, No. 4) **40.00**

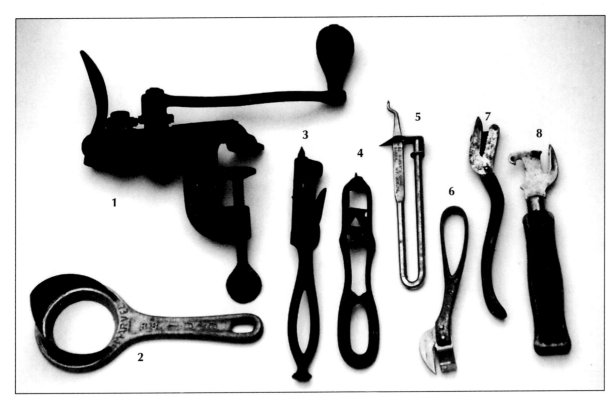

Fig. 16-5

Can opener, cast iron, "DELMONICO, PAT FEB
11 1898," available (Fig. 16-5, No. 7) **30.00**

Can opener, steel, marked "USE BAKER'S
COAL, F.H. BAKER, MT. JOY, PA," available
(Fig. 16-5, No. 5) **35.00**

Can opener, cast iron, Never Slip, "PAT MAY
17, 92," available (Fig. 16-5, No. 6) **25.00**

Can opener, wooden handle, marked cap lifter
& can opener, available (Fig. 16-5, No. 8) . . . **5.00**

Cherry pitter, cast iron, mechanical, marked
"NEW STANDARD CORP, MT JOY PA PATS.
PEND," common (Fig. 16-6, right) **145.00**

Cherry pitter, cast iron, mechanical 'wobble'
wheel, marked "NEW STANDARD CHERRY
STONER N.S. HDWE WKS," common
(Fig. 16-6, left) **95.00**

Chocolate grater, "The Edgar," spring-loaded
hood slides over tin grating surface, dated
1891-1896, 8½" l., rare **400.00**

Coffeepot or teapot stand, wrapped wire in a
star pattern, hard to find (Fig. 16-7, top) . . **65.00**

Coffeepot or teapot stand, wrapped wire
typical radiating design, common (Fig. 16-7,
left) **20.00**

Coffeepot or teapot stand, wrapped wire
w/scalloped sides, common (Fig. 16-7,
bottom) **45.00**

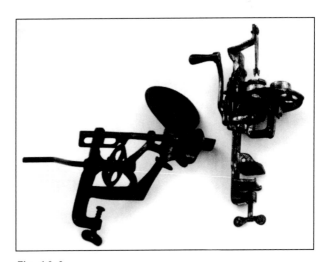

Fig. 16-6

Coffeepot or teapot stand, wrapped wire
w/diamond center, hard to find (Fig. 16-7,
right) **35.00**

Cookie cutter, tin, bird, handmade, common
(Fig. 16-8, No. 4) **45.00**

Cookie cutter, tin, heart in crimped circle,
common (Fig. 16-8, No. 1) **45.00**

Cookie cutter, tin, horse, handmade, late
1800s, common (Fig. 16-8, No. 2) **135.00**

Cookie cutter, tin, reindeer, manufactured,
common (Fig. 16-8, No. 3) **25.00**

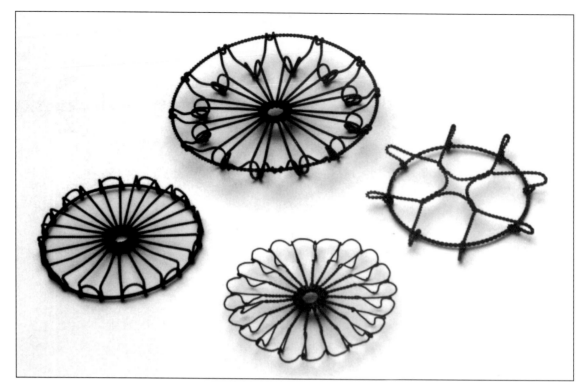

Fig. 16-7

Fig. 16-8

Fig. 16-9

Cookie cutter, tin, tulip, handmade, common (Fig. 16-8, No. 5) **75.00**

Cookie sheet, tin, marked "Kreamer," common **25.00**

Cornstick pan, aluminum "Griswold," no. 803, in original carton **25.00**

Cottage cheese mill, wooden dovetailed box covered w/mesh, iron turn handle & wood cylinder, marked "The Star," 5³⁄₄" sq. **155.00**

Dipper, glass bowl w/wood handle, marked "Marbury, pat. April 21, 1896," 13" l. **45.00**

Dish drainer, tin & wire, common (Fig. 16-9) . . **50.00**

Egg lifter, heavy twisted wire in diamond-shaped bowl, hard to find (Fig. 16-10, bottom) **40.00**

Egg lifter, thin wires in egg shaped bowl, available (Fig. 16-10, top) **35.00**

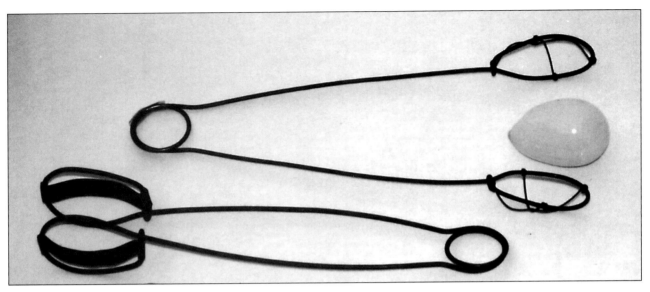

Fig. 16-10

Fig. 16-11

Egg lifter, tin, marked on straps "PAT DEC 16 1913," common (Fig. 16-10, center) **25.00**

Flour sifter, all-wooden with bottom screens marked "Bloods Improved Sifter" (Fig. 16-11, top) **295.00**

Flour sifter, concentric wire circles w/wooden handle, marked "JONES FLOUR & MEAL SIFTER, AP'L 17, 66," two pieces, hard to find (Fig. 16-11, left) **125.00**

Flour sifter, electric, plug-in, marked "Miracle," in original box **35.00**

Flour sifter, tin, marked "GEM SIFTER MANUF BY JL CLARK, MANU. CO ROCKFORD, ILL.," common (Fig. 16-11, bottom) **45.00**

Flour sifter, tin w/brass disc on handle marked "LIC'D BY NATL MFG. CO," hard to find (Fig. 16-11, right) **75.00**

Fork ejector, wood handle, push top projection to eject, hard to find (Fig. 16-12, top) **65.00**

Fork ejector, metal, squeeze to eject, common (Fig. 16-12, center) **25.00**

Fork ejector, twisted wire, squeeze to eject, common (Fig. 16-12, bottom) **35.00**

Fly swatter, wire handle & wire mesh w/three protrusions to keep fly from hitting against wall, hard to find (Fig. 16-13, left) **40.00**

Fly swatter, wire handle & wire screen, common (Fig. 16-13, center left) **15.00**

Fly swatter, wooden handles & fine wires, marked on brass "PAT'D JAN 8, 1895," common (Fig. 16-13, center right) **75.00**

Fly swatter, wooden handle & wire screen w/cloth edge, common (Fig. 16-13, right) **30.00**

Funnel, grater, apple corer, & cookie cutter, marked "PAT. APPD FOR," hard to find (Fig. 16-17, top center) **225.00**

Grater, tin, hand-punched, common (Fig. 16-14, left) **45.00**

Grater, tin, primitive hand-punched semi-circle mounted on walnut board w/hanging hole, board 24" l. **65.00**

Grater, tin, manufactured, common (Fig. 16-14, right) **20.00**

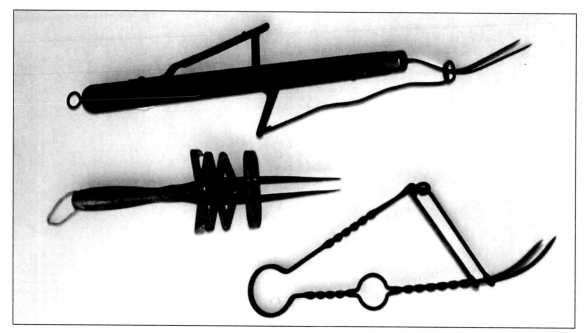

Fig. 16-12

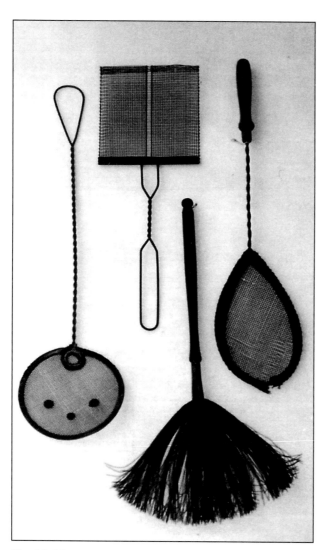

Fig. 16-13

Fig. 16-14

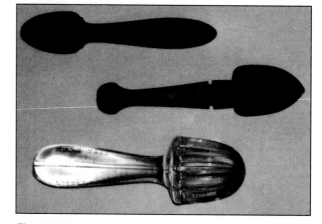

Fig. 16-15

Fig. 16-16

Kettle bail carrier, meat tenderizer, trivet, pudding dish carrier, removing pie pan from oven, & stove lid lifter, cast iron, marked "THAYERS PAT MAY 24, 1881," available (Fig. 16-17, top left) **85.00**

Lemon reamer, molded glass, marked "LITTLE HANDY LEMON SQUEEZER, SILVER & CO. NEW YORK," common (Fig. 16-15, bottom) **75.00**

Lemon reamer, wood handle w/tin pointed blades, sometimes serrated on edges, grooved around handle thwarted juice from running onto hand, hard to find (Fig. 16-15, center) **125.00**

Lemon reamer, wooden, conical grooved body, available (Fig. 16-15, top) **75.00**

Lemon squeezer, cast iron w/white porcelain interior, marked "E.M. Sammis," pat. Sept. 1878 . . . . **25.00**

Lunch pail, tin, sections held together by handle, marked "PAT FEB 26 1884" & "JUNE 26 1888," available (Fig. 16-16, two views) **95.00**

Meat tenderizer, beige crockery w/black painted wood handle, marked "Pat. Dec. 25, 1877," 8½" l. **85.00**

Mold, chocolate, darkened tin, bear climbing tree trunk, no. 1438, 2 pt., 8" h. **135.00**

Mold, chocolate, flat sheet, fourteen Father Christmas figures, marked "Booderas Ernotebruck No. 2214" **150.00**

Mold, chocolate, Rabbit standing w/long shotgun, marked "Solid Nickel Silver No. 25," 7" h. **85.00**

Mold, chocolate, tin, baby sitting w/thumb in mouth, marked "Anton Reich, No. 26359," 2 pt., 4" h. **70.00**

Mold, chocolate, tin flat sheet, Father Christmas & Black Peter in alternating rows, marked "Tilburg, Holland," 18 × 7¾" **150.00**

Mold, chocolate, tin flat sheet, thirty repeated turtles, marked "Tillburg, Holland," 22" l. . . **75.00**

Mold, chocolate, tin, greyhound jumping fence, marked "Van Emden, N.Y.," 2 pt., 8" l. **100.00**

Mold, chocolate, tin, locomotive engine, marked "Anton, Reiche," 2 pt., 6" l. **95.00**

Mold, chocolate, tin, monkey riding in child's scooter, marked "H. Walter, Berlin," 2 pt., 4¼" h. **65.00**

Fig. 16-17

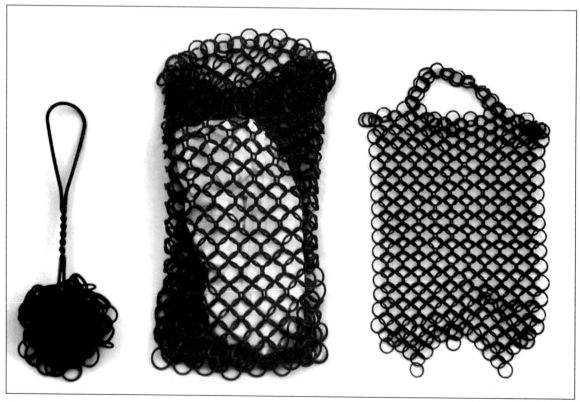

Fig. 16-18

Fig. 16-19

Mold, jelly, copper, circular bundt shape
w/nine ornate pillars, 5¹/₂" w., 6¹/₅" h. **60.00**

Mold, maple sugar, hand-carved wood, four
interlocking sides that fit into a cone,
interior carved w/hunting scenes, dated
1812 w/carver's initials **225.00**

Clear Toy Candy Molds: All clear toy candy
molds are in two pieces and made of heavy iron,
unless specified.

Elephants, group of three, No. 138 . . . . **55.00**

Horse pulling car w/rider, group of three
figures **65.00**

Rabbits, group of four standing, No. 18 . . . . . **42.00**

Rearing horse, large, No. 3 . . . . **70.00**

River paddle boat, group of three, No. 43 . . . **50.00**

President McKinley, group of three bust
figures, No. 259 . . . . **75.00**

Windmills, group of three, No. 251 . . . . **50.00**

Weasel at flour sack, group of three,
No. 103 . . . . **50.00**

Nutmeg grater, wood & brass, Champion,
Boston, MA, Pat Oct 9 1866, available . . . **375.00**

Nutmeg grater, wood & tin grater, swing arm,
M.H. Sexton, Utica NY, Pat'd May 1896,
rare **750.00**

Pan scraper, chains form a pocket in which
soap was placed, hard to find (Fig. 16-18,
center) **65.00**

Pan scraper, chains form single-layer scraper
w/small handle at end, patented Oct. 10,
1871, hard to find (Fig. 16-18, right) **45.00**

Pan scraper, chains in circle w/twisted wire
handle, available (Fig. 16-18, left) **35.00**

Pastry blender, wire w/tin handle, available . . **12.00**

Pie crimper, brass wheel & wood handle,
available (Fig. 16-19, bottom) **45.00**

Pie crimper, brass, wheel on one end, shaft
on other, shaft marked "Pat. Sept. 11, 1866,"
6" l. **140.00**

Pie crimper, cast-iron wheel w/wood handle,
ca. 1820, available (Fig. 16-19, top) **95.00**

Pie crimper, china wheel & wood handle,
wheel 2" d., handle 7" l. **28.00**

Pie crimper, tin wheel & handle, handmade,
may be 10th anniversary piece, 9" l., rare
(Fig. 16-19, top center) **250.00**

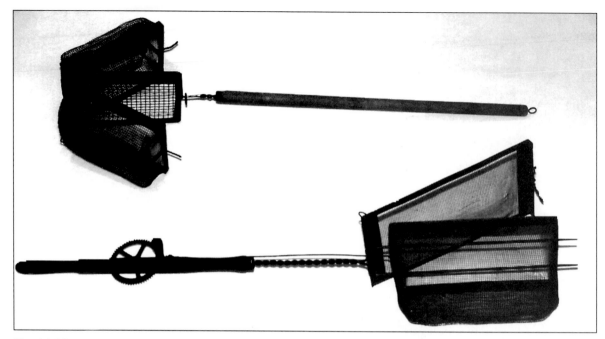

Fig. 16-20

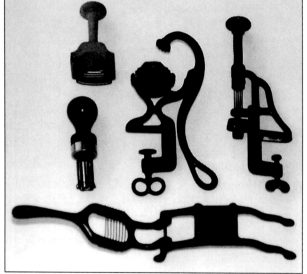

Fig. 16-21

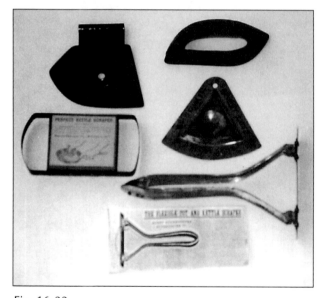

Fig. 16-22

Pie crimper, wood chip-carved wheel &
   handle, long end by crimping wheel is set
   on table as crimper rolled along edge of pie
   crust, rare (Fig. 16-19, bottom center) **125.00**

Popcorn popper, double sided mesh basket
   for popcorn & chestnuts w/long wood
   handle, hard to find (Fig. 16-20, top) **85.00**

Popcorn popper, mesh basket & wood handle,
   mechanical, turn crank on wheel to agitate
   basket back & forth, rare (Fig. 16-20,
   bottom) **385.00**

Potato masher, wooden, simple design,
   available **15.00**

Potato masher, wooden handle, spring-loaded
   double wire grid, available **40.00**

Raisin seeder, wire w/wood handle, marked
   "Everett," available (Fig. 16-21, top
   left) **50.00**

Raisin seeder, wire w/wood handle, marked
   "COLUMBIAN MAY 2, 1893," hard to find
   (Fig. 16-21, center left) **375.00**

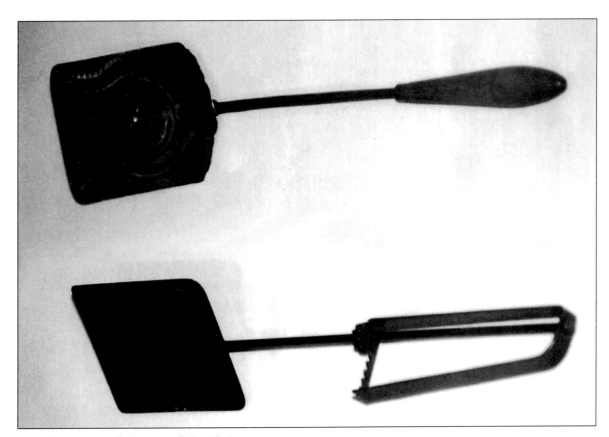

Fig. 16-23

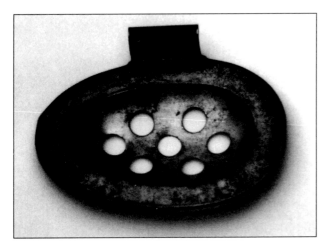

Fig. 16-24

Raisin seeder, wire w/cast-iron body & table clamp, marked "THE EZY PAT MAR 21 1895," available (Fig. 16-21, center) **300.00**

Raisin seeder, wire w/cast-iron body & table clamp, marked "FISKE, PAT AUG 16 1870," hard to find (Fig. 16-21, right) **495.00**

Raisin seeder, wire w/cast-iron body, known as 'Headless Horseman,' marked "PAT'D MAY 7, 95," available (Fig. 16-21, bottom) . . **450.00**

Rolling pin, wood, mounted wooden hopper across top that encloses mesh corked tube to hold flour, marked "Harlowe's Do Not Stick," 20" l. **225.00**

Rolling pin, wooden springerle w/twelve carved patterns including an eagle, sunburst, leaping cat & fish, 12" l. **65.00**

Rolling pin, wooden, simple design, available . . **15.00**

Rolling pin, yellowware cylinder w/wood handles, 11¾" l. (mint cond.) **325.00**

Scoop, tin, ice cream-type, cone-shaped disher w/tin handle & top turn key, marked "V. Clad, Phila" & "Pat. May 3, 1878," No. 5 . . . . **95.00**

Scraper, kettle, wood block body w/flexible steel bands at each end, paper label reads "PERFECT KETTLE SCRAPER" followed by short paragraph & illustration of pan & scraper, hard to find (Fig. 16-22, center left) **75.00**

Scraper, pot, cast iron, oblong shape w/pointed ends w/cut-out handle, marked "C.D. KENNY CO TEAS, COFFEES, SUGAR POT SCRAPER," hard to find (Fig. 16-22, top right) **175.00**

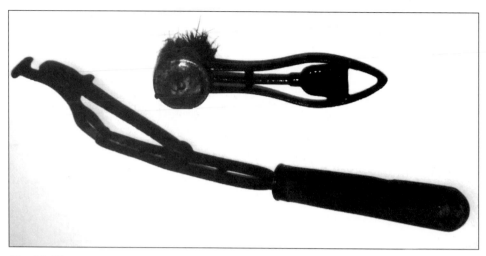

Fig. 16-25

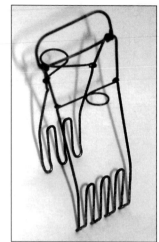

Fig. 16-26

Scraper, pot & kettle, tin, w/unattached label "THE FLEXIBLE POT AND KETTLE SCRAPER," followed by short paragraph & illustration of scraper, available (Fig. 16-22, bottom) **35.00**

Scraper, pot & kettle, tin w/swivelling handle, marked "PERFECT SCRAPER, PAT MAY 21, 89," available (Fig. 16-22, top left) **110.00**

Scraper, tin, advertising, triangular-shaped, marked "ENDICOTT JOHNSON SHOES FOR THE WHOLE FAMILY," available (Fig. 16-22, center right) **35.00**

Sifter, tin, two-cup measure w/wood handle, marked "Calumet Baking Powder" **38.00**

Spatula, tin w/tulip & star design, wood handle, hard to find (Fig. 16-23, top) **35.00**

Spatula, tin & cast iron, mechanical, push handle & it flips, available (Fig. 16-23, bottom) **75.00**

Spatula, spoon, & meat tenderizer, iron w/wooden handle, marked "PATENT JULY 11, 1916," hard to find (Fig. 16-17, right) . . **135.00**

Spoon, wire mesh center, wood handle, available **18.00**

Spoon-fork combination, twisted wire three prong fork on one end, wire spoon on other, available **45.00**

Spoon holder, tin, oval shaped seven holes & ridge around edge, w/hook, placed on side of kettle for drippings from spoon, unmarked, available (Fig. 16-24) **35.00**

Stove blackening brush, cast-iron handle & tin, "Pat. Aug 6 '95," available (Fig. 16-25, top) **30.00**

Stove lid lifter, cast iron w/wood handle, mechanical, hard to find (Fig. 16-25, bottom) **35.00**

Sugar auger, hand-wrought iron, twirled iron in center shaft divides into one straight prong, two beautifully curved swirls at bottom, wooden handle, mid-1800s, 20" l. **175.00**

Trivet, fish scaler (underneath), bottle opener, can opener, & hammer & tack pull, cast iron, marked "SIX IN ONE MFD BY PARK NOVELTY CO. BALTO MD," (has been reproduced) available (Fig. 16-17, bottom center) **75.00**

Vegetable lifter, wire, Handi-Hands, available (Fig. 16-26) **65.00**

Vegetable strainer, wire base, wood handle, available **18.00**

Wafer iron, cast iron, Griswold No. 955, w/stand **320.00**

COFFEE MILLS

Coffee mills, commonly called grinders, are perfectly collectible for many people. They are appealing to the eye and are frequently coveted by interior decorators and today's coffee-consuming homeowners. Compact, intricate, unique, ornate, and rooted in early Americana, coffee mills are intriguing to everyone and are rich and colorful.

Coffee milling devices have been available for hundreds of years. The Greek and Romans used rotating millstones for grinding coffee and grain. Turkish coffee mills with their familiar cylindrical brass shells appeared in the 15th century, and perhaps a century or two later came the earliest spice and coffee mills in Europe. Primitive mills were

Fig. 16-27

Fig. 16-28

handmade in this country by blacksmiths and carpenters in the late 1700s and the first half of the 19th century. These were followed by a host of commercially-produced mills which included wood-backed side mills and numerous kinds of box mills, many with machined dovetails or finger-joints. Characterized by the birth of upright cast-iron coffee mills, so beautiful with their magnificant colors and fly wheels, the period of coffee mill proliferation began around 1870. The next 50 years saw a staggering number of large and small manufacturers struggling to corner the popular home market for box and canister-type coffee mills. After that, the advent of electricity and other major advances in coffee grinding and packaging technology hastened the decline in poplurarity of small coffee mills.

Value-added features to look for when purchasing old coffee grinders include:

- good working order and no missing, broken, or obviously replaced parts
- original paint
- attractive identifying markings, label or brass emblem
- uncommon mill, rarely seen, or appealing unique characteristics
- known patent history, whether explicitly marked on the mill or not

—Mike White

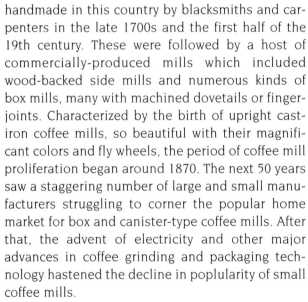

Fig. 16-29

◆ Primitive Coffee Mills

Box mill, w/raised iron hopper, signed
"J. Fisher" (Fig. 16-27) **$230.00**

Box mill, w/brass hopper & drawer front,
signed "ADAMS" on crank, 5½ × 5½" top
(Fig. 16-28) **110.00**

Box mill, w/pewter hopper, signed "G. Selsor
#2" on crank, 7 × 7" top (Fig. 16-29) **110.00**

Iron mill, post-mounted blacksmith's-type,
5" open hopper (Fig. 16-30) **150.00**

Fig. 16-30

Fig. 16-31

Fig. 16-32

◆ Side Mills

Side mill, w/wood back, "Increase Wilson's Best Quality No. 3" (Fig. 16-31) **80.00**

Side mill, w/wood block, marked "L&S Brighton" (Fig. 16-32) **60.00**

Side mill, w/sliding cover, "Kenrick & Sons (1815) Patent Coffee Mill" (Fig. 16-33) . . . **100.00**

Side mill, iron, double grinding gear, Parker Union, unmarked (Fig. 16-34) **100.00**

◆ Box Mills

Box mill, tapered iron box, English mill w/porcelainized hopper, marked "Kenrick & Sons Patent Coffee Mill" (Fig. 16-35) **140.00**

Fig. 16-33

Fig. 16-34

Fig. 16-35

Fig. 16-36

Fig. 16-37

Fig. 16-38

Fig. 16-39

Box mill, tin hopper & red label reads "Parker's Eagle No. 314," 6 × 6" top (Fig. 16-36) **80.00**

Box mill, tapered wood box w/brass hopper, Austrian, 3½ × 3½" top (Fig. 16-37) **170.00**

Box mill, all iron box w/original paint, raised hopper cover reads "Grand Union Tea Co.," 5 × 5" base (Fig. 16-38) **450.00**

Box mill, iron top, handle & covered hopper, "Parker's National No. 30," 6 × 6" top (Fig. 16-39) **120.00**

Box mill, tall wood box w/iron top, cover & handle, w/side crank, top embossed "Arcade Mfg. Co. IXL" (Fig. 16-40) **350.00**

Box mill, wood box, raised hopper w/pivoting cover, PS&W No. 350 (unmarked), 7 × 7" top (Fig. 16-41) **190.00**

Fig. 16-40

Fig. 16-41

Fig. 16-42

Fig. 16-43

Box mill, wood box w/handle on top, sunken tin hopper, label reads "Sun No. 1085 Challenge Fast Grinder" (Fig. 16-42) **120.00**

Box mill, wood box w/embossed covered hopper, marked "Logan & Strobridge Pat' Coffee Mill," some damage to box (Fig. 16-43) **70.00**

Box mill, wood box, tin hopper w/partial cover, well-marked "Arcade No. 367," 6¹/₂ × 6¹/₂" top (Fig. 16-44) **120.00**

Box mill, wood box w/tin dome & sliding cover, label marked "PeDe Dienes Mokka," 4 × 4" top (Fig. 16-45) **40.00**

Box mill, wood box w/wood hopper & pivoting wood cover, Peugot Freres, 5¹/₂ × 5¹/₂" top (Fig. 16-46) **140.00**

Box mill, tapered cast-iron box w/brass hopper, marked "T. & C. Clark Co.," England, 4¹/₂ × 4¹/₂" top (Fig. 16-47) **250.00**

Fig. 16-44

Fig. 16-45

Fig. 16-46

Fig. 16-47

Fig. 16-48

Box mill, wood box w/raised iron hopper & tin dust cover, straight handle, Arcade, unmarked (Fig. 16-48) **160.00**

◆ Upright Mills

Upright mill, cast-iron w/covered hopper, green w/gold trim, marked "LF&C Universal No. 11" (Fig. 16-49) **280.00**

Upright mill, cast iron, single-wheel mill w/wooden drawer & covered tin hopper, on wooden base, Elma, unmarked (Fig. 16-50) **160.00**

Upright mill, cast iron, spread-winged eagle perched atop brass hopper,

Fig. 16-49

Fig. 16-50

w/double 11" wheels repainted red, blue
& gold, replaced drawer, Enterprise No. 4
(Fig. 16-51) **400.00**

Upright mill, cast iron, w/wooden drawer & tin
covered hopper, painted green w/gold trim,
13" wheel w/gears, embossed "Peugot Freres
2A, Brevetes S.G.D.G." (Fig. 16-52) **700.00**

Upright mill, cast iron, decorative scrolls,
w/brass hopper, crank & single wheel, black
w/gold trim, 15" wheel embossed "Parnall &
Sons, Bristol (England)" (Fig. 16-53) **900.00**

Upright mill, cast-iron w/tin drawer, sliding
cover on hopper, double wheels, original
red, blue & gold paint, 9" wheel embossed
"The Cha's Parker Co., Meriden, Conn.
U.S.A.," model No. 200 (Fig. 16-54) **1,200.00**

Upright mill, cast iron, covered hopper &
double wheels, original red paint & decals,
1898 patent date, wheels embossed
"Enterprise Mfg. Co, Philadelphia, U.S.A."
(Fig. 16-55) **1,000.00**

Upright mill, cast iron, spread-winged eagle
atop brass hopper, tin catcher, double
wheels, original paint & decals, 1887 patent
date, wheels embossed "Coles Mfg. Co.,
Phila. Pa.," model No. 8, eagle replaced
(Fig. 16-56) **1,100.00**

Fig. 16-51

Fig. 16-52

Fig. 16-53

Fig. 16-54

Fig. 16-55

Fig. 16-56

◆ Wall Canister Mills

Wall canister mill, bronzed cast-iron canister w/glass window & cup, embossed canister reads "Golden Rule Blend Coffee The Finest Blend In The World, The Citizens Wholesale Supply Co., Columbus Ohio.," 18" h. (Fig. 16-57) **350.00**

Wall canister mill, ceramic canister w/glass cup, marked "PeDe" (Fig. 16-58) **110.00**

Wall canister mill, ceramic canister w/glass cup & wood backing board, cannister marked "KAFFEE," Leinbrock Ideal DRGM (Fig. 16-59) **240.00**

Wall canister mill, glass canister & cup, marked jar, Arcade Crystal No. 3, 18" h. (Fig. 16-60) **200.00**

Wall canister mill, glass canister & cup, embossed "Enterprise No. 100," 16" h. (Fig. 16-61) **130.00**

Fig. 16-57

Fig. 16-58

Fig. 16-59

Fig. 16-60

Fig. 16-61

Fig. 16-62

Fig. 16-63

Fig. 16-64

Fig. 16-65

Wall canister mill, steel canister w/glass cup, embossed "Pat 1891," Wilmot-Castle, 15" including glass cup (Fig. 16-62) **180.00**

Wall canister mill, steel canister w/steel cup, green label reads "Universal 0012 Coffee Mill Pat. Feb. 14, 1905, Landers, Frary & Clark, New Britain, Conn. U.S.A.," 13" h. (Fig. 16-63) **140.00**

Wall canister mill, tin lithographed canister, pictures a young girl wearing white dress, yellow apron & cap, yellow bonnet & dark cap, Bronson-Walton Beauty, 13" h. including cup (Fig. 16-64) **230.00**

◆ Miscellaneous

Box mill, child's, gold painted hopper & crank, labeled "Little Tot," Arcade 2¹/₂ × 2¹/₂" top (Fig. 16-65) **90.00**

Box mill, child's, painted tin, w/brass hopper, 3 × 3" top (Fig. 16-66) **40.00**

Fig. 16-66

Fig. 16-67

Fig. 16-68

Fig. 16-69

Fig. 16-70

Fig. 16-71

Clamp-on mill, open hopper, original red
paint w/label, LF&C No. 01 (Fig. 16-67) . . . **80.00**

Electric mill, aluminum hopper & tin catch
can, red w/gold trim, Holwick ¼ horsepower,
27" h. (Fig. 16-68) **120.00**

Turkish mill, brass, engraved cylindrical
casing w/folding crank (Fig. 16-69) **40.00**

Upright mill, miniature, cast-iron w/double
wheels, red w/gold trim, embossed
"ARCADE," 4" h. (Fig. 16-70) **150.00**

Wall mount mill, cast iron, open hopper &
cup, repainted red, embossed "Landers,
Frary & Clark," No. 001 (Fig. 16-71) **80.00**

EGGBEATERS

Eggbeaters are pure Americana! No other invention (although apple parers come close) represent America at its best from the mid-19th century to the 1930s or '40s. Eggbeaters tell the unbeatable story of America—the story of demand for a product, competition, success, retreat, failure, faith, and revival.

The mechanical (rotary) eggbeater is an American invention, and ranks up there with motherhood and apple pie, or at least up there where it counts—in the kitchen. American ingenuity produced more than 1,000 patents related to beating eggs, most before the 20th century.

To put it in perspective, try to imagine 1,000 plus ways to beat an egg. Here's a clue, and it's all due to Yankee tinkering: There are rotary cranks, archimedes (up and down) models, hand-helds, squeeze power, and rope and water power—and others. If you ever wanted a different way to beat an egg it was (and is) available.

Today, eggbeaters are a very popular Americana kitchen collectible—a piece of America still available to the collector, although he/she may have to scramble to find the rare ones.

But, beaters are out there, from the mainstay A & J to the cast-iron Dover to the rarer Express and Monroe. There is always an intriguing mix, ranging in price from less than under $10.00 to the hundreds of dollars.

—Don Thornton

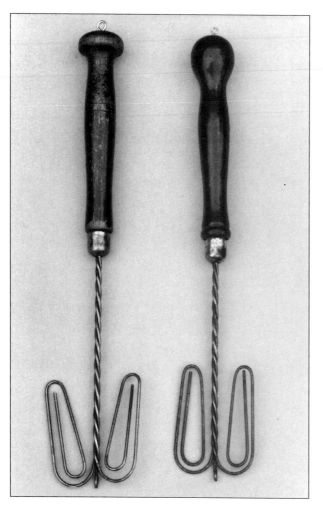

Fig. 16-72

Fig. 16-73

Items are listed alphabetically by manufacturer

A & J, archimedes "up & down" style, marked "A&J Pat'd Oct. 15 07 Other Pats Pending, 12½" (Fig. 16-72, left) **$30.00**

A & J, archimedes "up & down" style, marked "Patd Oct. 15 07 Other Pat Pend'g," 9¼" (Fig. 16-72, right) **50.00**

A & J, metal, rotary crank, marked "A&J Pat. Oct. 9, 1923 Made in U.S.A.," 8¼" to 10" . . . . **10.00 to 15.00**

A & J, ECKO, wood handle, rotary w/apron marked "A&J USA ECKO," on a two-cup measuring cup marked "A&J" (Fig. 16-73) . . **35.00**

Androck, Bakelite handle, metal rotary, marked "Androck," 11" (Fig. 16-74) **30.00**

Androck, metal rotary, wood handle, marked "Androck," 11" (Fig. 16-74) **15.00**

Androck, plastic handle, rotary, marked "Another Androck Product," 12½" (Fig. 16-74) **15.00**

Androck, wood handle rotary w/mesh dasher, marked "Another Androck Product," 12" (Fig. 16-74) **55.00**

F. Ashley, archemides, marked "F. Ashley Patent Appl For," 15" **525.00**

Aurelius Bros., wood handle, rotary w/double gearing, marked "Aurelius Bros., Braham, Minn. Pat. Nov. 9, 1926," 11½" h. (Fig. 16-75, left) **50.00**

Aurelius Bros., wood handle, rotary, rare triple dasher, rotary marked "Master Egg Beater Mfd. By Aurelius Bros., Braham, Minn. Pat. Appld. For," 11½" h. (Fig. 16-75, left center) **300.00**

Aurelius Bros., wood handle, rotary marked "Favorite Mfg. By Mille Lacs Lake Spinner Co (Aurelius)," 11¾" h. (Fig. 16-75, right center) **25.00**

Aurelius Bros., wood handle, rotary marked "Ideal Mille Lacs Mfg. (Aurelius)," 10¾" h. (Fig. 16-75, right) **30.00**

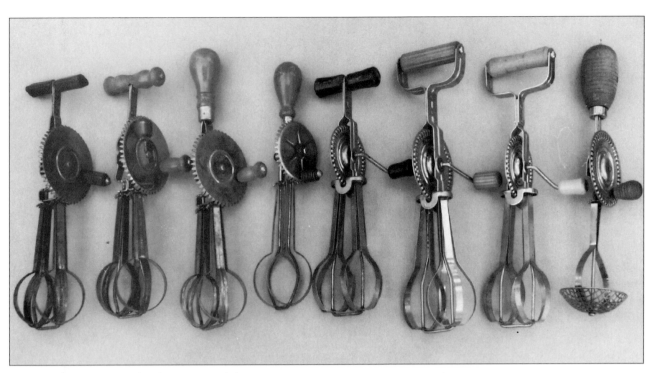

Fig. 16-74 – Various Androck rotary crank beaters.

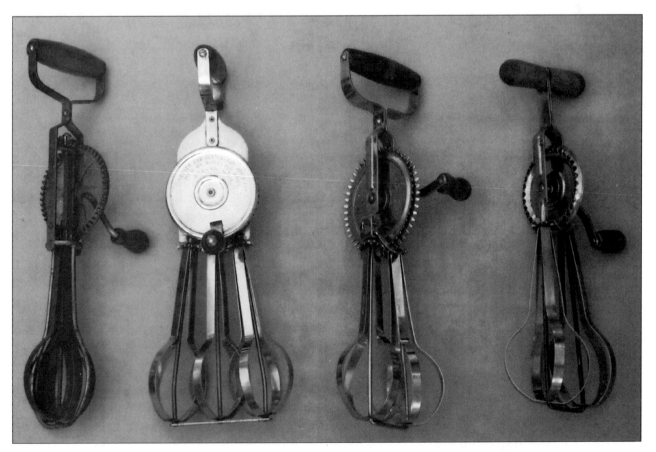

Fig. 16-75

Blisscraft of Hollywood, plastic, rotary, marked "Blisscraft of Hollywood Pat. USA Pend.," scarce, 12" h. (Fig. 16-76) **60.00**

Cyclone, cast iron, rotary marked "Cyclone Pat. 6-25 and 7-16 1901," 11½" h. (Fig. 16-77, center two) **75.00**

Cyclone, cast iron, rotary marked "Cyclone Pat 6-25-1901 Reissue 8-26-1902," 13½" h. (Fig. 16-77, far left & right) **90.00**

Dover, cast iron, rotary marked "Dover Egg Beater Pat. May 31 1870," 12½" h. **200.00**

Dover, cast iron, rotary marked "Dover Egg Beater Patd May 6th 1873 Apr 3d 1888 Nov. 24th 1891 Made in Boston U.S.A. Dover Egg Beater Co.," 11¼" h. **50.00**

Dover, cast iron, nickel-plated, D-handle, rotary marked "Genuine Dover, Dover Stamping Co.," 11¼" h. **50.00**

Dover, cast iron, rotary tumbler model (smaller dashers to fit in glass or tumbler), marked "Dover Egg Beater Patd Made in Boston U.S.A.," 9" **80.00**

Dream Cream, rotary turbine marked "The Dream Cream Trade Mark Whip Manufactured by A.D. Foyer & Company Chicago," 10" h. **40.00**

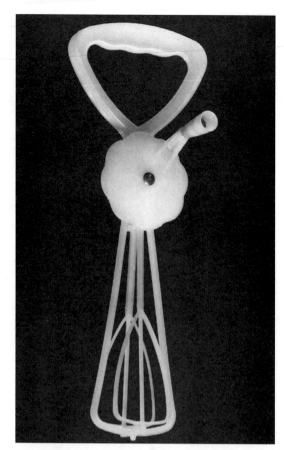

Fig. 16-76

Fig. 16-77 – Two sizes of Cyclone beaters.

Fig. 16-78

Fig. 16-79

Fig. 16-80

Express, cast iron, rotary w/fly swatter dasher, marked "Pat. Oct. 25, 1887" only, rare, 11½" h. (Fig. 16-78) . . . **550.00**

Hand-held, all-wire, unmarked, 13" h. **35.00**

Hand-held, plastic handle, marked "Patent No. 2906510" **5.00**

Holt-Lyon, cast-iron propeller, marked "Lyon Egg Beater Albany N.Y. Pat. Sep 7 '97," 10" h. (Fig. 16-79) **120.00**

Holt-Lyon, cast iron, side-handle, marked "Holt's Egg Beater & Cream Whip Pat. Aug. 22-'98 Apr. 3-00," 8½" h. (Fig. 16-80, left) **200.00**

Holt-Lyon, cast iron, side-handle, marked "H-L Co.," 8½" h. (Fig. 16-80, right) **225.00**

Jaquette Bros., scissors-type, cast iron, marked "Jaquette Bros No. 1," 7½" l. **400.00**

Jaquette Bros., scissors-type, cast iron, marked "Jaquette Bros No. 2," 8¾" l. **350.00**

Ladd, metal rotary, marked "No. 0 Ladd Beater Pat'd July 7, 1908 Feb. 2 1915 United Royalties Corp.," 9¾" h. (Fig. 16-81) **20.00**

Ladd, wood handle, metal rotary, marked "No. 00 Ladd beater Patd Oct. 18, 1921 United Royalties Corp.," 11" l. (Fig. 16-81) **12.00**

Ladd, metal rotary, marked "No. 1 Ladd Beater July 7, 1908, Oct, 1921," 11½" h. (Fig. 16-81) **15.00**

Ladd, tumbler model, metal rotary, marked "No. 5 Ladd Ball Bearing Beater Oct. 18 1921," 11½" h. (Fig. 16-81) **35.00**

Ladd, beater held in two-part apron marked "Ladd No. 2," embossed on pedestal jar "Ladd Mixer No. 2," 13½" h. (Fig. 16-81) **250.00**

Monroe, cast-iron rotary, shelf mount, marked "EP Monroe patented April 19 1859," 10½" h. (Fig. 16-82) **700.00**

P-D-&-Co., cast-iron rotary w/spring dasher bottom w/the word "E - A - S - Y" cut-out on spokes of main gear wheel & marked "Pat Sept. 28 26," 9¾" h. **500.00**

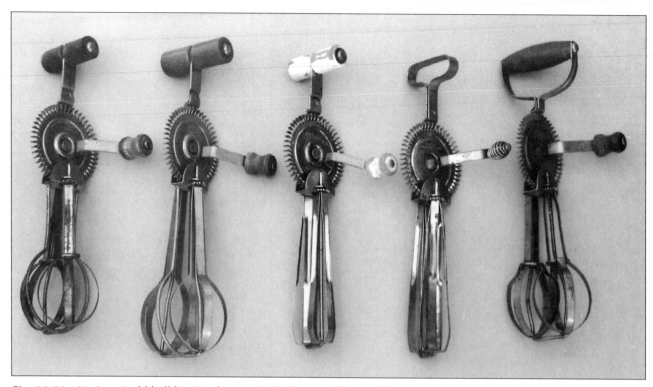

Fig. 16-81 – Various Ladd ball bearing beaters, including tumbler models.

S & S Hutchinson, cast-iron rotary (w/Hutchinson cut-out in wheel) marked "Hutchinson New York Pat. apld For," glass apron on bowl embossed "130 Worth St. New York J. Hutchinson S&S Trade Mark," 9½" h. **450.00**

S & S Hutchinson, heavy tin rotary marked "S&S Hutchinson No. 2 New York Pat. Sept. 2, 1913," w/heavy tin apron on ribbed glass jar embossed "National Indicator Co. No. 2 S&S Trade Mark Long Island City," 9½" h. (Fig. 16-83) **300.00**

Taplin, cast-iron rotary, marked "The Taplin Mfg. Co. New Britian Conn, U.S.A Light Running Pat. Nov. 24 '08," 12½" h. (Fig. 16-84) **50.00**

Taplin, cast-iron rotary, wood handle, marked "The Taplin Mfg. Co. New Britian Conn, U.S.A Light Running Pat. Nov. 24 '08," 11½" h. **35.00**

Taplin, cast-iron rotary, wood handle, marked "Pattern Improved April 14, 1903," 11¾" h. **30.00**

Turner & Seymour, cast-iron frame, metal gears, wood handle, marked

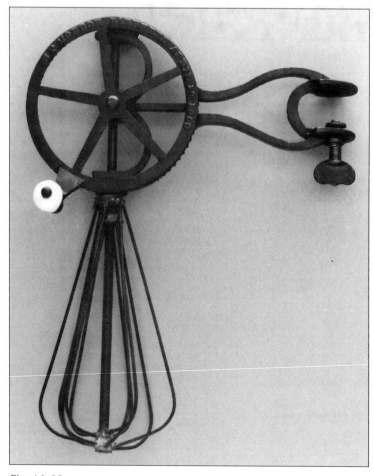

Fig. 16-82

Fig. 16-83

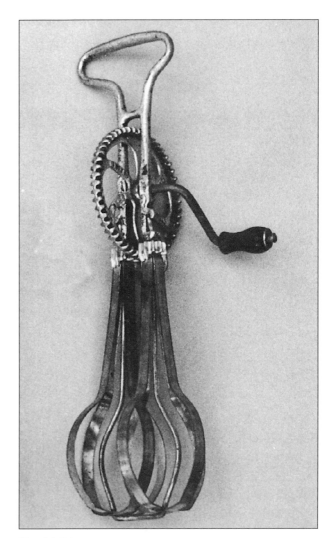

Fig. 16-84

"Merry Swirl Pat. 16-28-16 Other Pat.
Pending (T&S)," 11½" h. **20.00**

Turner & Seymour, cast-iron rotary, marked
"T&S Dover Beater," 10¼" h. **45.00**

Turner & Seymour, metal rotary, wood
handle, marked "T&S No. 39, Made in USA,"
11½" h. **10.00**

Turner & Seymour, tumbler model, metal
rotary, marked "Blue Swirl Pat. Nov. 28, 1916
Aug. 2, 1921 Pat. Pending Made in U.S.A.
(T&S)," 10¾" h. **15.00**

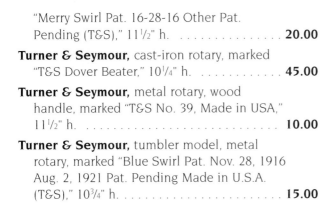

GRANITEWARE

Whether you prefer it as Graniteware, Agate Ware,
or Enameled Ware, the production was a process of
adhering single or multiple coats of enamel to
metal. This was done by using high temperatures in
a kiln drying system. When completed the items had
a glass-like finish. Even though they advertised it as
a very durable product, it does chip easily.
Production was carried on on a large scale in the
United States from the late 1870s through the
1950s. Even today there are a few companies still in
existence, but the majority of them are in foreign
countries.

In determining the values of Graniteware in this
price guide the following factors were used—condition, rarity, color, shape, size, age, dated, labeling,
and desirability. Values in the listing are based on
near-mint condition. Prices will vary according to
the condition of the piece.

—Jo Allers

Fig. 16-85

Fig. 16-87

◆ Blue & White Swirl

Baking pan, wire handles, 8³/₄" w, 12" l., 2¹/₂"
depth **$175.00**

Berry bucket, tin cov., wire handle, 4¹/₄" d.,
5³/₄" h. (Fig. 16-85) **225.00**

Bowl, mixing, 10" d., 3¹/₂" h. **100.00**

Bread raiser, tin cov., footed, 16" d., 9¹/₂" h. . . . **475.00**

Butter churn, wooden cov., 10" d., 18" h.
(Fig. 16-86) **1,800.00**

Chamber pail, cov., 10" d., 11¹/₂" h. **225.00**

Chamber pot, 10" d., 4³/₄" h. **125.00**

Coffee biggin, tin biggin & cover, 4" d., 9" h.
(Fig. 16-87) **800.00**

Coffee boiler, cov., Columbian Ware, 9" d.,
10¹/₂" h. **425.00**

Coffeepot, tin cov., goose neck, 4¹/₂" d.,
7³/₄" h. **265.00**

Colander, footed, 9¹/₂" d., 7³/₄" h. **250.00**

Cream can, tin cov., Columbian Ware, 4" d.,
7³/₄" h. (Fig. 16-88) **800.00**

Cream can, tin cov., 6¹/₂" d., 11" h. **425.00**

Creamer, Columbian Ware, 4" d., 5" h. **700.00**

Cup, Columbian Ware, 4" d., 3" h. **120.00**

Cuspidor, 2 pcs., 9¹/₂" d., 4¹/₂" h. **225.00**

Fig. 16-86

Fig. 16-88

Dipper, windsor, 6¼" d., 6¼" handle **120.00**
Dish pan, oval, 12¾" w., 5" h., 17" l. **250.00**
Funnel, bulbous shape, 4½" d., 3½" h.
   (Fig. 16-89) **190.00**
Jelly roll pan, 8¾" d., ¾" h. **65.00**
Kettle, straight sided cooking, Columbian
   Ware, 14" d., 13" h. **425.00**
Ladle, soup, 3½" d., 10½" handle **75.00**
Loaf pan, 6½" w., 11¾" l., 3½" depth. **300.00**
Lunch bucket, oval, wire & wood handle,
   3 pcs., 9" w., 8¼" l., 7" depth (Fig. 16-90) . . **600.00**
Measuring cup, 3½" d., 4½" h. (Fig. 16-91) . . **500.00**
Muffin pan, 6 cup (Fig. 16-92) **1,350.00**
Muffin pan, Columbian Ware, 8 cup **1,200.00**
Mug, 3½" d., 3" h. **60.00**
Mug, miner, 6" d., 5" h. **140.00**
Pail, water, 11½" d., 9" h. **150.00**
Pie pan, 10¾" d., 1¼" h. **60.00**
Pitcher, 6" h., 5" d., convex (Fig. 16-93) **300.00**
Pitcher, 9" h., 6" d., water, ... **275.00**
Roaster, oval, flat top, cover, 14" w., 7½" h.,
   9½" depth **175.00**
Salt box, wooden cov., marked "Sel," 6" d.,
   9¾" h. (Fig. 16-94) **500.00**
Salt & pepper shakers, 1½" d., 2½" h., pr.
   (Fig. 16-95) **2,400.00**
Sauce pan, w/long black handle, 10" d.,
   5¼" h. **125.00**

Fig. 16-89

Fig. 16-90

Fig. 16-91

Fig. 16-93

Fig. 16-94

Fig. 16-95

Soup bowl, white interior, 9¼" d., 1½" h. **125.00**

Spoon, 2½" d., 12" l. **225.00**

Strainer, 7¾" d., 5½" handle **225.00**

Teakettle, cov., wood & wire handle, 10" d.,
7" h. (Fig. 16-96) **300.00**

Teakettle, cov., wood & wire handle,
Columbian Ware, 10½" d., 7" h.
(Fig. 16-97) **625.00**

Teapot, tin cov., bulbous, 5" d., 5" h., ... **275.00**

Tea steeper, tin cov., 5" d., 5" h.,
(Fig. 16-98) **225.00**

Wash basin, 13¾" d., 3¾" h. **100.00**

Fig. 16-92

Fig. 16-96

Fig. 16-97

Fig. 16-98

Fig. 16-99

◆ Blue Diamond Ware (Iris Blue & White Swirl)

Baking pan, 7³/₄" w., 10" l., 2" depth
(Fig. 16-99) **225.00**

Berry bucket, cov., 5" d., 5¹/₂" h. **400.00**

Bowl, mixing, 5" d., 2" h. **75.00**

Chamber pot, cov., 10¹/₄" d., 8" h. **275.00**

Coffee boiler, cov., 9¹/₂" d., 12" h. **300.00**

Coffeepot, cov., 5¹/₂" d., 9³/₄" h. (Fig. 16-100) . **350.00**

Cream can, 5" d., 9" h. **575.00**

Creamer, 3¹/₂" d., 5" h. (Fig. 16-101, right) . . **325.00**

Cuspidor, 8³/₄" d., 5" h. **275.00**

Funnel, bulbous, 7¹/₄" d., 5" h. **225.00**

Kettle, cov., Berlin-style, 8¹/₄" d., 7" h. **200.00**

Measuring cup, 4¹/₄" d., 6" h. **600.00**

Measuring cup, 3" d., 4¹/₂" h. (Fig. 16-102) . . **625.00**

Molasses pitcher, cov., 3¹/₂" d., 6" h.
(Fig. 16-103) **900.00**

Mug, 3" d., 3" h. **100.00**

Mug, miner's, 6" d., 4³/₄" h. (Fig. 16-104) **225.00**

Mustard pot, cov., 2³/₄" d., 4" h.
(Fig. 16-105) **1,000.00**

Pitcher, water, 10¹/₂" h., 6" d., (Fig. 16-106) . . **575.00**

Fig. 16-101

Fig. 16-100

Fig. 16-102

Fig. 16-103

Fig. 16-104

Fig. 16-105

Fig. 16-106

Fig. 16-107

Platter, oval, 11 × 14", 1" depth **300.00**

Roaster, cov., oval, flat top, 17¹/₂" w., 7¹/₂" h.,
11³/₄" depth **250.00**

Soup bowl, white interior, 9¹/₄" d., 1¹/₂" h. **165.00**

Sugar bowl, cov., 4¹/₄" d., 6¹/₄" h. (Fig. 16-101,
left) **450.00**

Teapot, cov., bulbous body, 5¹/₂" d., 6" h.
(Fig. 16-107) **700.00**

Wash basin, 14¹/₂" d., 4" h. **200.00**

◆ Brown & White Swirl

Berry bucket, cov., wood & wire handle,
10¹/₂" d., 11¹/₂" h. **400.00**

Chamber pail, cov., 10¹/₂" d., 11¹/₂" h.
(Fig. 16-108) **300.00**

Coffee boiler, cov., 8¹/₂" d., 11¹/₂" h. **325.00**

Coffeepot, cov., goose neck, 5¹/₂" d., 9¹/₂" h. . **425.00**

Creamer, 3¹/₂" d., 5" h. **825.00**

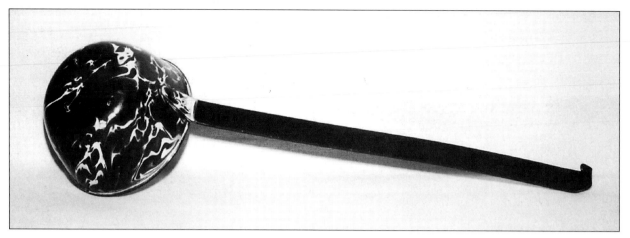

Fig. 16-109

Fig. 16-108

Fig. 16-110

Dipper, 4¹/₂" d., 12" handle (Fig. 16-109) **145.00**

Dish pan, oval, 14" w., 17³/₄" l., 7" h. **280.00**

Jelly roll pan, 10" d., 1¹/₄" h. **120.00**

Kettle, cov., Berlin-style, wood & wire handle,
    6¹/₄" d., 4¹/₄" h. (Fig. 16-110) **300.00**

Measuring cup, 4" d., 6¹/₄" h. **425.00**

Mug, miner's, 6" d., 4¹/₂" h. **225.00**

Pitcher, water, 8³/₄" h., 6¹/₄" d. **450.00**

Roaster, cov., round, 12" d., 8¹/₂" h. **300.00**

Soap dish, hangling, w/insert, 6" w., 3¹/₄" h.,
    4¹/₄" depth, 3 pcs. (Fig. 16-111) **240.00**

Spoon, 2¹/₄" d., 13¹/₄" h. **125.00**

Spooner, 4" d., 5¹/₄" h. (Fig. 16-112) **1,100.00**

Sugar bowl, cov., 4¹/₄" d., 6" h. **900.00**

Teakettle, cov., iron coiled handle, 7¹/₄" d.,
    7" h. **750.00**

Tumbler, 3¹/₄" d., 3¹/₂" h. (Fig. 16-113) **325.00**

Wash basin, 10¹/₂" d., 3¹/₄" h. **125.00**

◆ Chrysolite & White Swirl (Dark Green & White Swirl)

Baking pan, 8" w., 9¹/₂" l., 2" depth **225.00**

Berry bucket, cov., wood & wire handle, 5" d.,
    5¹/₄" h. (Fig. 16-114) **375.00**

Fig. 16-111

Fig. 16-112

Fig. 16-113

Fig. 16-114

Bowl, mixing, 10" d., 4" h. **125.00**

Butter churn, granite storage cover, 10¼" d.,
   19" h. **2,000.00**

Chamber pot, cov., 9" d., 6¾" h. (Fig. 16-115) . . **300.00**

Coffee boiler, cov., 9¼" d., 11¾" h. **350.00**

Coffeepot, cov., goose neck, 5¼" d., 8½" h. . . **450.00**

Cream can, tin cov., 5" d., 9½" h. **550.00**

Cup & saucer, 4" d., 2" h. cup, 6" d. saucer
   (Fig. 16-116) **125.00**

Cuspidor, 7½" d., 4¼" h. **400.00**

Lunch bucket, oval, 9" w., 7" h., 6¾" d. . . . **1,100.00**

Milk pan, 10" d., 2" h. **75.00**

Mug, railroad advertisement "C. & N. W. Ry.,"
   (Chicago & North Western Railroad), 2¾" d.,
   2¾" h. (Fig. 16-117, left) **200.00**

Mug, railroad advertisement, "Port Arthur
   Route," 2¾" d., 2¾" h., (Fig. 16-117,
   right) **200.00**

Pail, water, 9½" d., 8" h. **225.00**

Pitcher, water, 9" h., 5½" d. (Fig. 16-118) . . . **350.00**

Plate, 9" d., ¾" h. **125.00**

Skimmer, 4¾" d., 11" handle **200.00**

Fig. 16-115

Fig. 16-116

Fig. 16-118

Fig. 16-117

Fig. 16-119

Fig. 16-120

Fig. 16-121

Fig. 16-122

Soap dish, hanging, w/insert, 6" w., 3¼" h.,
  4¼" depth **250.00**

Tea steeper, cov., 4¼" d., 5" h. (Fig. 16-119) . . **400.00**

◆ Cobalt Blue & White Swirl

Baking dish, 8" w., 14" l., 2¼" depth **225.00**

Berry bucket, cov., 6" d., 6" h. **325.00**

Chamber pail, cov., 10¾" d., 12" h. **300.00**

Coffeepot, cov., belle-shape, 4½" d., 8¼" h.
  (Fig. 16-120) **650.00**

Coffeepot, cov., wooden handle, 5½" d., 9" h.
  (Fig. 16-121, right) **375.00**

Coffeepot, cov., wooden handle, 5¾" d.,
  9½" h. (Fig. 16-121, left) **350.00**

Colander, footed, 9½" d., 3¾" h. **300.00**

Creamer, 3½" d., 5" h. **875.00**

Cup & saucer, 2¼" h., 4¼" d. cup, 6" d.,
  saucer **125.00**

Dipper, windsor, 5¼" d., 9½" handle
  (Fig. 16-122) **175.00**

Double boiler, cov., 6¾" d., 8" h., 3 pcs. **400.00**

Funnel, tapered, 4¼" d., 4¾" h. (Fig. 16-123) . . **180.00**

Grocer's scoop, 6½" w., 13½" l., 2¼" depth . . **400.00**

Measuring cup, 3" d., 3½" h. **550.00**

Milk pan, 10½" d., 2½" h. **75.00**

Mold, flutted, round, 4¾" d., 2¼" h. **400.00**

Muffin pan, 9 cup **1,000.00**

Mug, 4" d., 3¼" h. **90.00**

Fig. 16-123

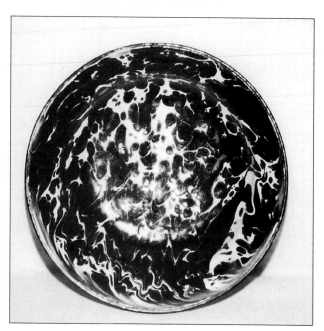

Fig. 16-125

Fig. 16-124

Pail, water, 11" d., 9" h. **200.00**

Pitcher, water, 10" h., 7¼" d. **750.00**

Platter, oval, 8" w., 12" l., 1" depth
   (Fig. 16-124) **275.00**

Roaster, cov., round, 12" d., 8½" h. **325.00**

Sauce pan, lipped, 6" d., 3" h., 6" handle **95.00**

Soup bowl, 9" d., 1½" h. (Fig. 16-125) **150.00**

Spoon, 2½" d., 11½" l. **125.00**

Spooner, 4" d., 5¼" h. **1,100.00**

Teakettle, cov., iron coiled handle, 7¼" d.,
   7¼" h. (Fig. 16-126) **750.00**

Teapot, cov., bulbous body, 4½" d.,
   6" h. **1,000.00**

Wash basin, 12¾" d., 3½" h. **125.00**

Fig. 16-126

Fig. 16-127

Fig. 16-128

Fig. 16-129

◆ Emerald Ware (Green & White Swirl)

Baking pan, 8½" w., 14¼" l., 2⅛" depth **325.00**

Berry bucket, cov., 5¾" d., 6½" h. **400.00**

Coffeepot, cov., goose neck, 5¾" d., 10" h.
(Fig. 16-127) **500.00**

Cream can, cov., wood & wire handle, 5" d.,
9¼" h. (Fig. 16-128) **850.00**

Funnel, bulbous, 5¾" d., 4" h. **375.00**

Jelly roll pan, 9" d., 1¼" h. **100.00**

Lunch bucket, round, 7¼" d., 10" h., 3 pcs. . **1,100.00**

Measuring cup, 4¼" d., 6½" h. (Fig. 16-129) . . **675.00**

Molasses pitcher, cov., 3½" d., 6" h. **1,100.00**

Pitcher, water, 6¼" d., 8¾" h. **500.00**

Sauce pan, cov., Berlin-style, 9" d., 6½" h. . . **250.00**

Skimmer, 5" d., 11" handle (Fig. 16-130) **225.00**

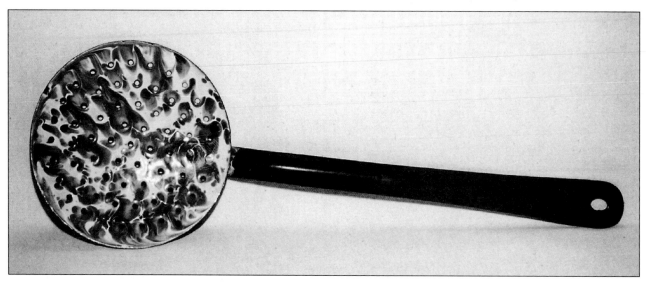

Fig. 16-130

Fig. 16-131

Fig. 16-133

Teakettle, cov., 9" d., 7½" h. **600.00**

Wash basin, 11" d., 3" h. **125.00**

◆ Red & White Swirl

Baking pan, 10¼" w., 15¼" l., 2¼" depth . . **2,000.00**

Berry bucket, tin cov., 6¼" d., 6½" h.
(Fig. 16-131) **2,000.00**

Chamber pot, 9" d., 5" h. (Fig. 16-132) . . . **1,800.00**

Coffee boiler, cov., 9¼" d., 12" h. **1,800.00**

Coffeepot, cov., goose neck, unattached
cover, light weight, ca. 1960s, 5" d., 8" h.
(Fig. 16-133) **100.00**

Fig. 16-132

Fig. 16-134

Fig. 16-135

Fig. 16-136

Fig. 16-137

Coffeepot, cov., goose-neck, 5¼" d., 8½" h.
(Fig. 16-134) **2,000.00**

Cup & saucer, 4¼" d., 2¼" h. cup, 6" d.
saucer **800.00**

Kettle, cov., swirled inside & out, light weight,
ca. 1950s, 8¼" d., 4" h. **40.00**

Mug, miner's, 6¼" d., 5" h. **800.00**

Pitcher, water, 6" d., 9¼" h. **2,000.00**

Plate, swirl inside & out, light weight,
ca. 1950s to 1960s, 10¼" d., 1" h. **30.00**

Sauce pan, wooden handle, swirl inside &
out, light weight, ca. 1950s, 13" w., 17½" l.,
1¼" depth **140.00**

Teakettle, cov., light weight, ca. 1960s, 8" d.,
1¼" h., 6" handle **80.00**

◆ Gray (Mottled)

Berry bucket, cov., 6½" d., 5¾" h. **80.00**

Biscuit cutter, 3½" d., 2¼" h. (Fig. 16-135) . . **550.00**

Butter carrier, cov., oval w/strap handle, 8" w.,
6½" h., 6" depth **250.00**

Butter churn, cov., floor model, wooden
frame, 19" w., 30" h., 13" depth **1,100.00**

Candlestick, 6¼" d., 2" h. **280.00**

Coffee boiler, cov., 8¾" d., 11" h. **100.00**

Fig. 16-139

Coffee flask, cov., round w/screw on cover,
  4³/₄" d., 5" h. **475.00**

Coffeepot, cov., 7¹/₂" d., 11¹/₄" h. **75.00**

Coffeepot, tin cov., 1 cup, 3" d., 4" h.
  (Fig. 16-136) **225.00**

Colander, footed, 10¹/₂" d., 4" h. **75.00**

Comb case, marked "The Jewel," 7³/₄" w.,
  5¹/₂" h., 3" depth (Fig. 16-137) **550.00**

Cream can, tin cov., 5¹/₄" d., 9" h. **110.00**

Cream can, tin cover, mottled steel ware,
  w/label, reads "EL-AN-GE," Boston
  (Fig. 16-138) **225.00**

Creamer, scalloped rim, pewter trim, 3¹/₂" d.,
  6" h. (Fig. 16-139, right) **325.00**

Cuspidor, 7¹/₄" d., 3³/₄" h. **120.00**

Funnel, canning, 4" d., 3" h. **25.00**

Grater, 4¹/₂" w., 11" h. **200.00**

Ladle, 3¹/₄" d., 10" handle **35.00**

Match holder, double pocket, 3³/₄" d., 4" h. . . . **550.00**

Measuring cup, 2¹/₄" d., 2³/₄" h. **300.00**

Measuring cup, embossed "For Household
  Use Only," w/measurement numbers, 4" d.,
  5¹/₂" h. (Fig. 16-140) **150.00**

Fig. 16-138

Fig. 16-140

Fig. 16-141

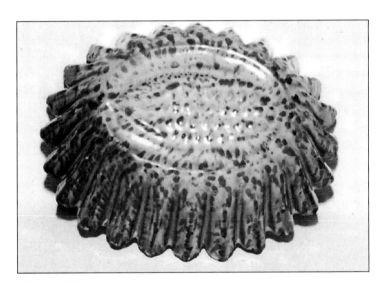

Fig. 16-142

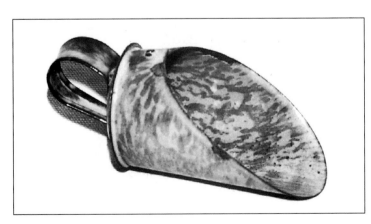

Fig. 16-143

Measuring cup, embossed "1 quart liguid," labeled "Royal Graniteware," 4¹/₂" d., 6¹/₄" h. (Fig. 16-141) **200.00**

Molasses pitcher, cov., 4" d., 6" h. **225.00**

Mold, oval, flutted w/corn design, 4³/₄" w., 6" l., 2¹/₂" h. (Fig. 16-142) . . **180.00**

Pitcher, 10¹/₂" h., 7" d. **150.00**

Plate, dinner, 9¹/₂" d. **30.00**

Platter, oval, 8¹/₂" w., 13" l., 1¹/₄" depth **100.00**

Scoop, spice, 2" w., 5" l. (Fig. 16-143) **250.00**

Scoop, thumb, 2³/₄" w., 4¹/₂" l. **140.00**

Skimmer, hand, 5" w., 5¹/₄" l. **200.00**

Soap dish, hanging, shell shaped, 5¹/₂" w., 2¹/₂" h., 3¹/₂" depth **100.00**

Strainer, screen bottom, labeled "Sterling Enameled Ware," 7¹/₄" d., 2¹/₂" h. (Fig. 16-144) **140.00**

Sugar bowl, cov., pewter scalloped rim, pewter cover & trim, 5" d., 8" h. (Fig. 16-139, left) **375.00**

Teakettle, cov., 5³/₄" d., 4" h. **200.00**

Teapot, cov., bulbous body, pewter trim & cover, 7¹/₄" d., 8¹/₂" h. **375.00**

Fig. 16-144

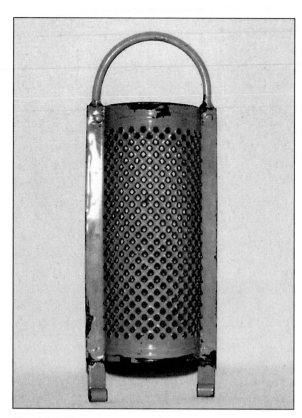

Fig. 16-145

Fig. 16-146

◆ Solid Colors

Baking pan, white w/red trim, 8" w., 13" l.,
2" depth **25.00**

Berry bucket, cov., cream w/green trim,
4¹/₂" d., 5" h. **70.00**

Butter churn, cov., solid blue, 9¹/₂" d., 18" h. . . **800.00**

Candlestick, cream w/green trim, 6¹/₂" d.,
1¹/₂" h. **95.00**

Coffee boiler, cov., solid blue, 8³/₄" d., 11" h. . . **125.00**

Coffee flask, round, solid blue, 3¹/₂" d.,
4¹/₂" h. **400.00**

Coffeepot, cov., cream w/green trim, 5¹/₂" d.,
7³/₄" h. **50.00**

Colander, footed, solid yellow w/black trim,
10" d., 5" h. **35.00**

Cream can, cov., cream w/green trim, 4³/₄" d.,
9" h. **120.00**

Cup & saucer, cream w/green trim, 4¹/₂" d.,
2¹/₄" h., 6" saucer **55.00**

Cuspidor, solid blue, inside & out w/black
trim, 7¹/₂" d., 4¹/₄" h. **75.00**

Double boiler, cov., red w/black trim, 6" d.,
7¹/₂" h., 3 pcs. **55.00**

Dust pan, solid red, 10¹/₂" w., 13¹/₄" h. **200.00**

Grater, solid blue, 3³/₄" d., 10" h. (Fig. 16-145) . . **75.00**

Ladle, white w/black trim & handle, 3" d.,
9" handle **30.00**

Lamp, hanging bracket lamp w/tin reflector,
solid blue, 5¹/₂" d., 10¹/₂" h. (Fig. 16-146) . . **225.00**

Fig. 16-148

Fig. 16-147

Measuring cup, solid cobalt blue, 3½" d.,
4¾" h. **70.00**

Molasses pitcher, cov., white w/navy trim,
3½" d., 5½" h. **120.00**

Mold, white, oval, fluted melon shape, 7½" w.,
11¼" l., 3¼" depth **95.00**

Mug, miner's, cream w/green trim, 5" d.,
4" h. **50.00**

Pail, water, cream w/green trim, 10½" d.,
9¼" h. **60.00**

Pie pan, solid red, 9" d., 1¼" h. **25.00**

Pitcher, water, 9" h., 6" d., solid blue **75.00**

Platter, 10" w., 14" l., 1" depth, oval, cream
w/green trim **20.00**

Salt box, cov., hanging, solid red, white
lettering, wood cover, 5¾" d., 8" h. **150.00**

Scoop, spice, solid blue, 2¼" d., 5¼" h. **100.00**

Skillet, white w/cobalt blue trim, 6" d.,
5" handle **45.00**

Soap dish, hanging, solid blue, 5¼" w., 5" h.,
3" depth **65.00**

Spoon, white w/red handle, 2½" d., 12" l. **25.00**

Strainer, triangular sink, yellow w/black trim,
10¾" d., 3½" h. **35.00**

Sugar bowl, cov., bulbous body, white
w/cobalt blue trim, 4½" d., 5" h. **100.00**

Teakettle, cov., cream w/green trim, 8" d.,
7" h. **80.00**

Teapot, cov., bulbous body, solid blue, 4½" d.,
5¼" h. (Fig. 16-147) **80.00**

Tumbler, solid blue w/black trim, 3¼" d.,
4¼" h. **65.00**

Wash basin, cream w/green trim, 12" d.,
3¼" h. **50.00**

◆ Children's Items, Miniatures & Salesman's Samples

Bowl, child's, feeding, cream w/green trim,
"Dickory Dickory Dock," 8" d. **40.00**

Colander, miniature, footed, blue w/white
specks, 2¾" d., 1¼" h. (Fig. 16-148, left) . . **325.00**

Colander, miniature, footed, solid blue,
3¼" d., 1¾" h. (Fig. 16-148, right) **325.00**

Colander, salesman's sample, footed, grey,
3¾" d., 1¾" h. (Fig. 16-149) **600.00**

Cuspidor, advertising, salesman's sample,
blue & white swirl, inside marked "United
States stamping Co., Moundsville, W. Va.,"
3½" d., 2" h. (Fig. 16-150) **700.00**

Fig. 16-149

Fig. 16-150

Fig. 16-153

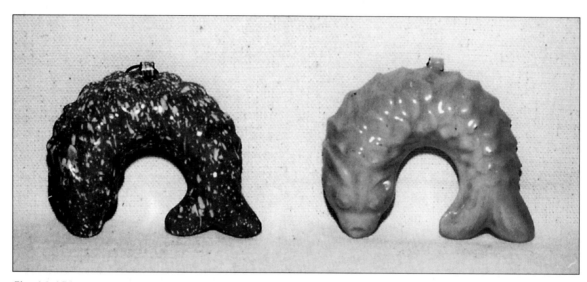

Fig. 16-151

Egg pan, miniature, blue w/white specks, 5
  eyes & handle, 2½" d., ½" h. **150.00**

Fish mold, miniature, blue w/white specks,
  3" l., 2½" h. (Fig. 16-151, left) **250.00**

Fish mold, miniature, solid light blue, 3" l.,
  2½" h. (Fig. 16-151, right) **250.00**

Funnel, miniature, solid blue, marked
  Germany, 1¾" d., 2¼" h. **60.00**

Grater, miniature, solid blue, 1¼" d., 3¾" h.
  (Fig. 16-152, right) **175.00**

Grater, miniature, solid light blue, 1¾" d.,
  4½" h. (Fig. 16-152, left) **175.00**

Mold, miniature, solid blue, Turk's head,
  2¼" d., 1" h. **200.00**

Mug, salesman's sample, brown & white swirl,
  1¼" d., 1" h. (Fig. 16-153) **675.00**

Mug, child's, red w/white interior, "Little Jack
  Horner," marked Sweden, 3" d., 3" h. **35.00**

Fig. 16-152

Fig. 16-155

Pail, water, miniature, solid blue w/bail
handle, 2¾" d., 2¼" h. **125.00**

Potty, salesman's sample, blue & white swirl,
2¾" d., 1¾" h. **550.00**

Roaster, salesman's sample, oval, cobalt &
white swirl, w/insert, 3½" w., 6¼" l., 3¼" h.,
3 pcs. (Fig. 16-154) **1,800.00**

Roaster, salesman's sample, oval, blue &
white mottled, w/insert, marked "LISK,"
4" w., 5¾" l., 2½" h. **1,000.00**

Spatula, miniature, blue w/white specks,
perforated, 1¾" w., 5½" l. **100.00**

Stove, wood burning, salesman's sample,
blue w/white specks, Karr Range Co.,
Bellville, Ill., 13" w., 21" h., 10" depth
(Fig. 16-155) **4,000.00**

Strainer, miniature, blue w/white specks,
w/handle & hook, 2" w., 5" l., 1¼" depth . . **100.00**

Teakettle, cov., miniature, blue, w/lid, bell-
shaped, 3" d., 2½" h. (Fig. 16-156) **400.00**

Tea set, miniature: cov. teapot, four cups, four
saucers, creamer, open sugar; blue, teapot,
3¼" h., 13 pcs. (Fig. 16-157) **450.00**

Fig. 16-154

Fig. 16-156

Fig. 16-157

Tea set, miniature: cov. teapot, four
cups, four saucers, creamer, open
sugar; white w/red floral & leaf design,
teapot 3¾" h., 13 pcs. **450.00**

Wash basin, salesman's sample, cobalt
& white swirl, 3¼" h. (Fig. 16-158,
left) **175.00**

Wash basin, salesman's sample,
chrysolite & white swirl, 3¼" h.
(Fig. 16-158, right) **235.00**

Wash basin, miniature, shaded blue
w/floral design, "Stewart Ware,"
4½" d. (Fig. 16-159, left) **125.00**

Wash basin, salesman's sample, blue
& white swirl, 4½" d. (Fig. 16-159,
right) **125.00**

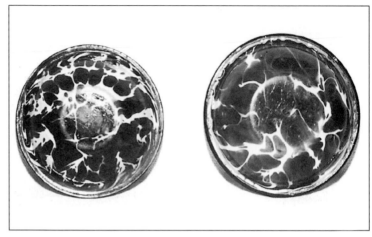

Fig. 16-158

◆ Miscellaneous Graniteware & Related Items

Berry bucket, cov., Bluebell Ware, blue
shading to lighter blue back to blue,
7⅕" d., 7½" h. **150.00**

Bread raiser, tin cov., cobalt & white
mottled, 17¼" d., 11" h. **275.00**

Candlestick, "Snow on the Mountain,"
white w/light blue swirl, 5¼" d.,
2¼" h. **300.00**

Chamber pot, cov., blue & white
mottled, 8" d., 6¾" h. **125.00**

Coaster, Emerald Swirl, 4" d.
(Fig. 16-160, right) **250.00**

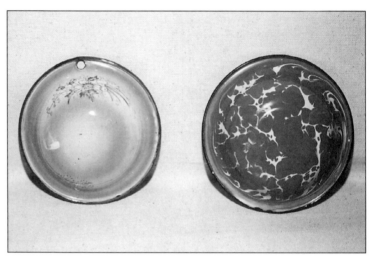

Fig. 16-159

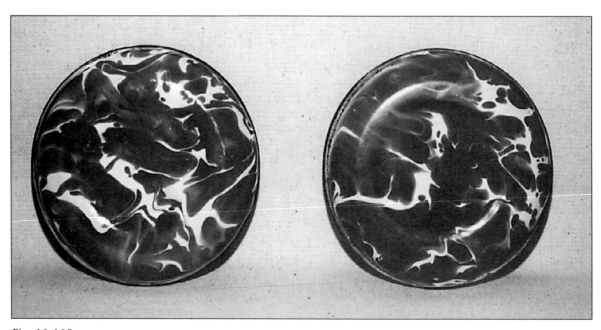

Fig. 16-160

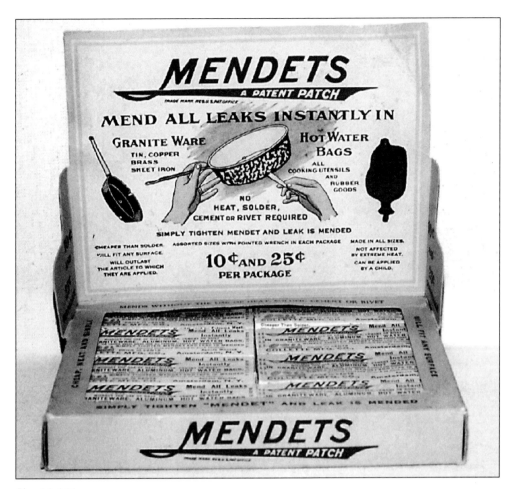

Fig. 16-161

Coaster, Iris Swirl, advertising "Norvell-Shapleigh Hdw., St. Loius, Distributors Blue Diamond Ware," 4" d. (Fig. 16-160, left) . . **250.00**

Coffeepot, cov., Shamrock Ware, dark green shading to lighter green back to dark green, goose neck, 5¼" d., 9" h. **250.00**

Colander, footed, blue & white mottled inside & out, 10" d., 3½" h. **160.00**

Cookbook, "Granite Iron Ware," dated 1883 . . **200.00**

Creamer, Thistle Ware, deep violet shading to a light violet, 3¼" d., 5¼" h. **175.00**

Custard cup, Bluebell Ware, blue shading to a lighter blue back to blue, 4" d., 2½" h. **50.00**

Double boiler, cov., Stewart Ware, shaded blue w/yellow & pink flowers, 7" d., 8" h., 3 pcs. **150.00**

Kettle, preserving, blue & white mottled, 17" d., 8½" h. **100.00**

Ladle, soup, Onyx Ware, brown & white mottled, 3½" d., 9½" handle **35.00**

Measuring cup, Shamrock Ware, dark green shading to a lighter green back to dark green, 3½" d., 4½" h. **200.00**

Mendets box, store display (Fig. 16-161) . . . **150.00**

Molasses pitcher, Bluebelle Ware, blue shading to a lighter blue back to blue, 3½" d., 6" h. **250.00**

Muffin pan, aqua & white swirl, 6 cup **575.00**

Mug, miner's, Duchess Ware, large blue dots w/white & brown veins, 5" d., 4½" h. **225.00**

Pail, water, Bonny Blue, white decorated w/scalloped blue design, 11¼" d., 9½" h. . . . **100.00**

Platter, 8½" w., 13¾" l., 1" depth, oval, End of Day, multicolors: red, yellow, green, cobalt blue & white large swirl **775.00**

Pot scraper, advertising, "Nesco and Pot Scraper," pictures Nesco boy holding Royal Granite Enameled Ware, 2⅞" d., 3½" h. . . . **500.00**

Roaster, Bonny Blue, white decorated w/a scalloped blue design, oval, 10" w., 15¼" l., 7½" h., 2 pcs. **150.00**

Fig. 16-162

Fig. 16-163

Sign, advertising, "Nesco Enameled Ware," wooden w/light blue w/cobalt blue lettering, 34" l., 8½" h. **300.00**

Skillet, Onyx Ware, dark brown & white mottled, 8" d., 1¾" h. **75.00**

Strainer, triangular sink, blue & white mottled, 10" d., 2½" h. **300.00**

Sugar bowl, cov., Shamrock Ware, dark green, shading to a lighter green back to a dark green, 3¾" d., 6" h. **250.00**

Teapot, cov., End of Day, multicolored, red, yellow, cobalt blue & black swirl, 4½" d., 4½" h. (Fig. 16-162) **475.00**

Tea strainer, blue & white mottled, screen bottom, 4½" d., 6¾" h. **155.00**

Tray, advertising, paper tip-type, "To the Patrons of Granite Iron Ware," copyright 1884, 7" w., 9¾" l. (Fig. 16-163) **250.00**

Washboard, "Soap Saver," solid cobalt blue w/wooden frame, 12½" w., 24" h. **140.00**

IRONS

What is the spark that inspires an interest in accumulating antique pressing irons? Once the mysterious process is in action, you are changed to the dedicated and possessed individual known as a collector.

One iron is not a collection. It seems lonely by itself. Perhaps it would be happier if others joined it. A collection begins to coalesce.

Most beginners start with common irons. Some remain at the entry level without moving to explore

Fig. 16-164

the higher delights of collecting. There is a tendency to acquire only one iron of a type and this is a common mistake. A representative collection should include a range of irons. Look for scarcity, attractiveness, interest and condition; emphasize quality. If you have pride in your collection, insist on the best and don't buy anything broken.

A quest for irons will lead to antiques shows, auctions and flea markets. These are chances to be exposed to various kinds of irons, possibly seeing one that will lead in an entirely new direction. Do not overlook any opportunity to get acquainted with the market. The real education begins by talking to other collectors, reading books and periodicals.

Traditionally, irons are used as book ends and doorstops and they look especially at home on the hearth or mantel. The more decorative pieces are proudly displayed where they can be seen in the entryway, living and dining rooms. Some of the finer irons were originally designed to be shown and admired. Today they still fulfill that purpose as well as they did when originally made a century or two ago.

By collecting irons, you are not only engaging in an absorbing hobby, but you are preserving the cultural and historical interest of antique pressing irons.

—Jimmy Walker

Box Iron, brass body, single post & swing
   gate, Germany **$150.00**

Box Iron, brass body w/lift gate & wood
   handle, Northern Europe (Fig. 16-164) . . . **100.00**

Box Iron, iron body w/brass trivet, drop in
   slug, wood handle, Belgium (Fig. 16-165) . . **650.00**

Fig. 16-165

Fig. 16-166

Fig. 16-167

Box Iron, lift-gate, pierced screw secure
    uprights, 18th c., England **150.00**

Charcoal iron, double chimney, marked "Ne
    Plus Ultra," pat. by George Finn July 9, 1902
    (Fig. 16-166) **200.00**

Charcoal iron, marked "Queen Carbon Sad
    Iron" **300.00**

Little iron, cast iron, figure of a swan,
    5" (Fig. 16-167) **500.00**

Little iron, model of a cross rib, 2¹/₂" **35.00**

Tailor iron, advertising-type, cast iron,
    embossed "J A Griffith & Co. Baltimore,"
    3¹/₂" (Fig. 16-168) **250.00**

Fig. 16-168

Fig. 16-169

Fig. 16-170

Tailor iron, cast iron, marked "Sensible"
w/removable wood & iron handle, 20 lb.
(Fig. 16-169) **200.00**

Combination iron, cast iron, marked "Acme
Carbon," w/fluter on side of iron, w/wood
handle (Fig. 16-170) **275.00**

Combination iron, charcoal w/chimney, fluter
bed on side, unmarked **175.00**

Combination iron, fluter/sad iron w/wire
latch (Fig. 16-171) **125.00**

Electric iron, Art Deco-style, streamlined body
w/black handle & red & black cord, marked
"Petipoint" (Fig. 16-172) **175.00**

Electric iron, General Mills w/steam
attachment **45.00**

Fig. 16-171

Fig. 16-172

Fig. 16-173

Fluter, crank, cast iron, w/C-clamp, marked "Crown" on base, Pat. Nov. 2, 1875 (Fig. 16-173) **125.00**

Fluter, crank, marked "American," Pat. Nov. 2, 1875 . . . . **125.00**

Fluter, rocking, cast iron, marked "Geneva" on top portion & "HEAT THIS. Pat.'d 1866" (Fig. 16-174) **45.00**

Fuel iron, iron base w/round tank mounted on top of iron, wood handle, Sears (Fig. 16-175) **175.00**

Polisher, cast iron w/embossed star on top of body, marked "Geneva" (Fig. 16-176) **65.00**

Sad iron, cast iron, coiled handle, marked "Ferris Cold Handle," Pat. Oct. 6, 1891, St Louis (Fig. 16-177) **175.00**

Fig. 16-174

Fig. 16-175

Fig. 16-176

Fig. 16-177

Fig. 16-178

Sad iron, cast iron, w/grid-like design on handle & star embossed on top of body, common (Fig. 16-178) **15.00**

Sad iron, dolphin handle **45.00**

Sad iron, detachable handle, bentwood, marked "Bless & Drake" **190.00**

Sad iron, detachable handle, Enterprise, A.C. Williams & others **25.00**

Sleeve iron, 'duck bill' model, marked "Geneva" on body & "GENEVA Pat. applied for" on toe **275.00**

Fig. 16-179

JUICE REAMERS

Everyone knows what they are...most people have owned one at one time or another...yet few people use them today—reamers! Your grandmother probably used a manual juicer every morning to start off her family's day. But even in today's health conscious society, the job of squeezing juice is relegated to fancy electronic models and good old orange and grapefruit juice often takes a backseat to carrot, mango and other exotic combinations.

However, nothing replaces the beauty or nostalgia of the manual reamer. Invented in the late 1760s to extract citrus juice to cure the maladies of French sailors, reamers eventually were adopted by almost every facet of society as an essential kitchen utensil.

It wasn't until the Civil War-era that the reamer surfaced in this country; and it took another 40-plus years before it was embraced by the average American household. Thanks to the clever marketing tactics of the California Fruit Growers Exchange, and its introduction of the now famous SUNKIST trademark, in 1916 they launched their "Drink An Orange" advertising campaign, and issued a reamer premium as a means to this end. As they say, the rest is his-

tory. The squeezing craze became an overnight success and reamers were produced by glasshouses, pottery factories, and even more elite precious metal manufacturers, both in the United States and abroad. From fine bone china, to whimsical Japanese imports and finely crafted sterling silver examples, reamers are a major collectible today. Prices range from fifty cents to thousands of dollars. Like most major collectibles, reproductions are abundant and the starting collector should get a good education before making any purchases.

—Bobby Zucker Bryson

Aluminum, red enamel, marked "Juice-O-Mat Single Action," ca. 1950s, 8½" h. **$20.00**

Ceramic, blue w/multi-colored flowers, marked "Crown Ducal, Made in England," ca. 1940s, 3½" h. (Fig. 16-179) **85.00**

Ceramic, figure of a clown, orange & white, Goebel, Germany, 5" h. (Fig. 16-181) . . . . **250.00 to 275.00**

Ceramic, figure of clown head, orange & white, Goebel, Germany, ca. 1939, 5" d. (Fig. 16-183) **215.00**

Fig. 16-180

Ceramic, figure of a clown, cream & multicolored w/a yellow & green hat, stamped "Made in Japan" & "Japan," ca. 1930s-40s, 8" h. (Fig. 16-182) **75.00**

Ceramic, green, marked "U.S.A. Ade-O-Matic Genuine Coorsite Porcelain," ca. 1933, 9" h. (Fig. 16-180) **125.00**

Ceramic, light & dark green turtle w/yellow trim, 4¹/₈" h. **50.00**

Ceramic, model of a windmill, beige, blue & green, marked "Made in Japan," ca. 1930s, 4¹/₂" h. **125.00**

Ceramic, model of an elephant, beige, inscribed "A Present from Southend" around rim, marked "Made in Czechoslovakia," 3¹/₂" h. **225.00**

Ceramic, multicolored flowers & black rim on beige ground, marked "Made in Japan," ca. 1930s, w/six tumblers, 8" h., set of 7 (Fig. 16-184 of part) **60.00**

Ceramic, white w/blue decoration of sailboat, marked "Mint," Germany, 3¹/₄" h. (Fig. 16-185) **75.00**

Fig. 16-181

Fig. 16-182

Fig. 16-183

Fig. 16-184

Fig. 16-186

Ceramic, yellow clown, inscribed "Florida," marked "Japan," 5" h. **100.00**

Ceramic, yellow lemon, marked "Germany," ca. 1940s, 3" h. **55.00**

Ceramic, yellow, marked "Red Wing USA," ca. 1928, 6¼" h. (Fig. 16-186) **100.00**

Ceramic, yellow, tan & white, marked "Shelley-England," 3½" h. **100.00**

Glass, amber, Federal Glass Co., 6⅛" d. **20.00**

Glass, amber, Westmoreland, 6¼" d. **250.00**

Glass, butterscotch, marked "Sunkist," McKee Glass Co., ca. 1925-1951, 6" d (Fig. 16-187) **850.00**

Glass, clear, marked "Little Handy Lemon Squeezer Silver & Co. NY," ca. 1885, 6½" l. **85.00**

Fig. 16-185

Fig. 16-187

Fig. 16-188

Fig. 16-189

Glass, cobalt blue, Crisscross patt., Hazel
Atlas Glass Co., 6⅛" d. (Fig. 16-188) **275.00**

Glass, green opaque glass, embossed "McK,"
McKee Glass Co., 5¼" d. **23.00**

Glass, pink, Hazel Atlas Glass Co., 5⅝" d. . . . **45.00**

Glass, pink, Paden City "Party Line," 4 cup
pitcher/floral etched on reverse side,
8¾" h. **150.00**

Glass, Seville yellow, McKee Glass Co.,
6" d. **225.00**

Glass & metal, electric, green metal body
w/white milk glass bowl, marked "Sunkist
Juicet," ca. 1934, 8¾" h. (Fig. 16-189) **40.00**

Plastic, yellow, marked "Bonny Products,
NY,17,NY," ca. 1970s, 4" h. **10.00**

Silver plate, marked "Meridien S.P. Co.
International S. Co.," 4⅝" d. **125.00**

Silver plate, marked Rio-Citro Patent, 3" l. . . . **12.00**

LIGHTING DEVICES

ALADDIN® MANTLE LAMPS

The Mantle Lamp Company of America, creator of the world famous Aladdin Lamp, was founded in Chicago in 1908. Like several of its competitors, the Aladdin coupled the round wick technology with a mantle to produce a bright incandescent light comparable to the illumination provided by a 60 to 75 watt bulb. Through aggressive national advertising and an intensive dealer network, the Aladdin Lamp quickly overcame its competitors to become the standard lighting fixture in the rural American home.

From the company's origin until 1926, Aladdin Lamps were produced in table, hanging, and wall bracket styles made mostly of brass and finished in either satin brass or nickel plate. With the purchase of an Indiana glass plant in the mid-1920s, the Mantle Lamp Company began to make their own glass shades and chimneys, in addition to the manufacture of glass lamp bases. Glass shades, both plain and decorated with reverse painting, were made in a variety of styles. Later, colorful parchment shades were produced in a myriad of colors and with decorations ranging from large, gaudy flowers in the early 1930s to delicate florals and intricate geometrics, sometimes with flocking, from the mid-1930s through the post-war years.

Aladdin kerosene lamps are probably best known for the colorful glass bases made from the late 1920s to the early 1950s. The earliest glass lamps were vase lamps that consisted of a glass vase finished in different colors that had a drop-in brass kerosene font. Later, seventeen different glass patterns were produced and

Fig. 17-2

most patterns were offered in a variety of different glass colors. Crystal glass lamp bases commonly came in clear, green, or amber colors, but for a few years crystal bases were produced in ruby red and cobalt blue. The latter two colors are especially prized by collectors. A translucent to opaque glass called moonstone was

Fig. 17-1

Fig. 17-3

Fig. 17-4

produced during the 1930s and was available in white, green, rose, and for one pattern in the late 1930s, yellow. A few styles had white moonstone fonts attached to a black stem and foot. Other lamps had a moonstone font mounted on a metallic base.

An ivory to white glass called Alacite is unique to the Aladdin Lamp. The late 1930s glass formula contained uranium oxide, and the ivory to marble-like appearance sometimes leads to its confusion with the Crown Tuscan glass of Cambridge. With the commencement of the Manhattan Project, this compound was placed on the restricted list and, as a consequence, the glass formula was changed. Early Alacite lamp bases will glow under a blacklight, whereas later ones will not. The later Alacite lamps also tend toward a white color rather than ivory.

Aladdin kerosene lamps are still being made today. The Mantle Lamp Company left Chicago in 1948 and was absorbed into Aladdin Industries, Inc., which today is headquartered in Nashville, Tennessee. Besides kerosene lighting produced for the domestic and foreign markets, the company also markets institutional food handling equipment and the well-known Stanley thermos bottle.

Aladdin kerosene lamps and their related accessories have been avidly collected over the last thirty years. As a consequence, prices have risen steadily even for the common lamps. Expectedly, condition of the lamp or shade is a very important consideration in determination of value. Glass damage, elec-trification, or missing parts can seriously depreciate value. By comparison, lamps in mint, unused condition and in the original carton fetch premium prices.

—Thomas W. Small

Hanging lamp, decorated w/hand painted roses on ball shade, Model No. 6 (Fig. 17-1) . . . . **$3,500.00 to 4,000.00**

Student lamp, original w/functional tank, unelectrified, Model No. 4 (Fig. 17-2) . . . . **6,500.00 to 7,000.00**

Table lamp, nickel finish, No. 10 flame spreader, Model No. 10 . . . . . . **400.00 to 450.00**

Table lamp, nickel plated w/embossed foot, ½ qt. font, Model No. 1 (Fig. 17-3) . . . . **600.00 to 650.00**

Table lamp, nickel plated, No. 6 flame spreader, Model No. 6 . . . . **80.00 to 100.00**

Table lamp, brass finish, No. 8 flame spreader & No. 401 shade, Model No. 8 (Fig. 17-4) . . . . **400.00 to 475.00**

Vase lamp, blue variegated, gold foot edge, three feet, 10¼" . . . . **550.00 to 600.00**

Vase lamp, green w/dark green foot edge, model No. 12, six feet, 10¼" h. . . . . **200.00 to 250.00**

Vase lamp, peach variegated, gold foot edge, three feet, 10¼" (Fig. 17-5) . . . . **275.00 to 325.00**

Fig. 17-5

Fig. 17-6

Vase lamp, variegated green, gold foot edge, three feet, 10¼" . . . . **250.00 to 300.00**

The following pattern glass names are from J.W. Courter reference books on Aladdin Lamps

Table lamp, Beehive patt., clear, Model B . . . . **100.00 to 125.00**

Table lamp, Beehive patt., green or amber crystal . . . . **125.00 to 175.00**

Table lamp, Cathedral patt., green or amber crystal . . . . **125.00 to 150.00**

Table lamp, Cathedral patt., rose moonstone . . . . **350.00 to 400.00**

Table lamp, Cathedral patt., white moonstone . . . . **300.00 to 350.00**

Table lamp, Corinthian patt., amber or green crystal . . . . **100.00 to 125.00**

Table lamp, Corinthian patt., clear . . . . **80.00 to 100.00**

Table lamp, Corinthian patt., white moonstone font w/green, rose or black foot . . . . **250.00 to 300.00**

Table lamp, Diamond Quilted patt., green moonstone . . . . **250.00 to 300.00**

Table lamp, Lincoln Drape patt., short, amber or ruby crystal w/metal collar at font top . . . . **100.00 to 125.00**

Table lamp, Lincoln Drape patt., short, ruby crystal, raised glass collar at font top . . . . **650.00 to 700.00**

Table lamp, Lincoln Drape patt., tall, cobalt blue, foot top w/circular ring . . . . **1,400.00 to 1,600.00**

Table lamp, Lincoln Drape patt., tall, cobalt blue, scalloped ring on foot top . . . . **1,800.00 to 2,000.00**

Table lamp, Lincoln Drape patt., tall, ruby crystal, lower value for light ruby, higher for dark . . . . **850.00 to 1000.00**

Table lamp, Lincoln Drape patt., tall, slightly tapered stem, Alacite . . . . **125.00 to 175.00**

Table lamp, Orientale patt., ivory, green, or bronze enamel, metallic finish (Fig. 17-6) . . . . **125.00 to 150.00**

Table lamp, Queen patt., green, white, or rose moonstone on metallic foot . . **250.00 to 300.00**

Table lamp, Simplicity patt., rose enamel . . . . **175.00 to 200.00**

Table lamp, Simplicity patt., Alacite, green or or white enamel . . . . **150.00 to 175.00**

Table lamp, Solitaire patt., white moonstone . . . . **2,000.00 to 2,200.00**

Table lamp, Venetian patt., clear, fused stem-foot/bowl, Model A . . . . **350.00 to 400.00**

Table lamp, Venetian patt., clear, green or peach enamel . . . . **125.00 to 150.00**

Fig. 17-7

Fig. 17-8

Fig. 17-9

Table lamp, Venetian patt., clear, white enamel . . . . **100.00 to 125.00**

Table lamp, Vertique patt., green moonstone . . . . **300.00 to 350.00**

Table lamp, Vertique patt., yellow moonstone . . . . **500.00 to 550.00**

Table lamp, Victoria patt., ceramic w/floral decoration & gold bands . . . . **600.00 to 650.00**

Table lamp, Washington Drape patt., clear crystal, plain stem, w/or without oil fill . . . . **75.00 to 100.00**

Table lamp, Washington Drape patt., clear, green, or amber w/open, thick round stem . . . . **100.00 to 150.00**

Table lamp, Washington Drape patt., green or amber crystal, plain stem . . . . **100.00 to 150.00**

◆ Miscellaneous

Chimneys, boxed (Fig. 17-8, left pair) each . . . . **75.00 to 100.00**

 Others, (Fig. 17-8) each . . **15.00 to 25.00**

Mantles, boxed (Fig. 17-7, left) each . . . . **50.00 to 75.00**

Mantles, boxed (Fig. 17-7, center) each . . . . **5.00 to 15.00**

Mantles, boxed (Fig. 17-7, right) each . . . . **20.00 to 30.00**

Matchholder, copper w/accessories & instruction booklet (Fig. 17-9) . . . . **100.00 to 150.00**

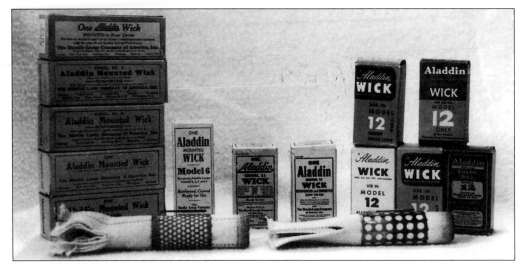

Fig. 17-10

Shades, floral, No. 601F roses, No. 616F
poppies, No. 620F roses . . . . . . **600.00 to 700.00**

Shades, green cased, No. 202 artichoke,
No. 204 eight panel . . . . **800.00 to 1,000.00**

Shades, plain, No. 201, No. 301, No. 401,
No. 501 (for Model No. 11),
No. 601 . . . . **100.00 to 125.00**

Shades, plain, opal No. 205 w/fire
polished bottom rim . . . . **400.00 to 500.00**

Shades, reverse painted, No. 601 Log
Cabin, No. 616 Gristmill, No. 620
Windmill . . . . **300.00 to 350.00**

Shades, Whip-O-Lite parchment, floral,
geometric, or scenic, 14" . . . . . **150.00 to 200.00**

Wicks, boxed, mounted, (Fig. 17-10,
left stack) each . . . . **30.00 to 40.00**

Wicks, boxed, No. 6, mounted
(Fig. 17-10, left center) each . . . . . **20.00 to 25.00**

Wicks, boxed, No. 11 & No. 12, (Fig. 17-10,
right center & right) each . . . . **5.00 to 10.00**

Kerosene & Related Lighting

Kerosene lamps were used from about 1860 until replaced by electric lighting when it became available. In cities and towns this was generally from about the turn-of-the-century until 1920. Rural electrification occurred in the 1930s or later.

Today, kerosene lamps are sought after for their appearance and function. Some owners light them occasionally, while a few enjoy them every night. Certainly experimenting with the lamps can add another dimension to collecting. Try placing lamps strategically—not just to illuminate a room but to create dramatic shadows.

If a hanging lamp is the only source of illumination in a room, patterns of light and shadow and perhaps colors will be splayed out on the ceilings and walls. The flickering of an open flame will create shadows in motion which can give a favorite piece of folk art or furnishings, such as a clock or collectible, a different nighttime look. Natural wood finishes which can look flat under incandescent light will glow with a warm sheen to create the mood of a century ago. Most examples shown here are ones that would have been relatively inexpensive when they were made and are compatible with country furnishings. There was tremendous competition and production in the kerosene lamp business. This led to the creation of an astounding variety of lamps and accessories. Because electric lighting was not perfect, kerosene lamps were preserved for emergencies. Thus Americans are blessed with a good supply and an appreciation that will ensure a continuing demand.

—Catherine Thuro-Gripton

Note: Lamps do not include burner & chimney, unless otherwise noted.

◆ Pre-Kerosene Lamps

Hand lamp, pressed waffle design, flared font
w/applied handle, burning fluid burner,
ca. 1850 (Fig. 17-11, right) **$250.00**

Fig. 17-11

Fig. 17-12

Fig. 17-13

Table lamp, free-blown squatty bulbous font above a flared columnar standard, w/whale oil burner, ca. 1850 (Fig. 17-11, left) **175.00**

Table lamp, pressed Star-and-Punty patt., slightly flared font w/smooth domed top, w/burning fluid burner, ca. 1850 (Fig. 17-11, center) **250.00**

◆ Kerosene Lamps

Hand lamp, blue opalescent pressed glass, Sheldon Swirl patt., footed . . . **500.00 to 550.00**

Hand lamp, blue pressed glass, Whirlpool patt., footed . . . . **250.00 to 300.00**

Hand lamp, clear pressed glass, Bullseye patt. . . . . **125.00 to 150.00**

Hand lamp, clear pressed glass, Polka Dot patt., ovoid font decorated w/opalescent cranberry or ruby dots, applied handle, all above circular domed base, kerosene burner & baluster-shaped chimney w/slightly scalloped rim (Fig. 17-12) . . . . . **1,550.00 and up**

Hand lamp, clear pressed glass, Quartered Block patt., w/handle, flat bottom, kerosene burner & "pie crust" chimney, ca. 1880s (Fig. 17-13, center) . . . . **150.00 to 200.00**

Hand lamp, clear glass, Quartered Block patt., w/handle, footed, kerosene burner & "pie crust" chimney, ca. 1880s (Fig. 17-13, far right) . . . . **150.00 to 200.00**

Hand lamp, clear pressed glass, Ribbed patt., bulbous globular font tapering into flared foot, ca. 1850s-1870s (Fig. 17-14, center front) . . . . **75.00 to 100.00**

Hand lamp, clear glass, Ribbed patt., globular font w/applied handle, ca. 1850s-1870s (Fig. 17-14, right front) . . . . **125.00 to 150.00**

Hand lamp, clear pressed glass, Ribbed patt., squatty bulbous font, applied handle, ca. 1850s-1870s (Fig. 17-14, left front) . . . . **75.00 to 100.00**

Hand lamp, clear pressed glass, squatty ovoid font w/ribbed center ring, tapering to domed foot w/applied handle, patented, marked, Atterbury & Co., ca. late 1860s-1870s (Fig. 17-15) . . . . **75.00 to 100.00**

Hand lamp, milk glass, flared foot below angular font w/handle & wide lip below clear glass top, Collin's burner & milk glass Sun chimney tapering at top, Adams & Company, rare complete (Fig. 17-16) . . . . **950.00 to 1,000.00**

Hand lamp, tin & glass, painted tin w/handle & removable glass font, w/Columbia burner & cylindrical glass chimney combination, font & holder marked "Bradley's Security Factory Lamp" (Fig. 17-17, left) . . . . **200.00 to 250.00**

Hanging lamp, adjustable, cast iron & glass, elaborately cut-out cast-iron arms holding two lamps, etched glass fonts decorated w/star- and cross-like designs, glass chimneys & glass shades, original finish & shades, ca. 1860s-1880s (Fig. 17-18) . . . . **1,500.00 to 2,000.00**

Fig. 17-14

Fig. 17-15

Fig. 17-16

Fig. 17-17

Mechanical lamp, Wanzer Mechanical lamp, metal base w/forced draft for operation even without a shade, shown w/a 5" d. opalescent Hobnail shade (Fig. 17-17, far right)

Lamp base . . . .**450.00 to 550.00**

Opalescent Hobnail shade . . . . . .**75.00 and up**

Parlor lamp, milk glass, squatty ovoid shade tapering to slightly flaring rim above squatty pear-shaped bottom, both decorated w/raised & painted flowers, ca. 1880s-1890s (Fig. 17-19) **275.00**

Fig. 17-18

Fig. 17-19

Fig. 17-20

Fig. 17-21

Parlor vase lamp, globular white glass shade w/hand-painted roses w/cylindrical glass chimney, above baluster-shaped vase w/scroll-cut lip & scrolled handles, all on elaborately scroll-cut footed base (Fig. 17-20) **275.00**

Student lamp, brass & glass, cylindrical chimney w/milk glass shade, original finish & parts, kerosene burner, ca. 1879 (Fig. 17-21) . . . . **600.00 to 700.00**

Student lamp, brass & glass, Manhattan Brass Co., original nickel-plate base & cased green glass shade (Fig. 17-17, center back) . . . . **450.00 and up**

Table lamp, clear blown glass, globular font, brass standard on square marble base, or chimney, the appropriate chimneys & burners (as shown here) could easily double or triple the value, ca. 1860s (Fig. 17-22, w/chimney & burner) each . . . . **75.00 to 100.00**

Table lamp, clear pressed glass, Bullseye & Fleur-de-lis patt., font tapering to baluster-shaped standard, late 1860s (Fig. 17-23) . . . . **100.00 to 150.00**

Table lamp, clear pressed glass, Chadwick patt., w/milk glass base . . . . **175.00 to 200.00**

Table lamp, clear pressed glass, Corn patt., ovoid font tapering to ridge at top w/bulging below burner, glass standard & base, marked w/patent date of 1873, La Belle Glass Company, Bridgeport, Ohio (Fig. 17-24) . . . . **150.00 to 200.00**

Table lamp, clear pressed glass, Corn-in-Shield patt., Oval Band patt. base . . . . **175.00 to 225.00**

Table lamp, clear pressed glass, Daisy and Button patt., glass font w/domed top & angled bottom above paneled standard & base, ca. 1890s (Fig. 17-25) . . . . **100.00 to 125.00**

Table lamp, clear pressed glass, Eyewinker patt., cylindrical font above baluster-shaped standard & base, Dalzell, Gilmore & Leighton Company (Fig. 17-26) . . . **125.00 to 150.00**

Table lamp, clear pressed glass, Gaiety patt., angular ribbed font decorated w/opalescent feathered design, cylindrical glass standard on circular base, kerosene burner & baluster-shaped chimney w/scalloped rim (Flg. 17-27) . . . . **370.00 to 420.00**

Fig. 17-22

Fig. 17-23

Fig. 17-24

Fig. 17-25

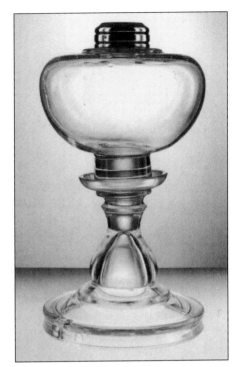

Fig. 17-26   Fig. 17-27   Fig. 17-28

Table lamp, clear pressed glass, McKee Tulip
patt. . . . . **300.00 and up**

Table lamp, clear pressed glass, Moon and
Crescents patt., w/brass stem & marble
base . . . . **300.00 to 350.00**

Table lamp, clear pressed glass, ovoid font
above Ewing patent drip catcher above
clear glass baluster-shaped standard,
ca. 1870s (Fig. 17-28) . . . . **150.00 to 200.00**

Table lamp, clear pressed glass, Quartered
Block patt., one-piece, kerosene burner &
"pie crust" chimney, ca. 1880s (Fig. 17-13,
back left) . . . . **125.00 to 150.00**

Table lamp, clear pressed glass, Ribbed patt.,
globular font, columnar standard w/flared
ribbed base, ca. 1850s-1870s (Fig. 17-14,
back left) . . . . **75.00 to 100.00**

Table lamp, clear pressed glass, Ribbed patt.,
inverted pear-shaped font, on baluster-
shaped standard, ca. 1850s-1870s
(Fig. 17-14, back right) . . . . **125.00 to 150.00**

Table lamp, clear pressed glass, Riverside
Wild Rose patt. . . . . **175.00 to 225.00**

Table lamp, clear pressed glass, Sawtooth
patt., globular font w/diamond-like pattern
on lower half, tapering brass connector,
slightly flared columnar milk glass standard
& base, includes burner & tall, thin
cylindrical chimney (Fig. 17-29) . . **250.00 to 300.00**

Fig. 17-29   Fig. 17-30

Table lamp, clear & cranberry opalescent
pressed glass, Snowflake patt., squatty
ovoid font in opalescent cranberry,
above ribbed clear standard, Hobbs
(Fig. 17-30) . . . . **600.00 to 700.00**

Table lamp, clear pressed glass (on inside of
lamp), Veronica patt., ovoid font tapering to
brass standard on a marble base, Hobbs
Brockunier & Company, ca. mid-1860s -
mid-1870s (Fig. 17-31) . . . . **150.00 to 200.00**

Fig. 17-31

Fig. 17-32

Fig. 17-33

Table lamp, cut-overlay, inverted pear font in white cut to green, tapering brass connector, tapering to slightly flared columnar green alabaster standard & base, (Fig. 17-32) . . . . **1,500.00 and up**

Table lamp, green pressed glass, Vera patt. . . . . **175.00 to 225.00**

Table lamp, marigold Carnival pressed glass, Zipper Loop patt. . . . . **650.00 to 750.00**

Table lamp, figural, angular etched clear glass font w/star- and cross-like designs, above spelter fisherwoman holding spear w/a basket full of fish at her feet, all on tiered square base, Bradley & Hubbard Mfg., ca. 1888 (Fig. 17-33) . . . . **200.00 to 250.00**

Table lamp, figural, clear pressed glass font & spelter figure of Mary & her Lamb . . . . **125.00 to 225.00**

Table lamp, figural, clear frosted glass font w/Greek Key design above spelter bust of Empress Eugenie (wife of Napoleon III), ca. 1870s (Fig. 17-34) . . . . **150.00 to 170.00**

Table lamp, Ripley Wedding Lamp, blue & clear pressed glass, two matching blue fonts flanking toothpick holder, above white glass base **1,400.00**

Fig. 17-34

CHAPTER 18

LIGHTNING ROD BALLS

These decorative glass ornaments were used to dress-up lightning rods used on the farm structures and homes of rural America. Many were round with embossed designs such as stars or swirls but some were odd shapes. Amber and dark blue were fairly common colors but other rarer colors can also be found. Today there is a serious core of collectors for these fascinating glass objects and values depend on the rarity of the shape and color. Our thanks to Phil Steiner of Weather or Knot Antiques, Wanatah, Indiana for the information and illustrations provided here.

Amber mast (Fig. 18-1, top left) **$500.00**

Amber RHF (Fig. 18-1, top right) 500.00

Chestnut, milk glass, blue 50.00

Chestnut, milk glass, white 30.00

Chestnut, red . . . . 200.00 to 325.00

D&S, cobalt blue 150.00

Doorknob, milk glass, blue 50.00

Doorknob, milk glass, white 30.00

Diddie Blitzen, orange, marked "BLITZEN"
    (Fig. 18-1, bottom left) 1,750.00

Flat quilt patt., grey green mercury (Fig. 18-1,
    top center) 750.00

Hawkeye, amber 150.00

Hawkeye, bright orange (Fig. 18-1,
    center middle row) 2,000.00

Hawkeye, milk glass, blue 50.00

Hawkeye, milk glass, white 35.00

Fig. 18-1

Hawkeye, sun-colored amethyst 100.00

Moon & Star patt., amber (Fig. 18-2, top
    right) 150.00

Moon & Star patt., cobalt blue (Fig. 18-2,
    bottom left) 3,500.00

Fig. 18-2

Moon & Star patt., gold (Fig. 18-2, center) . . **500.00**

Moon & Star patt., milk glass, flash blue over white (Fig. 18-2, top left) **50.00**

Moon & Star patt., milk glass, grey, rare (Fig. 18-2, bottom right) **7,500.00**

Moon & Star patt., milk glass, orange, rare (Fig. 18-2, bottom center) **5,000.00**

Moon & Star patt., red (Fig. 18-2, left center) **300.00**

Moon & Star patt., silver (Fig. 18-2, right center) **550.00**

Moon & Star patt., sun-colored amethyst (Fig. 18-2, top center) **75.00**

Onion-shaped, cobalt blue (Fig. 18-1, left center) **2,250.00**

Plain, "7-Up" green, 4½" **150.00**

Plain, amber, 4½" **25.00**

Plain, cobalt blue, 4½" **60.00**

Plain, flashed orange, 4½" (Fig. 18-1, bottom right) **500.00**

Plain, milk glass, blue, 4½" **20.00**

Plain, milk glass, white, 3½" **10.00**

Plain, milk glass, white, 4½" **15.00**

Plain, red, 4½" . . . . **60.00 to 75.00**

Plain, sun-colored amethyst, 4½" **20.00**

Pleat patt., amber, Barnett (Fig. 18-1, bottom center) **750.00**

Swirl patt., cobalt blue (Fig. 18-1, right center) **2,500.00**

Rugs–Hooked & Other

Fig. 19-1

In most colonial American homes rugs and carpeting were a rarity, reserved mainly for the wealthy. It wasn't until the first half of the 19th century that less expensive commercial carpeting became widely available in this country. At that time hooking and weaving of small rugs and runners also became a popular handicraft and provided some added comfort and color in often austere rooms. Rug hooking became a popular pastime for women with more leisure time by the late 19th century and the handicraft was common right through the Depression era when preprinted background designs were often used. Today the "folksy" designs of many hooked and sewn rugs have made them popular and sometimes expensive collectors' items.

HOOKED

Angel standing over & slaying the devil, holding a shield w/"Quis ut Deus," cross w/ eye, brown, blue, purple, yellow & black on light ground, wear & fading, 29 × 40" . . . **$495.00**

Animals, rectangular, primitive center design of facing flying birds flanked by cats, worked in pale blue, tan & white on black & olive-green ground, light colored scalloped border, mounted on a stretcher, found in Maryland, some wear, 16¼ × 37" **688.00**

Animals, rectangular, center design of two cats w/a pig in each upper corner & a dog in

283

Fig. 19-2

Fig. 19-3

Fig. 19-4

each lower corner, all worked in black
w/yellow & pink floral designs & "1924" in
red, grey ground w/black striped border,
some wear & edge damage, mounted on a
stretcher, 21 × 35" **440.00**

Birds & florals, Waldoboro-type, three-
dimensional sculpted surface w/raised floral
design w/four birds & nest w/stuffed eggs,
yellow, red, green, magenta, orange, purple
& black on a brown ground, some of the
colors & details executed w/applied paint or
dye, "1910" sewn in black thread to back,
mounted on linen-covered foam core board,
21 × 37" (Fig. 19-1) **1,430.00**

Boy in pony cart center scene, rectangular,
crocheted brown yarn edge, black, grey,
blue, beige & brown on a grey ground,
red & purple in details, 17 × 33¾"
(Fig. 19-2) **413.00**

Compote of flowers, urn-shaped vase
containing large & small stylized flowers
surrounded w/leafy stems & flowers in red,
green, pink & white on a multicolored black
& dark-colored ground, found in New
England, wear, damage & repair, 33 × 49"
(Fig. 19-3, top) **605.00**

Deer, rectangular, wool yarn on canvas, finely
detailed oval scene of recumbent stag &

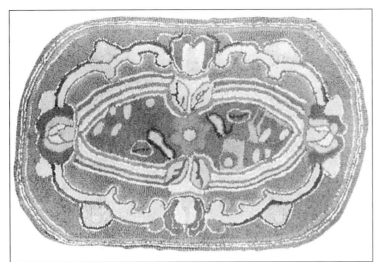

Fig. 19-5

Fig. 19-6

Fig. 19-7

standing doe in landscape, flanked by flower-filled cornucopias, worked in subtle shading of red, blue, brown, green, black, rebacked & some edge damage & repairs, 27 × 63" **578.00**

Dog, rectangular, oval center scene depicting reclining Golden Retriever, dark outer border, early 20th c., 29 × 53" (Fig. 19-4) **920.00**

Floral design, oval, cotton & wool, center panel design of red, green & pink flowers & leaves in a crimson, white, pink, blue & black oval, alternating C-scrolled lozenge surround, brown ground enclosed by a crimson, blue, pink, black & olive-green border, probably Pennsylvania, 19th c., 24¹/₂ × 37" (Fig. 19-5) **185.00**

Florals, semi-circular, a large stylized flowerhead in center flanked by similar flowers & surrounded by leaves & flower buds in shades of red, tan, pale green & grey on a black ground, red & white border stripe, 22 × 37" (Fig. 19-6) **303.00**

Horse, rectangular, w/a black running horse on a beige ground, vining border worked w/red & green yarn, mounted on a stretcher, wear & edge damage, 26¹/₂ × 41" (Fig. 19-7) **550.00**

Indians, rectangular, center design of an Indian maiden w/long dark hair facing an Indian brave w/headdress, worked in multicolors on a light ground & a green maple leaf in the center & on each side, scalloped black border, some age, 18 × 37" (Fig. 19-3, bottom) **165.00**

Lions, rectangular, worked in brown tones, red, green, cream & black depicting a central recumbent lion & another standing to one side in an exotic landscape of palm trees & flowering plants within a striped border, late 19th c., mounted on a rectangular backing, some fabric loss & wear, minor repairs throughout, 36¹/₄ × 65¹/₂" (Fig. 19-8) **1,725.00**

Noah's Ark, rectangular, worked in blue, pink, green, yellow, grey, brown

Fig. 19-9

& white wool threads w/stylized figures of
a black Noah w/his family & a watermelon-
form ark surrounded by exotic animals, a
sun, a moon & rain clouds in the sky,
framed by a scalloped blue edge, red
striped border w/fringed edges, initialed
"EHR" & "MGT," Charlotte, North Carolina,
ca. 1930-40, approximately 44 × 68"
(Fig. 19-9) **10,350.00**

Ship, rectangular, all-wool w/center design of
three-masted sailing ship w/red, white &
blue American flag, on rolling waves,
mountains in background, worked in yarn
of black, several shades of blue, yellow &
white, surrounded by an elaborate border
of purple, white, beige & red w/pink stars
in corners, minor wear, some stains &
reds have bled in areas, 40 × 59"
(Fig. 19-10) **1,155.00**

Stag & doe, rectangular, an idyllic pastoral
scene w/recumbent stag & standing doe,
corner floral designs, leafy branch & trees,
worked in several shades of brown, green,
black, red & pink w/light blue sky, some
wear, edge damage & repair, minor stains,
36 × 66" **242.00**

Fig. 19-8

Fig. 19-10

Fig. 19-11   *Courtesy of Garth's Auctions*

Fig. 19-12   *Courtesy of Garth's Auctions*

HOOKED RUG GROUP PHOTOS

Cat & dog, rectangular, each wearing a large bow around their neck, worked in browns & greys w/magenta, black, blue, orange on bluish black ground w/brown & grey border, dated "1938" in white, some wear & colors have bled slightly, 28 × 38½" (Fig. 19-11, bottom) **358.00**

Geese, rectangular, scene of flying geese above pine trees, worked in tan, blue, green, black & yellow w/black border, labeled "Grenfell Labrador Industries," some wear & edge damage on top corners from hanging, 27¼ × 38½" (Fig. 19-11 top) **688.00**

Roosters, rectangular, facing pair of crowing roosters worked in white, brown, yellow & red on a brown ground, segmented border of bright colors, 19 × 34" (Fig. 19-11, center) **495.00**

Cabin, rectangular, a landscape w/snow-covered ground & trees, cloudy sky, worked in shades of blue, green, red, white, black & light brown, rebound, minor wear, 24½ × 33½" (Fig. 19-12, center) **303.00**

Couple in horse-drawn sleigh, rectangular, oval center scene w/sleigh, house & trees in background, worked in white, black, blue & grey w/magenta, purple & maroon, some wear & light stains, 27 × 40" (Fig. 19-12, bottom) **275.00**

Kittens, rectangular, scene of three kittens worked in greys, black, brown & yellow w/red ball of yarn, background stripes of many shades of greyish blue bordered in yellow, pink & black w/stripes of brown, some wear, 23 × 33" (Fig. 19-12, top) **770.00**

Dogs, rectangular, two black dogs, one standing & one recumbent before a white picket fence, green & red flowers & blue sky, red & black border, some wear & fading, 26 × 47½" (Fig. 19-13, row 3) **330.00**

Florals, rectangular, stylized floral design w/two three-blossom stems in white, pink, red & blue on striped ground w/sheared stitches, dated "1919," some wear, rebacked & rebound, 25 × 58" (Fig. 19-13, row 2) **468.00**

Florals, rectangular, center basket of Waldoboro-type sculptured flowers & elaborate scroll border worked in yarn, red, pink, yellow, blue & green w/beige ground & olive-green border, minor wear & damage, slight fading, 30 × 60" (Fig. 19-13, bottom) **220.00**

Interior home scene, rectangular, worked in yarn, shows a fireplace, pictures on wall, cobbler at work, woman at spinning wheel, cat on table, a colorful design on a yellow ground, 19 × 69" (Fig. 19-13, top) **578.00**

OTHER

Appliqué all-wool rug, rectangular, center w/large fish, surrounded w/white floss embroidery stitches enclosing a series of appliquéd circles, squirrel appliqué in two corners, bird & floral appliqués in alternate corners, border & fishscale edge w/white floss embroidery stitches, white, red, yellow, green & blue on black ground, mounted on fabric-covered foam core, wear, moth damage & old repairs, 22 × 43" (Fig. 19-14) **1,925.00**

Fig. 19-13   *Courtesy of Garth's Auctions*

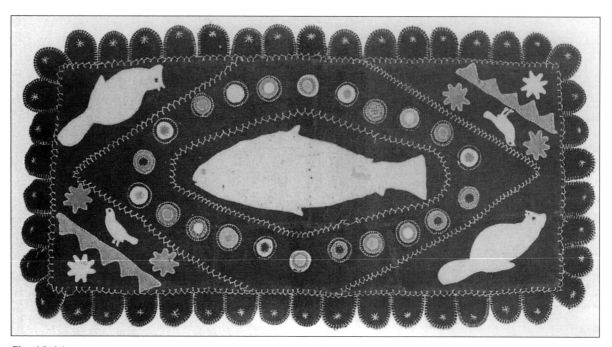

Fig. 19-14

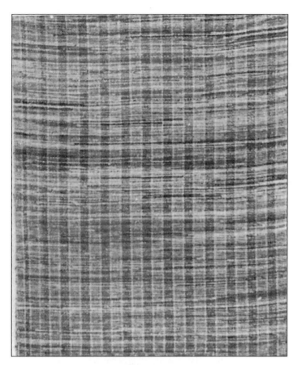

Fig. 19-15

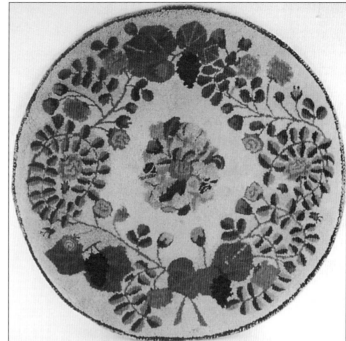

Fig. 19-16

Woven rag carpet, ivory ground w/wide stripes composed of red, purple, yellowish green, white & lavender stripes, two strips joined to make the carpet, Pennsylvania, 70 × 75" (binding on one end replaced, some wear & damage) **165.00**

Woven rag runner, stripes of olive & blue w/narrow orange bands, unused, one end w/finished border & tied fringe, Pennsylvania, unfinished end has started to fray, 36" × approximately 40' (Fig. 19-15) **440.00**

Yarn-sewn rug, circular, center floral bouquet surrounded by trailing leafy branches, large leaves, roses & rosebuds, multicolored yarns w/dark border, 19th c., patch to backing, 42" d. (Fig. 19-16) **1,380.00**

Yarn-sewn rug, rectangular, center w/early floral design hooked on canvas, worked in shades of red, blue, brown & green on a multicolored predominately olive & brown background, professionally mounted on stretcher, worn & edges worn bare in places, 24 × 42" **149.00**

SALESMAN SAMPLES

Fig. 20-1

Collecting salesman samples is a very fascinating hobby because one not only collects farm and construction samples, one studies history. These salesmen samples are a perfect replica of what American farmers and road builders used in the past. Nearly all were made of brass, because it was easy to work with and does not rust. There is somewhat of a misunderstanding about salesman samples. They are thought of as being carried by salesman, which was true, but farm and construction samples were used another way. Years ago, there were not large equipment dealers as we know them today. A good share of the farm equipment (such as plows, mowers, rakes, wind mills, etc.) was sold by hardware stores. They stocked a few smaller items, but the larger items had to be ordered. Salesman samples were set on the shelves and allowed the customer to see exactly what they were buying.

On the whole, salesman samples are quite difficult to find. Not many of them were made because they were expensive to produce and over the years most of them have been discarded. Also see: GRANITEWARE.

—Allan Hoover

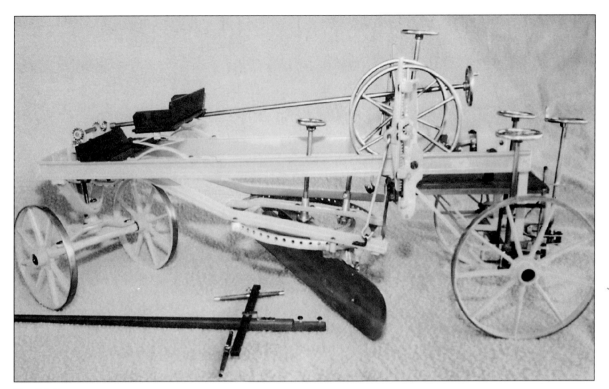

Fig. 20-2

Fig. 20-4

Corn Planter, brass & wood, "Check Row Corn Planter," seat behind levers flanked by large wheels behind two seed bins, patent model, patented December 9, 1890, 15" l. (Fig. 20-1) . . . . **$1,500.00 and up**

Grader, brass, "Case Grader," painted yellow, ca. 1905, restored & repainted, approx. 20" l. (Fig. 20-2) . . . . **800.00 to 2,000.00**

Hay loader, brass, Rock Island Plow, mounted on wood base, ca. 1900, 10" h. (Fig. 20-3) . . . . **800.00 to 1,500.00**

Plow, brass, "Sulkey Plow," raised seat next to two levers & flanked by one large spoke wheel & one small raised spoke wheel, all above plow blade, unusual because plow is raised & lowered for depth (Fig. 20-4) . . . . **800.00 to 1,400.00**

Table rake, brass & wood, "Buckeye Table Rake," ca. 1893, 18" w., rare (Fig. 20-5) . . **5,000.00**

Fig. 20-3

Fig. 20-5

CHAPTER
21

SEWING ADJUNCTS

The first needlework was created when prehistoric man first joined animal pelts together with vegetable fiber or animal sinews. The first needlework tool was invented around the end of the Stone Age, when a resourceful seamstress (seamster?) discovered that joining pelts together was facilitated by the use of a needle made of fish bone, animal bone, or bristle. It was from this humble beginning that the huge variety of needlework and the almost endless types of needlework tools evolved, with needleworking reaching the height of interest in the late 1800s.

Not only did adults do needlework, but young girls and boys were trained in the art, often by their mothers and grandmothers, instructors, teachers at boarding schools, or nuns in girls academies.

After 1912, when the Girl Scouts of the United States was established, some young girls learned needleworking while earning their patches in "Sewing," or perhaps in "Textiles and Fibers." One strategy used to motivate a young girl to discover the joys of needleworking was to provide her with all the sewing accessories that Mother had. She would receive needles, spools of thread, scissors, thimbles, darners, emery balls, pincushions, and perhaps even an odd bodkin, all contained in a fancy sewing box, basket or bag.

Needlework skill was considered a virtue, a 'proper' activity regardless of social or economic status. Even in the most prosperous households, although there might be live-in girls, the ladies of the household also did needlework. Eleanor Roosevelt, when she was 6 years old, was taught by her nurse to darn stockings.

There are two basic types of needlework, 'utilitarian' and 'decorative,' plus some that are a combination of the two. Decorative needlework tended to be a form of recreation and relaxation, giving the needleworker a sense of accomplishment and satisfaction by creating an item of beauty and artistry and it still is for a great many. The superb quilts produced by the ladies at the quilting bee were both utilitarian and decorative. These beautiful creations provided warmth on a cold winter night, and color and beauty during the daytime.

While interest in needlework—particularly the utilitarian type—may have declined, interest in the tools of needlework most assuredly has not. Collectors worldwide, engrossed by the enormous variety and charm, have made sewing implements an avidly pursued collectible.

—Wayne Muller

EMERIES

Bog wood, kettle-shaped, black w/metal
handle w/three legs **$75.00**

Fig. 21-1

Strawberry, silk, sterling filigree on top &
loop **25.00**
Black mammy's head **45.00**

PINCUSHIONS

Linen pincushion, embroidered, 12" l. **20.00**
Advertising folder, paper, Prudential
Insurance **5.00**
Coquella nut (vegetable ivory) basket, blue
velvet cushion w/carved detail on handle &
all over basket **75.00**
Silver-plated pincushion (some plating
wear) **22.00**
Beaded pincushion, American Indian, heart-
shaped, w/"NIAGARA FALLS" written out in
beads above a flower, some beads missing
(Fig. 21-1) **25.00**

SEWING KITS & BOXES

Figure of a flapper, celluloid, the thimble is
her hat **25.00**
World War I mending kit, olive drab painted
metal, 1912 patent date (Fig. 21-2) **25.00**
Lydia Pinkham sewing kit, matchbook-
shaped **20.00**
Tramp art sewing kit, including pincushion &
thread holder **95.00**
Bullet-shaped sewing kit, sterling silver,
includes three spools of thread & thimble,
1³/₄" **125.00**
Sewing case, tooled leather, including
scissors, bodkin, needle case & thimble,
marked "LADY'S COMPANION" **100.00**
Sewing kit, wood bullet-shaped standing
container, including thread & needle,
marked "KALAMITY KATE" (Fig. 21-3) **25.00**

Fig. 21-2

Fig. 21-3

Fig. 21-4

Fig. 21-5

Sewing kit, in the form of a General Electric vacuum cleaner **30.00**

SOCK DARNERS

Black egg on handle, plasticized black by being dipped in proxylin-shellac solution, ca. 1890, 6" (Fig. 21-4) . . . **18.00**

Celluloid, pink egg on ornate yellow handle, ca. 1900, 6⅞" **30.00**

Darner w/fabric holder, "Queen," japanned black, wheel shape on handle w/bicycle clip to hold fabric, by William H. Snyder, marked "Pat'd Dec. 18, 1900," 4⅜" (Fig. 21-5) **25.00**

Ebony & mother of pearl, ebony egg on mother-of-pearl (nacre) handle, ca. 1880, 5" (Fig. 21-6) **90.00**

Ebony & sterling silver, ebony egg on sterling silver handle set w/½" amethyst, ca. 1900, 6¼" (Fig. 21-7) **140.00**

Fig. 21-6

Fig. 21-7

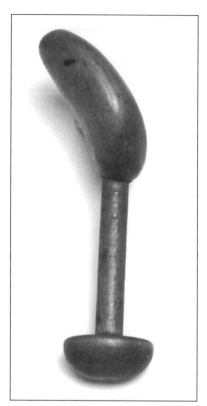

Fig. 21-8

Foot form, stained & lightly varnished
birch, standard form, marked "FOOT-
FORM Pat. Nov. 1907," 5¹/₂" **15.00**

Foot form, lightly varnished maple,
elliptical foot form on dowel handle
w/small mushroom, ca. 1860, 6¹/₂"
(Fig. 21-8) **30.00**

Glass, Steuben "Blue Aurene," large
ball on handle, developed by Frederick
Carder, ca. 1905, 6³/₄" (Fig. 21-9) . . **600.00**

Hollow, unfinished bass wood egg,
pyrographed "For Ruth - Souvenir
Revere Beach - 1906," 2³/₈" **35.00**

Primitive, wood, beehive on needle
holder handle, South Carolina,
ca. 1872, 4¹/₂" **25.00**

Primitive, wood, mushroom & beehive
on dowel handle, stained dark &
lightly varnished, ca. 1840, 5"
(Fig. 21-10) **25.00**

Primitive, varnished maple, egg on
Shaker-type handle, ca. 1860, 5³/₄"
(Fig. 21-11) **25.00**

Primitive, stained cherry wood ball on
handle, carved from single block of
wood, ca. 1850, 5⁷/₈" **15.00**

Fig. 21-9

Fig. 21-10

Fig. 21-11

Fig. 21-13

Fig. 21-12

Fig. 21-14

Shaker, Ball & Block, small, from Shaker Church Family of Mount Lebanon, New York, ca. 1905 (Fig. 21-12) **100.00**

Wood, large egg on glove darner handle, handle holds needles & thimble, patented by George F. Atkinson of San Francisco on June 30, 1885, marked "Atkinson Darner U.S. Pat. June 30, 85," 6½" (Fig. 21-13) **40.00**

TAPE MEASURERS

Advertising tape, celluloid, 1¾" d. . . **11.00 to 17.00**

Clamshell, silver-plated brass, ca. 1920, 2½" l. **150.00**

Fawn sitting, celluloid, w/cream color body, pink back & brown spot **45.00**

Flower basket, celluloid, ca. 1920, 1½" d. . . . **60.00**

Mill house, brass, wheel is winder, 1½" h. . . **150.00**

Pig, sliver-plated brass, tail is winder **88.00**

Pinkham, Lydia, celluloid **60.00**

Refrigerator, G.E. Monitro top-type **100.00**

Sailing ship, celluloid, pull is in the aft of the ship (Fig. 21-14) **88.00**

Straw hat, marked "Covers the Feet," brass bow on band is pull, 2" w. **77.00**

"Three Feet in One," 2¼" l. **90.00**

Vacuum, Hoover-type **45.00**

THIMBLES

Advertising, aluminum, painted band, raised letters read "Butternut the Coffee Delicious" **3.00**

Advertising, brass, "Gold Thimble Scotch" **6.00**

Advertising, silver, for "Needlecraft" magazine, ca. 1915 . . . . **100.00**

Brass, raised floral band **20.00**

Gold, 14k, plain band **75.00**

Gold, scenic band decorated w/houses, trees & a sun rise **100.00**

Ivory, scrimshaw, whale's tooth, ca. 1860 . . . **200.00**

Metal, marked "DIRAGOLD" **200.00**

Metal, nickel plated, marked "SBC" in a keystone **8.00**

Porcelain, decorated w/bird, signed by William Powell, by Royal Worchester **400.00**

Porcelain, modern, hand-painted design, by Meissen **125.00**

Silver, decorated w/Atlantic Cable Pattern . . **150.00**

Silver, decorated w/birds in high relief **50.00**

POLITICAL

Political, Aluminum, painted band, raised letters read "COOLIDGE and DAWS," from Calvin Coolidge presidential campaign . . . **15.00**

SOUVENIR & COMMEMORATIVE

Silver, Chicago World's Fair, marked "CENTURY OF PROGRESS" **300.00**

Silver, marked, "Golden Gate International Exposition, San Francisco," image of Golden Gate Bridge & the skyline of San Francisco, by Simons, ca. 1939 . . . . **600.00**

Silver, marked "Atlantic City," decorated w/the Boardwalk, steel pier, hotels & beach, by Ketchem & McDougall, ca. 1930 . . . . **400.00**

THIMBLE HOLDERS

Glass, clear, in the shape of a slipper **150.00**

Silver, round, w/elaborate filigree marked "F&B" & a banner **150.00**

CHAPTER
22

SHAKER ITEMS

The Shakers, a religious sect founded by Ann Lee, first settled in this country at Watervliet, New York (near Albany) in 1774 and by 1880 there were nine settlements in America. Workmanship in Shaker crafts is an extension of their religious beliefs and features plain and simple designs reflecting a chaste elegance that is now much in demand though relatively few items are available.

Apple corer & slicer, round base, riveted construction, four quarter-round cutting blades surround hollow stem handle, circular brown leather guard fits over handle, acquired at Canterbury, New Hampshire, 4⅝" d., 5" h. **$86.00**

Basket, black ash, rectangular bottom, oval top, shaped handle, single notch, single wrap rim, 1" wide uprights, narrow weavers, "C.F.S." painted in 2" letters on side & initialed "CSF" on handle & on bottom in pencil, 11½ × 17", 5¾" h. **460.00**

Basket, round, ash, wrapped ear handles, double bottom, straight sides, single wrap over shaped rims, written in ink on outside "For the Meeting Room in the Meeting House," inscribed on weavers "Office" & "F.L.," 12½" d., 8½" h. **403.00**

Basket, black ash, rectangular bottom, oval top, shaped ear handles notched & fitted to outside of basket, single wrap rim, wide uprights, narrow weavers, probably Canterbury, New Hampshire, 14 × 12½", 5½" h. **173.00**

Bench, pine, grain painted, red over olive-green paint, single board seat w/legs set into dado, foot cut in bootjack pattern, half-dovetailed braces, possibly Harvard, Massachusetts, 9¼ × 81¼", 15½" **546.00**

Blanket chest, original reddish orange paint, iron hinges & lock, brass escutcheon, w/through mortised paneled lid, dovetailed case w/applied broken ogee-shaped bracket base, three dovetailed drawers w/hardwood pulls, two half-width over one full-width drawer w/molded lips, ogee-shaped moldings on applied base & lip molding, original key & tag reads "key belongs to red chest large," Enfield or Canterbury, New Hampshire, ca. 1848, rare, 21⅝ × 49⅝", 29¼" h. **140.00**

Box, cov., pine & maple or birch, oval bentwood, yellow paint, two fingers, copper points & tacks, inscribed in pencil on inside cover "Presented by Eld'r Grove Wright to Martha Johnson," Hancock, Massachusetts, rare, 2¹⁄₁₆ × 3¹⁄₆", 1¼" **5,175.00**

Box, cov., pine & birch, bentwood, yellow stain w/varnish finish, copper points & tacks, lined w/padded blue satin, probably made by George Robert, New Lebanon, New York, 2¾ × 4½", 2" h. **374.00**

Box, cov., pine & maple, oval bentwood, original yellowish green paint, three fingers, copper points & tacks, 8⅛ × 11⅞", 4⅝" h. **1,725.00**

Box, cov., pine & maple, bentwood, olive-green paint, fingers (left handed), copper tacks, 8½ × 11⅜", 4⅝" h. **1,265.00**

Box, cov., round bentwood, ash or hickory sides, pine top & bottom, bluish green paint, straight seam, iron tacks, 8⅜" d., 4" h. **230.00**

Box, cov., round bentwood, maple sides, pine top & bottom, dark red over bluish green, three fingers, copper tacks, 10¼" d., 4¾" h. **518.00**

Brush, wood & horsehair, red paint, long slender swelled handle w/two scribe lines around the widest section & at narrow section below knob, one scribe line around ball end, probably Canterbury, New Hampshire, 14¼" l. **1,840.00**

Carrier, pine, maple, ash handle, oval bentwood, yellow paint, four fingers (left handed), copper nails, shaped handle has break, inscribed on bottom "Ministry Shop," 8 × 11", 3⅝" h. **863.00**

Carrier, pine, maple or birch, ash handle, oval bentwood, brown stain, shellac finish, four fingers, copper points & tacks, delicately shaped fixed handle, Caterbury, New Hampshire, 9 × 13¼", 4" h. **805.00**

Chest & cupboard, pine, brass hardware, old varnish finish, cupboard has two paneled doors, each w/sliding spring latch & original lock, two different size keys for locks inside, ends terminate in double-arched skirt, chest has lift top & molded overhanging rim on two sides, ends of chest are dovetailed front & back, applied ogee-shaped brackets on end & backboard, single board bottom to entire piece, salmon wash on back, interior has red wash, exterior probably old refinish w/varnish, Canterbury star-shaped paper tag reads "$20," 23¼ × 56⅝" chest, 81" l., 63⅝" h. overall (hinges replaced, brackets missing from front legs) **4,600.00**

Chip box, pine, ash handle, copper tacks, red stain, finely shaped & tapered handle, dovetail construction w/nailed bottom, "Pegs" faintly written in chalk on one end, 9⅜ × 15", 9¼" h. (small chip in handle) **1,840.00**

Cupboard, pine, old blue paint over red, iron hinges, brass pulls, single small raised

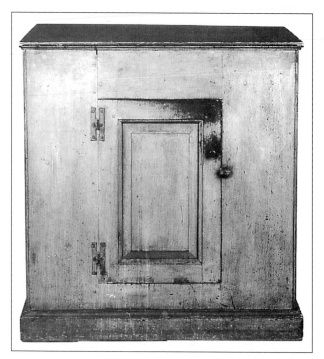

Fig. 22-1

panel door set into front of case, case is pegged together, single board overhanging top finely molded on three sides, interior unpainted, fitted w/single central shelf, back is notched out on bottom to fit as baseboard, probably Sabbathday Lake, Maine, ca. 1790, 17⅛ × 36½", 37¼" h. (Fig. 22-1) **17,250.00**

Cupboard, pine, original brown paint, hardwood pulls, built in two sections w/removable cupboard top w/complex cornice molding & two thin shelves, the dovetailed cupboard case is held in place by a cove molding, the case houses two deep half-width drawers over three full-width graduated drawers, drawers are dovetailed w/thumbnail molded lips, bold applied bracket base w/arched cut-outs dovetailed in rear, probably Groveland, New York, ca. 1840, 17⅛ × 36½", 37¼" h. (extensive use of glue on blocks & drawer construction, small splinter missing from cove molding, replaced pulls) **27,600.00**

Cupboard, pine, door over door, two raised panel doors double-pinned through mortise, w/two H-hinges per door, turned wooden knobs, toggle clasps on cupboard close over brass plates tacked to doors, both doors have locks, corners of base are mitered & nailed, beaded corners on case, one shelf in each cupboard compartment, ogee molding form on both cornice & base,

Fig. 22-2

ship lapped back boards, applied bracket base w/arched cut-outs, ca. 1800, escutcheons missing, 21 × 49¼", 77" h. (Fig. 22-2) **17,250.00**

Dipper, heavy gauge tin, straight sides, flat bottom, rolled rim, long hollow handle attached w/supporting bracket terminating in D-shaped wide ring for hanging, "S 20" stamped near rim, acquired near Canterbury, New Hampshire, 4¼" d. bowl, 12¾" h. **345.00**

Dust pan, birch, small size, folded corners, rolled top rim, finely turned handle w/scribe lines & small knob at end painted red, inscribed on bottom "Harriet Johns 1880," acquired at Canterbury, New Hampshire, 5 × 13" (small split in side) **3,680.00**

Engraving, stipple-line, "SHAKERS near LEBANON state of N YORK - their mode of worship - Drawn from Life," hand-colored, clouds but no trees visible through windows, arched line depicting the barrel vaulted ceiling, artist unknown, ca. 1830, 8¾ × 12¾" (sheet glued to cardboard backing, wrinkle in upper left & at top left margin) **1,955.00**

Firkin, pine staves & bottom, original blue paint, diamond-shaped bail plates, iron hoops w/ends clipped to a V, hardwood concave-shaped turned handle stained red w/scribe line at center, staves joined w/V-shaped tongue and groove joints, Canterbury or Enfield, New Hampshire, 11¼" d. top, 12⅞" d. bottom, 11" h. **1,610.00**

Foot stool, pine, brown stain, nailed five-board construction, sides have semi-circular cut-outs at feet, slight overhang on top, bottom step set into dado in sides, 8 × 14¾", 9½" h. **748.00**

Footwarmer, soapstone w/cotton cover, w/three layers, pattern-woven olive green outer layer, pink inner lining, blue & white print lining, two handsome button holes, 5½ × 10", 1" h. (small burn mark) **626.00**

Grain measure, oak & pine, round, natural color, stenciled in black on bottom "Shaker Society, Sealed, W. Gloucester, ME.," ca. 1880-1896 . . . . **230.00**

Lap Desk, butternut, cherry & poplar, old varnish finish, finely dovetailed, slant top writing surface has breadboard end, case contains a pencil till w/ink compartment, w/secret compartment beneath, opposing drawers for writing paper, turned hardwood pulls on drawer & till lid, 17¾ × 21", 3½" h. (Fig. 22-3) **3,738.00**

Pail, cov., wood w/heavy wire bail, wooden handle, painted red on outside, staves jointed w/tongue and groove joints, cover w/knob recessed in center, 9¾" d., 7⅝" h. . . . **230.00**

Pail, pine staves & bottom, original ochre-brown paint, rare coffin-shaped bail plates, iron hoops w/clipped ends, hardwood shaped handle stained brown, staves jointed w/square tongue and groove joints, possibly New Lebanon, New York, 12" d., 9¼" h. . . **1,380.00**

Pail, pine staves & bottom, original ochre-orange paint, diamond-shaped bail plates, iron hoops w/ends clipped to a V, hardwood convex-shaped handle stained red w/scribe line in center, staves joined w/V-shaped tongue and groove joints, Caterbury or Enfield, New Hampshire, 10" d., 7¼" h. . . **1,380.00**

Rocking chair w/arms, maple, black paint, stamped "#6," on back top slat, Mount Lebanon, New York, ca. 1880, 41¾" h. (replaced seat) **1,380.00**

Fig. 22-3

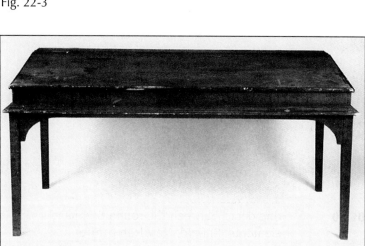

Fig. 22-4

Fig. 22-5

Rocking chair without arms, maple, ebony
stain, three-slat back, olive tape seat
covered w/olive velveteen, rockers pinned
through legs, marked w/"#4" on back of slat,
Mount Lebanon, New York, 34¼" h. **403.00**

School desk, pine, grain-painted reddish
orange, slant top, lift top fitted w/leather
straps on each side, center divider & narrow
shelf at back of interior compartment, lift
top has remnants of oilcloth covering, upper
case is dovetailed w/lock at center front,
upper case is secured to table base
w/applied cove molding, four square tapered
legs, apron on front & sides, possibly
Harvard, Massachusetts, repairs to mortised
leg joints, one small section of front apron
replaced, 31¼ × 66", 31⅝" h. (Fig. 22-4) . . **1,150.00**

Seed box, pine, red paint, top has splines
which run full width at both ends to prevent
warping, machine cut dovetails, labeled on
front "SHAKERS GENUINE GARDEN SEED,
MOUNT LEBANON, N.Y.," remains of labels
inside lid, six compartments labeled at front

edge left to right: "BEETS, CARROTS, SAGE
& PEPPER, TOMATO, FLOWERS, CORN," in
black script at bottom "W.B. Harris, Highland
[illeg]," 11½ × 23½", 3¾" h. **776.00**

Sewing desk, pine, fruitwood pulls, salmon
paint, plank-sided case w/ogee-shaped
base, sliding work surface, scrolled side
panels & recessed upper gallery of two
small drawers raised above work surface,
case houses four graduated drawers of
nailed construction w/bottom chamfered in
at front, single turned pull in the center of
each drawer, drawer blades set in w/half-
dovetails, Canterbury, New Hampshire or
Sabbathday Lake, Maine, ca. 1840, acquired
at Sabbathday Lake, Maine ca. 1950s-1960s,
18 × 26", 36" h. (sliding surface repaired,
one half-dovetail replaced) **8,625.00**

Side chair, maple, salmon paint, three arched
slats, egg-shaped finials, scribe lines
visible, olive colored taped seat, probably
Canterbury, New Hampshire, 40¾" h.
(bottom slat split w/old repair) **978.00**

Fig. 22-6

Side chair, maple, red stain, tilters, three
graduated arched slats, front legs are
tapered, multi-colored seat, Canterbury
New Hampshire, 40¾" h. (repaired break to
top slat, paint worn from finials, leather
thongs on tilters replaced) **805.00**

Side Chairs, maple, old brown stain, tilters,
three graduated slats, stretchers slightly
tapered at ends, cane seats, one chair
stamped "3" on right front post, Canterbury,
New Hampshire, ca. 1840, 13⅜ × 18¾",
40¾" h., pr. (Fig. 22-5, of one) **8,625.00**

Spool rack, maple & fruitwood, including nine
turned wooden spools (one spool has paper
label "M.O."), rectangular base w/dark stain,
two rows of six handcarved spindles each
pegged through base, 3 × 7", 4" h. **1,092.00**

Spools, various hardwood, one retains yellow
wash, one salmon wash, ranging in size
34" h. to 2¼" h., set of 10 . . . . **690.00**

Stove, small size, cast iron, canted sides,
hinged door w/latch, handle fitted w/turned
wooden knob, circular hearth, 12 × 28¾",
16⅜" h. **460.00**

Stove tools: tongs & shovel; iron, shaft of
shovel swells below knob, half-domed knob
at ends, much wear, 21¾" l. tongs, 21½" l.
shovel **138.00**

Strainer, formed flared bowl w/integral
punched-screen bottom, flange for handle,
turned handle painted black, acquired at
Canterbury, New Hampshire, 4¼" d.
bowl, 9⅛" h. **46.00**

Table, side, curly birch & pine, old red wash,
well-shaped deep ogee apron one-board
top attached w/shaped cleats, above
single drawer, finely turned legs
w/characteristic Enfield, New Hampshire
ring detail between the round & square
elements, Enfield, New Hampshire,
ca. 1840, 22¾ × 36", 26¾" h. **8,050.00**

Table, work, pine, red paint, two-board top,
mortised case, finely turned tapered legs, top
of drawer fits flush w/underside of table top,
single turned knob in center of drawer,
Canterbury tag attached to drawer knob
which reads "$10" in faded script, Canterbury,
New Hampshire, ca. 1850, major repair to
right rear leg, 35⅝ × 60¾", 30¾" h.
(Fig. 22-6) **2,300.00**

Trundle bed, oak, dark olive-green paint,
non-swivel wooden wheels, side rails
drilled for roping, solid headboard panel
between rails, posts at foot of bed are
chamfered to octagonal shape at top,
headboard tapered on front side, acquired
at Mount Lebanon, New York, 30¾ × 68"
(legs reduced, wooden wheeled casters
added) **403.00**

Utility basket, black ash, round bottom,
round top, finely shaped handle double-
notched, alternating wide & narrow
uprights turned down alternately inside
& outside, uprights w/beveled edges,
single wrap over shaped rims, 12" d.,
8½" h. **2,645.00**

CHAPTER
23

STOVES

A Kitchen Jewel cook stove, ca. 1893.

I f you're like most people, you've turned to this section to find out what a particular stove is worth. Over a thousand stove manufacturers were in business during the antique era, each producing dozens and dozens of different models and unfortunately no price guide could even begin to list them all. The best we can do is show you the major stove types.

One must also realize that the market for antiques is a thin market, where realized prices vary all over the lot; the market for antique stoves is even thinner. Unfortunately, most antiques dealers won't handle stoves because they are too heavy and bulky to lug around conveniently, and they don't turn over quickly in inventory. In a market this thin, the proper role of a price guide is not to

DESIRABLE	UNDESIRABLE
Cast iron	Sheet metal
Mica windows	No illumination
Nickel plated trim	All black
Victorian embossed design	1920s plain style
a. Animals & people	a. Vines & leaves only
Decorative ceramic tiles	No tiles
Colored porcelain, especially blue	White or pseudo grain
Fuel: wood, coal, gas	Fuel: Kerosene, gasoline
Big and spectacular	Small and unpretentious
Golden age of stoves: 1870-1910	Appliance era: 1935 and beyond
Ranges:	Ranges:
a. Reservoir	a. No water heating capability
b. Warming closet	b. Shelf only, no high back
c. Glass panel in oven door	c. Food not visible
d. Wood/coal/gas combination	d. Wood/coal only
Top-of-the-line model	Cheap
Excellent condition	Fire damage, deep rust pits, missing parts

give you some particular figure as being THE value of the stove, but to help you deal with the very unhelpful truth that antique stoves are only worth something *to somebody.* What the stove is worth to you is as good a figure as anything an expert could come up with, because in a market this thin, *you are the market.* You'll find prices in this section, but please recognize them as estimates.

When buying or selling a stove keep in mind what is desirable and undesirable as shown above.

—Clifford Boram

PARLOR STOVES

Base burner, 1887 Art Garland, Michigan Stove Co., Detroit, Michigan. (Fig. 23-1)

Complete, rusty, unrestored . . **$500.00 to 1,000.00**

Fully restored without optional oven . . **9,000.00**

Complete, fully restored **9,800.00**

Fig. 23-1

Fig. 23-2

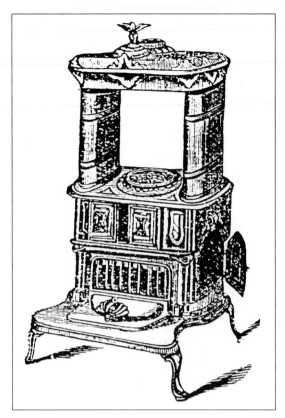

Fig. 23-3

Cannon Stove, 1902 Station Agent, Union Stove Works, New York, New York, this type, commonly known as "potbelly" stove, was an industrial stove, not of high demand (Fig. 23-2)

> **Complete,** original condition **500.00**

> **Complete,** restored condition **1,000.00**

Column stove, 1874 Little Corporal Column Stove, Cooperative Foundry Association, Beaver Falls, Pennsylvania (Fig. 23-3)

> **Complete,** good condition **950.00**

> **Complete,** fully restored, cast iron, four column w/animal designs **5,000.00**

Cottage stove, 1949 Parlor Glow Cottage Stove, Southern Cooperative Foundry Co., Rome Georgia (Fig. 23-4)

> **Complete,** good original condition **150.00**

Cylinder stove, 1869 Arctic Cylinder Stove, Heldenbrand & Wolf, Beaver Falls, Pennsylvania, sheet iron w/cast-iron decorations (Fig. 23-5)

> **Complete,** unrestored rusty condition **75.00**

> **Complete,** fully restored . . **2,000.00 to 4,000.00**

Fig. 23-4

Fig. 23-5

Fig. 23-6

Fig. 23-7

Fig. 23-8

Double cased heaters, 1900 Moore's Air Tight Heater, Joliet Stove Works, Joliet, Illinois, cast-iron outer case, highly decorative, w/optional vertical nickel plated wings flanking feed door (Fig. 23-6)

Complete, unrestored **350.00**

Complete, restored . . . . . . **2,500.00 to 4,500.00**

Double cased heater, 1926 Sentrola, James R. Wotherspoon Inc., Sinking Spring, Pennsylvania, pseudo wood-grain porcelain on sheet metal outer case, became popular ca. 1920s (Fig. 23-7)

Basic utility value **200.00**

Oak stove, 1927 Palm Oak heater, Standard Stove & Range Co., Rome, Georgia, legs mounted directly to ashpit (Fig. 23-8)

Basic utility value . . . . **60.00 to 300.00**

Oval airtight, 1923 Maple Clermont, Gem City Stove Co., Dayton, Ohio, cast-iron & nickel plated parts (Fig. 23-9)

Basic utility value . . . . **7.00 and up**

Fig. 23-9

KITCHEN RANGES

Box stove, 1921 Champion, Sears & Roebuck Co., made for Sears by The Wehrle Co., Newark Ohio, w/swelled sides, undesirable (Fig. 23-10)

> **Complete,** good original condition . . . . **50.00 to 250.00**

Cook stove, 1893 Kitchen Jewel, Detroit Stove Works, Detroit, Michigan, w/optional reservoir & low warming closet (Fig. 23-11)

> **Complete,** unrestored rusty condition . . . **250.00**
>
> **Complete,** fully restored **1,400.00**

Combination range, 1926 Peninsular, Peninsular Stove Co., Detroit, Michigan, four gas burners, four wood holes (Fig. 23-12)

> **Complete,** good original condition **1,000.00**
>
> **Complete,** fully restored **3,400.00**

Fig. 23-10

Fig. 23-11

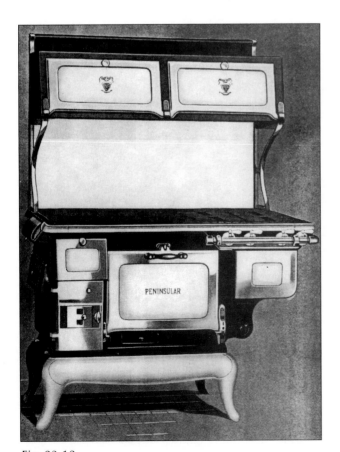

Fig. 23-12

Fig. 23-13

Gas range, 1937 Magic Chef, American Stove
 Co., Cleveland, Ohio, commercial size, very
 desirable (Fig. 23-13)

 Excellent condition, 6 burner **6,000.00**

 Excellent condition, 8 burner **8,000.00**

Oil range, 1926 Clark Jewel, George M. Clark &
 Co. (division of American Stove Co.),

Fig. 23-14

Fig. 23-15

Chicago, Illinois, 4 burner, these were rarely used outside Amish community, so demand is low (Fig. 23-14)

Complete in original condition **25.00**

Wood-burning range, 1923 Prizer Regal, Prizer-Printer Stoveworks, Reading, Pennsylvania, swing door, enameled high chest, loose nickel trim (Fig. 23-15)

Complete, unrestored . . . . **100.00 to 500.00**

Complete, fully restored **1,500.00**

Complete, fully restored, blue **2,000.00**

FRANKLIN & FIREPLACE STOVES

Franklin stove, Floral Estate, 1893, F&L Kahn & Bros., Hamilton Ohio, very fancy,

Fig. 23-16

Fig. 23-17

numerous tiles, mica windows, illuminated 'glass' jewels & faces molded in cast iron, very vulnerable to fire damage, so good ones are hard to find (Fig. 23-16)

Complete, rusty unrestored condition . . . **200.00**

Complete, fully restored **1,200.00**

Fireplace heater, 1897 Improved Original Baltimore Heater, S.B. Sexton & Son, Baltimore, Maryland, mantel & fireplace surround were not included w/stove (Fig. 23-17)

Complete, unrestored **1,000.00**

Complete, fully restored **4,000.00**

LAUNDRY STOVES

Iron heater, No. 8, 1893, J.L. Mott Iron Works, New York, New York, w/flat sides for heating flat irons (Fig. 23-18)

Complete w/flatirons, fully restored . . . . **400.00 to 600.00**

Fig. 23-18

CHAPTER
24

THEOREMS

Theorem painting, a form of stencil painting, was a popular pastime for Victorian ladies, especially in the first half of the 19th century. Hollow-cut patterns were laid over paper or cotton velvet and paint was then applied over the stencil designs. The most commonly found type of theorem features baskets, bowls or compotes of fruits or vases of flowers, but some landscapes and religious scenes were also made. For amateur artists who had limited skill with free-hand painting, this craft provided an outlet for their artistic inclinations and today the best examples of theorems in good condition sell for high prices and are considered charming "folk art."

Fig. 24-1

Basket of fruit, pen & ink & water-color on paper mounted on board, a colorful array of large fruits including grapes & a melon overflowing a lattice-sided basket w/S-scroll handles, unsigned, unframed, some discoloration, 19th c., 13½ × 16½" (Fig. 24-1) **$1,495.00**

Basket of fruit, water-color on paper, a large cross-woven basket w/center loop handle filled to overflowing w/colorful fruits including grapes, peaches & pears, in shades of green, brown, blue & red, 19th c., in beveled frame w/original red flame

graining, 13½ × 16¾" (minor age stains & water stains) **1,760.00**

Basket of fruit w/a bird, water-color on velvet, a wide & deep waisted-form splint basket filled to overflowing w/colorful fruits including grapes & a pineapple, a bird perched at the top, the basket resting on a green marble slab w/a knife & cut peach shown, signed "D. Ellinger," David Ellinger, 20th c., 19¼ × 24" (Fig. 24-3) **2,300.00**

Basket of fruit w/a parrot, water-color &
stencil on white velvet, a wide yellow
slat-sided basket filled to overflowing
w/leafy clusters of fruit, a large parrot
perched on the top of the fruit & a
butterfly flying to one side, the basket
resting on a blue-spotted rectangular
mat, in the apparently original
giltwood & gesso frame, paper label
on back inscribed "Marshfield Oct. 30,
1838. Received of John Lord Jr. thirty-
five dollars in full payment for a carry
all and sleigh. Ruth Winsor.," ca. 1830
(Fig. 24-2) **12,650.00**

Bowl of fruit, water-color on paper, a
wide shallow bowl filled to
overflowing w/colorful fruits &
berries in red, yellow, orange, green
& brown, ink inscription "Friendship,
Laura M. Lord," in old beveled frame
w/alligatored red & yellow paint,
19th c., $10^3/_8 \times 12^3/_4$" (three vertical

Fig. 24-2

Fig. 24-3

Fig. 24-4

Fig. 24-5

fold lines, some minor tears &
stains) **3,135.00**

Compote of fruit, water-color on paper, the
compote w/a deep, ribbed bowl raised on a
short pedestal w/a round foot, filled to
overflowing w/colorful fruits in shades of
blue, green, brown & red, old label taped to
back of frame "Painted by Mary Ellen
Fuller...," 19th c., old narrow giltwood frame,
14 × 16" (minor fading & stains, some frame
damage) **1,650.00**

Compote of fruit, water-color & pen & ink on
paper, a wide shallow-bowled pale blue
ribbed compote raised on a wide pedestal
& foot, filled to overflowing w/leafy fruits
including grapes, cherries, peaches & a
pineapple, on a green ruffled ground,
some staining & discoloration, ca. 1830,
15$\frac{1}{2}$ × 17" (Fig. 24-4) **4,312.00**

Cornucopia of fruit, water-color & stencil on
paper, the spiraled upright cornucopia filled
to overflowing w/colorful fruits including
grapes, peaches, pears & strawberries,
ca. 1860, framed, 13$\frac{1}{4}$ × 16$\frac{1}{2}$"
(Fig. 24-5) **1,840.00**

Platter of fruit, water-color on velvet, an oval
platter w/pierced end handles filled to
overflowing w/colorful fruits including a
large watermelon, grapes, apples, a small
plate of strawberries & a small basket of
berries, late 19th c., in a grain-painted
frame by Peter Finnegan, 19$\frac{1}{2}$ × 21$\frac{5}{8}$"
(Fig. 24-6) **3,162.00**

Fig. 24-6

Still life of fruit, water-color on paper, a
cluster of three large fruits, a pear, peach &
an apple, against a leafy background
w/flowering vines above, 19th c., framed,
8$\frac{3}{4}$ × 10$\frac{3}{4}$" (old repair) **495.00**

Still life of fruit, stencil & free-hand water-
color on paper, a large grouping of colorful
fruits including grapes, peaches & cherries,
signed, dated & inscribed on the back
"Agnes Carpenter 1864. Presented to Mr. &
Mrs. Gardner, Little Mountain, Ohio,"
appears to retain original giltwood frame,
11$\frac{1}{4}$ × 14$\frac{5}{8}$" **690.00**

C H A P T E R
25

TOBACCIANA

Tobacco was grown, manufactured, sold, and used in all regions of the world. If you are an active shopper you will discover more than 50 different types of tobacco related collectibles and, if you keep at it long enough, at least 50,000,000 different individual items. This guide can be but a hint at the richness of the various hobbies and collections related to tobacco growing, manufacture, selling, and use. Both rare and common items have been included to give you a sampling of items available.

Collectibles are second-hand goods and have no fixed price. There is no all-knowing grocery clerk able to stamp each of the world's billions of second hand items with an absolute value. The value of things is determined by who is buying and who is selling and where and under what circumstances a transaction is taking place. There is no "value" except what a buyer and seller agree to. Values in this section are given as a range of wholesale and retail prices likely to be offered and/or paid by pickers, dealers, and collectors of tobacciana.

—Tony Hyman

TOBACCO PRODUCT TINS

Smoking tobacco tins are among the more expensive tobacco collectibles. Plenty of tobacco tins are worth only a few dollars, but a surprising number are worth more than $100.00 and a significant handful worth $1,000.00 or more. Tobacco tins that are rusty, damaged, or badly scratched have no value. Condition is absolutely vital in the world of tin cans. A can worth $1,000.00 in mint condition may sit on your shelf unsold for years at $100.00 if it has condition problems.

To qualify as "excellent condition" the printed surface of the can should be unmarked or with slight soil and/or use wear outside the image area. The revenue stamp may be scratched or removed. A can is not "excellent" if the image is scratched or if "paint" [ink] is flaking off. Values given are for retail of cans in excellent condition. Cans in less than excellent condition retail for 25% to 50% of the prices shown.

Alumni Burley Cut, vertical pocket tin in unusual concave configuration, predominantly silver tin with bust of man in cap & gown, United States Tobacco Co., Virginia, approximately 4 × 3 × 1", good condition . . . . **$700.00 to 1,500.00**

Bulwark cut plug, tin horizontal box, predominantly gold & blue, depicting a sailor looking through a spyglass, made in England by W.D. & H.O. Wills, approximately 6 × 4 × 1½", excellent condition (Fig. 25-1) . . . . **10.00 to 20.00**

George Washington cut plug, tin lunch box, w/wire & wood handle & metal clasp, R.J. Reynolds, Winston-Salem, NC, after 1910, common, approximately 7½ × 4½ × 4½", excellent-mint condition . . . . **30.00 to 40.00**

Fig. 25-1

Hi-Plane smooth cut tobacco, vertical pocket tin, lithograph on tin in white on red background w/single engine, near mint condition **10.00**

Hi-Plane smooth cut tobacco, vertical pocket tin, lithograph on tin in white on red background w/China clipper, good condition . . . . **200.00 to 1,000.00 and up**

Just Suits cut plug, tin lunch box, w/wire handle & metal clasp on end of box, Buchanon & Lyall, New York (div of P.Lorillard, Virginia), after 1910, approximately 8 × 5¹/₄ × 4", common, mint condition . . . . . . **20.00 to 35.00**

Lucky Strike cigarettes, flat tin box called a "Flat Fifties," American Tobacco Company, regularly found in white, green, black, white & Christmas versions, approximately 6 × 4", full, near mint condition . . . . **15.00 to 25.00**

Lucky Strike (smoking tobacco), small green box w/red circle, some gold trim, "R.A. Patterson Tobacco Co. Rich'd, VA" (div. of American Tobacco Co.), ca. early 20th c., approximately 4¹/₄" l., 3" w., excellent condition (Fig. 25-2) . . . . **10.00 to 30.00**

Niggerhair Tobacco, tin can w/bail handle & slip-top lid, black on brown, pictures South Sea Islander w/nose bone, earrings & predominant hair-do, American Tobacco Company, ca. 1920s -1946 when name changed to Biggerhair, approximately 6³/₄ × 5¹/₂" d., common (Fig. 25-3) . . . . **125.00 to 200.00**

Prince Albert crimp cut (smoking tobacco), vertical pocket tin & other configurations, in various sizes. R.J. Reynolds Tobacco Co., Winston-Salem, North Carolina, ca. 1910 to 1960s, full, near mint condition . . . **5.00 to 15.00**

Prince Albert Now King (smoking tobacco), "Now King" printed under portrait of Albert, most valuable as a vertical pocket tin (but known in other configurations), R.J. Reynolds Tobacco Co., Winston-Salem, North Carolina, ca. 1910s, good condition . . . . . **200.00 to 400.00**

Rex pipe & cigarette tobacco, vertical pocket tin, Spaulding & Merrick, Chicago (div. of Liggett & Myers), approximately 5 × 2" w., 5" h., excellent condition . . . . **25.00 to 35.00**

Stag tobacco, small lightly oval upright pocket tin w/flip-top cover, predominantly red, depicting a large stag, numerous other varieties of Stag are found (Fig. 25-4) . . . . **50.00 to 75.00**

Stanwix ground plug, vertical pocket tin w/flip-top lid, Falk Tobacco Co., Richmond, approximately 4¹/₂ × 3 × 1", excellent condition (Fig. 25-5) . . . . **150.00 to 250.00**

White Ash cigar, round woodgrained tin can w/slip-top lid, newspaper-style black & white photo of Snyder in suit & tie is central oval image on can, originally held 50 5¢ cigars upright, made by Snyder in Pennsylvania, a large well-known company, ca. 1930s, approximately 5¹/₂" h., common, excellent condition . . . . **10.00 to 20.00**

Fig. 25-2

Fig. 25-3

Fig. 25-4

Fig. 25-5

Fig. 25-6

CIGAR BOXES

Between 1860 and 1940, the collectible era of cigar boxes, more than a million and a half different brand names were sold in containers made of wood, tin, cardboard, aluminum, china, glass, and other materials. To qualify as "excellent condition" the inside label should be unmarked or with slight soil outside the image area. The inside paper liner in bottom of box should be present and the outside of the box should be clean; the Revenue stamp may be scratched or removed. A box is not "excellent" if the liner is missing; if words are written in ink on the outside and/or inside of the box; or if there are grease or water stains on the box. Values given are for retail of excellent boxes. Boxes in less than excellent condition retail for 25% to 50% of the prices shown.

Alcazar, nailed wood/cardboard box of 50 cigars in four rows, label depicts famous race horse in full color, ca. 1950s, common, full, excellent condition (some minor external scuffing) . . . . **50.00 to 75.00**

Brooks & Co, Tebson/Coronas, standard *boite nature* box w/interlocked corners, hinges & clasp, collar & no paper label, popular national brand from 1920s through 1960s, near mint condition . . . . **3.00 to 5.00**

Corina Larks, Western shape, sports or other size/shape boxes of 50 cigars, standard *boite nature* box w/hinges, clasp, collar & no or little inside label, Jose Escalante & Co., New Orleans, ca. 1940s & 50s, common, mint condition (Fig. 25-6) . . . . **3.00 to 5.00**

Floradora, nailed wood box of 100 cigars, label depicts bundle of three cigars held together w/pictorial band depicting woman's head, cigars priced at 3/10¢, P. Lorillard, factory 17, Virginia, ca. 1901-1909, excellent condition . . . . **30.00 to 40.00**

General U.S. Grant, nailed wood cigar box made to hold 100 cigars in six rows, overall lid & vertical end label, black & white outer label depicts General Ulysses Grant in Civil War uniform, plain white inner label, made by Wescott, Wise & Kent, Binghampton, NY, 1866, signature canceled 1866 revenue stamp in fine condition, handsome end label on an

Fig. 25-8

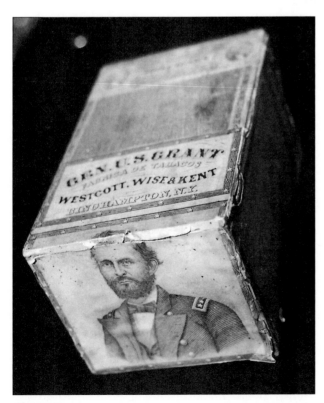

Fig. 25-7

important box made between the war & his presidency (Fig. 25-7) . . . . **125.00 to 250.00**

House of Windsor Palmas or Mark IV Magnates, plastic box, either brown or black, designed to hold 50 cigars four rows deep, ca. 1970s & 80s, mint condition . . . . **3.00 to 5.00**

Metal box, w/top picture frame inset w/various color pictures, hinges, clasp & inside mirror, known in green, red, other colors, w/a wide variety of subject matter on pictures from English cottages, French court scenes, sports, etc., held 100 cigars, box used by variety of Florida & Pennsylvania factories during 1930s, inside mirror had label glued on, but usually removed, excellent condition (cracked mirror) . . . . **20.00 to 30.00**

Phillies Perfecto, tin box of 50 cigars packed four rows high, minor varieties; made by Bayuk Brothers, Philadelphia, ca. 1920s & 1930s, common, mint condition . . . **5.00 to 10.00**

Merry Christmas, book-shaped wooden box of 25 cigars packed two deep, F.M. Howell label depicts windblown pretty girl in Santa outfit

Fig. 25-9

carrying holly, unknown western New York cigarmaker, factory 973, 28th tax district . . . . **30.00 to 50.00**

Sam'l Davis 1886, wooden box, held 50 cigars packed in four rows, w/hinges, often w/a button clasp, no inside pictorial label, made by Sam'l Davis, Pennsylvania, ca. 1950s, mint condition . . . . **3.00 to 5.00**

Unique Hermann Göring Box with Cigars
Sonderanferligung Reichsmarschall **Hermann Göring,** nailed wood box of 10 large cigars packed in glass tubes, inside label depicts Göring's crest in red & gold, German revenue stamp, Gildemann cigar factory, Berlin-Hamburg, ca. 1940s. Excellent condition (Fig. 25-8) . . . . . . **1,000.00 to 1,500.00**

Women's Rights *Concha Regalia*, nailed wood box of 100 cigars, black & white label depicting street scene w/picketers from Democratic & Independent parties soliciting women's attention, John Rauch, factory 97 in the 6th tax district of Indiana, ca. 1880, excellent condition . . . . **400.00 to 600.00**

Yellow Kid Reina Victoria, nailed wood box of 100 cigars, colorful label depicts the Yellow Kid smoking a cigar, plus front page of New York Journal, signed by R.F. Outcault, ca. 1901-1909, unknown New York City cigarmaker, desirable box. **600.00 to 800.00**

Pipes & Cheroot Holders

To be considered in excellent condition, Meerschaum pipes should have no damage & should be smoothly colored, not mottled. The amber or plastic stem should be in place as, ideally, is the case in which it originally came. Briar pipes should show no evidence of reddish colored fill (it looks like clay) to correct blemishes. Pipes should not be dented around the bowl, the result of being banged to loosen tobacco.

Cheroot holder, Meerschaum, w/carving of three nondescript dogs sitting sideways on straight stem, amber bit, approximately $3\frac{1}{2}$" l. (missing case) . . . . **30.00 to 40.00**

Cheroot holder, Meerschaum, w/carving of two riders in hunting costume & seven dogs looking for a fox, seen peeking from around the bow, bowl at 45° angle to stem, original fitted wooden case lined w/satin, covered w/split leather, inside marked "Paris," European origin, ca. 1890-1910, approximately 5" l. . . . . **250.00 to 400.00**

Cheroot holder, Meerschaum, w/amber stem, three deer w/large three-dimensional carving of antlers in crook of holder, exceptionally carved, ca. 1890-1910, $4\frac{3}{4} \times 3$" in original case, mint condition . . . . **40.00 to 60.00**

Fig. 25-10

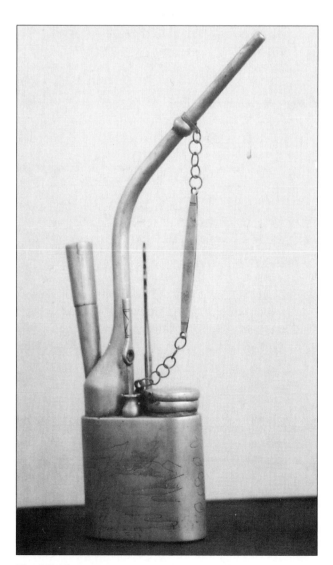

Fig. 25-11

Pipe, Meerschaum, w/slightly bent plastic stem, w/two carved bare breasted ladies swooping about garlands of roses, European origin, ca. late 1800s, approximately 6¼ × 4" (Fig. 25-9) . . . . **400.00 to 650.00**

Pipe, Meerschaum, w/slightly bent amber stem & bit, carved in the form of a hand holding a skull, good detail, stands upright when resting, without case, ca. early 20th c. **75.00 to 150.00**

Meerschaum pipe, carved w/face of Napoleon, excellent turn-of-the-century likeness, European origin, approximately 6" l. (Fig. 25-10) . . . . **150.00 to 300.00**

Pipe, Meerschaum, carved in the form of an elephant w/bead eyes, approximately 14" l. w/plastic bit, no case, Turkish, ca. 1960-1990 . . . . **60.00 to 150.00**

Pipe, water w/tools, made of paktong, Chinese origin, 20th c., approximately 10" h. (Fig. 25-11) . . . . **50.00 to 125.00**

MATCH BOXES & COVERS

Advertising, Bell's Waterproof Wax Vestas, tin matchbox, w/slip-top & striker on bottom, litho in blue, white & tan w/three lines of lettering, English, ca. 1900-1910, approximately 2¾ × 1½" . . . . **5.00 to 20.00**

Dewey for President, cover w/photo of Dewey, ca. 1948. . . . . **10.00 to 15.00**

First Nite-Life match cover, set of famous personalities on standard covers, colored in pastel, complete w/original strikers, Diamond Match Co., 1938, set of 24 . . . . . . **20.00 to 40.00**

Girlie matchbook cover, w/original strikers, "It's great to be an American" on one side, pin-up girls by Merlin on the other, Maryland Match Company, ca. 1940, excellent condition . . . . **3.00 to 8.00**

Lux Super fosforos match box, cardboard box w/sliding drawer, label depicts baseball player, Cuban, ca. 1940s-1950s, good condition . . . . **10.00 to 20.00**

NBC/CBS stars match cover, famous radio personalities on standard match covers complete w/original strikers, Diamond Match Co., 1935, part of set . . . . **1.00 to 5.00**

Fig. 25-12

Fig. 25-13

CIGARETTE DISPENSERS & ASHTRAYS

Ashtray, advertising, clear glass w/black imprint "Biloxi Belle Casino" (Biloxi, MS), after 1992, 3¼" . . . . **2.00 to 4.00**

Ashtray, advertising, amethyst glass w/smooth bottom & white imprint "Hotel Fremont, Las Vegas, Nevada," ca. 1970s, 3½" d. . . . **2.00 to 4.00**

Ashtray, advertising, clear glass, w/red on white imprint "The Fabulous Flamingo, The Showplace of the Nation, Las Vegas, Nevada" & artwork of flamingo w/head lowered, ca. 1947-1967, 4" d. . . . . **10.00 to 20.00**

Ashtray, advertising, smoked glass, imprinted in red, "Flamingo Hilton, Las Vegas-Nevada" w/the three flamingos logo, after 1971, 4" d. . . . . **3.00 to 6.00**

Ashtray, ceramic, three-dimensional figure of poodle's head w/mouth open to receive cigarette, smoke comes out dog's eyes when cigarette left in ashtray, brown & white glaze (Fig. 25-12) . . . . **10.00 to 12.00**

Ashtray, ceramic, three dimensional figure of Ubangi, smoke comes out his pursed lips when cigarette left in ashtray, brown glaze, approximately 7" h., unusual . . . . **10.00 to 25.00**

Ashtray, ceramic, in shape of the state of New York, w/decals picturing state capitol, state flower & state fish, ca. 1950s, approximately 5" . . . . **5.00 to 15.00**

Ashtray, ceramic, multi-colored, shaped as a tobacco leaf w/three dimensional figures of Uncle Sam & Cuban man carrying a giant cigar, ca. 1920s, approximately 8" l., excellent condition . . . . **50.00 to 85.00**

Dispenser, cast-iron elephant dispenses cigarette under his belly when tail is cranked, holds approximately one pack in howdah on his back, known in red, black & green, ca. 1920s-1930s, 7" l. (Fig. 25-13) . . **50.00 to 75.00**

ADVERTISING & STORE ITEMS

Advertising figure, Admiration cigars, composition Indian vigorously striding w/box of cigars under his arm, S. Fernandez & Co., Tampa, ca. 1940s, 18" h. . . . . . . **150.00 to 250.00**

Advertising sign, cigar, "Robert Burns 10¢ Cigar," lithographed on tin, 1901-1909, 24" d., very good condition (Fig. 25-14) . . . . **450.00 to 800.00**

Advertising sign, snuff, paper, "Lorillard's Snuff" above handsome red, white, blue & black depiction of snuff taking seniors, reads "Won the Only Gold Medal Awarded on Snuff at the Atlanta Exposition" below, professionally framed, intended for tobacconist's wall, P.Lorillard, New York, ca. 1905-1910, 24 × 32" . . . . **300.00 to 450.00**

Fig. 25-14

Fig. 25-16

Fig. 25-15

Advertising sign, tobacco, " 'You'll Like it Too!' Prince Albert," linen-backed, outdoor sign or indoor banner depicting pipe smoker & Prince Albert can, 4 × 8', excellent condition (Fig. 25-15) . . . . **30.00 to 75.00**

Cigar store Indian, full-size, wood, Indian maiden holding bunch of cigars, fair carving by unidentified workman, ca. late 19th century manufacture, repainted before WWII, 5' h. including base . . . . **7,500.00 to 15,000.00**

Tobacco container, Bull Durham, cardboard, designed to hold 64 cloth bags of smoking tobacco, intended as display pieces, various cowboy & racist Negro scenes, ca. 1910-1920s, excellent condition, widely reproduced (Fig. 25-16) . . . . **400.00 to 1,000.00 and up**

Cigar box opener, "El Verso Cigars" on one side & "San Felice Cigars" on the other, nickel plated, ca. 1950s, 3" l. . . . . **3.00 to 5.00**

Tobacco plug cutter, counter-top, cast iron, figural of an imp, w/original paint, ca. late 1800s, has been reproduced . . . **150.00 to 200.00**

Fig. 25-17

Fig. 25-18

Paper Goods

Cigar bands, mounted in album without glue, bands complete w/white tabs at end, more than half are pictorial bands of Presidents, animals, kings, famous persons, etc., approximately 1,000 in set . . . . . **50.00 to 100.00**

Postcard, "A Modern Tobacco Factory, Tampa, Fla.," color . . . . **2.00 to 3.00**

Postcard, real photo, black & white, shows tobacco buyer, reads "Our Mr. Levy Pres. Enterprise Cigar Co. Buying Havana in Cuba for the Celebrated Lord Stirling & Taking Cigars" (Fig. 25-17) . . . . **5.00 to 10.00**

Poster, L & M cigarettes, featuring Matt Dillon & Miss Kitty from Gunsmoke, reads "They Said It Couldn't Be Done But L&M Did It! - Don't settle for one...without the other!," ca. 1960s, excellent condition . . . . **50.00 to 75.00**

Fig. 25-19

Personal Items

Cigar case, aluminum, holds three cigars, decoration cut into the aluminum along w/inscription "Jamestown, 1907," apparently purchased or received as a prize at the Jamestown Exposition honoring the 300th anniversary of the first colony, $2^{1}/_{2} \times 4^{1}/_{2}$" (Fig. 25-18, bottom) . . . . **30.00 to 50.00**

Cigar case, nickel plated metal, w/space for name or inscription, ca. 1900-1930, $2^{1}/_{2} \times 4^{1}/_{2}$" (Fig. 25-18, top) . . . . **15.00 to 30.00**

Cigar case, silver plated, gold wash inside, holds three cigars, minor decoration, ca. 1900-1930, $2^{1}/_{2} \times 4^{1}/_{2}$" . . . . **20.00 to 45.00**

Fig. 25-20

Fig. 25-21

Fig. 25-22

Cigar clipper, brass, shaped like scissors, made in U.S. & Europe, ca. 1890s-1920 . . **25.00 to 40.00**

Cigar clipper, shaped like man sitting on chamber pot, clip cigar by putting it in hole in his stomach, push down on his head & cigar trimming falls into chamber pot, European origin, turn-of-the-century, 6" h. (Fig. 25-19) . . . . **150.00 to 400.00**

Matchbox grip, silver plated, three-sided, device for protecting matchboxes, w/embossed design of the United Brotherhood of Carpenters & Joiners of America, reads "See That This Label Appears On All Wood Work," 1¼ × 2¼", rare (Fig. 25-20, bottom) . . . . **60.00 to 100.00**

Matchsafe, nickel plated w/celluloid wrap-around, depicts brewery worker's union label, reads "International Union of the United Brewery Workmen of America ask your Support against Prohibition As it is Detrimental to All," ca. 1920, 1½ × 2½", excellent condition (Fig. 25-20, top) . . . . **100.00 to 300.00**

CIGARETTE LIGHTERS

Figural, pot metal, shape of a dachshund, made to imitate its much more valuable Vienna bronze counterpart, tag has 1912 patent & is marked "Austria," 4¼" l. (Fig. 25-21) . . . . **50.00 to 100.00**

Evans cigarette lighter/cigarette case, mother-of-pearl squares, excellent condition, set of 2 (Fig. 25-22) . . . . **50.00 to 125.00**

Fig. 25-23

Fig. 25-24

Ronson, pocket, Diana model, ca.
1950s . . . . **10.00 to 20.00**

Ronson, table-type, Queen Anne model,
ca. 1936-1959 . . . . **10.00 to 20.00**

TOBACCIANA FOLK ARTS

Dish, glass, covered w/cigar bands in
carefully chosen geometric pattern.
ca. 1910-1920, 6½" d., excellent unfaded
condition (Fig. 25-23) . . . . **25.00 to 50.00**

Pillow cover, made from satin cigar ribbons.
ca. 1900-1920, value depends on condition
(no less than excellent is acceptable), the
selection of ribbons & the artistry of
presentation, 2' sq. (Fig. 25-24) . . **75.00 to 250.00**

Vase, glass, covered w/cigar bands in random
patterns, ca. 1910-1920, 6" h., excellent
unfaded condition . . . . **20.00 to 30.00**

MISCELLANEOUS

Cigar mold, ten cigar size, hardwood, made by
Miller, Dubrul & Peters, ca. 1880s through
1920s, common . . . . **20.00 to 35.00**

Cigarette pack, Twenty Grand, paper cup-
type package, image on pack depicts race

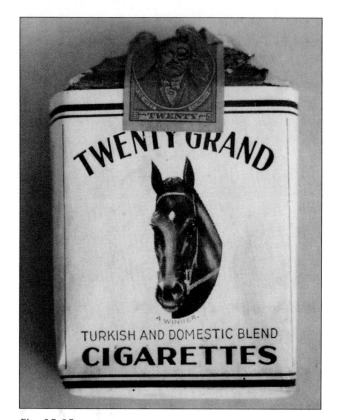

Fig. 25-25

horse, printed brown on white
(Fig. 25-25) . . . . **3.00 to 5.00**

Tray, advertising Cigar Maker's Union &
Union, tin 10½ × 13¼", ca. 1902-1905
(Fig. 25-26) . . . . **100.00 to 150.00**

Fig. 25-26

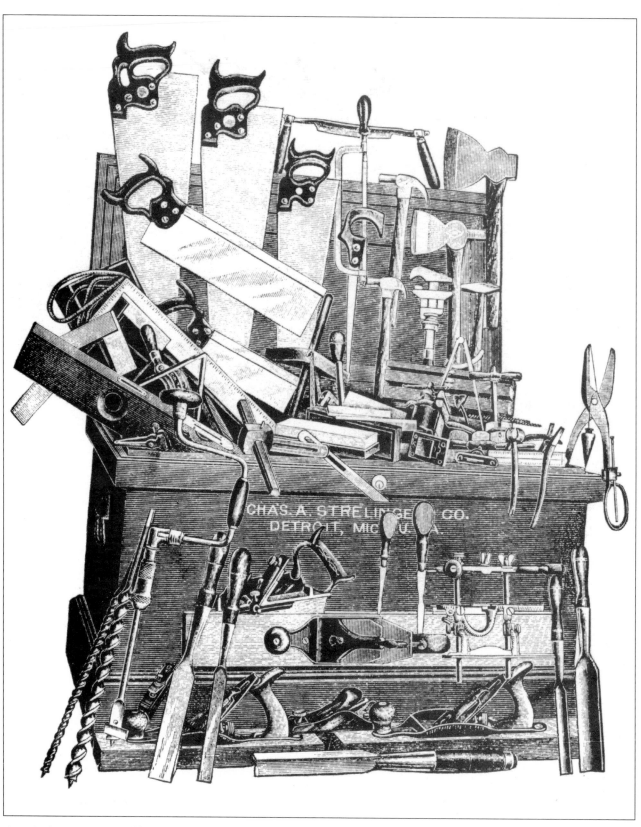

A typical carpenter's tool kit of the 1890s.

CHAPTER
26

TOOLS

Contrary to popular belief, not all woodworking, blacksmith or farm tools are collectible. Some common items held in low esteem, include: plumber's tools, automotive tools, pliers, screwdrivers, socket wrenches, taps, and dies, etc.

Twenty years ago there was a demand for primitive handmade tools of obvious form and function. But today's sophisticated collectors are looking for complex patented woodworking tools by high-quality manufacturers such as Baily, Chapin, Disston, Davis, Greenfield, KeenKutter, Sargent, Stanley, and Winchester. Wooden planes need a rare maker's mark to attract strong interest. The "high-flyers" are metallic woodworking planes, brass-bound or ivory rulers, rosewood levels with extra trim or gages and giant brass plumb bobs.

Wooden jack planes, panel planes, fore planes (all shaped like a long 4 × 4" length of lumber) are common. So are simple narrow wooden moulding planes by the Auburn, Ohio and Chapin Tool Companies. Millions of core, round, and beading planes were factory-made between 1860 and 1920. It is the 18th century makers that are rare today.

Double-bodied plow planes with adjustable screw-arms are very desirable. Ivory trim can quickly boost them to a $1,000.00 or more. Wide complex-moulders with wavy ornamental-shaped irons are quite scarce, whereas straight blades and half-round blades are common forms.

Farm tools are not scarce because they were produced in huge numbers, made of indestructible materials (oak and iron) and sold to most of the population a hundred years ago. However, there are a few higher-ticket items in this field. Certain items such as old cream separators, fancy churns, butter molds, cast-iron tractor seats, cookware, figural weathervanes, and windmill weights; and the latest fad, spurs, chaps, saddles, and other cowboy gear, all bring top dollar from dealers, decorators, museums, and collectors.

Blacksmith tools, with few exceptions, are not worth a whole lot more than scrap iron unless they have decorative appeal as wall hangers. Exceptions are wheel-shaped "travelers," post drills, cage-head braces and certain special-function anvils. The average long-handled horseshoe pincer or pliers are not hot items and most of these rusty branding irons are clever forgeries recently made in Mexico (socket handles are a clue to the real thing).

There are several ways to familiarize yourself with the thousands of old tools which make up our industrial and agricultural heritage. You can join clubs, subscribe to dealer catalogs, attend tool auctions or read popular price guides and reference books.

Condition is a big factor when pricing old tools. Excessive cleaning, sanding, wire-brush marks, or refinishing can drastically reduce value to a seasoned collector. Do not try for top dollar if your old tool has a cracked handle, missing or broken parts, weathered wood, heavy rust, cracked glass vials, or repainted surfaces. It is acceptable to rub on a little furniture polish or oil, but avoid soap and water.

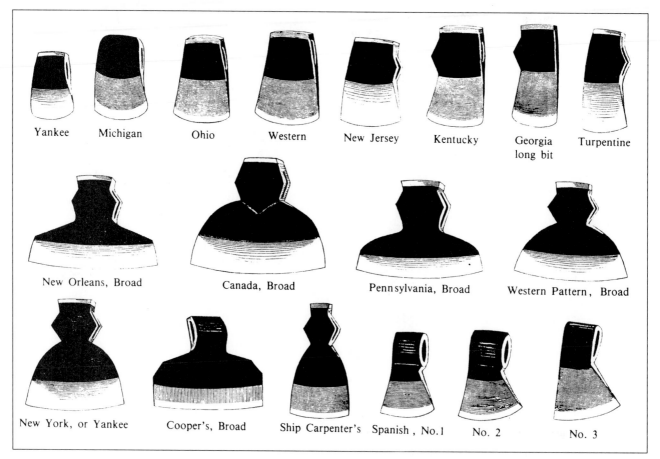

Yankee   Michigan   Ohio   Western   New Jersey   Kentucky   Georgia long bit   Turpentine

New Orleans, Broad   Canada, Broad   Pennsylvania, Broad   Western Pattern, Broad

New York, or Yankee   Cooper's, Broad   Ship Carpenter's   Spanish, No.1   No. 2   No. 3

Fig. 26-1 – Various styles of ax heads.

Soap can raise the wood's surface and remove patina. Never use any abrasive stronger than a soft wire brush or fine steel wool. A thin coat of matte spray lacquer actually improves the look of rusty surfaces; no other treatment is necessary.

—Ron Barlow

Adze, bowl-type w/curved blade, 6" w. blade .. **$75.00**

Adze, Cooper's rounding-type, 1½" square face, 9½" curved head, 3" w. bit, 10" handle **55.00**

Auger, "Gedge's Patent" tap-type, wood handle, tapered funnel w/bit at end . . . . **15.00 to 20.00**

Auger, carpenters-type, "T-handle," 14" to 24" l. . . . . **25.00 to 45.00**

Ax, broad-type, factory-made, American . . . . **45.00 to 75.00**

Ax, "Cast Steel, Oswego," broad-type, Pennsylvania patt., made by Farnham (Fig. 26-1) **75.00**

Ax, Cooper's side ax w/rectangular blade, 5 × 10" blade (pitted & weld repair) **50.00**

Ax, "E.C. Simmons," broad-type, Pittsburgh patt., Keen Kutter, head only **60.00**

Ax, goosewing-style w/punched star & wheat patterns, 10" head, 11" blade (pitted condition) **350.00**

Ax, "Keen Kutter," California patt., double-bit **30.00**

Ax, "Keen Kutter," Michigan patt., single-bit (Fig. 26-1) . . . .**25.00 to 45.00**

Ax, "Shapleighs" logo, Michigan patt., single-bit (Fig. 26-1) **15.00**

Ax, shipwright's style, marked "Gilpin," 5" bit, 12" head (pitted condition) **175.00**

Ax, "Vaughan VB" adze-eye, w/original handle **30.00**

Ax, "Winchester" Dayton patt., single-bit . . . . **45.00 to 60.00**

Blacksmith's top swedge, handmade, wire handle, 19" l. **24.00**

Blow torch, "Shapleigh," solid brass, 1909 patent, in good working order **75.00**

Boring machine, wood-frame upright auger w/bit, egg-shaped hardwood crank handles, 2" bit **85.00**

Brace, "Millers Falls," No. 502B, corner-type (gear cover missing) **25.00**

Brace, Sheffield-style beechwood w/brass & Lignum Vitae wood head **95.00**

Brace, "Stanley," No. 921, ratchet brace, 1906 patent **25.00**

Calipers, steel, without maker mark, 18" **25.00**

Calipers, Wheelright's, large curved bell-shaped, steel legs, slotted bow, 12½" w. .. **75.00**

Chisel, "Buck Brothers" bevel edge, 7/16" socket firmer **14.00**

Chisel, "Diamond-edge," pocket butt, ½" edge .. **9.00**

Chisel, "Diamond-edge," pocket butt, ½" edge (no handle) **5.00**

Chisel, "Stanley," everlasting 3/8" butt chisel w/black plastic handle **9.00**

Chisel, "Winchester," socket firmer, bevel edge 5/8", good logo & handle **38.00**

Coachmaker's router, draw-knife-shape w/1½" w/blade in the center, 18" l. overall **45.00**

Compass, "P.S. & W. Company," No. 15, 15" l. . **35.00**

Cooper's adze, "D.R. Barton," replaced handle **25.00**

Cooper's hollowing knife, "D.R. Barton," walnut handles, no rust **35.00**

Corn-husking gloves, leather, w/rivets & pin .... **10.00 to 25.00**

Corn sheller, floor model, hand-cranked w/fly wheel, ca. 1880 .... **100.00 to 250.00**

Corn sheller, table model, iron, portable w/coil spring .... **45.00 to 75.00**

Dowell sharpener, "Stanley," No. 22, ¼" shaft **25.00**

Draw knife, "D.R. Barton," mast-style w/brass ferrules, 14" blade, 22" l. .... **40.00 to 60.00**

Drill, archimedean-type, tin w/steel counter weights, unmarked, 9" overall **25.00**

Drill, egg beater-style, metal-spoked-wheels, geared w/hollow wooden handle for bit storage .... **14.00 to 20.00**

Drill, "Post drill," mounted on indoor barn post for blacksmith-type repairs to farm equipment (Fig. 26-2) ...... **85.00 to 150.00**

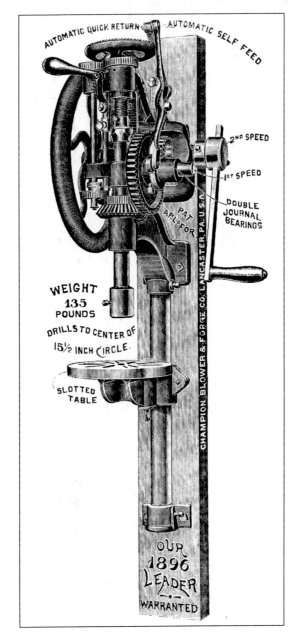

Fig. 26-2

Drill, push-type, "Johnson & Tainters," brass, ca. 1880 .... **22.00**

Fencing pliers, combination hipper, hammer, ax, tackpuller, screwdriver & wire cutter, common **15.00**

Gauge, leather-cutting, iron-framed, pistol-shaped w/sliding gauge & blade .. **25.00 to 30.00**

Gauge, "Stanley," No. 71, double-bar beechwood & brass marking & mortise gauge **35.00**

Gauge, "Stanley," No. 77, rosewood & brass mortise gauge, ca. 1872-1920s ... **25.00 to 40.00**

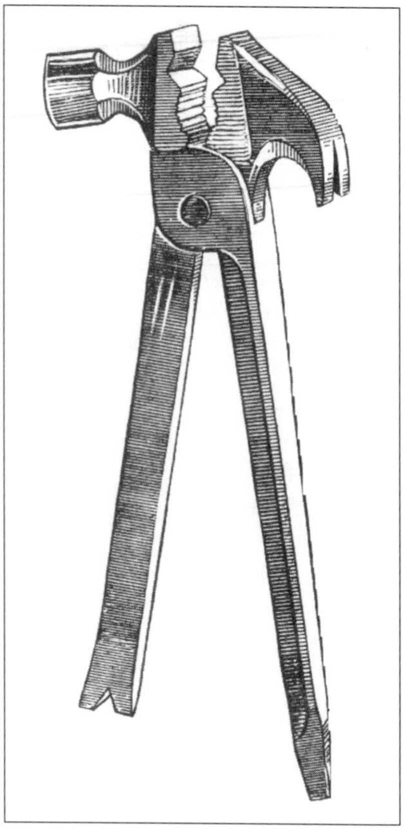

Fig. 26-3

Fig. 26-4

Grinder, "Deering," peddle-powered, chain drive, wood frame w/steel seat **150.00**

Grindstone, wheel-mounted on oak frame w/foot pump lever .... **100.00 to 250.00**

Grindstone, wheel-mounted on oak frame w/foot pump lever, metal frame w/sheet metal tractor seat & pedals .... **75.00 to 150.00**

Hammer, Adams Claw Hammer, w/gas pliers, screw driver, wrench, tack puller & box opener, ca. 1887 (Fig. 26-3) ..... **25.00 to 45.00**

Hammer, "Blue Grass," nail-type, No. BG47-16, label on handle, mint condition **18.00**

Hammer, coachmaker's tack-type w/thin head & delicate nail claw, 8½" l. head **40.00**

Hammer, common ball-peen style 16 oz. .... **8.00 to 10.00**

Hammer, Kent patt., English strap-handled claw-type **48.00**

Hammer, "Shapleigh's," straight pein-type, wedge & round, flat head **35.00**

Hammer, "Snow Knocker," iron, blacksmith-made, used for cleaning ice from horse's hooves, 6" head **45.00**

Hammer head, handmade by blacksmith, 5" claw (pitted condition) **24.00**

Hatchet, "Boy Scout"-style .... **30.00 to 45.00**

Hatchet, English bow-tie style, marked "Charles Thompson," 10" head w/4" blade on each end **35.00**

Hatchet, "Keen Kutter," flat-top flooring-type, 4" blade **25.00**

Hatchet, shingling-type, round neck & poll, bell-face, 3" blade .... **10.00 to 15.00**

Hay hooks (bale hooks), steel blades w/wooden handles, set of 2 ..... **10.00 to 19.00**

Jig saw, "Seneca Falls," Rival model, treadle-style, iron frame, pat. 1877 & 1855 .... **350.00 to 550.00**

Knife, "E.C. Simmons," iron-handled farrier's hoof-type, rare **10.00**

Knife, leather cutting, traditional half-moon blade, turned wood handle & brass ferrule (Fig. 26-4) .... **8.00 to 15.00**

Knife, race knife or timber scribe, two blades, brass ferrule **37.00**

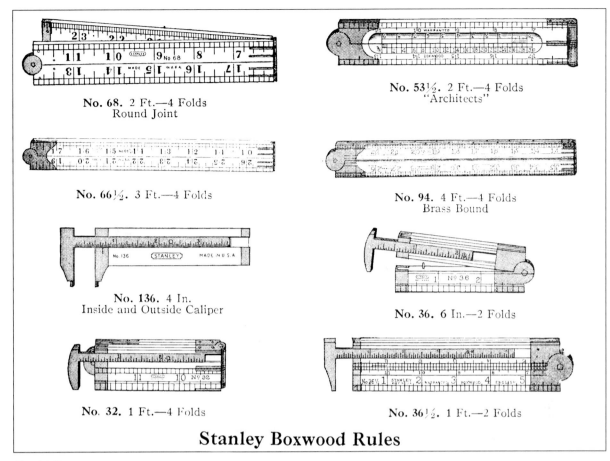

No. 68. 2 Ft.—4 Folds
Round Joint

No. 53½. 2 Ft.—4 Folds
"Architects"

No. 66½. 3 Ft.—4 Folds

No. 94. 4 Ft.—4 Folds
Brass Bound

No. 136. 4 In.
Inside and Outside Caliper

No. 36. 6 In.—2 Folds

No. 32. 1 Ft.—4 Folds

No. 36½. 1 Ft.—2 Folds

Stanley Boxwood Rules

Fig. 26-5

Note: Lantern prices depend on date & number of brass parts. Metallic paint & poor-quality wicks and adjusting wheels are indications of more modern manufacture. Look for maker's names & patent dates.

Lantern, "Cold Blast" style w/tubular sheet metal frame, globe intact . . . . **25.00 to 65.00**

Lantern, searchlight-style, large dish reflector, dash-clamp . . . . **75.00 to 125.00**

Note: Levels are priced by the number of dials & the amount of brass trim present. The most common "Stanley" Nos. 01, 02, 03 & 04 were made by the millions and prices range from $15.00 to $22.00. Higher numbers, fully bound on all sides can go for $100.00 or more. In between are lots of models from $30.00 to $50.00

Level, "Diamond Edge," walnut, duplex-type, marked "Norvel-Shapeigh" on brass trim, ca. 1910, 24" **45.00**

Level, "Stratton," No. 1, brass bound plumb-type, pat. 1888, 28" l. **25.00**

Lock, "Eagle" brand, ca. 1870 . . . . **20.00**

Lock, "Keen Kutter," triangular-shaped solid brass **125.00**

Mallet, carpenter's wood-type w/iron-banded head 3" to 6" l. head **15.00**

Oil stone, "Keen Kutter" embossed into smooth side **22.00**

Pitch fork, all wood w/three tines (often reproduced) . . . . **30.00 to 60.00**

Pliers, "Keen Kutter," slip joint water-pump-style **18.00**

Pliers, "Winchester," nickel-plated, universal style w/wire cutter in handle **48.00**

Plumb bob, "K 7 E," brass w/steel point, 9 oz. . **15.00**

Plumb bob, pitcher-spout-type, iron pump for indoor use . . . . **15.00 to 40.00**

Plumb bob, "Stanley," No. 2, brass w/built-in reel in head, 4" l. . . . . **125.00 to 225.00**

Rope machine, "New Era," hand-cranked rope twister . . . . **100.00 to 150.00**

Router, "Keen Kutter," nickel-plated frame w/two mahogany knobs, pat. 1901, 7" w. . . . **95.00**

Router, oak, D-shaped w/carved initials & brass wingnut, 3½" w. **60.00**

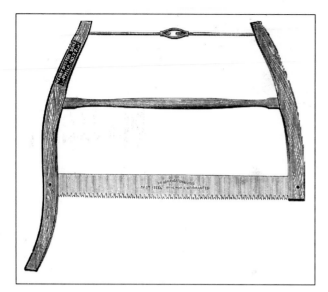

Fig. 26-6

Router, woman's tooth-style, beechwood, unmarked, nice patina, $3\frac{3}{4} \times 2\frac{5}{8}$" . . **20.00 to 30.00**

Rule, "Lufkin," No. 38, caliper-style, boxwood, four-fold, 1 foot **20.00**

Rule, "Stanley," No. 36, square joint w/folding six-foot caliper rule (Fig. 26-5) . . . **20.00 to 30.00**

Rule, "Stanley," No. 66½, arch joint, three-foot, four-fold w/heart logo (Fig. 26-5) **25.00**

Saw, "Blue Grass," No. 2 panel saw, rosewood handle, 15 points to the inch . . . . **50.00 to 70.00**

Saw, brass back-type, turned handle, 5" l. blade, 9½" l. **39.00**

Saw, "E.C. Simmons, Keen Kutter," oak handled hand saw, 8 points, 26" blade **35.00**

Saw, H-frame turning saw w/cord & tension stick, 12" to 14" blade . . . . **40.00 to 55.00**

Saw, "Henry Disston & Sons," buck saw, cast-steel blade, ca. 1880-1930 (Fig. 26-6) . . . . **20.00 to 30.00**

Saw, "Henry Disston," cross-cut, 8-point w/large Federal Eagle medallion & split slot bolts (minor pitting) **25.00**

Saw, stair saw, fruitwood, 11" l. **50.00**

Saw set, "Morril's Patent," pliers-type, ca. 1900 . . . . **6.00**

Scales, farmer's "steelyards" w/three hooks & pear-shaped weight on steel bar, 50 lbs. to 200 lbs. . . . . **25.00 to 65.00**

Scales, "Sargent" or "Chatillions," brass circular dial w/dairy or feed store advertising & hanging brass pan . . . . **150.00 to 200.00**

Scales, "Chatillions Ice Balance," heavy-duty hanging style, 1876 patent, 300 lbs. capacity . . . . **35.00 to 75.00**

Scales, "Frary's Improved," balance w/hanging ring & bottom hook, brass face reads to 24 lbs. . . . . **15.00 to 20.00**

Scales, "Turnbull's Market," cast iron, glass face, marble slab, pat. 1859, 16 lbs. . . . . **150.00 to 200.00**

Screwdriver, flat-bladed early style w/brass ferrule on turned handle, 12" . . . . . **8.00 to 12.00**

Screwdriver, "Yankee," spiral ratcheting-type w/wood handle . . . . **10.00 to 20.00**

Scythe, factory-made w/attached grain cradle arms . . . . **100.00 to 200.00**

Spoke shave, "Stanley," No. 53, adjustable iron **15.00**

Spoke shave, "Stanley," No. 60, all metal, double-bladed **35.00**

Spoke shave, wooden, non-adjustable 10" to 12" . . . . **10.00 to 15.00**

Spoke shave, wooden, adjustable w/brass trim, 10" to 12" **20.00**

Square, "Diamond edge," try- & mitre-type, rosewood handle & brass trim, 6" **25.00**

Square, "Fox," mitre-type w/E.C. logo **20.00**

Square, "Stanley," try square, solid iron, blue blade **15.00**

Tip snips, "Diamond-edge," forged steel, 10½" overall **9.00**

Tip snips, "Diamond-edge," forged steel, pocket-sized 7" **12.00**

Tool chest, machinists-type, "Gerstner's," seven drawer oak chest w/diamond shaped mirror in lid . . . . **195.00 to 250.00**

Tool holder, "Aiken's Patent," wooden handle w/a variety of tool tips, ca. 1880-1920 (Fig. 26-7) . . . . **25.00 to 45.00**

Traps, bear, w/toothed jaws . . . . . **100.00 to 450.00**

Traps, mouse & rat, catch 'em-alive cage-type . . . . **25.00 to 50.00**

Traveler, steel w/five curved spokes, open shaped handle (Fig. 26-8) . . . . **35.00 to 50.00**

Try square, ebony stock, blue-black blade, brass inlay, 14" overall **25.00**

Vise, iron, portable, ornamental turned knob on end of main shaft, 14" l. including screw-clamp base, 3½" jaws **200.00**

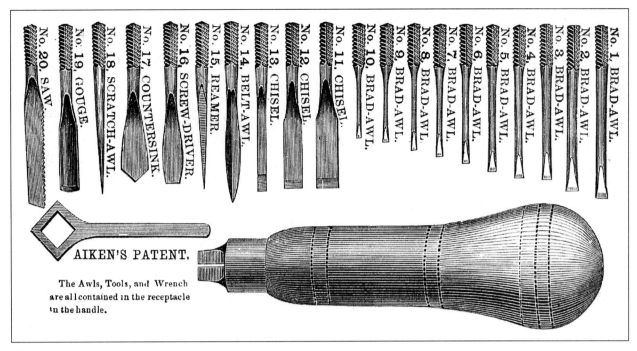

No. 20. SAW. No. 19. GOUGE. No. 18. SCRATCH-AWL. No. 17. COUNTERSINK. No. 16. SCREW-DRIVER. No. 15. REAMER. No. 14. BELT-AWL. No. 13. CHISEL. No. 12. CHISEL. No. 11. CHISEL. No. 10. BRAD-AWL. No. 9. BRAD-AWL. No. 8. BRAD-AWL. No. 7. BRAD-AWL. No. 6. BRAD-AWL. No. 5. BRAD-AWL. No. 4. BRAD-AWL. No. 3. BRAD-AWL. No. 2. BRAD-AWL. No. 1. BRAD-AWL.

AIKEN'S PATENT.

The Awls, Tools, and Wrench are all contained in the receptacle in the handle.

Fig. 26-7

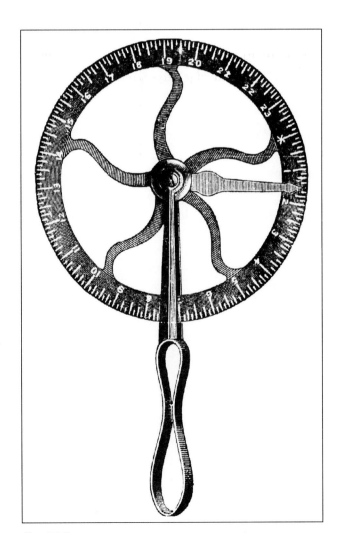

Fig. 26-8

Vise, saw filer's cam-action lever-type . . . . **15.00 to 18.00**

Wrench, "Deering," No. D203 iron implement-type, 8½" **10.00**

Wrench, "Keen Kutter," crescent-style, 10" l. **22.00**

Wrench, "Keen Kutter," pipe-type, 10" to 24" . . . . **18.00 to 24.00**

Wrench, "Maydole," pipe-type w/wood-handle, 6" overall **50.00**

Wrench, "Pexto," pipe-type, 10" **5.00**

Wrench, "Pierce Arrow," one-end, 6" **15.00**

Wrench, "Sargent," No. 66, tiny wood handled monkey-type, 6½" l. . . . . **25.00 to 40.00**

Wrench, "Sattley Golden Harvest," cream separator-type **35.00**

Wrench, "Winchester," No. 1005, wood handled monkey-type, 15" l. **150.00**

◆ **Planes**

Woodworking planes are by far and away the most popular tools being collected today.

Early Americans used mostly English-made woodworking tools prior to the year 1800. Between 1810 and 1840 about two dozen planemakers were engaged full-time at the activity, mostly around

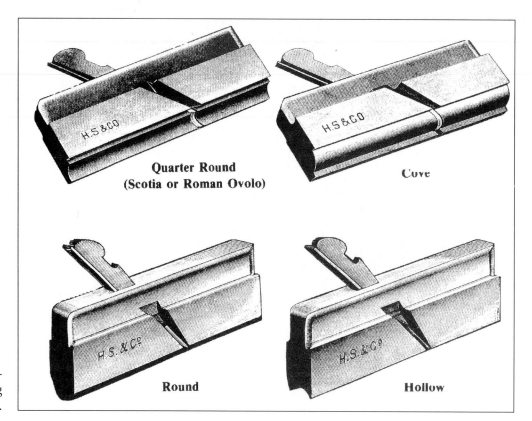

Quarter Round
(Scotia or Roman Ovolo)

Cove

Round

Hollow

Simple factory-made moulding planes, 1860-1920.

Philadelphia and New York City. The first plane making factories were founded in the 1840s and 50s, primarily in Connecticut where the industrial leadership had already been established. The average sized firm was capitalized at about $10,000.00 and employed fifteen workmen, who produced from five to twenty completed tools per day. They were, of course, beechwood, with few if any metal parts.

Wooden plane production peaked a couple of decades later and then plummeted when Stanley began to mass-produce Leonard Bailey's iron-bodied planes in 1870. A massive advertising program, coupled with aggressive pricing and a nationwide distribution network, soon eliminated most of the competition. By the year 1900 over 3 million Stanley "Bailey" planes had been sold.

In order to prepare readers unfamiliar with the terminology used by tool dealers and auctioneers, when referring to the Stanley planes, we list the following definitions:

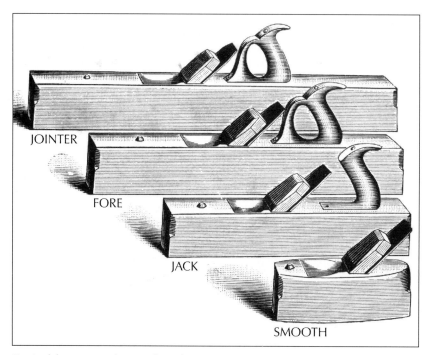

JOINTER

FORE

JACK

SMOOTH

Typical factory-made wooden planes, 1865-1925.

Bailey name was cast on the toe of iron planes starting in 1902.

Block Planes come in wood or metal and are straight-bladed and under 7½" long.

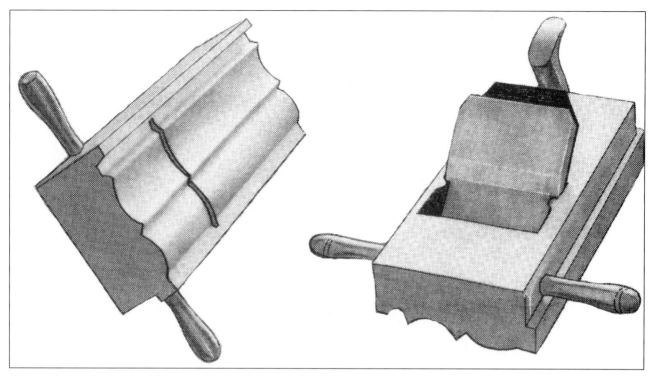

A pair of 5" Complex moulding planes, ca. 1864. This pair might sell for around $3,000.00 today.

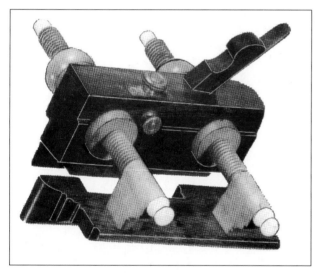

Ivory-trimmed plow planes of the 1850s, such as this example, can be worth $2,000.00 to $6,000.00. The same style in plain beechwood or boxwood only bring $100.00 to $150.00.

Compass Planes, in wood, are non-adjustable curved bottom planes. The metal variety have an adjustable sole-plate for different radius curves and coach work.

Eagle Trademark appears on the most prelateral models of the wood-bottom-type made from 1869 to about 1887.

Fore Planes can be wood or metal and have open or closed-style handles. They generally range in length from 18" to 24" and have flat straight blades.

Jack Planes are from 14" to 18" long in the older wooden style and a uniform 14" in the metal variety. Their 1³/₄" to 2" cutting iron (blade) is slightly convex for rapid removal of excess stock.

Jointer Planes of the factory-made beechwood style are 22" to 28" in length. Their long bodies reduce the hills and valleys left by shorter planes, giving uniform joints.

Kidney Cap is a term describing the kidney-shaped hole in lever caps made after 1933.

Liberty Bell emblem appears on the lever caps of some models made for the 1876 Centennial and continued on through World War I.

Low Knob refers to the lower height front-knob design of planes produced prior to 1922.

Moulding Planes have been used to cut ornamental profiles into wooden trim stock since Roman times. Factory production of wood-bodied moulding planes began in London in the 18th century. American moulders became a standard 9¹/₂" long by the mid-19th century. There are two basic kinds of moulding planes—"simple" and "complex." Simple moulders are usually narrow, common, un-handled shapes, in beechwood such as round, hollow, bead, cove, casing, snipe bill, etc. Complex moulders are

Fig. 26-9

wider, cornice-cutting planes of complex combinations of curves up to 5" in width. They often have handles and/or thru-the-nose tow-bars for an apprentice to pull, while the master pushed.

Common factory-made moulding planes were produced at a rate of thousands per week between 1865 and 1900. The simple shapes usually bring no more than $8.00 to $20.00, while complex moulders by famous makers can fetch up to $2,000.00 or more.

Plow Planes were invented to cut uniform grooves in the drawer, door and chest frames. All plows have "fences" to keep the groove a preset distance from the edge of a board. The earliest British and American plow planes had wedges to lock these fences in place. Between 1800 and 1840 screw-arm plow planes evolved. Metal plow planes came into widespread use between 1870 and 1880.

Prelateral models without a lateral blade adjusting lever, made prior to 1884.

Smoothing Planes are the final tools used on flat surfaces. Their 6" to 10" length allows them to move in small areas. They came in wood or metal and have approximately 2" wide straight cutters and open-style handles, or no handles at all.

Sweetheart trademark adopted in 1920 and discontinued ca. 1935.

Transitional Planes are wood bodied planes with metal tops or blade housings. They were a transition between all-wood and all-metal planes. Most of them were out of production by 1920.

Plane, "Auburn Tool Co.," No. 180, moulding-type, double boxwood inserts, custom blade profile, ca. 1870, 1⅝" w. **25.00**

Plane, "Barton Tool Co.," wood rabbet-type, 2" w. **24.00**

Plane, "D.R. Barton," beechwood toothing-type, coffin-shaped **32.00**

Plane, "Hermon Chapin," double-iron wooden match-type, steel skate **38.00**

Plane, "Keen Kutter," fore-type, solid beechwood, 2⅜" cutter, 26" l. **45.00**

Plane, "G. White," bead moulding-type, ca. 1820, ¼" blade **50.00**

Plane, "Greenfield Tool Co.," Greek ogee moulding-type, beechwood, 2¼" w. **28.00**

Plane, "Ohio Tool Co.," Greek ovolo moulding-type, 1½" **38.00**

Plane, "Ohio Tool Co.," half-round nosing-type, 1" cutter **15.00**

Plane, "Sargent," No. 106, metal block-type . . **15.00**

Plane, "Sheneman, Market St, Phila," mitre-type, coffin-shaped beechwood ca. 1850, 2¹/₈" **150.00**

"Stanley Rule & Level Company" made millions of woodworking planes between 1860 & 1960. It would take a separate book to list all the varieties & prices. We have listed some common types, but there are rare numbers, of which only a few were made, that sell for $500.00 to $3,000.00.

Plane, "Stanley," No. 1, smoothing-type, metal w/wood handle & knob, 5¹/₂" l., rare (Fig. 26-9) . . . . **800.00 to 2,000.00**

Plane, "Stanley," No. 3, metal smoothing-type, ca. 1935 . . . . **30.00 to 45.00**

Plane, "Stanley," No. 10, carriage maker's rabbet w/heart logo **145.00**

Plane, "Stanley," No. 13, circular-type, ca. 1890 . . . . **135.00**

Plane, "Stanley," No. 26, wood bottom, iron top, early model . . . . **35.00 to 45.00**

Plane, "Stanley," No. 55, combination-type, without blades **295.00**

Plane, "Stanley," No. 55, combination-type, in original box **450.00**

Plane, "Stanley," No. 122, un-handled, wood bottomed, smoothing-type **26.00**

Plane, "Stanley," No. 135, smoothing-type, Liberty Bell logo on cap . . . . **800.00 to 2,000.00**

Plane, "Winchester," iron fore-type, rosewood handle & knob, 2³/₄" cutter, 18" l. **125.00**

Plane, wooden horned, smoothing-type, crown logo, Germany **23.00**

Romeo and Juliet.

Singer "Romeo and Juliet" trade card; valued at $15.00.

340

CHAPTER
27

TRADE CARDS

Trade cards were the dominant form of advertising throughout most of the late-Victorian period. A number of companies exhibiting at the 1876 Centennial Exposition experimented with color advertising cards. Consumers were intrigued by these free "chromolithographed" cards and brought them home to paste into scrapbooks as souvenirs of their visit. Advertisers were quick to take note. Within five years, most American firms were issuing full-color advertising cards. The widespread availability of trade cards in turn fueled the scrapbook craze until nearly every middle-class Victorian parlor had an album of tastefully-arranged trade cards somewhere on display.

The charm of Victorian culture is captured by trade cards of all sizes and shapes, including some with moving parts and flaps that open and shut to create changing illustrations. Most are rectangular and slightly smaller than a postcard. Many trade cards used delightful illustrations of children, pets and landscapes and were printed in huge quantities to be sold in bulk as "stock cards" that could have different ads stamped on them locally. Major companies paid more to have cards custom designed for their use only. These "private issue" cards are the most valuable and popular with collectors because they often show the product and are frequently of exceptional quality. Trade cards were distributed by merchants who handed them out to customers and traveling "drummers" who gave them away like samples. Some cards were also sent through the mail or inserted in packages with products.

Most stock cards in good condition sell for $1.00 to $6.00. Privately issued cards typically bring $5.00 to $25.00. Cards with tears, creases or damage on the back from glue are much cheaper. Rare and desirable cards like those advertising clipper ships voyages and mechanical banks sell for hundreds, or even thousands, of dollars.

—Dave Cheadle

Centennial Exposition Stock Card, color, imprint, Prang card, shows Main Building, Horticultural Hall, Agricultural Hall, Machinery Hall, & the Art Gallery, all surrounding the words "Methodist Book Concern, - Nelson & Phillips, Agents, Publishers, Booksellers, and Stationers, - 805 Broadway, N.Y." all above "International Exhibition - Fairmount Park Philadelphia, PA. - 1876" (Fig. 27-1) **$20.00**

Clothing, Pearl Shirts, color, wife in blue presents shirt to sitting man, "George, I have just bought six of those celebrated Pearl Shirts for you" (Fig. 27-2) **18.00**

Farm, Buckeye Force Pumps, color, shows a crying child sitting beside pump in the grass holding plate & frog in his lap in the background a rabbit is running away, marked "Buckeye Force Pumps - manufactured by - Mast, Foos & Co. - Springfield, O." (Fig. 27-3) **16.00**

Fig. 27-1

Fig. 27-2

Fig. 27-3

Fig. 27-4

Fig. 27-5

Farm, Corliss Engine Oil-Brooks Oil Co., black & white, harvest scene of two men, one sitting in horse cart w/two horses cracking a whip, the other holding sickle, storm brewing in the background, reads "Corliss Engine Oil - For all Farm Machinery - is the best Oil - Brooks Oil Co - Cleveland, O" (Fig. 27-4) **30.00**

Farm, Livingston's Rices Seeds, color, depicts farm couple waking up to find huge tomato growing through bedroom window, tomato marked "Livingston's Perfection (New)," reads "Warranted to produce - Ripe Fruit In 100 days From - The Sowing Of The Seed." in bottom left corner (Fig. 27-5) **15.00**

Fig. 27-6

Farm, Peckham Farmer's Boiler, color, shows farmer in frumpy hat lifting lid on agricultural boiler w/steam rising from boiler, marked "J.S. & M. Peckham, Utica, N.Y." (Fig. 27-6) **20.00**

Farm, Vermont Farm Machine, shows three children w/blue cream separator in cow pasture, upper right corner reads "The Vermont Farm Machine Co. - Bellows Falls, Vermont.," lower left corner reads "Improved - United States Cream Separator No. 5" (Fig. 27-7) **30.00**

Food, Albion Milling, color, shows woman wearing pink dress with grain in arm and holding a small sickle in her hand, sash around grain reads "Albion.," top of card reads "Goods Not Genuine Unless Our Card is found in Every Package," Bottom reads "Albion Milling Co. - Albion, Mich. Merchant Millers." (Fig. 27-8) **16.00**

Food, Carnrick's Lacto-Preparata, color, from Columbian Exposition, depicts old farmer milking cow holding child in his lap while he squirts milk into cat's mouth, reads "Carnrick's Lacto-Preparata - and Carnrick's Soluble Food - Will Nourish A Child As Perfectly As Mother's Milk." above & "Prepared By Reed & Carnrick, New York." below, statement at bottom of card states that the Board of Lady Managers of the

Fig. 27-7

Fig. 27-8

Fig. 27-9

Fig. 27-11

Fig. 27-10

World's Columbus Exposition used Reed &
Carnrick's infant foods in the Fair Crech or
nursery (Fig. 27-9) **25.00**

Food, Magic Yeast, color, depicts four young
girls waiting at table for biscuits brought by
house servant, yeast package placed in the
middle of the table (Fig. 27-10) **18.00**

Ice Cream Freezer, White Mountain, color,
shows young farm boy kissing a young
girl in a field, marked "Coming through
the Rye" beneath his foot, reads "Use
the White Mountain Ice Cream Freezer"
across the top & "The World's Best" below
(Fig. 27-11) **16.00**

Fig. 27-12

Fig. 27-13

Fig. 27-14

Iron, Geneva Hand Fluter, color, shows young woman using hot fluter to iron white ruffles, while two kittens play beneath table, inset box in upper left corner reads "Geneva Hand Fluter" (Fig. 27-12) **20.00**

Kitchen, Sterling Meat Chopper, color, woman in red dress and white apron grinds meat into bowl while young girl watches & points, reads "The Sterling Chopper" in upper left corner (Fig. 27-13) **25.00**

Medicine, Boschee's German Syrup, color, shows mother w/stick walking son home by ear from swimming hole, reads "4,000,000 bottles sold annually - German Syrup - cures consumption and August Flower for Dyspepsia," stock card (Fig. 27-14) **10.00**

Medicine, Dr. Morse's Indian Root, color, 1883 calendar card below Indian spearing a bear while on rearing white horse, card reads "Dr. Morse's Indian Root Pills" & "Comstocks Dead Shot Worm Pellets" (Fig. 27-15) **30.00**

Medicine, Maltine, color, shows cherub in wheat field holding big bottle of Maltine over shoulder (Fig. 27-16) **12.00**

Medicine, Uncle Sam's Powder, shows two horses, a cow & sheep in pasture w/barn in the distance, card reads "Uncle Sam's Condition Powder, Keeps Stock Healthy & Fat" across bottom (Fig. 27-17) **30.00**

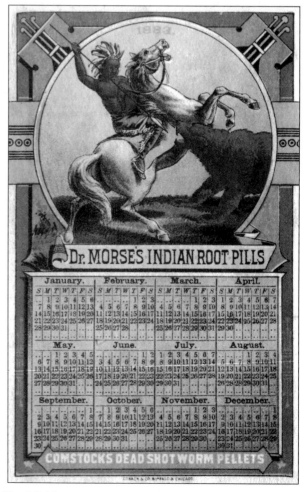

Fig. 27-15

Fig. 27-16

Santa Claus, Zinn Stores, color, shows Santa wearing a blue coat, his sleigh being pulled by two reindeer, as he stuffs package down chimney, card reads "Wm. H. Zinn, Connecting Stores. - Washington St., Temple - Pl., and West St., - Boston," stock card (Fig. 27-18) **12.00**

Sewing Machine, Domestic, color, depicts farm scenes of man showing livestock, vegetable inset, harvesting scene & Victorian house in the background, reads "Compliments of the Domestic Sewing Machine Co." (Fig. 27-19) . . **12.00**

Soap, Draper Jasmine Toilet Soap, color, shows young girl in blue hat holding basket full of straw w/three kittens on top, front of basket reads "NO! - There is no better than - Jasmine or Violet Water - Toilet Soaps - J.O. Draper & Co.," stock card (Fig. 27-20) . . . **5.00**

Soap, James Pyles Pearline, color, shows young farm boy in straw hat teasing dog under his arm w/a crawfish as cat watches, small rectangle in upper left corner reads "James Pyle's Pearline" (Fig. 27-21) **5.00**

Stove Polish, Dixon's, color, shows black woman bathing young girl standing on table surrounded by boxes of Dixon's polish, card reads "Dixon's - Carburet of Iron - Stove Polish." (Fig. 27-22) **15.00**

Fig. 27-17

Fig. 27-18

Fig. 27-20

Fig. 27-19

Fig. 27-21

Fig. 27-22

Fig. 27-23

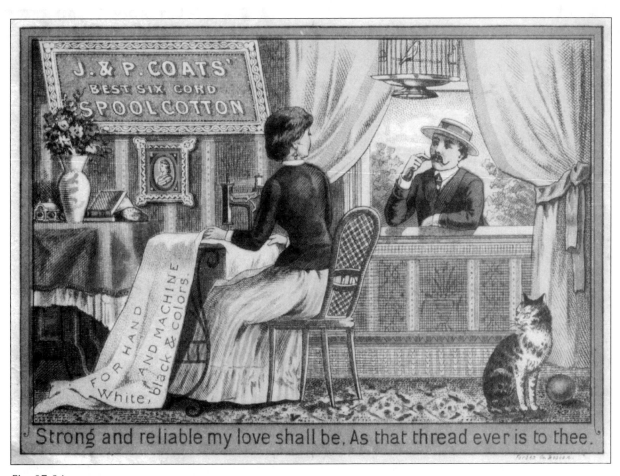

Fig. 27-24

Thread, Chadwick's Spool Cotton, shows young boy in sailor suit & young girl in white dress ready to fly kite in field, reads "Use - Chadwick's - Spool Cotton." (Fig. 27-23) **12.00**

Thread, J. & P. Coats Spool Cotton, color, shows man courting woman through window, card reads "J. & P. Coats' Best Six Cord Spool Cotton," in upper left corner & "Strong and reliable my love shall be, As that thread ever is to thee." (Fig. 27-24) . . . **15.00**

Thread, Merrick's Thread, color, shows woman in fancy hat on green bench w/big spool in her lap & young girl holds thread, upper left corner reads "Use Merrick's Thread" (Fig. 27-25) **15.00**

Thread, Merrick's Thread, depicts black boy hanging by thread and fishing pole above alligator, reads "Fooled Dis Time Cully. Dis Cotton Aint Gwine To Break" (Fig. 27-26) . . **15.00**

Washing, Spurlock's Bluing, depicts father wearing nightshirt pacing w/crying baby & nursing bottle while mom sleeps, card reads "This Picture is given to each Purchaser of - A 'Night' of Labor. (Ready to Arbitrate) - Spurlock's No. 5 Bluing - Ask for No: 5." (Fig. 27-27) **15.00**

Fig. 27-26

Fig. 27-25

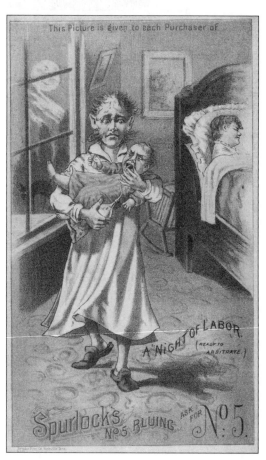

Fig. 27-27

TRAMP ART

A pair of crate wood urns, ca. 1930-40, 4¹/₂" h.; pair valued at $140.00

"Tramp Art," used as a term to describe the articles made from edge-notched and layered cigar box and packing crate wood, was coined by Frances Lichten in 1959. Interest in this strange craft grew immensely during the 1970s, when a traveling exhibit organized by the Museum of American Folk Art focused the first scholarly attention on it. Subsequently, decorators seized on its bold, eccentric look, perfect for the eclectic "folksy" interiors coming into vogue. Prices soared, and a relatively small group of serious collectors began assembling large quantities of the work. Values leveled somewhat at the beginning of this decade, but are again escalating, with the market strongest for out-of-the-ordinary specimens.

Tramp art has indistinct origins in the traditions of chip-carving as practiced by the peoples of Northern Europe. In fact, many of its earliest practitioners were immigrants from Germany and Scandinavia. But what primarily gave rise to the enormous popularity of this craft was the sudden availability of cigar boxes made from Honduras mahogany and Spanish cedar. Previously sold in bundles tied with ribbons, a government tax act requiring non-reusable boxes for cigars precipitated this new, handsome free material which was gladly adopted by the whittlers. With the simplicity of its techniques practically guaranteeing success, tramp art tempted many newcomers to the knife.

In order to achieve appreciable size or sculptural mass with these small, thin sheets of wood, they had to be spliced, by overlapping, or stacked into many layered "pyramids" of various shapes. The layers were usually first carved with tiny V's around their edge, so that each step had a zigzag profile. Shiny varnish and shellac emphasized the multifaceted surface thus created, producing a rather gaudy appearance. (Today's collectors are, no doubt, grateful for the changes wrought by time; darkened, oxidized and crackled finishes are the norm.) Crate wood was also frequently employed, especially as the base or armature, but sometimes comprising the entire construction and decoration.

The rapid dissemination of this craft, and its remarkable pervasion, still defy a definitive explanation. Although plans for many similar handicrafts appeared in late Victorian periodicals, no published instructions or patterns for tramp art have ever been found. Once considered to have been made mainly by the itinerants with specialized training, a popular legend crediting the work to wandering hobos during economic hard times has so gripped the public imagination that, despite evidence to the contrary, it is often still repeated. Actually, all but a handful of the identified craftsmen were working family men who created these things at home. As a domestic handicraft, it coincided with fretsawing and paralleled women's quilting.

The oldest known piece of tramp art is a birdcage dated 1868. (The hitherto accepted date of 1862 has been proven false.) However, it wasn't until the mid-1880s that its practice was widespread. By then, and until the time of World War I, cigar smoking was at its zenith, and the plentitude of recyclable material must have been tantalizing, challenging men's imaginations in an era before easy distractions like television. Projects in this style were made as sentimental or romantic love tokens, out of religious devotion and patriotic zeal, to answer utilitarian household needs, as tour de force demonstrations of carving, and functionless and whimsical, "just for nice."

Although it enjoyed several peaks and wanes, a resurgence of tramp art during the Great Depression produced some of its most ambitious artifacts. Gradually, though, cigarettes eclipsed cigars as the smoke of choice, cardboard packaging replaced wooden containers, and by World War II the craft, for the most part, ceased. Today, it is being made in revival by artisans in Texas, New York, Wisconsin, Ohio, and Massachusetts.

In terms of current value, age isn't as critical as ingeniousness, complexity, condition and patina to

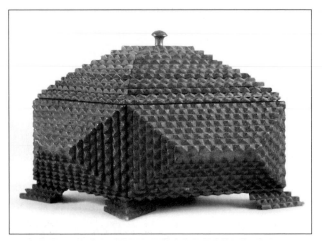

Fig. 28-1

collectors. Provenance is just becoming an important criteria; scarce signatures and dates are finally affecting the worth of pieces carrying them. Usually, outsized examples and those with designs leaning toward the bizarre are most sought-after. Tramp art is not for the timid! Old pieces made in Sweden, Denmark, Czechoslovakia, France, and especially Germany and Canada are constantly being imported by antiques dealers, and once mixed in with the domestic variety are fairly indistinguishable. Collectors, however, don't seem to express the prejudice for American origin that afflicts most other categories of folk art (whether this is indifference or ignorance). German boxes and frames, though, often characterized by velvet-covered panels and applied stamped metal decorations, have undeniably less appeal.

Though restorations are rare, they do not compromise the value much when neatly done. Old refinishes are acceptable, but new alterations or repaints are not. Since many of these things were refurbished or modernized by their owners over the years, greater than usual allowance for the lack of complete originality is made. Still quite affordable, especially when compared to 18th and early-to-mid 19th century folk art, the novice collector can take some chances without great risk. Look for polychrome finishes, unusual inclusions, exceptional or wild forms and a comfortable level of intactness.

—Micheal Cornish

Box, trapezoid shape, lid fits either direction, turned-out feet, original medium brown varnish w/fine craquelure, ca. 1895-1915, one foot damaged, 5½ x 11½", 6½" h. (Fig. 28-1) **$250.00**

Fig. 28-2

Fig. 28-4

Fig. 28-3

Box, common-form, multiple pyramids on ends & cross-hatched patterning on tips, ca. 1915-35, 7½ × 9½", 6" h. **150.00**

Box, w/curvilinear pyramid & dozens of whittled knobs decorating exterior, framed mirror under lid & interior decoupage w/colorful cigar box labels, original varnish w/fine craquelure, exceptional quality & design, ca. 1880-1900, 10 × 12½", 6" h. (Fig. 28-2) **725.00**

Boxes, pedestal base w/tiny lift-top w/restrained chamfered layering, dated 1941, all approx. 4" h., the set (Fig. 28-3) **225.00**

Boxes, both have drawers w/same unusual stop mechanism, taller is crate wood w/metal balls for finials, knob & feet, shorter alternates softwood & plywood, has

whittled finials, knob & feet, ca. 1930-40, 8½ × 8½", 6½" h. & 6¼ × 6½", 4½" h., pr. **300.00**

Chest, small, edge-notched diamonds attached w/brass escutcheon pins, over deep burgundy velvet, on bracket feet, velvet lined, 7 × 11", 6½" h. (Fig. 28-4) . . . **375.00**

Chest of drawers, three drawers made from cigar boxes w/ceramic pulls, very large notching, flat-topped w/overhang on thick layered base, ca. 1905-25, 6 × 14½", 15" h. (Fig. 28-5) **425.00**

Clock case, hexagonal case supported by turned spindles on platform base, made to hold alarm clock, missing face moldings professionally restored, Nova Scotia origin, possibly sailor-made, ca. 1905-25, 4½ × 7½", 11" h. (Fig. 28-6) **600.00**

Fig. 28-5

Fig. 28-6

Fig. 28-7

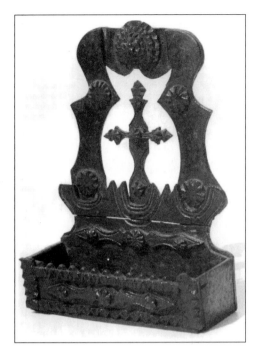

Fig. 28-8

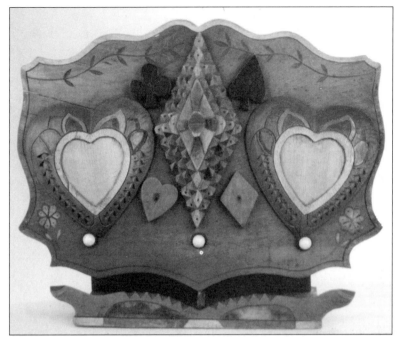

Fig. 28-9

Clock case, crate wood, cathedral-form, model of a church w/twin steeples, dormers, spires, peaked roof, arched doorway & large round 'window' opening for alarm clock, w/access to clock by removing small roof section, stained dark brown, on plywood platform base, dated 1932, 17 × 22", 28½" h. (Fig. 28-7) **2,200.00**

Comb box, cigar box wood, delicate cross in opening, cinched nail construction, w/incised & applied carving, typical of kind found in eastern Pennsylvania, ca. 1870-1890, darkened varnish w/some losses, 3 × 8½", 10½" h. (Fig. 28-8) **150.00**

Frame, standing, crate wood, mounted at 30° angle via whittled peg to circular pyramid base, stained alternating colors, exceptionally large double-sided notching, ca. 1920-40, minor losses, sight size approx. 2 × 3", 4 × 6", 6½" h. overall **150.00**

Frame, standing, double-type, two openings for pictures on carved hearts, applied cut-out shapes of playing card symbols, painted & incised vines & flowers, one-piece crate wood backboard w/undulating profile, wood pivoting mechanism in stand, signed on back "CHARLES CHABOT - COCHRANE, ONT.," ca. 1920-40, 4½ × 13", 10" h. (Fig. 28-9) **275.00**

Fig. 28-10

Frame, densely & highly layered w/hearts & circles, marked "YOUNGSTOWN, OH" on back, ca. 1890-1910, sight size 3¼ × 5", 7 × 11" overall (Fig. 28-10) **375.00**

Fig. 28-11

Fig. 28-12

Frame, openwork, lattice-type construction
w/fine zigzag carving, tip layers highlighted
in gold, ca. 1910-1930, sight size 5 × 3",
10 × 12" overall (Fig. 28-11) **225.00**

Frame, 'antennae crest' w/even pyramiding
w/dark varnish finish bordering panels of
faded rust-colored velvet, decorative
porcelain buttons, ca. 1880-1900, sight size
3¼ × 5½", 10½ × 20" overall (Fig. 28-12) . . **875.00**

Frame, elaboration of crossed-corner style
w/double rows of pyramiding, gold ribbon-
carved outline, large triangular shoulders
w/'all-seeing' eyes (possibly Masonic or
fraternal) & 'onion-dome' crest w/curvilinear
pyramiding, ca. 1885-1915, sight size
6 × 7½", 14 × 21" overall (Fig. 28-13) **775.00**

Frame, cigar box wood, star-shaped, six-
pointed star, built up to thirteen layers,
sight size 6 × 6", 18½ × 18½" overall
(Fig. 28-14) **800.00**

Frame, scalloped perimeter w/mirrors inlaid at
sides, bas relief eagle & Arabic inscription
"Habib & Adale - 1924 - Alexander Alckazi,"
made as wedding present by craftsman of

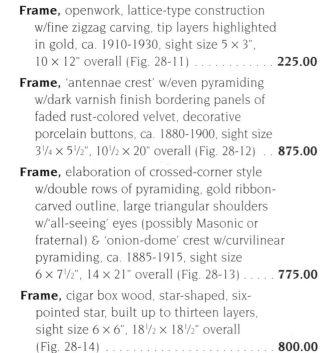

Fig. 28-13

Fig. 28-14

Fig. 28-15

Fig. 28-16

Lebanese descent, sight size 13 × 17",
20¹/₂ × 27" **525.00**

Frames, zigzag strips bordering panels filled
w/chamfered diamonds, darkened oxidized
finish, Danish origin, ca. 1930-40, approx.
8 × 10", pr. **275.00**

Lamp, table-type, made from crate wood in
the form of a stagecoach without wheels,
recycled furniture spindle used for socket
support, ca. 1930-1950, minor damage,
5¹/₄ × 10", 11" h. **100.00**

Lamp base, table-type, crate wood, sculptural
design made from thick dark stained wood,
uppermost tip split & socket missing,
ca. 1930-1940, ca. 8 × 8", 15¹/₂" h.
(Fig. 28-15) **375.00**

Lunch counter menu holder, pivoting four-
sided card display w/sixteen slotted
openings all on a pyramid base, original
gold & silver painted finish, ca. 1930s,
probably one of lost set, 6 × 6", 19" h.
(Fig. 28-16) **325.00**

Medicine chest, exterior completely
decorated, mirrored door w/shelved interior,
drawer w/ceramic pulls, facade crest
w/undulating profile & tall circular
pyramids, ca. 1930s, original white enamel
finish replaced by pale brown wash, mirror
removed for photo, 9¹/₂ × 22", 38" h.
(Fig. 28-17) **950.00**

Fig. 28-17

358 ★ Country Americana

Fig. 28-19

Fig. 28-18

Fig. 28-20

Planter, miniature, layered triangles create crosses on front & back, trapezoidal extensions at corners form integral short legs, cigar brand imprints visible through original light green paint, ca. 1925-40, unfinished interior, 3½ × 7¼", 5" h. **125.00**

Planter, thick wood from crates or lumber & enormous notching, weathered w/vestiges of several paint colors, meant for outdoors, ca. 1925-40, unusual, two tip pieces missing, 17 × 17", 10½" h. **325.00**

Planter, pedestal-form w/ladyfinger-shaped pyramids comprising the sides, on a stacked neck w/platform base, interior painted dark green, original glossy clear finish, pristine condition, ca. 1920-1940, 7 × 7", 9½" h. (Fig. 28-18) **425.00**

Sewing box w/drawer, eight whittled spindles on truncated pyramids on top, holding red- and black-painted thread spools around original faded burgundy pincushion, early cigar box markings in drawer compartment, sans finish, ca. 1880-1900, 6 × 6", 5" h. **250.00**

Sewing box, double-walled construction w/green slag glass panels, large drawer w/brass pull, hinged top w/yellow velvet pincushion, three lift-out partitioned trays, cigar box mahogany on a thick softwood base, brass roundhead tacks & escutcheon pins used decoratively, ca. 1880-1900, sight size 2 × 3", 11½ × 12", 9½" h. overall **1,050.00**

Sewing or jewelry box, very delicate carving, alternate beveled & notched layers, some tips missing, fretwork initials "MK," & date "1897," highlighted in gold, original purple velvet pincushion, 6 × 10", 6" h. (Fig. 28-19) **425.00**

Urn, thick pine crate wood, square layered body, stem cut from a banister turning, layered base w/feet, all held together by threaded rod & nuts, ca. 1930s, lumpy black repaint w/flower decals on tips, 8½ × 8¼", 12" h. **140.00**

Urn, "Cross of Thorns," made from thousands of thin strips of wood, notched to interlock without glue, unfinished softwood, ca. 1885-1915, some breaks & losses, but unusually intact for its age & complexity, 17 × 17", 22" h. **650.00**

Fig. 28-21

Wall cabinet, body made from U.S. Government surplus food crate wood, glazed door on brass hinges overlaid w/large heart, scallop-edged shelf inside, meant for recessed installation, unfinished sides, ca. 1930s, 4½ × 13½", 16½" h. (Fig. 28-20) **750.00**

Wall pocket, design is busy & dense combination of pyramid & mosaic styles, w/precisely layered hearts, stars, diamonds & circles of zigzag strips, original uniform opaque pale brown finish, made by Arsene Coll, Manchester, NH, ca. 1920s, 3½ × 8¼", 16" h. (Fig. 28-21) **450.00**

CHAPTER
29

WEATHERVANES & ROOF ORNAMENTS

WEATHERVANES

Weathervanes were widely popular with American farmers at a time when agriculture dominated the workforce of America in the 19th and early 20th centuries. This rooftop adjunct was not only decorative but provided a reliable guide to wind direction from afar. Today farming employs less than 5% of the American workforce but the old adage, "You can take the boy out of the farm, but not the farm out of the boy" still holds true as evidenced by the continued popularity of farm-related antiques. Today valuable old weathervanes adorn walls above fireplaces, in kitchens and family rooms and even, on a few rooftops.

As in the past, vanes in the forms of animals remain the most popular with collectors. Farmers sometimes used vanes which represented the stock they raised, so cows and horses were the most common forms, with chickens and pigs also widely seen. Eagles, of course, were popular with the patriotic-minded. Sheep, ears of corn and mules can also be found quite often but more rare are beavers, fish, and wolverines.

Today when you are looking at old weathervanes you are likely to find them with bullet holes since they were popular targets for little boys and hunters

of the past. The rarest examples can be found in undamaged condition with an original finish and perhaps traces of original gilding.

In addition to animal-form vanes, beautiful glass-tailed arrow vanes were popular. Found in basically two shapes, rectangular and kite-tail, the framed, colored glass was often etched. The six most common etched designs include:

1. Company names such as Barnett, Electra, Kretzer, and Shinn

2. Fleur-de-lis

3. Moon and comet

4. Star in diamond

5. Hearts and balls

6. Maltese cross

What better way to market your company name than perched high atop a few barns around the farming community? In fact, the design of the ball, the arrow and the system was a mark of the company that installed the system. Often reproduced, an original glass-tail vane should show the stains that result from the rusting of the frame around the glass, unless the arrow frame is of a later example made of aluminum.

—Phil Steiner

Fig. 29-1

Pricing:

Current market prices for smaller vanes, dependent on the condition and rarity of form, may run as follows:

Animals:

Common horse	$175.00
Circus horse	300.00
Copper horse (standing or running)	450.00
Small cow	175.00
Large cow	250.00
Small pig	250.00
Medium pig	350.00
Large 14" pig	500.00
Small chicken	250.00
Large chicken	350.00
Ear of corn	450.00

Glass-tail:

Company names:

Barnett Systems	375.00
Kretzer	300.00
Electra	350.00
Shinn	300.00
Plain kite-tail	125.00
Plain rectangular	165.00

Etched:

Snowflake	125.00
Fleur-de-lis	150.00
Moon & comet	250.00

Fig. 29-2

Star in diamond	275.00
Hearts & balls	350.00
Maltese Cross	250.00

Wolverine, sheep, fish, mule, eagle, beaver and the more rare large vanes are valued at $1,000.00 for more.

Fascinating, decorative and pleasing to both male and female tastes, weathervanes are majestic reminders of our country heritage.

Additional Price Listings:

Arrow, sheet metal, the silhouetted arrow cut w/circles, scrolls, fleur-de-lis & an arrowhead, mounted on a later metal rod & base, some corrosion, late 19th c., 74¼" l., 18½" h. (Fig. 29-1) **$1,725.00**

Bull, molded & gilded copper, full-bodied animal covered in old weathered gilding, mounted on a repaired rod & a later black metal base, third quarter 19th c., 24½" l., 17¼" h. **4,887.00**

Cod Fish, gilt copper, New England, late 19th century (a few minor dents), 30" l. (Fig. 29-2) .... **1,500.00 to 2,500.00**

Fig. 29-3

Fig. 29-4

Fig. 29-5

Fig. 29-6

Cow, large, standing on end of arrow rod
w/arrow point & pierced diamond "King"
logo (Fig. 29-5, center) **300.00**

Horse, copper, Black Hawk, America,
19th c., verdigris surface, 26" l.
(Fig. 29-3) . . . .**800.00 to 1,200.00**

Horse, circus-type, standing on end of arrow
rod w/arrow point & pierced diamond "King"
logo (Fig. 29-5, bottom) **350.00**

Horse, hackney-type, molded & gilded copper,
the full-bodied figure of a running horse w/a
zinc head & a cropped tail, w/old gilding,
mounted on a later rod & a black metal
base, third quarter 19th c., 30½" l.,
21" h. **6,325.00**

Horse, prancing, molded & silvered zinc, the
swell-bodied model of a horse w/sheet
metal ears, ridged mane & stylized leaf
fitted between its ears, mounted on a rod,
third quarter 19th c., 40½" l., 23" h. (minor
repairs, tail loose) **9,200.00**

Horse, running, carved & painted pine, the
flattened animal w/incised mane & tail
detail, the saddle, reins & hoofs painted in
black & silver, mounted on a rod & later

black metal base, retains traces of brown &
white paint, cracks, 19th c., 37¼" l., 21¾" h.
(Fig. 29-4) **3,450.00**

Rooster, copper, America, 19th c., 19½" h.
(Fig. 29-6) . . . . **700.00 to 900.00**

Rooster, realistically molded silver-colored
body standing on end of arrow rod w/arrow
point & pierced diamond "King" logo
(Fig. 29-5, top) **500.00**

◆ Roof Glass

Roof glass was the creation of a gentleman from
Crawfordville, Indiana in the late 19th century.
Scores of pieces adorned the roof peak, front
porch, front doors and windows of charming
Victorian homes during the 1890s. All of these
pieces carried the mark "Dec. 1, 91," the date of the
original patent.

A range of colors was available including dark
red, light and dark blue, green opaque glass, amber,
white with a vaseline tint, and clear, which over the
years has often turned a light purple due to exposure to sunlight.

Roof pieces slid into a bent metal (usually tin)
track which was also stamped with the 1891 patent
date. Large upside-down "J's" might be seen standing, some 14" high, at the outer edges of the roof
which was then lined with arrowhead-shaped
pieces about 4½" to 6" high. Where two peaks met,
a double-wheel shape sometimes adorned the
intersection. Also common were fan-shaped pieces
that fit in the ninety degree angles of porch
columns. These fans were sometimes used in
groups of four to make a circular window for a door
or hallway.

Other unusual pieces included sections used
above doorways and a glass ornament that was
used in conjunction with a large 3' scrolled brace.
This brace elevated itself above the roof crest
arrowhead glass and held a ball in its center. The

Fig. 29-7

ball was designed in a Dot and Dash design that
matched the pattern of the roof crest glass. This
metal scrolling and the glass ball were not ground-
ed like a lightning rod system and served a decorative purpose only.

Current values:

4½" l. Arrowheads $50.00
6" l. Arrowheads 75.00
14" h. Upside-down "J" (Fig. 29-7) 300.00
Fan-shaped pieces 250.00
Double-wheels 400.00

WINDMILL WEIGHTS

Various windmill weights.

Windmill weights were manufactured primarily between about 1875 and 1925 for use as counterbalance or governor weights on windmills. Yet, until about 1985, few persons outside the Midwest had ever heard of them. Since that time, they have attracted interest from collectors of folk art and farm equipment as an art form and as a reminder of a way of life which has long since disappeared. This interest has resulted in a dramatic increase in their value and in a like decrease in availability.

Windmill weights, always cast in iron, with two exceptions, can be classified into two categories—counterbalance and governor or regulator weights.

The counterbalance weights, which were utilized on vaneless mills as a method of counterbalancing the weight of the windmill's wheels, are primarily figural in form—horses, roosters, bulls, buffaloes, squirrels, spears, arrows, and stars, among others. The governor or regulator weights are primarily non-figural and attract interest primarily from windmill restorers and advanced collectors.

The windmill manufacturers, and farms using windmill weight-type windmills, were concentrated primarily in the Midwest. Hence, the vast majority of weights found today appear in farm sales or in local auctions in Nebraska, Kansas, Minnesota, and the

Dakotas. As with most antiques and collectibles which attract and increase prices, reproductions and artfully repaired weights are now somewhat commonplace. Therefore, weight purchasers should be wary of getting "something for nothing" or of any weights which have new paint or new rust.

The following rules should be observed:

1. Don't purchase anything in new paint unless you can remove it to determine age and condition.

2. Avoid weights which have uniform grind marks on the edge.

3. Don't sandblast weights or remove old paint. Patina or surface is acquired through a long aging process by exposure to the elements and is highly regarded by collector. Removing the paint or sandblasting destroys the character, personality, and historical significance.

4. Don't pass on items because they are not described in a book or because the actual weight or dimensions differ from that indicated in the book. New forms (or variations of known forms) are continually being discovered. Windmill weights were produced at foundries using unsophisticated production techniques (by today's standards).

5. Don't buy a weight because someone says it is rare—it frequently isn't rare or even a weight. I have seen "rare" short-tail horses (the most common forms) and have heard of camels, pigs, and rabbits (which to my knowledge do not exist).

6. Buy the very best you can afford. Don't sacrifice quality, rarity, and condition for price. The great pieces will almost always increase in value while the average or mediocre pieces almost always do not.

7. Lastly, talk to and deal with knowledgeable and reputable dealers. They are generally happy to share their knowledge and enthusiasm.

Values are estimated retail prices and are based upon form, condition and rarity. Prices tend to be higher in large metropolitan areas, such as the East Coast.

—Richard S. Tucker

Arrow, original red paint, w/three small holes in the neck, 22$\frac{1}{2}$ lbs. (including base), Leach Windmill Company, Joliet, Illinois, very rare, 1$\frac{3}{8}$ × 25", 9$\frac{1}{2}$" h. (Fig. 30-1) . . . . **$2,001.00 to 2,500.00**

Battleship, Monitor, concrete & cast-iron frame & turret, 62 lbs., Baker Manufacturing Company, Evansville, Wisconsin, 12$\frac{1}{2}$ (at bracket) × 28$\frac{3}{4}$", 8" h., to top of turret (Fig. 30-2) . . . . **2,001.00 to 2,500.00**

Bell, marked "6," 43 lbs., Breyer Brothers, Whiting & Company, Waupun, Wisconsin, rare, 2 × 11$\frac{3}{4}$", 14$\frac{1}{2}$" h. (Fig. 30-3) . . . . **3,501.00 to 5,000.00**

Bell, rounded corners, 15$\frac{1}{2}$ lbs., maker unknown, very rare, some rusting, 2$\frac{3}{8}$ × 5$\frac{1}{4}$", 5$\frac{1}{2}$" h. (Fig. 30-4) . . . . **1,001.00 to 1,500.00**

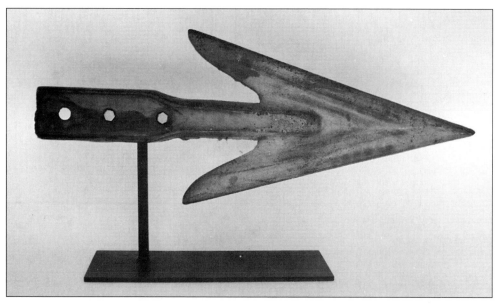

Fig. 30-1

Fig. 30-2

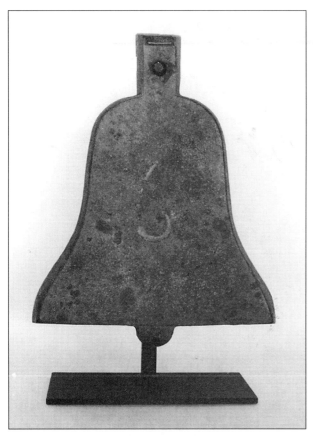

Fig. 30-3

Fig. 30-4

Fig. 30-5

Fig. 30-6

Fig. 30-7

Bull, marked "FAIRBURY NEBR.," 53½ lbs. (including base), Fairbury Windmill Company, Fairbury, Nebraska, bull ⅝ × 24½", 17¾" h., base 9¾ × 17⅝", ⅜" h. (Fig. 30-5) . . . . **1,001.00 to 1,500.00**

Bull, thick w/separated tail, unmarked, 71 lbs. (including base), Fairbury Windmill Company, Fairbury, Nebraska, rare, rusted, bull 1¼ × 24½", 17¾" h., base 9¾ × 17⅝", ⅜" h. (Fig. 30-6) . . . . **2,001.00 to 2,500.00**

Bull, unmarked, 96½ lbs., Fairbury Windmill Company, Fairbury, Nebraska, rare, original paint worn & rust, bull 1½" × 24¼", 18" h., base 10 × 17⅞", ¾" h. . . . . **2,001.00 to 2,500.00**

Buffalo, w/molded 'hair,' 13½ lbs. (without base), maker unknown, rare, ½ × 16", 10⅞" h. (Fig. 30-7) . . . . **3,501.00 to 5,000.00**

Canister, marked "Fairbanks Morse," 17½ lbs., Fairbanks, Morse & Company, Chicago, Illinois, rare, 11¾" d. (Fig. 30-8) .**1,001.00 to 1,500.00**

Fig. 30-8

Fig. 30-9

Fig. 30-10

Cow, original white & black paint, w/embossed lettering "FAIRBURY" on side of cow, 54 lbs., Fairbury Windmill Company, Fairbury, Nebraska, very rare, cow ⁵⁄₈ × 24³⁄₄", 17⁵⁄₈" h., base 9³⁄₄ × 17⁵⁄₈", ³⁄₈" h. (Fig. 30-9) . . . . **2,001.00 to 2,500.00**

Crescent moon, points down, marked "AA13 - Standard," 14¹⁄₂ lbs., F.W. Axtell Manufacturing Company, Fort Worth, Texas, rare, 2¹⁄₈ × 10¹⁄₂", 6¹⁄₂" h. (Fig. 30-10) . . . . **251.00 to 500.00**

Crescent moon, points up, marked "A13 - SUCCESS," 24 lbs., Challenge Company, Batavia, Illinois, rare, 2⁵⁄₈ × 10⁵⁄₈", 6¹⁄₂" h. . . . . **251.00 to 500.00**

Disc, 40¹⁄₂ lbs., Baker Manufacturing Company, Evansville, Wisconsin, 3 × 10¹⁄₄" . . . . **Under 100.00**

Eagle, 13 lbs., maker unknown, rare, ¹⁄₂ × 7¹⁄₈", 15³⁄₄" h., 17" h. including lid (Fig. 30-11) . . . . **5,000.00 and up**

Fig. 30-11

Fig. 30-12

Governor weight, marked "MFG BY BREYER BROS WHITING & CO WAUPUN WIS USA," 7½ lbs., rare, 1⅝ × 3¼", 5⅝" h. . . . . **501.00 to 750.00**

Governor weight, model E S262, 17½ lbs., U.S. Wind Engine & Pump Company, Batavia, Illinois, 7⅞" d., 10½" including bracket . . . . **100.00 to 250.00**

Governor weight, success, D17, 34½ lbs., Hastings Foundry & Iron Works, Hastings, Nebraska, 8½" d. . . . . **100.00 to 250.00**

Heart, one of two sizes, marked "The Co. L. Houston Montgomery PA Patented June 1 1884 April 14 1885," maker unknown, 13 lbs., rare, 2¼ × 9⅛", 10" h. (Fig. 30-12) . . . . **3,501.00 to 5,000.00**

Horse, running, smaller version of two sizes, 33 lbs., attributed to Benjamin Danforth, Beatrice, Nebraska, rare, 1½ × 19½", 21½" h. (Fig. 30-13) . . . . **5,000.00 and up**

Horse, long-tail w/large base, 57½ lbs., Dempster Mill Manufacturing Company, Beatrice, Nebraska, rare, base 2½ × 17¼", 21½" h. (Fig. 30-14) . . . . . **2,501.00 to 3,500.00**

Horseshoe, w/bar across middle, 17½ lbs., maker unknown, 1¹/₁₆ × 8¾" (including bracket), 10¾" h. (Fig. 30-15) . . **3,501.00 to 5,000.00**

Letter—Ozark "O," smallest of three sizes, 28½ lbs., Breyer Brothers, Whiting & Company, Waupun, Wisconsin, rare, excluding base, 12" d. (Fig. 30-16) . . . . **1,501.00 to 2,000.00**

Letter—B, marked "Hildbreth Iron Works - Hildreth Neb," 54 lbs., Hildreth Iron Works, Hildreth, Nebraska, very rare, 2⅝ × 12¾" (including bracket), 15⅞" h. . . . . . **5,000.00 and up**

Letters—CWS, 53 lbs. (including base), Cornell-Wigman-Searl Company, Lincoln, Nebraska, rare, weight 1 × 23", 10⅞" h., base 12 × 18", ½" h. (Fig. 30-17) . . . . **3,501.00 to 5,000.00**

Fig. 30-13

Fig. 30-14

Fig. 30-15

Fig. 30-16

Fig. 30-17

Fig. 30-18

Fig. 30-19

Regulator weight, Stover B13, 26½ lbs., Stover Manufacturing Company, Freeport, Illinois, 2¾ × 7" . . . . **100.00 to 250.00**

Rooster, long-stem, marked "Hummer E 184" on tail, 9½ lbs., Elgin Wind Power & Pump Company, Elgin, Illinois, 9½ lbs., Elgin Wind Power & Pump Company, Elgin, Illinois (Fig. 30-18) . . . . **751.00 to 1,000.00**

Rooster, small mogul w/base, 21½ lbs., 7 × 12½", 8" h. . . . . **3,501.00 to 5,000.00**

Rooster, w/original yellow & red paint, marked "10 ft. No. 2" on tail, on red base, 34 lbs., Elgin Wind Power & Pump Company, Elgin, Illinois, 4⅜ (at base) × 17", 15¾" h. . . . . **751.00 to 1,000.00**

Rooster, large base, original red & white paint, marked "Hummer" on tail, 48 lbs., Elgin Wind Power & Pump Company, Elgin, Illinois, paint slightly worn, 4⅜" (at base) × 17", 17¾" h. (Fig. 30-19) . . . . **1,501.00 to 2,000.00**

Rooster, barnacle-eye, w/original white & red paint, 52 lbs., Elgin Wind Power & Pump Company, Elgin, Illinois, paint worn, 2¾ × 18", 18½" h. (Fig. 30-20) . . . **3,501.00 to 5,000.00**

Rooster, small mogul, 60 lbs., 4¾ × 10½", 18" h. (Fig. 30-21) . . . . **3,501.00 to 5,000.00**

Fig. 30-20

Rooster, Woodmanse, large, original paint, 63 lbs., Elgin Wind Power & Pump Company, Elgin, Illinois, some rust & paint worn, 3¾ × 18", 19⅜" h. (Fig. 30-22) . . . . **1,001.00 to 1,500.00**

Fig. 30-21

Fig. 30-22

Fig. 30-23

Fig. 30-24

Fig. 30-25

Rooster, duplex (A20), w/original red & white paint, 64 lbs., Elgin Wind Power & Pump Company, Elgin, Illinois, paint worn, 2½ × 19", 19¼" h. (Fig. 30-23) . . . . **3,501.00 to 5,000.00**

Rooster, screw leg, 64 lbs., Elgin Wind Power & Pump Company, Elgin, Illinois, rare, 3¼ × 17½", 20" h. (Fig. 30-24) . . . . . . **5,000.00 and up**

Rooster, duplex, thick, w/original red & white paint, 100½ lbs., Elgin Wind Power & Pump Company, Elgin, Illinois, rare, paint worn, 4⅜ × 19", 19½" h. (Fig. 30-25) . . **5,000.00 and up**

Shield, decorated w/stars & stripes, w/original paint, 16 lbs. (including base), attributed to Challenge Wind Mill & Feed Mill Co., Batavia, Illinois, rare, excluding base, some rust & paint worn, 1⅜ × 7¼", 8⅜" h. (Fig. 30-26) . . . . **2,501.00 to 3,500.00**

Spear, w/original white paint, embossed letters read "New Century Sauk Centre Minn," 34½ lbs. (without base), maker unknown, rare, 2 × 15¼", 11" h. (Fig. 30-27) . . . . **2,001.00 to 2,500.00**

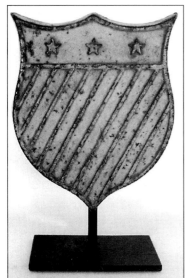

Fig. 30-26

Fig. 30-27

Fig. 30-28

Spear, marked "MODEL - 1912," 39 lbs.,
Challenge Company, Batavia, Illinois, rare,
3¹/₂ (at rear bracket) × 35³/₄", 14" h.
(Fig. 30-28) . . . . **3,501.00 to 5,000.00**

Spear, marked "Model 1913," 39 lbs.,
Challenge Company, Batavia, Illinois,
3¹/₂ × 35³/₄", 14" h. . . . . **1,001.00 to 1,500.00**

Squirrel, small w/original paint, 35¹/₂ lbs.,
Elgin Wind & Pump Company, Elgin,
Illinois, 3 (at base) × 13³/₄", 17" h.
(Fig. 30-29) . . . . **3,501.00 to 5,000.00**

Star, Halladay, five-pointed star w/original
paint, 38¹/₂ lbs., U.S. Wind Engine &
Pump Company, paint worn & some
rusting, 2³/₄ × 14³/₄", 2³/₄"
(Fig. 30-30) . . . . **501.00 to 750.00**

Star, (C24), five-pointed star w/remnants
of original white paint, 38¹/₂ lbs., Flint
& Walling Manufacturing Company,
Kendellville, Indiana, rare, some
rusting, 2³/₄ × 14³/₄", 14³/₄" h.
(Fig. 30-31) . . . . **1,001.00 to 1,500.00**

Fig. 30-29

Fig. 30-30

Fig. 30-31

Clubs, Organizations & Newsletters

Bottle & Openers

Figural Bottle Openers Club
Nancy Robb
3 Ave. A
Latrobe, Pennsylvania 15650

Just For Openers
John Stanley
3712 Sunning Dale Way
Durham, North Carolina 27707

Ceramics

Blue & White Pottery

Blue & White Pottery Club—Secretary
224 12th Street NW
Cedar Rapids, Iowa 52405
Club dues: $12/year
For free introductory brochure,
    call: (303) 690-8649

Red Wing

Red Wing Collectors Society, Inc.
P.O. Box 14
Galesburg, Illinois 61402-0184
(309) 342-1601

Watt Pottery

Watt Collectors Association
P.O. Box 184
Galesburg, Illinois 61401
Club dues: $10/year

Watt Pottery Collectors
Dennis Thompson
P.O. Box 26067
Cleveland, Ohio 44126-0067
(216) 235-8548

Christmas Collectibles

Golden Glow of Christmas Past
Robert Dalluge
6401 Winsdale Street
Golden Valley, Minnesota 55427
Club dues: $20.00/year

Graniteware

National Graniteware Society
P.O. Box 10013
Cedar Rapids, Iowa 52410
(319) 393-0252

Irons

Iron Talk®
P.O. Box
Waelder, Texas 78959
Club dues: $25.00/year; $30.00/year outside
    United States

Kitchen Collectibles

Kollectors of Old Kitchen Stuff (KOOKS)
Carol Bohn
501 Market Street
Mifflinburg, Pennsylvania 17844
Send long self addressed envelope for information

The National Reamers Collectors Association
(NRCA)
Bobbie Zucker
1 St. Eleanoras Lane
Tuckahoe, New York 10707
(914) 779-1405

or

Debbie Gillham
47 Midlane Court
Gaithersburg, Maryland 20878
(301) 977-5727

Lightning Rod Balls

Weather or Knot Antiques
15832 S. C.R. 900 W
Wanatah, Indiana 46390
(219) 733-2713

Trade Cards

Trade Card Collector's Association
The Advertising Trade Card Quarterly
P.O. Box 284
Marlton, New Jersey 08053

Tools

The Early American Industries Association
For more information & a book list, write:
John S. Watson, Treasurer
EAIA
P.O. Box 143
Delmar, New York 12054

The Missouri Valley Wrench Club
H. Klein, President
832 Ash Street
Granville, Iowa 51022

Midwest Tool Collectors Association
Rt. 2, Box 152
Wartrace, Tennessee 37183-9406
(614) 455-1935

Ohio Tool Collectors Association
P.O. Box 261
London, Ohio 43140
(614) 852-3180

Rocky Mountain Tool Collectors
2024 Owens Court
Denver, Colorado 80227-1910
(303) 988-5053

AUCTION HOUSES

Barberiana

Anthony J. Nard & Co.
US Route 220
Milan, Pennsylvania 18831
(717) 888-9404

Ceramics

Historical & Commemorative Wares

Collector's Sales and Service
P.O. Box 4037
Middleton, Rhode Island 02842
(401) 849-5012

Stoneware

Bruce & Vicki Waasdorp
P.O. Box 434
Clarence, New York 14031
(716) 759-2361

Decoys

Decoys Unlimited
Theodore S. Harmon
2320 Main Street
West Barnstable, Massachusetts 02668
(508) 362-2766

Guyette & Schmidt, Inc.
P.O. Box 522
West Farmington, Maine 04992
(207) 778-6256 or (207) 778-6266

Furniture, Fine & Decorative Art

Christie's
502 Park Avenue
New York, New York 10022
(212) 546-1000

Dunning's
755 Church Road
Elgin, Illinois 60123
(708) 741-3483 or (312) 664-8400

Garth's Auctions
2690 Stratford Road
Box 369
Delaware, Ohio 43015
(614) 362-4771 or (614) 548-6778

Skinner, Inc.
357 Main Street
Bolton, Massachusetts 01740
(508)779-6214

Sotheby's
1334 York Avenue
New York, New York 10021
(212) 606-7000

Lightning Rod Balls

Russell Barnes
P.O. Box 141994
Austin, Texas 78714
(512) 835-9510 (please call between 8:00 to 10:00
    p.m. CST)

Tools

Barry Hurchalla
RD2, Box 558
Botertown, Pennsylvania 19512

Richard Crane
63 Poor Farm Road
Hilsboro, New Hampshire 03244
(603) 478-5723

Bud Brown
4729 Kutztown Road
Temple, Pennsylvania 19560

Tom Witte
P.O. Box 399
Front St. West
Mattawan, Michigan 49071
(616) 668-4161

FURTHER READING

Books are organized alphabetically by category

Baskets

Johnson, Frances. *Wallace-Homestead Price Guide to Baskets*, Second Edition. Radnor, Pennsylvania: Wallace-Homestead Book Company, 1989

Lawrence, Martha R. *Lightship Baskets of Nantucket*. West Chester, Pennsylvania: Schiffer Publishing, Ltd., 1990

McGuire, John. *Basketry—The Shaker Tradition*. Asheville, NC: Lark Books, 1988

McGuire, John E. *Old New England Splint Basket and how to make them*. West Chester, Pennsylvania: Schiffer Publishing, Ltd., 1985

Schiffer, Nancy. *Baskets*. Exton, Pennsylvania: Schiffer Publishing, Ltd., 1984

Teleki, Gloria Roth. *Collecting Traditional American Basketry*. New York, New York: E.P. Dutton, 1979

Ceramics

Bennington Pottery

Barret, Richard Carter. *Bennington Pottery and Porcelain*. New York, New York: Crown Publishers, 1958

Blue & White Pottery

Alexander, M.H. *Stoneware in the Blue and White*. Paducah, Kentucky: Image Graphics, Inc., 1993 reprint

Harbin, Edith. *Blue & White Stoneware Pottery Crockery. Identification and Value Guide*. Paducah, Kentucky: Collector Books, 1977

Harbin, Joseph, M. & E. *Blue & White Pottery*. 1973

McNerney, Kathryn. *Blue & White Stoneware*. Paducah, Kentucky: Collector Books, 1995 reprint

Sanford, Steve & Martha. *The Guide to Brush-McCoy Pottery*. 1992

Pennsbury Pottery

Henzke, Lucile. *Pennsbury Pottery*. West Chester, Pennsylvania: Schiffer Publishing, 1990

Myers, Esther. "Pennsbury Pottery," *American Clay Exchange* (January 30, 1986)

Cox, Susan N. "Pennsbury Pottery Pictorial," *American Clay Exchange* (June 15, 1985)

Company catalogs and invoices from 1960 through 1965.

Redware Pottery

McConnell, Kevin. *Redware—America's Folk Art Pottery*. West Chester, Pennsylvania: Schiffer Publishing, Ltd., 1988

Rockingham Pottery

Brewer, Mary. *Collector's Guide to Rockingham— The Enduring Ware—Identification & Values*. Paducah, Kentucky: Collector Books, 1996

Children's Dishes

Lechler, Doris Anderson. *English Toy China*. Marietta, Ohio: Antique Publications, 1989

Lechler, Doris Anderson. *Children's Glass Dishes, China, and Furniture*, Vol. 1., Paducah, Kentucky: Collector Books, 1986

Lechler, Doris Anderson. *Children's Glass Dishes, China, and Furniture*. Vol. 2., Paducah, Kentucky: Collector Books, 1986

Lechler, Doris Anderson. *Toy Glass*. Marietta, Ohio: Antique Publications, 1989

Lechler, Doris Anderson. *French & German Dolls, Dishes and Accessories*. Marietta, Ohio: Antique Publications, 1991

Christmas Collectibles

Brenner, Robert. *Christmas Past*. Exton, Pennsylvania: Schiffer Publishing, 1985

_____. *Christmas Revisited*. Exton, Pennsylvania: Schiffer Publishing, 1986

_____. *Christmas through the Decades*. Atglen, Pennsylvania: Schiffer Publishing, 1993

Decoys

Huxford, Bob & Sharon. *The Collector's Guide to Decoys*. Paducah, Kentucky: Collector Books, 1990

_____. *The Collector's Guide to Decoys, Book II*. Paducah, Kentucky: Collector Books, 1992

Kangas, Linda & Gene. *Decoys*. Paducah, Kentucky: Collector Books, 1992

Kerosene Lamps

Thuro, Catherine, M.V. *Oil Lamps: The Kerosene Era in North America*. Des Moines, Iowa: Wallace-Homestead Book Company, 1976

Thuro, Catherine, M.V. *Oil Lamps II: Glass Kerosene Lamps*. Toronto, Ontario: Thorncliffe House, Inc., 1983

Kitchen Collectibles

Coffee Mills

MacMillan, Joseph. *The MacMillan Index of Antique Coffee Mills*. 1995

White, Derek and Micheal, *Early American Coffee Mills*. 1994

Egg Beaters

Thornton, Don. Beat This, *The Eggbeater Chronicles*. Sunnyvale, California: Off Beat Books (to order, send $24.95 to Off Beat Books, 1345 Poplar Ave., Sunnyvale, CA 94087 or call (408) 737-0434)

Rugs

Kopp, Joel and Kate. *American Hooked and Sewn Rugs—Folk Art Underfoot*. New York, New York: E.P. Dutton, 1975.

Sewing Adjuncts

Muller, Wayne. *Darn It! The History and Romance of Darners*. L-W Book Sales: 1995 (to order, send $22.25 to Darn It!, P.O. Box 903, Pacific Palisades, CA 90272)

Zalkin, Eselle. *Zalkin's Handbook of Thimbles & Sewing Implements*. Willow Grove, Pennsylvania: Warman Publishing Co., 1988 ($24.95)

Tobacciana

Alsford, Denis. *Match Holders*. Exton, Pennsylvania: Schiffer Publishing

Hyman, Tony. *Handbook of American Cigar Boxes*. Pismo Beach, California: Treasure Hunt Publications (to order, send $25.00 to Tony Hyman, P.O. Box 3028, Shell Beach, CA 93448)

Martin-Congdon, Douglas. *Tobacco Tins*. Exton, Pennsylvania: Schiffer Publishing

Storino, Louis. *Chewing Tobacco Tin Tag*. Exton, Pennsylvania: Schiffer Publishing

Tools

Barlow, Ronald S. *The Antique Tool Collector's Guide to Value*. El Cajon, California: Windmill Publishing (to order, contact the publisher at 2147 Windmill View Rd., El Cajon, CA 92020)

Tramp Art

Cornish, Micheal, and Clifford Wallach. *They Call it Tramp Art*. Columbia University Press, 1996

Windmill Weights

Lindsay, T. A *Field Guide to American Windmills*. Norman, Oklahoma: The University of Oklahoma Press, 1985.

Simpson, Milt. *Windmill Weights*. 1985 (out of print)